THE ART OF BEING KUNA

LAYERS OF MEANING

AMONG THE KUNA OF PANAMA

MARI LYN SALVADOR

EDITOR

UCLA FOWLER MUSEUM OF CULTURAL HISTORY

LOS ANGELES

**This publication and related exhibition
were supported by funding from**

The National Endowment for the Humanities
  *Dedicated to expanding American understanding
  of history and culture*
The Ahmanson Foundation
The Times-Mirror Foundation
Manus, the Support Group of the UCLA Fowler
  Museum of Cultural History

Lenders to the Exhibition

Mac Chapin
The Field Museum, Chicago
Ann and Monroe Morgan
Jim and Jeanne Pieper
National Museum of the American Indian,
  Smithsonian Institution
2 Private collectors

Daniel R. Brauer *Design and Production*
Corinne Lightweaver *Editing*
Don Cole *Principal Photography*

UCLA Fowler Museum of Cultural History
Box 951549
Los Angeles, California, USA 90095-1549

Requests for permission to reproduce material from this work should be sent to the UCLA
Fowler Museum Publications Department at the above address.

The paper used in this publication meets the minimum requirements of the American
National Standard for Information Sciences—Permanence of Paper for Printed Library
Materials, ANSI Z39.48-1984.

Portions of Chapter 2 © 1995 by the University of Texas Press

Printed and bound in Hong Kong by South Sea International Press, Ltd.

Library of Congress Cataloguing-in-Publication Data

Salvador, Mari Lyn.
    The art of being kuna : layers of meaning among the Kuna of Panama
    / Mari Lyn Salvador , editor.
        p. cm.
      Publication is also an exhibition catalog.
      Includes bibliographical references.
      ISBN 0-930741-60-9. – ISBN 0-930741-61-7 (pbk.)
  1. Cuna art–Exhibitions. 2. Cuna Indians–Material culture–Exhibitions. 3. Cuna
  textile fabrics–Exhibitions. 4. Molas–Exhibitions. 5. San Blas Islands (Panama)–
  Social life and customs–Exhibitions. 6. San Blas Coast (Panama)–Social life and
  customs–Exhibitions.   I. University of California, Los Angeles. Fowler Museum of
  Cultural History. II. Title.
  F1565.2.C8S23 1997
  306'.0899707287–dc21   97-36368
                                                                    CIP

Front cover: Berta Alicia Avila. Photo by Mari Lyn Salvador, Suitupu, 1997.
Front and back cover (background): See Cat. 48, p. 342.
Back cover (birds and fish mola panel): See Fig. 2.14, p. 63.
Endsheet image (foliage): Vernon Salvador, 1974.
Endsheet image (palm frond): Vernon Salvador, 1974.
Page i: Photo by Mari Lyn Salvador, Ubigandup, 1997.
Pages ii-iii: James Howe, Niatupu, 1971.
Pages iv-v: Vernon Salvador, 1974.
Pages vi-vii: Mari Lyn Salvador, Tupile, 1974.
Pages viii-ix: Mola (detail) by Delia Méndez, Ailigandi, 1986. See Fig. 6.78, p. 182.
Page x: Doralia Garcia. Photo by Mari Lyn Salvador, Suitupu, 1997.
Pages x-xi: Skirt (*sabured*). Cotton cloth. 80.5 x 134.0 cm. FMCH X83.511. Gift of Dorothy
M. Cordry in memory of Donald B. Cordry.
Page xvi: The island of Nalunega. Mari Lyn Salvador, 1997.
Page xix: Noga Kope dancers. James Howe, Niatupu, 1995.
Page 354: Photo by Mari Lyn Salvador, Ailigandi, 1974.
Page 355: Photo by Mari Lyn Salvador, Suitupu, 1974.
Page 356: Photo by Vernon Salvador, 1974 (left), photo by Sergio Salvador, 1997 (right).
Page 357: Photo by Mari Lyn Salvador, 1994 (left), photo by Sergio Salvador, 1997 (right).
Page 358: Photo by James Howe, 1972.
Page 359: Photo by James Howe, 1972.
Page 360: Photo by Mari Lyn Salvador, 1967.

A Note on Photograph Captions

    All measurements are to the nearest half centimeter.

    Unless otherwise noted, all mola blouses and mola panels are composed of some
    or all of the following materials: cotton fabric, cotton thread, synthetic fabric,
    synthetic thread, string, rickrack.

    Mola dimensions are height x width. For all other objects, the dimension given is
    the single longest measurement.

    The following abbreviations have been used:

    FMCH: UCLA Fowler Museum of Cultural History
    NMAI: National Museum of the American Indian, Smithsonian Institution
    EMB: Etnografiska Museet i Götegorg, Sweden

    Complete photographer credits for studio photographs may be found on page 347.

Contents

Director's Acknowledgment

The Kuna peoples are best known for their intricately appliquéd blouses, called *molas*. Nevertheless, this exhibition and associated publication hope to make the *whole* of Kuna society better known to the general public. Still, of all Kuna expressive culture it will probably be the molas that leave the lasting impression with our audiences. This is certainly due in part to the easy appreciation of the delight of the Kuna people in pure form and color. But beyond that is the wide ranging subject matter of the textiles. Very few non-western indigenous arts feature such a thorough representation of a people's worldview. The mola genre includes virtually all Kuna material culture, ritual life, and social, political, and economic experiences. The molas provide detailed and near comprehensive pictures of Kuna society and negate any view of Kuna as a "traditional," "isolated" culture frozen in time. To the contrary, they reveal an energetic, dynamic people who are both resilient and adaptable when confronted by the late twentieth-century "global village."

Although I was well aware of Kuna textiles in the 1970s, it was not until attending a slide lecture in 1983 by Dr. Mari Lyn Salvador that I gained any real appreciation for the people and their culture. Mari Lyn's presentation was visually dazzling and intellectually captivating. It immediately prompted thoughts of a major exhibition and publication that could bring this material to a wider audience. Mari Lyn was clearly the obvious choice to curate this project. I want to thank her for her tremendous energy in bringing *The Art of Being Kuna* to fruition. Her diligence, thoughtfulness, and good humor prevailed in the face of difficult deadlines and financial constraints. We are highly appreciative of all her efforts. I am also extremely grateful for Mari Lyn's selection of project consultants whose research and scholarship informed both exhibition and publication. I would like to thank Mac Chapin, Marta Lucía de

Gerdes, Alexander Moore, Carlo Severi, Sandra Smith, Jorge Ventocilla, and especially James Howe and Joel Sherzer for their many valued contributions.

The support and guidance of the National Endowment for the Humanities have been the foundation of many of the Fowler Museum of Cultural History's most important projects. This vital federal agency provided both planning and implementation grants without which this exhibition and publication could not have happened. I would especially like to thank Marsha Semmel and Suzi Jones for their help in shaping the proposals and for being stimulating colleagues in the process.

The Kuna holdings of the Fowler Museum were built through the generosity of a number of donors. An important collection of molas was given by Thomas K. Curtis, Todd P. Curtis, Caroline C. Bramhall, Sandra G. Lovell, and S. Premena in memory of Caroline P. Green. Another major collection of Kuna arts was given by Dorothy M. Cordry in memory of Donald B. Cordry. And a very fine group of molas were a museum purchase in memory of Sidney S. Kallick.

I join Mari Lyn Salvador in thanking the staff of the Fowler Museum, listed at the back of this volume, for their exceptional efforts on behalf of this project. Their consistent professionalism continues to be a profoundly rewarding experience. Beyond the museum staff I would like to single out the work of editor Corinne Lightweaver for her usual excellence and Janice Klein, Registrar at the Field Museum, Chicago, for a substantial dose of last minute magic.

Doran H. Ross
Director

Curator's Acknowledgment

Exhibitions, like opera, depend on many talented people each with their own creative energy. Inspired performances can only be achieved if each enters at just the right moment. *The Art of Being Kuna* was such a production. Anthropologists and the staff of the Fowler Museum worked together with Kuna men and women—specialists in history, politics, ritual, and mola making—to create a project that highlights Kuna verbal and visual arts over time. Although the pace varied throughout the ten years of planning and production, at the end it seemed to go faster and faster, moving ever forward to the day the manuscript was "off to Hong Kong." What seemed a culmination, however, was only the end of the second act with just enough time in the intermission for an espresso before it all started up again. We hoped to reflect Kuna ideas and aesthetic sensibilities in subtle and engaging ways—to David Mayo who designed the exhibition and Danny Brauer who designed the book I say *"Yer dailege!"* Beautiful.

My special thanks to the staff of the Fowler Museum for their incredible efforts. It has been a pleasure to work with such an extraordinary group of people. I will always be grateful to Doran Ross, colleague and friend, for giving me the opportunity to dream of such a project, encouraging me to do an exhibition that placed Kuna arts in a historic context, and offering his unrelenting support of the book. Never did I hear "Don't you think this is too much color, Mari Lyn?" He worked his magic and we pressed forward.

Director of Education Betsy Quick, whose insights enhanced the educational goals of the project from the beginning, brought a sense of discovery and exuberance to the interpretive text for the exhibition. Sheila Egan, Kim Herzog, and Alicia Katano worked on the ever changing object list; and Stacey Hong, Kristin Quine, and Lyn Avins developed educational programs. Kathlene Kolian planned a wonderful opening, and Karyn Zarubica made arrangements for the exhibition to travel. Special thanks to Christine Sellin for creating public interest in Kuna culture and to Linda Lee for her work on materials for the press.

The logistics of dealing with objects were handled by Sarah Kennington and Farida Sunada in Registration and Fran Krystock and Dwight Gorden in Collections Management. Jo Hill worked with Andy Williams, Linda Clougherty, Batyah Shtrum, and Tania Collas on artifact preparation.

The exhibition was designed by David Mayo who made it all sing with color, and form, and grace. A masterful teacher, he reminded me that exhibits, like sculpture, benefit from what you remove. His design was carried out by Don Simmons, Victor Lozano, Ann McNamara, and Luciana Scrutchen. Jim Sudalnik and David Mayo created the video programs; photo production was done by Olson Color Expansions, Los Angeles, and Camera Graphics, Albuquerque.

Danny Brauer brought to the book insightful as well as artful design and kept me going with a wonderful sense of humor and early morning emails from "Tiki D." The authors are grateful to Corinne Lightweaver for taking on the difficult task of editing such a volume. Levon Mardikyan, Vernon Salvador, David Mayo, Norbert and Betty Sperlich, and Sergio Salvador provided contemporary field photographs. Don Cole of the Fowler Museum and Pam Dewey, Gina Fuentes, and Shilice Clinkscales of the

National Museum of the American Indian photographed the objects. Thanks to Ilford for providing film.

Projects of this scale require heroic efforts in the area of fundraising. My thanks to Richard Chute for work on the planning grant and Kirin Ealy Hobson for work on the implementation grant. We are especially grateful to the National Endowment for the Humanities, a Federal Agency. Special thanks to Marsha Semmel for guidance on planning and to Suzi Jones for encouraging our efforts to create an opportunity for Kuna artists to speak in their own voices. I am grateful to the National Museum of the American Indian and the Inter-American Foundation for funding the Kuna research project in New York. Thanks to Lic. Julieta de Arango, director of the Patrimonio Histórico del Instituto Nacional de Cultura, Panama, for her cooperation and sponsorship; to Ben Howe for collecting musical instruments; and to Prudence and Max Heffron for their support.

My special thanks to Clarissa Coyoca for keeping things running smoothly; to Dina Ogle and Michael Bermudez for wading through piles of receipts and paying the bills; and to Betsy Escandor, Lori LaVelle, Barbara Underwood, and Millicent Besser for always making me feel welcome at the Fowler.

I am grateful to the consultants who have worked together in various configurations for decades. Special thanks to Joel Sherzer who provided guidance on the presentation of the verbal arts. James Howe, an eloquent speaker of Kuna and integral member of the research teams in New York and Kuna Yala, took on the burden of ensuring, even in the intensity and haste of impending deadlines, that we were "getting it right." This project could never have been done without him and it is with fondness that I extend my thanks.

My appreciation and affection to "the New Mexico team." William Calhoon's creative spirit enhanced the planning, Julie Griffin spent tedious hours scanning slides, and Joseph Kinsella attacked the task of locating photographs and obtaining permissions. Special thanks to Angelle Khachadoorian for her work on manuscript preparation and for bringing moments of hilarity to the team. To Jenny Sanborn, my thanks for brainstorming, and for long hours at the computer, editing, re-writing, editing again. I am most grateful for her willingness to debate and challenge me, and for her critical eye for the aesthetics of representation. Thanks to June-el Piper, Jasmine Gartner, Nelson Graburn, Alessandro Falassi, and Chris Musello for their helpful comments on the manuscript. Loving thanks to Melina Salvador for her work in the European collections and to Sergio Salvador who returned to Kuna Yala, a land he enjoyed as a child, to take photographs for the exhibition.

Colleagues in museums in Europe facilitated the research on early Kuna collections. Special thanks to Jean-Loup Rousselot, Staatliches Museum für Volkerkunde, Munich, and Jonathan King, The British Museum, London, for their advice. I would like to thank Sara Posey and Hans Rushbrook, Museum of Mankind, London; Linda Mowat, Pitt Rivers Museum, Oxford; Vita Ferdaliz, Musée de l'Homme, Paris; Carmen Huera, Museo de Santa Madrona, Barcelona; and Dra. Paz Cabello Carro, Museo de America, Madrid; Richard Haas and Maria Geida, Museum für Volkerkunde, Berlin; and Sven Erik-Issacson and Gunilla Amnehal, Göteborgs Etnografiska Museum.

Research also led us to museums in the United States. Thanks to Anne Rowe, Textile Museum, Washington, D.C.; Felicia Pickering, National Museum of Natural History, Smithsonian Institution, Washington, D.C.; and Janice Klein, Field

Museum, Chicago. The National Museum of the American Indian in New York sponsored the Kuna visit which involved the entire staff for one hectic week. Scott Merritt and Terry Snowball took care of collections management issues while registration was handled by Ann Drumheller, Kenn Yazzi, and Marcus Monenerkit. Marian Kaminitz and Susan Heald developed a mounting system for the early molas, and Anna Marie Strankman and Angie Pearce worked on conservation. Thanks to Mark Clark for help with photography over the years. Nancy Rosoff has been an integral part of the project from the beginning. Whether brainstorming about planning and conceptualization, facilitating research, or navigating through the rapids of museum logistics, she never ceases to amaze me. To her, a heartfelt thanks from the Kuna research group.

I am particularly grateful to Cacique Carlos López and Cacique Leonidas Valdéz of the General Congress for their participation throughout the project; Caciques Paulino González, Daniel Ramires, Niga Pereira, and General Secretary Iguayokiler Ferrer of the Cultural Congress, Gilberto Arias and the Chiefs from Mandi Ubigandupu, Suitupu and Tigre, the Noga Kope dance society of Tigre and Rodolfo Herrera for facilitating the work of the documentation team in 1997; Elegio Alvarado Parades for his participation in the planning; Nicanor González, Serafina López, Rodolfina Andreve, Elvira Torres, and Balbina Denis for their interpretation of museum collections. My special thanks and affection to the women of the Mola Co-op.

The authors would like to express our appreciation to the Kuna men and women who have worked closely with us over the years, often sitting for hours as teacher and apprentice, talking and clarifying the most subtle details with patience and care. We thank you for opening your homes and receiving us with gracious hospitality, and most of all for the friendship and playful moments that add to our lives in so many ways.

Mari Lyn Salvador

Preface

The ideas behind this project have been developing from several directions for years. For me it started in 1967 when members of the Mola Co-op, the community of Tupile, and I worked together on an exhibition that was shown at the Casa de Escultura in Panama City. The Kuna decided what was to be shown, explained the objects and their meaning, and guided the photography. I wrote the labels, took photographs, and installed the exhibit.

Thirty years after that exhibition in Panama, the Kuna collaborated with outside scholars again on a new exhibition, this time working in a more formal way with the Kuna General and Cultural congresses and a second generation of women from the Co-op. Throughout the planning and development of the project, fond memories of the early work that drew me to anthropology often came to mind. Collaborative exhibitions, because of their multi-dimensional nature and expressive possibilities, provide an extraordinary arena for presenting the results of scholarly research and highlighting interpretation in their own voice the artists themselves. Scholarly researchers, like Joel Sherzer and James Howe in this book, have an opportunity to reach a wider audience and make their research accessible and interesting to the general public.

During the 1960s, interest in Kuna material culture was building at UCLA. In 1966 the Fowler Museum of Cultural History started its Kuna collection, which expanded over the next thirty years through museum purchases and gifts. In 1980, "Yer Dailege! Kuna Women's Art," a mola exhibition based on the original exhibit and my ethnoaesthetic research, was shown at UCLA. In 1987 Doran Ross, then deputy director of the museum, suggested an exhibition to highlight the verbal arts as well as molas and take a historical perspective, and he invited me to participate. Over the next ten years, the Fowler Museum brought a team of Kuna specialists and anthropologists—most of whom have been working in Kuna Yala since the 1970s—together with the Fowler staff to work on the project.

A planning grant from the National Endowment for the Humanities in 1990 enabled us to continue to research, photograph, and document collections. In the summer of 1992, I visited the Kuna collections in European museums with Melina Salvador as a research assistant. Over the next five years, research centered on collections in American museums. At the planning meeting held at UCLA in 1992, project consultants, Kuna sociologist Elegio Alvarado, and members of the Fowler Museum's staff made key decisions that set the parameters of the project, in form as well as content.

We agreed to follow Kuna preferences regarding the appropriate representation of their language. Kuna Yala, the name they use to refer to their land replaced San Blas, a term imposed by outsiders. In order to be consistent in this volume we agreed to follow the system linguist Joel Sherzer recommends for the spelling of Kuna words. During this process, Sherzer and James Howe emerged as special consultants, with the former taking responsibility for issues regarding language and Howe working closely with me on all aspects of the project.

In 1994 the Fowler Museum received an implementation grant from the National Endowment for the Humanities. Over the next three years James Howe and I made several trips to Panama to present the results of planning and refine details through a series of informal meetings at village and regional gatherings in Kuna Yala, and with representatives of the Cultural Congress in Panama City. In January 1997, exhibition designer David Mayo, videographer Jim Sudalnik, and photographer Sergio Salvador joined James Howe, researcher Rodolfo Herrera of Kuna Yala, and me on a journey through the Carti area of Kuna Yala. The Cultural Congress and the chiefs of the islands of Mandi Ubigandup, Suitupu, and Tigre planned and facilitated the trip and ensured collaboration in each community. Loaded with detailed "shoot lists" and more camera and video equipment than even the expert pilots who fly in and out of Kuna Yala felt very happy about, we set off to collect ethnographic materials needed for the exhibit, and to do additional still photography and video documentation. With the cooperation of the Cultural Congress and the Chiefs of the islands of Mandi Ubigandup, Suitupu, and Tigre we were able to accomplish more than any of us thought possible.

Our project draws on research and collections from the 1920s by European and American scholars, scientists, and visitors to Kuna Yala, as well as to field research done over the past thirty years by the project consultants and other scholars. The range of historical materials, photographs, and collections from the early 1900s to the present make it possible to document Kuna expressive culture from this period. Objects and images from several early collections are included. For example, materials from the Field Museum including an elaborate feather headdress, curing objects, and mola blouses were collected prior to 1918 by G.L. Fitz-William, a chemical and mining engineer, and donated in 1919 in honor of his son William.

The earliest collection of molas at the National Museum of Natural History, Smithsonian Institution, was made by Eleanor Yorke Bell, an American woman who visited the Kuna in 1906. In 1918 and 1924, A. Hyatt Verill collected ethnographic materials in Panama for the Heye Foundation; his letters and unpublished reports are included in the documentation.

In 1922, Lady Richmond Brown, an adventurous British woman, and her companion, Frederick Mitchell Hedges, traveled to Panama and collected sixteen hundred molas and other objects. While most of the collection was given to the Museum of Mankind and the Pitt Rivers Museum in England, many of the molas in the exhibition were transferred to the Heye Foundation, now the National Museum of the American Indian. Extensive collections were also made during the Marsh Darién Expedition for the Smithsonian Institution in 1925.

Perhaps the largest documented collection of early Kuna materials in Europe is at the Göteborgs Etnografiska Museum, Sweden. In 1927 Baron Erland Nordenskiöld, a Swedish ethnographer, collected ethnographic objects including musical instruments, ritual objects, examples of picture-writing, and mola blouses. To further his collaborative research with the Kuna, Nordenskiöld invited Ruben Perez Kantule, a Kuna cultural specialist who had been working with him in Kuna Yala, to Sweden to work in the museum with him; Kuna specialist Guillermo Hayans continued that documentation.

Central to the interpretation in the present exhibition is an ethnoaesthetic approach to the study of early molas and ethnographic collections as well as contemporary examples. Research focused on how Kuna women interpret mola designs and how they evaluate their own work and the work of their peers, addressing the issue of what Kuna women consider to be beautiful and why. In the summers of 1992 and 1993, photographs of early molas (from the collections from the Göteborgs Etnografiska Museum, Sweden; the National Museum of the American Indian; and the National Museum of Natural History) were used to discuss the names and meaning of the designs as well as artistic criteria.

Building on this research, Kuna specialists were invited to go the United States to document the collections. In 1994, while representing the Kuna at the Festival of American Folklife in Washington, D.C., Cacique Leonidas Valdéz, first chief at the time; Serafina López, manager of the Mola Co-op; Rodolfina Andreve, a mola maker selected by the Co-op; and Nicanor González, spokesperson for the group, interpreted examples from the Kuna collections of the National Museum of Natural History. In 1996, Cacique Carlos López, first chief and renowned Kuna traditionalist; Elvira López, spokesperson for women throughout Kuna Yala; Balbina Denis, president of the Mola Co-op in 1996, and Nicanor González documented the entire Kuna collection at the National Museum of the American Indian in New York. It is their commentary that informs this exhibition and publication.

Currently throughout Kuna Yala there is debate surrounding issues of representation and multi-vocality. Who should speak for the group? How should Kuna culture be represented to the outside world? These questions, of concern to the consultants as well, guided us to work closely with specialists from Kuna Yala to insure that the project was in keeping with Kuna ways of presenting their culture. Kuna concerns regarding representation center on having appropriate people, who are properly prepared, speak on their behalf, ensuring that these spokespersons fully understand the issues and that they "get things right." The Kuna insist on being integrally involved in this and any other form of representation of their culture, and have demonstrated their willingness to collaborate on projects with outsiders for decades. They assert that their voice or voices be not only apparent in the final product but resonant throughout the process. They are interested in their culture and assume that others will be as well. Their concern is to provide a better understanding of Kuna society and accomplishments and to make cultural arguments as a rationale for the maintenance of their integrity, to support their rights, and to protect their political autonomy. By working in this way we hope that we were able to bring to the exhibition and the book a sense of the artfulness and beauty the Kuna bring to their everyday lives.

Mari Lyn Salvador

In the Words of Carlos López

Carlos López, first Cacique (high chief of Kuna Yala, is one of the greatest living Kuna traditionalists. A master of Father's Way, the sacred narrative, he has spent several decades interviewing participants of the rebellion of 1925, in which the Kuna threw off a police program aimed at eradicating their culture. The history of this rebellion, carried by Cacique López as oral tradition, which he relates to his followers on each anniversary of the 1925 rebellion, has recently been published in Panama as *Así lo ví, y así me lo contaron* (Thus I saw it, and thus they told me).

Cacique López participated throughout the planning and preparation of this volume and the exhibition at the UCLA Fowler Museum of Cultural History. In October 1996, he traveled to New York, as a member of the research team, to interpret and document the Kuna collections from the 1920s. In January 1997, he graciously agreed to an interview in Panama City to speak about Kuna culture for the benefit of the North American public.

Seated in front of the Panamanian flag, Cacique Carlos López, Cacique Leonidas Valdéz, and Argar Gilberto Arias attend a regional meeting. The Kuna flag, created during the 1925 Revolution, has a traditional decorative motif taken from Kuna basketry.
Mari Lyn Salvador, Suitupu, 1994.

In excerpts included here, Cacique López discusses the Kuna relationship with nature, as well as the origin of three primary elements in their culture: house-building, political leadership, and mola-making. Like everything good in the world, the Kuna attribute these gifts to their relationship as a people with the deities, Great Father and Great Mother. Great Mother sits with Father above in heaven, called Father's Place, but she is also the earth, and like her human counterparts, Great Mother inspires devotion from her Kuna children.

Where do we come from? We come from Great Mother, it is said, We come for the earth. The great seers of the past discovered this. That is what we come for, they said. I will tell you. The earth is Great Mother, they say. Everything is born from her, they say. Everything is born in her, they say. The trees are born, corn, sweet potato—every last thing, to the very end, they say… Everything that is born of Mother will end in Mother. Mother is the earth. The trees are her kin. The rivers are her kin, it is said. There is a layer of gold [underground]; there is a silver layer, there is an iron layer; there is a copper layer—it is the earth's heart, they say. The elders say this: [the earth] has bile, it has lungs…. It is truly alive. The great seers discovered all of this. "The soul of the place, what is it? The land, what is it? How was the land made?" This was the seers' message for us…And the fathers learned this, and caring for the land had truly come.

Teachers like Carlos López find the essence of what the Kuna do today in its historical origins, with the series of prophets and seers sent to earth by Great Father to instruct and reform the animal-peoples who preceded the Kuna. One of the greatest of these culture heroes was named Ibeorgun. With his sister Kikadiryai, Ibeorgun did away with crude bestial habits; taught the verbal, visual, and musical arts; and gave the correct names for all the parts of the social and natural world. Here Cacique López tells how Ibeorgun showed people to make houses and then how to use the most important of those buildings, the village gathering house, to manage their affairs and communicate with Great Father. Just as a house has many named parts forming a unified whole, so the village as instituted by Ibeorgun includes multiple, named leaders working for the common good. Not surprisingly, the Kuna often refer to the gathering house as Ibeorgun's house.

Then Ibeorgun came. Ibeorgun came. Father sent him…. People's dwellings were made of palm leaves piled one on top of the other, that's what they slept on. There weren't any houses yet like those we live in. Their dwellings were just the palm fronds….

Then Ibeorgun came, and he said, "Elders this isn't how it is. We will sleep in houses…. First you get a center post [buar]," he said. "It's the leader," he said. "Get a sidepost [usor]," he said. "Get rafters [maket]," he said. "Get purlins [sagirbir]…. Get a ridge pole [asubir]."…The elders were learning…. The house was built….

"In this house, three people will lead: the chief; the argar [chief's spokesman or interpreter]; and the master-of-the-staves [constable]. Three of them."…

Ibeorgun said, "This house, I will give it a name," he said. "I'll call it the Golden Listening House…. He was speaking of the gathering house. "I'll call it the Golden Speech House. Inside this house, speech will be put in order, one word after another….

"Truly said. This house that we will place here, it is for admonishing the members," he said. "To call the Father," he said. "That's why a hammock has been strung there. That's why it has another hammock as its counterpart. For the chief who leads [in chanting] and the chief who follows. We will choose eight chiefs," he said…. "For you to help each other. In order for you to manage things as a group…. It can't be done by one person by himself. So you will be sitting and consulting with each other."

"Here people will be admonished. They will be admonished,"…Ibeorgun said, "If someone breaks the rules, you will call to him… 'Young man, this is how you went wrong.'…If someone has struck his wife, you will call to him," he said, "'That is not the way, if you thought so. Hitting your wife, that's not the way.'…If someone marries two wives, 'That's not the way either,' you will say. 'You will marry only one wife.' That's what Father said…. That's what this house was put here for."

"Everyone can be admonished: an elder medicine man, a flute man [puberty chanter]-all will be admonished. The grandmothers who catch junglefowl [midwives], everyone will be admonished. A chief will be admonished too. It is a world in which anyone can do wrong. That's why this house is truly communal….

"That's why this house was built. Every day you will open it…. This hammock here, it doesn't hang here for no reason. If you come here and you are a chief, right away you lower it down [to get into it]…. They say about that, don't let the hammock be just to gather mold, don't let the hammock be just for spiders."… Speaking in metaphors had come too. Ibeorgun said all this. "That's what I have come to put this house here for."

"You will call Father. There will be chanting about Father's Way. There will be singing every day…. And the argar, he is the chief's interpreter. He is your second in command." He began to put things in order like that…. That's how it was born,

Ibeorgun's House. You hear.

Cacique López also narrates the origin of clothing and mola-making, describing how Ibeorgun and Kikadiryai taught women to make cloth from pounded tree bark, and to make needles, thread, and dyes from other trees and plants. Kikadiryai went on to teach women how to cut mola designs, which she named after the elements of the natural world from which they were taken. As with house construction, the narrative underlines the central importance of language in Kuna life, because the people had to learn what to call things as well as how to use them.

Our grandfathers [ancestors] lived there. They have always lived on this land. There were no molas then like those today. The grandmothers, the clothes they wore were animal skins, it is said. Heron skins, pelican skins, parrot skins, macaw skins, jungle fowl skins—that's what they used for clothes....

Then Iheorgun arrived.... He saw when he arrived that they wore animal skins, the grandmothers did.... "Young bwiba-*tree, it will become your clothing," he said. "Young* urtu *will become clothing," he said. "Ikor-tree will become clothing," he said.... "You put this in water for awhile. You scrape its bark and put it in water, for eight days."... In this way Iheorgun was...really putting the grandmothers to work. They did it, and it turned out well.... Those trees were turned into clothing....*

"You will boil it in [the juice of] the disgela *plant," he said. "You will boil it in* abgi," *he said. "You will boil it in* goka," *he said..."So it will turn black...So it will turn white."*

"Where will we find thread?" he said. To sew it. Oa-plant leaves began to be cut. Nila leaves began to sew cut. They split the nila *leaves. It was made into thread. Molas were sewn with it.... "And where will we find needles?" he said. We will make needles from* sinyu" *[a tree with long thorns].... Then molas began to be sewed for the first time....*

Iheorgun did this, and then [his sister] Kikadiryai worked on it.... Women all became mola makers.... Grandmother Kikadriyai said, "Now, I will tell you the names of molas. Where does this mola come from?-from the invisible world. I was ready to come here from the world above. Star girls live up there. You will wear star molas," she said. "We will cut star molas."... Rainbow molas came here. Kikadiryai introduced them. "Mist molas," she said. "It looks white," she said. "You will cut mist molas," she said. Molas began to come out like that. "They come from the soul of the place," she said. ... "Basket-weave molas," she said. "Snail-path molas," she said. Kikadiryai was truly bringing out every last kind of mola..."Crayfish molas," she said. She was setting them all out. Every last one, by how it looked....

Then cut molas were introduced. There were still no scissors. "What will we use for scissors?" Signu-tree wood came to be used as scissors. To cut out molas. The grandmothers were working.... At one river after another, at every village, they started to do these things.

Interview translated and transcribed by James Howe

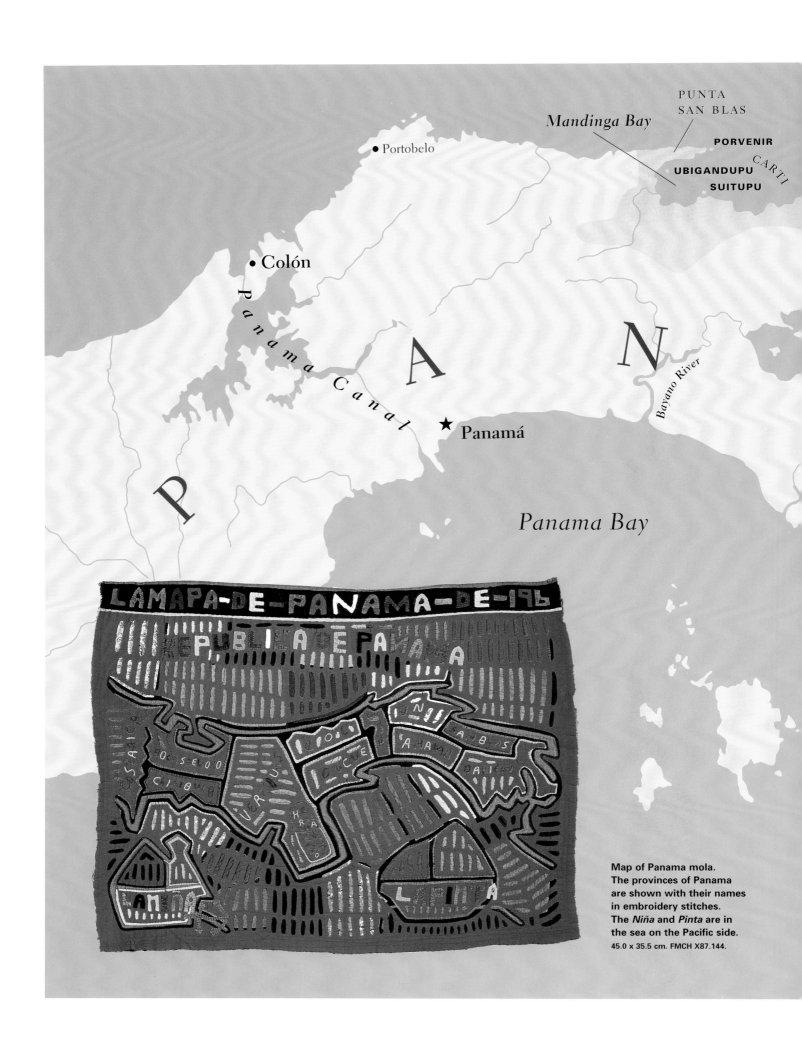

PUNTA
SAN BLAS

Mandinga Bay

PORVENIR

CARTI

UBIGANDUPU

SUITUPU

● Portobelo

● Colón

Panama Canal

P   A   N

Bayano River

★ Panamá

P

Panama Bay

Map of Panama mola.
The provinces of Panama
are shown with their names
in embroidery stitches.
The *Niña* and *Pinta* are in
the sea on the Pacific side.
45.0 x 35.5 cm. FMCH X87.144.

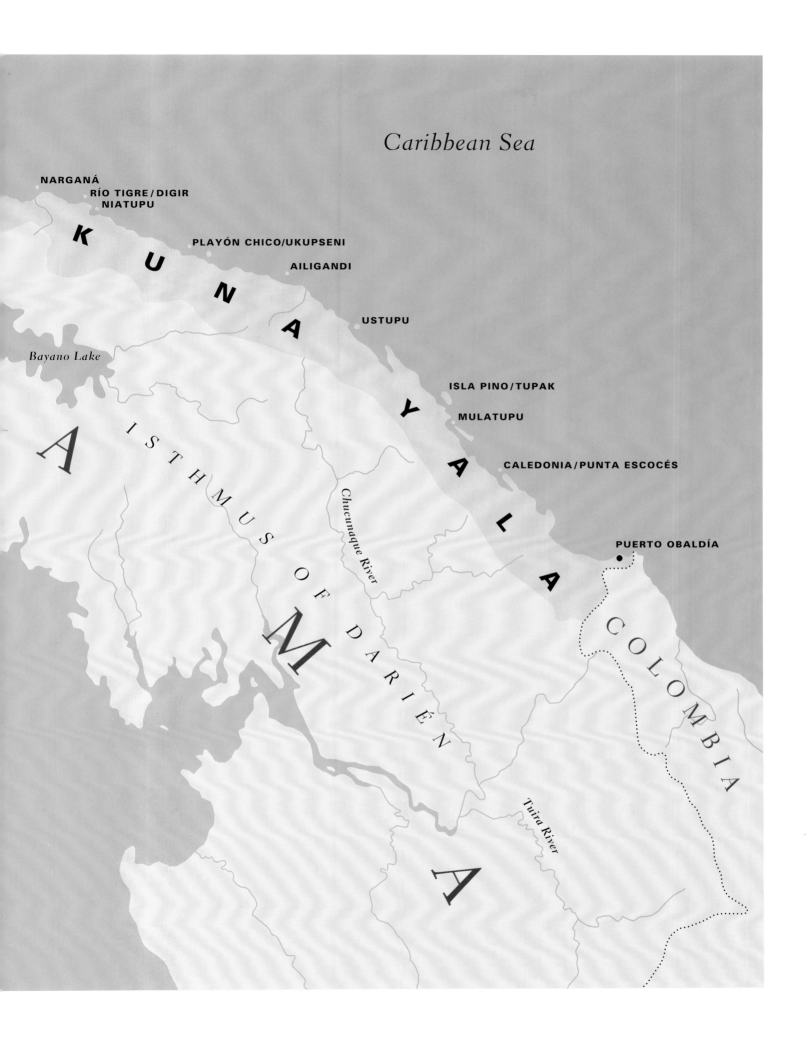

Caribbean Sea

NARGANÁ
RÍO TIGRE / DIGIR
NIATUPU

K U N A

PLAYÓN CHICO/UKUPSENI
AILIGANDI

USTUPU

Bayano Lake

Y A L A

ISLA PINO/TUPAK
MULATUPU

A

I S T H M U S   O F   D A R I É N

CALEDONIA / PUNTA ESCOCÉS

Chucunaque River

PUERTO OBALDÍA

M

COLOMBIA

A

Tuira River

Introduction

Artful Lives

The Kuna of Panama

Mari Lyn Salvador and James Howe

sunna ukupa dar baryosa dar itole an soge itole.
demmar billigan akuma soku ukuparbi dar daniki gudaylee.

    degii.

inso mubilli de nue dar marwe mai soku nega nabir dayle an soge idole.
bela ukub arradiki bilid bardakedani sunyee.

    degii

an aiye Enrique ambogwa dani dayle "aiye babadi nega dar sade be dake" soge itole.
"mai baba arbasa dayleye" obaryee.

    degii

In truth we began to walk again along the great beach it is heard I say it is heard.
We were observing the tranquil tops [waves] of the sea I say coming along the beach.

    So it is.

Thus the waves were so tranquil that the place seemed beautiful I say it is heard.
On the beach it was all blue as we came truly seeing it.

    So it is.

I was coming along with my friend Enrique see "Friend it is Father who made
    this wonderful world you see" it is said it is heard.
"One can recognize this as the work of Father" I pronounce.

    So it is.[1]

        — A ritual greeting between two Kuna chiefs, Muladupu, 5 July 1970;
        the first chants a verse and the second responds *degii*.

1.1. **Dad Ibe mola blouse (detail).
Dad Ibe, the sun, is represented with
radiating golden rays within a star
between two crescent moons. The
design on the other side of the
blouse, shown in Figure 6.48, has
stars and moons but no central figure.
By Doralina Denis, Suitupu, 1997.**
63.0 x 108.0 cm. Private collection.

The Kuna of Panama live in a land of remarkable beauty, a beauty expressed and celebrated in their verbal and visual arts. They have created an aesthetic system that crosscuts all aspects of their culture and is linked to their worldview.

To the Kuna, each part of the natural world—rainforest, rivers, and mountains, birds and animals, their own farms and coconut groves, the islands on which they live, the sea and its fish—each is a gift from their deities, Great Father and Great Mother. Through the verbal arts, they express their feelings of admiration and appreciation for the natural environment, as well their responsibility to protect the earth, which they say is the body of the Great Mother. When Kuna chiefs sing to their followers, they remind them of Father's generosity and Mother's bounty, of the land's fruitfulness, of the pleasure they take from its cool winds and sweet smells, of the mist that hangs over the forest, of the earth's response to the rising sun. The following passage, typical of chiefly discourse, comes from a narrative about a great past leader, Cimral Colman:

> In the morning Grandfather Colman would sing about how Father had given them the land. About the rising of Dad Ibe, the sun, how Dad Ibe came renewing his headdress…he came waking up the trees. "The birds respond, 'A great person is coming…' the birds respond. 'This person, a good person is coming, he is the one who gave us bread, he is the one who gave us drink, he has cared for us,' they sing…. We people, we are here too," he said. As for us, Father put us here too. "In the whole world…only through the sun do they have food to eat. Only through Father can they eat. We are the same…he established the world, he came to give us the world…. He put wild pig here, we came to hold the land. 'This you will eat,' following Father's words…. He put the fish there for us. He gave us the sea. 'Care for the fish,' Father said." Thus Grandfather sang.[2]

In another narrative, Cacique Enrique Guerrero (Ventocilla, 1995) refers to the earth:

> The earth is the mother of all things, the Great Mother.
> She is the guardian who caringly watches over all that exists.
>
> The Great Mother helps us stay in equilibrium.

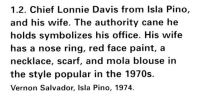

1.2. Chief Lonnie Davis from Isla Pino, and his wife. The authority cane he holds symbolizes his office. His wife has a nose ring, red face paint, a necklace, scarf, and mola blouse in the style popular in the 1970s.
Vernon Salvador, Isla Pino, 1974.

1.3. Noga Kope dancers. Men playing panpipes and women playing rattles form two parallel lines as they dance. James Howe, Niatupu, 1995.

The Kuna have created a remarkable range of verbal, visual, and performance arts that gives us insights into what they value, what they think, and how they feel. Expressive culture enriches all aspects of Kuna life, reflects ideology and worldview, communicates with the spirit world, and provides the context for demonstrating skill and distinguishing personal achievement.

Visual and verbal artistry is integrated into everyday dress, adornment, housing, politics, and ritual; each element has its spiritual dimension and its place in Great Father's plan for his people, and each task is carried out with expressive creativity and aesthetic discernment. In the Kuna cosmos, everything in the world, whether natural, cultural, or spiritual, is divided by gender, and almost every specific kind of verbal or visual art belongs either to males or females but not to both. Moreover, although women sing and men produce objects, verbal art is predominantly associated with men, and visual arts with women.

The Kuna enjoy speaking in the artful language of everyday life, and take pleasure in joking and playful conversation. The primary verbal arts of the men include singing and eloquent political oratory, and the chanting that animates and guides activities in the spirit world. Kuna women sew elaborate mola blouses and have created a unique dress style that is an art form in and of itself. The performance arts, music and dance, which bring verbal and visual elements together and involve the participation of both men and women, are generally associated with girls' puberty ceremonies. Recently established inter-island dance festivals offer opportunities to celebrate and publicly demonstrate musical ability and finesse (Fig. 1.3).

The Kuna in the world

The Kuna are for the most part a coastal people, poised at the border between sea and land. They remember a time, however, when their ancestors lived along great mainland rivers all across the eastern Isthmus at places that even today have Indian names. For more than two hundred years the Kuna resisted Spanish attempts to missionize and subdue them, finding allies in the British and French pirates who preyed on Panama's mines and colonies. Peace did not come until the end of the

1.4. In addition to providing transportation routes, mainland rivers are a source of fresh water. Vernon Salvador, 1974.

eighteenth century, after the pirates had disappeared and the field of international conflict moved elsewhere.

When Latin America gained its independence early in the nineteenth century, some of the Kuna lived at the headwaters of rivers that flow to the Pacific or just off the Isthmus to the east, but many inhabited the northern Caribbean coast, in communities prudently sited a few miles inland. Toward the middle of the century, some people began to move their villages a few hundred yards offshore onto small islands. The thorny brush, mangrove swamps, and evil spirits thought to inhabit many of these islands hindered settlement, and a few villages even disappeared underwater during a great earthquake in 1882, but the Kuna persisted, anxious to escape snakes, mosquitoes, and endemic disease, as well as to increase contact with foreign trading boats. Today, of forty-nine coastal villages, only eleven remain on the shore.

This northern strip of the Darién, between the Caribbean and the mountain spine of the Isthmus, has since colonial times been known to outsiders as the Coast of San Blas. The Kuna call it "the long land" (*yar suid*) or simply the land or mountain (*yala*); in the 1980s they replaced the foreign term of San Blas with Kuna Yala, the name we use in this volume. Between Cabo Tiburón at the Colombian border in the east and Punta San Blas 130 miles to the west, the crest of the mountains is never

1.5. Clouds swell up over the mainland and the island village of Nusatupu.
James Howe, 1978.

more than ten miles inland, and in most places the hills come down to the sea (Fig. 1.5). They are drained by clear rocky streams and rivers which, with a few exceptions, never attain much size except during downpours in the rainy season, when they overflow their banks and send muddy floodwater miles out to sea.

The inshore waters are dotted with hundreds of small islands. A very few such as Tupak or "Whale Island" (*Isla Pino* in Spanish) in the east have their own hills and streams, but the rest are flat coral outcroppings a foot or two above sea level (Figs. 1.6, 1.7). In the western third of Kuna Yala, the coastal zone begins to widen, protected by parallel chains of offshore islands and ending in a broad expanse of deep water called Mandinga Bay or the Gulf of San Blas.

The Kuna, traveling on the ocean in small dugout canoes, have become accomplished sailors (Figs. 1.8, 1.9). They paddle and sail between neighboring islands and to and from the mainland but now often use outboards for longer trips. Colombian traders in vessels known locally as *canoas* arrive regularly to buy coconuts, and communities on a number of the largest and most enterprising Kuna islands run their own

1.6 (ABOVE LEFT). In 1922 Lady Richmond Brown and her companion Frederick Mitchell Hedges visited several small islands. They noted that three families lived on this island at the time of their visit.
F.A. Mitchell Hedges, 1922.

1.7 (ABOVE RIGHT). A small island in the Carti area.
Sergio Salvador, 1997.

1.8. Boys fishing from the front of a *cayuco* docked at island's edge.
Vernon Salvador, Ailigandi, 1974.

1.9. Just before sunrise, men prepare to sail to the mainland to prepare the fields, plant, care for and harvest crops, and tend the coconut trees. Here, men about to go fishing are netting minnows for bait.
James Howe, Ubigandup, 1997.

trading boats between Colon and Kuna Yala (Fig. 1.11). During the dry season from January to April, which is also the tourist season, massive cruise ships arrive regularly in Mandinga Bay; European- and North American-owned yachts are ubiquitous throughout the year, and small planes from Panama City land each day at village-owned airstrips up and down the coast.

To feed their families, Kuna men return each day to the mainland for slash-and-burn agriculture, in which the great staples—bananas, plantains, and root crops—are supplemented by corn, rice, and seasonal fruits (Figs. 1.12-14). From the shore up into

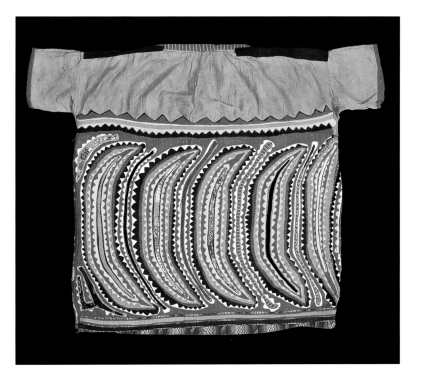

the hills, the land is covered by a dense patchwork of banana and coconut groves, scattered fruit trees, corn and rice fields, woodlands being cleared for burning and planting, older fallow plots covered with second growth, and swatches of forest set aside for the spirits and botanical medicines. Only several miles inland and uphill does the old rain forest reassert itself.

Some men hunt, but game is scarce near the coast, and most animal protein in the Kuna diet comes from the sea. In the nineteenth and early twentieth centuries, the Kuna took abundant conch and lobster in shallow water, netted sea turtles for their shells, and harpooned huge tarpon that they drove into aquatic corrals on the sand flats. Today some cooperative groups net schooling fish, and divers take shellfish and reef fish, but tarpon, lobster, and turtle are diminishing, and most of the catch is taken on hook and line baited with minnows netted in shallow waters.

Having traded with outsiders for several hundred years, the Kuna began in the late nineteenth century to produce coconuts for the international market, eventually planting almost every uninhabited island and usable stretch of mainland shore with palms (Figs. 1.13, 1.14). Coconut cropping, the mainstay of the cash economy through much of the present century, has increasingly been supplemented by diving for lobster and octopus, and by tourism, as well as by wage labor outside of Kuna Yala. Further, Kuna women have developed a brisk business of selling molas and mola products to tourists and outside buyers. In recent years, as cash needs have increased and coconut production has suffered from endemic blight and a weakening market, these alternative pursuits have all intensified.

As the Kuna see it, they have a duty to protect the land and the coastal seas. The fear that outsiders would violate Great Mother's body has repeatedly motivated them to counter intruders who would exploit the land: invasive rubber-tappers and turtlers in the 1910s and 1920s; in recent years, Colombian immigrants, ranchers and peasants

1.10. *Ulu,* canoe mola blouse. Kuna women illustrate all types of boats used in Kuna Yala in their molas. Here the design is based on the side view of the dugout canoe, which is used as the primary mode of transportation by women as well as men.
67.5 x 80.0 cm. NMAI 16/6434. Collected and presented by Lady Richmond Brown and F.A. Mitchell Hedges.

1.11. *Coveñas,* a Colombian trade boat docked in Kuna Yala.
Vernon Salvador, Ailigandi, 1974.

1.12. Harvesting rice on the mainland.
James Howe, c. 1970.

1.13. Man carrying a netted bag full of coconuts on one end of a pole balances his cargo with bananas on the other end.
Mari Lyn Salvador, Ailigandi, 1974.

1.14. Husking a coconut. Baskets are often used for carrying and storing fruits and other agricultural products as well as for medicinal plants.
James Howe, 1970.

from western Panama, and multinational mining companies. In the course of this struggle, the Kuna have seen their own ties with nature weaken, as traditional medicinalists die out and many young men abandon agriculture for the cash economy, and the Kuna have begun to recognize a duty to protect Great Mother not just from outsiders but from themselves, from their own carelessness and over-exploitation of her resources.

Island living

Most villages lie a few hundred yards offshore, near the mouth of a mainland river: the one closest in is connected to the mainland by a footbridge, while a handful in western Kuna Yala lie much further out, several miles into Mandinga Bay (Fig. 1.15).

1.15. Kuna women use their scarves for privacy as well as to protect them from the sun.
Mari Lyn Salvador, Ailigandi, 1974.

1.16. Houses are so tightly clustered on many islands that the thatched roofs almost touch.
Mari Lyn Salvador, Suitupu, 1997.

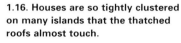

Except for a few fortunate communities that still retain a little open space for coconut groves or a landing field, most are packed tightly from one side to the other with houses, and today anyone who wants to build must create a new site by filling in shallow water with rocks and sand. Traditional dwellings constructed on a frame of massive tree trunks, with thatched roofs and walls of cane or bamboo, predominate almost everywhere, though cement houses with roofs composed of artificial materials (i.e., tin, plastic, asbestos) grow increasingly common, particularly for churches and public buildings (Figs. 1.16–18).

On some islands, homes are arranged in neat rows facing onto wide streets, a smaller cookhouse hiding behind each massive sleeping house; on others, a cookhouse, sleeping house, and satellite structures are loosely grouped into small fenced

1.17 (ABOVE LEFT). **Electric plant on the island of Suitupu, the island of the crab.**
Sergio Salvador, 1997.

1.18 (RIGHT). Baptist church on the island of Ailigandi.
Mari Lyn Salvador, 1984.

1.19 (BELOW). Corn, bundles of rice, and cacao beans are often dried in the streets in the afternoon sun.
Vernon Salvador, Ailigandi, 1974.

1.20 (BELOW RIGHT). Sorting dried corn kernels.
Mari Lyn Salvador, Ailigandi, 1974.

1.21 (BOTTOM RIGHT). Women outside the gathering house. If the topic pertains to them they attend and sit inside.
Mari Lyn Salvador, Ailigandi, 1974.

1.22. Although fish are traditionally exchanged between households, cooperative societies also sell fish caught in seine nets.
Mari Lyn Salvador, Ailigandi, 1974.

compounds, separated only by narrow alleyways. The corners of family compounds and the spaces between houses are devoted to coconut palms and banana plants; gourd, mango, and breadfruit trees; hot pepper plants and medicinal herbs; and when the sun is out, lines of drying clothes and basins of corn and rice (Figs. 1.19, 1.20).

Every island has at least two public buildings, both of them enlarged versions of a traditional dwelling: a gathering house (*onmaked nega*) or congress house, where the community manages its affairs and assembles as a religious congregation, and a *chicha* house (*inna nega*), where the community celebrates the coming-of-age of its young girls. Today all but one or two villages also have elementary schools; many have Baptist,

1.23. Cinder block stores are often painted in bright colors.
Mari Lyn Salvador, Tupile, 1984.

Catholic, or Mormon missions; and all of them construct public docks for trading boats (Fig. 1.22). Even the most crowded villages reserve space for a basketball court. Stores are plentiful. They range from tiny operations run out of a home, where neighbors can buy sugar and salt, dry goods, soft drinks, and kerosene, to much larger shops in concrete buildings stocked with clothing, fabric, canned foods, sundries, and an occasional restaurant. Many of these stores are owned and staffed by members of cooperative societies (Fig. 1.23).

In the morning, when children are in school and men are off-island fishing or working in mainland farms, most villages are quiet, with only scattered individuals passing through the streets (Fig. 1.25). Groups of women paddle to nearby rivers to fill water bottles and wash clothes, except on islands that now have aqueducts to bring fresh water from the mainland (Fig. 1.26). By midday or early afternoon, fishermen begin returning, and as the day wears on, agriculturalists sail and paddle home with canoeloads of bananas, coconuts, and firewood. After workers and schoolchildren have changed clothes and eaten, the streets begin to fill with children at play and

1.27 (OPPOSITE, TOP LEFT). **Rinsing grated coconut for *dule masi,* a traditional fish stew.**
Mari Lyn Salvador, Ubigandup, 1997.

1.28 (OPPOSITE, TOP RIGHT). **In the late afternoon children play in the street.**
Sergio Salvador, Suitupu, 1997.

1.24 (TOP). **A school parade on a rainy day.**
James Howe, Niatupu, 1970.

1.25 (ABOVE LEFT). **Women visiting in the shade outside a store.**
Vernon Salvador, Ailigandi, 1974.

1.26 (ABOVE RIGHT). **Women going to the mainland to get water in 1922.**
F.A. Mitchell Hedges, 1922.

adults who are visiting friends, attending meetings, shopping, playing basketball, and, most of all, talking. The noise and activity do not cease until well after sunset (Figs. 1.28, 1.29).

Many men and women also live far from Kuna Yala, in cities or on the banana plantations of Bocas del Toro. For many years, Kuna men have left home in small numbers for months or years of wage labor, the great majority eventually returning home to their families. Since the 1970s, the flow of migrants has greatly increased, encompassing whole families drawn by the greater educational opportunities of the city as well as by paid employment. Today, many urban Kuna have chosen to live close to each other, sometimes in the same apartment building or in the same neighborhoods as well as in settlements on the city outskirts (Fig. 1.31) (see Marta Lucía de Gerdes, this volume).

1.29. Many islands have basketball teams.
Sergio Salvador, Suitupu, 1997.

1.30. Basketball mola. A favorite sport in Kuna Yala, basketball is often depicted on molas.
61.0 x 68.0 cm. NMAI 24/7986. Presented by Elena Eritta.

1.31. Kuna women shopping in downtown Panama City. Many fabric stores have special sections with the imported material the women use for their skirts and scarves, as well as poplin for making molas.
Sergio Salvador, 1997.

1.32. Colorful painted design on the prow of a canoe.
Mari Lyn Salvador, Ubigandup, 1997.

The artfulness of life

Each sphere of Kuna life has its associated art forms, even the domestic sphere. In addition to fashioning household implements and cooking utensils, Kuna men also make and use baskets, canoes, and dwellings. Basketry is treated as an explicit marker of Kuna identity, a skill traditionally expected of all grown males: one often sees men quietly weaving firefans and baskets with complex designs while listening to a meeting or attending a ritual (Fig. 1.33). Canoe making, the ability to shape a tree trunk into the graceful form of a sea-going dugout, is a rare skill of high prestige. Each owner, however, decorates his own canoe and, if needed, sews elegant sails out of old flour sacks and other scraps of material (Fig. 1.32).

House construction is a collective enterprise, one in which some men have special knowledge but all play their roles, just as the house itself is a collection of named and symbolically significant pieces that when lashed together create an aesthetically pleasing whole standing for the solidarity of kin and community. The household is also the main context for making molas. Women, sitting in their hammocks or on long benches, spend hours each day sewing. Talking all the while, they learn from each other. Over the past hundred years, they have developed a beautiful art form that is a visual expression of their identity.

Other than conversation, the domestic verbal arts are largely female. Women wail for the dead; women and girls sing little songs to the parakeets found in many homes; and most of all they sing lullabies. In passing through the streets of a Kuna village, one hears over and over the creaking of house timbers as they are pulled back and forth by swinging hammocks, the sound of rattles, and the rapid, high-pitched voices of young girls singing to to the babies in the family about all the things they will do when they grow up.

The village gathering house is the center for politics and religion, which are intertwined in Kuna culture (see the chapters by Howe and

Sherzer) (Fig. 1.35). Several nights a week and often in the morning as well, one of several village chiefs sings to his followers about history or cosmology and about how they should act as Kuna men and women. Mola-making and basket-weaving continue while women and men listen. The men elected as chiefs function not only as sacred leaders and repositories of tradition but also as poets, composing their chants as they sing them and working variations on traditional themes and metaphors. On other nights, when village men hold talking meetings, followers as well as chiefs create verbal arts in the form of oratory, admonishments, reports, greetings, storytelling, and jokes (Howe 1986). Although village politics has traditionally been a male domain, women now speak in meetings, such as those of the mola cooperative, and some progressive villages have elected female leaders.

Outside the gathering house, ritual focuses on curing and female puberty, both of which connect humans with the world of spirit. In Kuna thought, illness follows from the action of hostile spirits, who kidnap, damage, or invade human souls (see Chapin, in this volume). For relief, the Kuna call most often on practitioners called *ina duled* (medicine persons), who cure with physical medicines, which they "admonish" (*unae*) or instruct during short chants. Since most of the substances they collect come from trees and plants, medicinalists acquire a deep and wide-ranging knowledge of botany and the world of the forest. Other specialists called *igar wisid* (chant knowers) cure by performing long narratives to expel evil spirits or rescue a patient's soul.

Curing of all sorts depends on the help of familiar spirits, who are represented by objects of various sorts, most of all by small carved figures called *nuchu, suar nuchu,* or *suar mimmi* (Fig. 1.36). Although many outsiders have noted the striking resemblance of these

1.33 (ABOVE LEFT). Man making a basket at a curing ceremony. The curer is chanting at the end of the patient's hammock.
James Howe, Niatupu, 1970.

1.34 (ABOVE RIGHT). Celina Porras, a member of the Mola Co-op, starting a mola. Small gold pendants have become popular for everyday wear.
Mari Lyn Salvador, 1994.

1.35. Regional meeting in the gathering house on the island of Suitupu. The sign reads, "A people that loses its tradition loses its soul."
Mari Lyn Salvador, 1994.

carvings to eighteenth- or nineteenth-century Europeans, the Kuna insist that it is not external form that matters, but the spiritual qualities represented by the woods from which the figures are carved. Every household has its box of figures which, when not actively following the instructions of the igar wisid, guard the household members against spirit intrusion. Every few years, when epidemics threaten or the spirit world is "heated up," villages hold mass exorcisms, in which specialists called *absoged* (conversers) chant for eight nights. For these crisis rituals, villages carve much larger, human-sized figures out of balsa logs called *ukur war* (see Chapin, in this volume).

The visual arts associated with healing also include picture-writing (discussed by Carlo Severi, in this volume), which is used to represent medicines and chants, and wooden canes carved with designs reminiscent of nuchu figures. Each time an igar wisid goes to chant at the foot of a patient's hammock, he carries with him a cane representing his prestige and cultural authority. Similar canes of a slightly different design belong to the realm of politics: although chiefs today are less likely than in the past to bear a staff of office, village constables or policemen are so identified with their canes that they are called *sual ibgana* (masters of the staffs).

Puberty rituals given for Kuna girls when they come of age are held in the chicha house, a large structure much like the gathering house but used only for this event. These events provide the occasion for a profusion of visual and especially verbal arts, as well as for participation by the community-at-large, alongside ritual specialists. In the longest ceremonies, the central figure, called *gandule* (flute person), performs a chant cycle of three or four days' duration. The festivities are orchestrated by the

1.36. *Nuchu* in wooden boxes in a family home. Alongside them, a brazier contains the ashes from burnt cocoa beans and behind is a box with objects used for medicine.
Mari Lyn Salvador, Suitupu, 1994.

1.37. Women dancing at a girl's puberty ceremony. They are wearing headdresses like those used by the *gandule,* the ritual specialists, and his assistants.
James Howe, Isla Tigre, 1970.

gandule, the ritual specialist who, chanting to the sprit of his long flute, guides the activities in the spirit world (Fig. 1.37).

Many other men and women play specialized ritual roles—blowing smoke from long homemade cigars, dancing with clattering necklaces of bird bones, cutting the hair of the pubescent girl—while the village at large enjoys dancing, drinking, and engaging in verbal art. Women sing to each other of kinship and friendship, while men play panpipes and other flutes or perform excerpts from the curing chants in their repertoires. At intervals during the festivities, men and women stand up and join in vigorous stomping dances called *gwile* (see Smith, in this volume).

Traditionally, the Kuna did not dance in secular settings outside the puberty ceremonies. After World War II, however, a dance group was formed on the island of Río Tigre, which performed new dances called *noga kope* (drink the cup) combining traditional steps and panpipe music with folkloric figures. In the beginning, many other Kuna fervently opposed this new art form, but over the last half-century it has gained acceptance, and on many islands, dance troupes perform outdoors in the village center several days a week. The musicians play flutes and gourd rattles and the groups often wear coordinated outfits, performing in spaces decorated with mola panels and flags made from colorful pieces of fabric.

Kuna aesthetics

The Kuna have a lively aesthetic and sensory appreciation of both Great Father's creation and their own. Whether speaking of the fragrant scent of herbs, the feel of a cool wind, the brilliance of the sun in early morning over the forest, the look of a finely stitched mola, the sound of chanting, or the appeal of a new metaphor, they readily say that something *yer dailege* (looks great, beautiful) or *nabir itolege* (feels, sounds fine)—or, if something displeases them, that it *isdar yapane* (smells terrible) or *isdar dailege* (looks bad). Mola makers observe everything around them, thinking always about new designs and motifs, just as orators and chiefly chanters devise new poetic figures to capture their audiences' imaginations.

As the Kuna see it, aesthetic goodness has a moral dimension, one that goes back to the original creation. "In the beginning, Tiolele [Great Father] unfolded the surface of the earth, it looked beautiful, he was thinking of our future well-being" (Chapin 1983, 262). At each stage of the sacred history of creation and destruction that leads eventually to "The Golden People," moral goodness goes with soft earth, mild winds, sweet smells, and human order, while corruption is signaled by foul winds and slovenliness as well as immorality, leading inevitably to Great Father's anger, destruction, and a new beginning. In each day, the rising of the sun and its life-giving voyage across the sky manifest the beneficence of creation. And in each lifetime, good Kuna are confident of seeing their heavenly parents in "Father's Place" above, which is filled with gold and silver flags and flowers.

Spirits share the same aesthetic appreciation, which is evident in the chants used to direct and control them. In his chapter on curing, Mac Chapin illustrates the power of poetic language to

1.38. Geometric mola blouse, with a basket design. Collected by Baron Erland Nordenskiöld in 1927.
85.5 x 86.0 cm. EMG 1927.27.877.

1.39. Flowers are used as a metaphor to describe the beauty and character of Kuna women.
Sergio Salvador, Mainland in Carti, 1997.

1.40. Relaxing after cooking. Elder women as well as young girls take care with the way they dress and express their identity through their clothing.
Mari Lyn Salvador, Ubigandup, 1997.

encourage spirit participation in the curing process. As he notes, "The most effective specialists are those who can converse with the spirits in their own tongue and, in so doing, delight them by weaving complex tapestries of metaphor, poetry, and elaborate descriptions. The spirits appreciate this talent for intricate description. It 'makes them feel good' and bends them to the curative tasks they are being asked to perform." The more the spirits enjoy what they hear, the more ready they are to cooperate.

The chants used to communicate with the spirits are filled with lavish detail, and with reference to the senses and to pleasurable experiences, as is evident in an excerpt from the chant directed toward Muu, the spirit grandmother-midwife who controls childbirth and the formation of new humans (Chapin 1983, 518):

> On Muu's table, Muu's golden flowers are standing in rows.
> On Muu's table, Muu's golden flowers are becoming yellow.
> With the wind against them, Muu's golden flowers are singing.
> With the wind against them, Muu's golden flowers are making noise,
> they are all like the winds of the golden keli bird
> With the wind against them they are all fragrant,
> all the golden flowers on the table are fragrant
> All are fragrant, Muu's house is fragrant.

Several of the dominant principles of Kuna aesthetics that have been noted by anthropologists over the years are discussed by authors of this volume.[3] Perhaps the most apparent principle is balance, especially balance between pairs, of which the prime example is man and woman. This principle emerged strongly in discussion with Kuna experts who came to the National Museum of the American Indian in October 1996 to comment on materials in the collections there. Balbina Denis noted, "*Iberogun nos dijo que no se vivan sólos, ni hombre ni mujer, siempre en pares, y por eso todo viene en pares*" (Ibeorgun told us not to live alone, neither man nor woman, and for that reason everything comes in pairs).[4]

Thus, as Sandra Smith points out, panpipes are played in pairs, called man and woman, leader and follower. Mola blouses have similar designs on front and back, as well as balance between the sides of a panel. Chiefs and flute players chant in pairs, each responding to the other in turn. Even curing chants, which are performed by a single ritualist, are understood as one half of a dialogue with the spirit world. Balance, however, is not static or complete. Male and female panpipes have different pitches, and chanting chiefs take different roles. The symmetry between the two sides of a mola panel, similarly, is never exact, nor are the two panels of a blouse ever identical. Rather, symmetry and repetition are the fields against which small significant variations can be elaborated, creating tension and a complex texture of similarity and difference.

In Kuna chanting, this combination of repetition with change is the basis for parallelism, the dominant poetic principle in the oral literature of many societies. In the chants, the extended series of parallel verses encourages length, complexity, and detail, which are all valued in visual as well as verbal art. Just as a puberty chant may list the actions of the ritual haircutter as she prepares for the young girl's ceremony, and a curing chant may detail all the subspecies of a plant, so expert mola makers create designs with a profusion of decoration, filling all the space with the smallest motifs (see Fig. 1.1). As Dina Sherzer and Joel Sherzer (1976, 34) have noted, even Kuna villages display the same density and aversion to unfilled space.

From a slightly different perspective, density and repetition are aspects of the intensity and controlled exuberance of Kuna art. A chief singing to his followers may seem restrained, even repressed, until one takes note of the sometimes riotous profusion of his metaphors as he develops analogies between women and flowers, or chiefs and trees, into almost surrealistic descriptions (Figs. 1.39, 1.40).

Kuna dancers, as Sandra Smith notes, create patterns like the concentric outlining images of mola designs, these patterns growing increasingly vivid as the dance grows in intensity. Kuna art, finally, is intertextual, in that works of one sort refer to and borrow from others. In the gathering house, chiefs often chant about the importance of mola making and tell women that needle and thread are their pen and paper. They sometimes remark on the striking impression made by the women in their bright head scarves sitting together in the half light. Conversely, women sometimes illustrate themes from narratives in

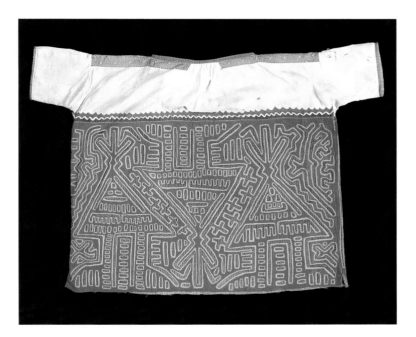

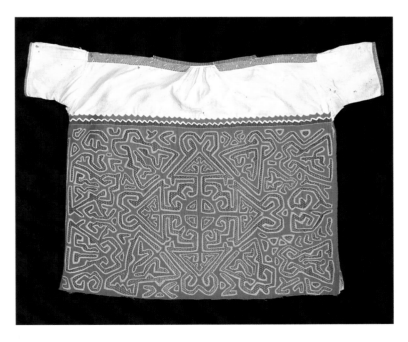

1.41A,B. *Galu mor,* spirit house mola. On one side (TOP) the spirit strong hold is shown from the front with a ladder ready for the spirits to enter. The other side (BOTTOM) shows the same structure opened from the center to show the space inside. 76.0 x 89.0 cm. NMAI 22/4829. Gift of Herbert H. Evans.

their molas, as shown in Figure 1.1. Spirit strongholds called *galu*, which figure prominently in picture-writing, also appear in molas.

Talent, learning, and performance

The Kuna say that when the souls of unborn children are being formed by Muu, the great spirit midwife, she places on each a gurgin. In other contexts gurgin refers to a "hat" or "brain," but here it means either "destiny" or " talent." In the first of these two senses, one may have a destiny to marry at a certain age or move to another community, and in the second, one may have a gift for playing the panpipes, sewing molas, or learning chants. It is sometimes said that one has as many gurgin as one has natural abilities.

Although gurgin in the sense of destiny is supposedly fixed at birth, the Kuna are in practice anything but fatalistic. Each individual strives to make the most of his or her life and talents, not least in the sphere of artistic expression. Just as parents may bathe their children in certain medicines to make them hard workers or good hunters, so do high school students and mola makers wash their eyes in water steeped with forest leaves called *sapigarda*, whose patterns evoke the marks of pen

1.42. Altagracia surrounded by a sea of molas. She is selling molas to visitors from a cruise ship docked at the island of Yandup in Carti.
Mari Lyn Salvador, 1997.

on paper. Men learning a curing chant often bathe in water soaked in sweet-smelling herbs, and a prospective orator may take medicines made from the tongue of a loquacious bird.

Medicine baths, however important, matter less than apprenticeship. For every pursuit, whether canoe making or puberty chanting, a would-be specialist must find a teacher willing to take him on as a student. If he wishes to master a single narrative in chiefly tradition or in one medicinal cure, he may acquire it in a few hours or days, but mastery of a long curing chant can take years, memorization of the puberty cycle two decades, and of medicinal curing, the Kuna say "it has no end." Some things, such as puberty chanting, are best learned on-island, while other bodies of knowledge, like chiefly tradition, can be learned far from home. The most ambitious learners, who want to avoid comparison with local rivals or to acquire the cachet of distant knowledge, apprentice themselves in Colombia or across the mountains in the Darién.

For the women, who distinguish themselves by making fine molas, learning starts at home at an early age. Young girls begin by sewing patterns cut for them by women in the family. As they learn, they gradually sew more and more complex designs and are sometimes allowed to sew small sections of molas the women are working on, progressing eventually to cutting and sewing their own blouses. As the women sew, they talk, share designs, and scrutinize each other's work, but no one takes on a formal mentor or apprentice.

1.43. Leaves used for medicine.
Norbert and Betty Sperlich, 1970.

Verbal artistry is important in all Kuna discourse: "Kuna consider themselves verbally 'on stage' and attempt to heighten the quality of their own verbal artistry and critically evaluate the artistry of others" (see Sherzer, "Kuna Language and Literature," in this volume). This is also the case for the visual and performance arts. Kuna women, who create lavish mola blouses that reflect their interest in beauty and demonstrate their artistic abilities, are keenly aware that their blouses will be judged by other mola makers according to shared aesthetic sensibilities (see Salvador, in this volume).

Kuna society combines egalitarianism and hierarchy in an uneasy combination. Villages have ranked chiefs and other leaders, as does Kuna Yala as a whole, but no one lets those leaders put on airs or order their followers around. Similarly, men compete for recognition by what they learn and how they perform it: rivals assess and quietly criticize each other's proficiency, and everyone knows who the great teachers and performers are. A chief with a weak voice or little talent for metaphor will be criticized behind his back, and women frankly discuss the strengths and weaknesses of the molas they see. Nevertheless, overt competition and public challenges are strongly discouraged. In admonishing their followers, chiefs insist that there is room for everyone and that everyone has skills. Remarkably, almost every woman sews molas, and until recently, almost every man made a name for himself by learning and performing ritual.

Audience and boundaries

In making art, the Kuna address variable and multiple audiences—personal and social, human and spirit, Kuna and foreign. Mola makers aim first of all to please themselves, along with their friends and family, taking pleasure in combining skirts and scarves as well as in designing the mola panels themselves. After wearing blouses

1.44A,B. "Arabia" mola. Carlos Lopez, first chief, remembered the "Arabia" and thought it may have belonged to the United Fruit Company.

53.0 x 66.5 cm. NMAI 16/6523. Collected in 1922 and presented by Lady Richmond Brown and F.A. Mitchell Hedges.

for some time, however, some women cut out the panels and sell them to tourists or merchants: thus foreigners constitute a significant second audience. Many women today also sew panels expressly for sale, as well as products with mola work, such as stuffed animals, Christmas ornaments, and T-shirts; in this last instance, foreign audiences, or Kuna perceptions of these audiences, influence production (Fig. 1.42).

Similarly, as the chapters on music (Smith), curing (Chapin), and language (Sherzer) all show, both chant curers and the gandule or "flute person" of the puberty ceremonies communicate with the spirits, and it is these spirits who are said to take pleasure in the profusion of imagery and metaphor in the chants. Simultaneously, however, a chanter demonstrates his mastery to human listeners, and in the last analysis, whether in the chant itself or the picture-writing discussed by Severi, which is closely guarded in private notebooks, it is himself that the ritualist most pleases.

Like molas and chanting, much of Kuna art crosses social and cultural boundaries, speaking not only to deities and spirits, but to non-Kuna humans who are ready to look and listen. Thus, for instance, the dance troupes discussed by Sandra Smith, in addition to linking different villages in regional competitions, have always performed for outsiders. Kuna oratory, similarly, plays an increasingly large role in national politics and international gatherings of native peoples.

The Kuna have been dealing with non-Indian outsiders for several hundred years, often in the face of attempts to conquer them or suppress their culture. As they have struggled to preserve their autonomy and capacity for self-determination, the Kuna have set boundaries, isolating themselves and rejecting foreign influence. But they have also crossed those boundaries, seeking controlled contact and limited innovation. Kuna women's dress, as unique as it is, incorporates skirts and scarves made of fabric originally imported from England, trade beads from the former Czech Republic, and gold jewelry from Panama and Colombia. The mola itself is made from imported cloth using purchased thread and needles.

Kuna women's interest in representing elements from outside their environment is evident in molas from museum collections as early as the 1920s. Figure 6.46 (p. 168), a mola collected in 1924, shows two umbrellas, and Figure 1.44 illustrates the "Arabia," a commercial boat that traveled to Kuna Yala in the 1920s. Today, Kuna women continue to illustrate helicopters, spaceships, product labels, books, political posters, etc., in their molas. The mola in Figure 1.45 shows one of the Teenage Mutant Ninja Turtles relaxing in a hammock under coconut trees.

In an article on molas written in the 1970s, Sherzer and Sherzer (1976, 34) found the same creative eclecticism throughout Kuna culture:

> It is characteristic of the Cuna and a measure of their dynamism to welcome and enjoy novelty, but to transform it into something Cuna, into Cunaité. Precisely this same process occurs in Cuna literature, the rich oral system of chanting and speaking, in which all kinds of new elements are introduced—dreams, travels, aspects of life in Panama City—and made a part of and relevant to traditional themes in Cuna religion and politics.

Even on Nargana, one of the few communities in Kuna Yala that rejected tradition in favor of Panamanian national culture, the Panamanian custom of electing a queen for a saint's day has been adapted to Kuna ends, in effect taking the place of traditional puberty ceremonies (Moore, in this volume).

The Kuna are keenly aware of how outsiders observe and represent them, and that their survival as a people depends not just on the internal strength of their society but also on a dialogue with the outside world. They cannot share their poetry and chanting with others as readily as they have shared their mola art, but it matters very much to them that outsiders understand the worth and richness of their culture. Anthropologists and museums have played an important role in advancing this goal, and those Kuna who know of this exhibit or have contributed to it are glad it is taking place. The following chapters are intended as a contribution to that dialogue.

1.45. Teenage Mutant Ninja Turtle Mola. Leonardo relaxes in a hammock. Made in Río Sidra, 1992.
36.0 x 42.0 cm. FMCH X96.25.5.

Baba's Creation
Flora and Fauna of Kuna Yala

Jorge Ventocilla

The Kuna people

It is estimated that when the Europeans arrived in the New World, approximately fifty-seven million people were living on this continent. Of these, five to six million inhabited Central America. A century and a half later, due to the adverse impact of the European invasion, the central American population was reduced to three and a half million.

After five hundred years, forty-five indigenous cultures still survive, with an estimated total population of five million people. In Central America, only Guatemala and Belize have a proportionately larger indigenous population than does Panama. Several Panamanian native communities are considered to be the least acculturated in the region.

According to the National Census of 1990, Panama has an indigenous population of no less than 225,373 people composed of seven groups: Ngobe (Guaymí), Kuna, Embera, Buglé (Bokota), Bounaan, Nasos (Teribe), and Bribri. Therefore, one of every ten Panamanians belongs to an indigenous group. The Ngobe (or Guaymí), with a population of 123,000, are the most numerous.

The Kuna are the most well known ethnic group both within and outside of the Panamanian context. They collectively own the Comarca Kuna Yala (the territory of Kuna Yala, also known as San Blas): 320,600 hectares on the mainland and the adjacent marine waters. Kuna Yala extends from northeastern to southeastern Panama, from Punta de San Blas (79° west) to Puerto Obaldia, near the Colombian border (77° west). From one extreme to the other, the distance by sea is approximately 226 kilometers (140 miles).

2.2. Coconut palm on the mainland near Suitupu.
Mari Lyn Salvador, 1997.

2.1 (OPPOSITE). Coconut mola panel. Emphasis is on the coconuts shown in enlarged clusters hanging from the palm tree.
50.5 x 37.0 cm. FMCH X83.451. Gift of Dorothy M. Cordry in memory of Donald B. Cordry.

2.3. Uninhabited islands used for raising coconuts among the western islands of Kuna Yala.
James Howe, 1975.

The population census taken by the Ministry of Health in 1989 indicates that the population living in the Comarca is at least 40,864 persons. Most of the Kuna live on roughly forty islands. However, eight communities are located on the coast of the Comarca adjacent to the islands and two (Gangandi and Mandi) are situated a few kilometers inland. According to the 1990 national census, the total Kuna population of Panama is 47,298. Certainly those who are familiar with the figures provided by the census and with the indigenous populations to which they refer, realize that they are approximate, and lower than the actual numbers.

In Kuna Yala, communities are strategically situated near the coast, where agricultural areas and vital natural resources such as water, wood, and construction materials are easily accessible. Roughly three thousand additional Kuna inhabit the Pacific slope of Panama in the watersheds of the Bayano, Chucunaque, and Tuira rivers. They live in a different environment and are considered to be remnants of the ancient Kuna emigration from the Pacific to the Caribbean. A minor population of a few thousand people lives in northern Colombia. From a cultural standpoint, the three groups of Kuna do not differ greatly and are recognized as a single ethnic group.

For years there has been extra-commarcal migration, but today it is becoming more evident. It is estimated that up to thirty percent of the Kuna population live outside of their original homelands, whether in the cities of Panama and Colon or in the banana plantations of Changuinola.

It is useful to note that Kuna communities are composed, in large part, of children and young people, as is the case in all of Latin America today.

The debate as to whether the indigenous peoples that Spanish chroniclers met in the Darién in the beginning of the sixteenth century were ancestors of the Kuna is still unresolved. One school of thought maintains that the Kuna are their direct descendants—regardless of cultural and linguistic differences. The other claims that the Kuna emigrated from Columbia after the sixteenth century. In addition, ethnolinguistic evidence strongly supports the theory of a Kuna origin to the north of Panama, even that the Kuna could have settled in present day Columbia and later returned to the territories in Panama that they occupy today.

According to oral tradition, the *dule* (Kuna) people originated in the Sierra Nevada de Santa Marta in northern Columbia. One of the most notable experts in Kuna culture, the *sayla* (the person with highest authority in the community) Horacio Mendez, agrees that the Kuna originally came from five areas in the Sierra Nevada, and that due to pressure from neighboring tribes, they were forced to emigrate to the plains of Amukadiuar (the present day Atrato river). Much later, persecution by other indigenous groups and flooding of the Atrato river drove them to take refuge in the mountains of the Darién, especially on Cerro Tacarcuna (at 1,875 meters, the highest mountain in western Panama), a mountain that, even today, is a sacred place for the *olodulegan*. About their time in the lands of the Darién, we are told of Durien, a *nele* (traditional doctor, shaman) who instructed the group in the art of self-defense. The Tuira River takes its name from Durien (which some traditional teachers indicate is the nickname of the great Olonekikinya). In stories about this epoch, the *saylamala* (plural of sayla) speak of dispersed groups of Kuna, rather than of a single entity. In the Congress (*onmaked nega*), the meeting place in each Kuna community, the elders say: "We are not from these small islands. We are from the great rivers. Enemy forces imprisoned us and reduced emigration. Our lands are there, across the frontier."

2.4. Moss covered tree trunk on the mainland near Ailigandi.
Vernon Salvador, 1974.

In the last few centuries the dule have been displaced toward the Caribbean, and it is only relatively recently that they arrived and established themselves on the islands which they inhabit today. For many years before, they frequented these coasts but the gradual movement of the population to the islands started as recently as the middle of the nineteenth century.

It is important to take into account that the dule have been associated with the mainland environment, and that their cultural heritage is based in mainland areas, in forested environments along rivers. Nevertheless, many aspects of Kuna culture are derived from the coastal environment. There are strong sentimental roots within Kuna Yala. The Kuna often speak with feeling about *yar suid*, the "long land."

Since the arrival of the Europeans, the dulegan have maintained partial geographic isolation with respect to foreign societies. By monitoring and managing their contact with other societies, they have succeeded in maintaining a degree of political and cultural autonomy which is extremely exceptional for the indigenous peoples of America today. Through trial and error, they have adapted to the radical changes of Latin America in the twentieth century, preserving a good part of their cultural identity and unity.

2.5. View from the rainforest looking toward the coast near Suitupu.
Sergio Salvador, 1997.

2.6. Young man poling a canoe toward the mainland.
James Howe, Niatupu, 1974.

The other famous characteristic of the dule is the production of the mola, the blouse panels used by women in their traditional dress and sold as crafts. Molas still symbolize the identity of the Kuna people to outsiders, and their designs may be very elaborate. However, to the Kuna themselves, it is the songs and stories that are part of the meetings of the community congress that maintain the essential themes of the culture and reveal its basic religious and moral character.

It is also quite common that intrinsic characteristics which define an indigenous group are overlooked. For example, the dule traditionally celebrate the solidarity and unity of their communities. There are still communities in which barter of food and assistance among community members strongly binds individuals and groups. As an

Baba's Creation

The following text represents the testimony of the Kuna Cacique Enrique Guerrero (1912–1992), Second Cacique General, recorded by Valerio Nuñez in the community of Ogobsukun in April 1992. The cacique died two months later.

The earth is the mother of all things, the Great Mother. She is the guardian who caringly watches over all that exists; she has *burba* [spirit, force, vigor] and we live in her.

The Great Mother has an attractive force that allows us to stay in balance. Our fathers teach us that the world has eight spiritual levels where one finds gold, silver, iron, and many other minerals that sustain Mother Earth. If we allow all of this to be exploited, the trees will dry up and production will dwindle. Therefore, we have to care for them, and not abuse them.

Our body is the same. We, too, are made of iron and gold. Once you break an arm or a leg, you will never be able to move it as you once did. Therefore, remember that your body and Mother Earth are one. They are the creation of Bab Dummad, the Great Father, whom we also call "Baba." He and his wife, Nan Dummad, the Great Mother, created it all.

The rain passes over, just as clouds and winds do, and they are attracted by the trees that refresh the environment. Thus, trees are indispensable and we cannot mistreat them. Trees are not here by chance. Their roots penetrate the earth through the sixth level and grow on the surface as well. Trees renew their sap by drinking river water through their roots. Water circulates through all of their branches and leaves.

Trees have sap, resin, and who do you think drinks the sap?

Mother Earth. That is how she strengthens herself.

The earth is covered with trees of all kinds that give it life and strength. This is Baba's Creation. So our fathers tell us: "You have to learn all of this to truly love Mother Earth."

The thick threads, like ropes that you see hanging from the trees, are medicinal vines that serve as perches for birds who come to enjoy the surroundings and the trees. Trees never harm anyone. They protect us and provide the remedies to treat our ills.

Trees give their fruit to feed the animals. They don't produce fruit needlessly. If trees didn't produce so much

there would be no collared or white-lipped peccaries, no birds. Therefore, we must take care: trees are your life, they feed you and protect you.

All of this is so essential. If, by chance, the breezes don't blow, the mists won't fall. Many times a torrential rain falls, and after a while the sun shines again. The sun is also necessary, our life depends on it.

Nan Gabsus, Mother of the Night who cares for the children, the darkness, is essential as well. We sleep until Mother Earth gives the sign for us to wake up.

2.7. **Cacique Enrique Guerrero**.

Our prophet Ibeler or Dad Ibe, who was transformed into the sun, wakes us and invites us to work. Ibeler gave us all of the songs and traditions. Everything that we do is not our own doing: someone compels us to do it.

Ibeler loved nature. He cared for them all: the smallest insects like the fire ants, the scorpions, the spiders, the vipers. He could not bear to see floating branches. He rescued them and put them in a place where they could grow.

The jungle where the wild animals live—the snake, the puma, the jaguar—rarely frightens us when we go into her interior because Ibeler guides and protects us.

Olodualigipileler, the moon, father of Ibeler, is also important to us. He registers our ages. When I see a small child I ask: "How many moons does this child have?"

The elements of nature are not here in vain. Each has its function. When a hard rain falls, it is to let us rest. But even more so, it is to clean the natural world which gets dirty during the summer. Thus, the rivers overflow their banks, dumping the debris that has fallen in during the dry season.

Our forefathers lived on the mainland on the banks of the great rivers in the mountains, before they came to know the sea. The rivers were places that were chosen for their pleasant environment. Our fathers were strong because they were nourished by the plants and trees that surrounded them.

The rivers that they cared for so much were full of stones and had strong currents. Our fathers drank from these rivers and therefore they were strong and they understood the natural world well. The rivers touch the roots of many medicinal plants and therefore we have *akwanusagana*, medicinal stones. This is why the old people then were much stronger than the men of today who live on the islands.

The elders also knew of the existence of other continents and that one day white people would arrive in Abya Yala, as we call the American continent. All of this was prophesied by the *neles*, our traditional doctors who see by means of dreams. Our fathers saw tall bearded men in their dreams.

The Spanish sacked our towns, killed our wise grandmothers who wove hammocks and made marvelous things with clay. They were makers of necklaces. The Spanish came to claim ownership of the gold in our rivers. They also killed the great specialists in botany and sacred song.

We know, as our fathers have told us, that there would be those who would offer us money and promises in exchange for the resources that we had in our territory. None of us are millionaires. We work the earth. This is our tradition and our culture.

We are talking about lobsters and iguanas. Our fathers did not sell lobsters. And the iguanas were abundant in the *suu*, the fig trees. One could find them in great numbers.

Our fathers did not use the hunting weapons that are used today. That is, they only hunted to survive.

If we begin to hunt indiscriminately we will run out of lobsters and iguanas. We know this from messages that come to our fathers who are well informed about these subjects. The same thing will happen to the turtles. We ought to let them reproduce. We cannot collect all of the eggs that they lay on the beaches. We would like to regulate the sale of lobster but we have not been able to restrain the buyers. Our General Congress has made statements to this effect. It is not true that the caciques are not doing anything. The Government is familiar with the problem and has acted in our favor, but beyond that, nothing happens.

In essence, the sea is like a forest populated with different plants and animals. We should take care of our natural resources.

In 1925, [Cimral] Colman and Nele Kantule launched the Revolution.

Why? They did it to oppose the abuses and the racism of the Colonial Police. Nele Kantule said: "Bab Dummad gave us culture. So that my culture is not lost and so that we recognize ourselves as the *olodulegan*, our sisters must continue to wear their molas, their gold nose rings, their earrings, and gold breastplates.

"I am happy that we have *gandurgan*, singers and performers of the Ceremony of Puberty, and that there is mutual cooperation in the building of houses and canoes. This is how we establish our self-worth, the feeling that we are brothers and sisters and that we have a culture. If we start to lose our culture we will be going down another road that won't be the same and everyone will think in terms of money. This is why the school has been started, to defend the culture."

This is the way Nele Kantule and Colman spoke.

Our grandmothers and grandfathers went to Panama City and I don't know what they are doing there. They didn't need to go. They don't think about coming back now that they have made the city their home. They have forgotten their culture.

No one is here forever.

I know that I'm going to die.

I want to leave all that I know to the new generation.

I want to leave ideas so that everyone can benefit from them. This way they will remember me forever as an individual who dedicated himself to planting mangoes, cocoa, and coconuts. He dies, but his plants remain for the good of his children.

anthropologist who worked with them remarked, the Kuna "talk about their generosity constantly" and the absence of exchange "marks the limits of their social world."

But these customs have begun to diminish as relationships become more oriented toward money than toward solidarity. In this process which is neither recent nor limited to this group of people, the logic, if we can call it that, of the consumer society puts pressure on the Kuna lifestyle and the way the Kuna relate to each other, and modifies it.

2.8. Gonzalo Salcedo harvesting rice on the mainland.
James Howe, 1970.

2.9. An agriculturist carries harvested rice across a river near Tigandiki.
James Howe, 1970.

Working with the environment

The Kuna are primarily farmers and fishermen, practicing slash-and-burn agriculture and obtaining a large part of their protein from ocean fish. Activities such as hunting and gathering of forest products are secondary.

Their lifestyle is definitely conditioned by their location on islands near the coast. Their subsistence requires almost daily visits to agricultural plots. They must travel from homes on the islands to their farms (*nainu*) on the mainland. The canoe trip from the ocean to the farm may take several hours.

If they are working far inland they may construct a shelter to stay in at night. In Kuna Yala there are only a few burros and mules in the communities near the Colombian border and in Mandi and Gangandi, areas where *campesinos* live nearby.

The Kuna farm along a coastal strip that extends several kilometers inland. The worked lands are concentrated along rivers or near the coast, facilitating the transport of agricultural products to island communities. Agriculture is better characterized as extensive than intensive, with *masi* (bananas) as the principal product. Besides masi, *oba* (corn), *mama* (yucca), *oros* (rice), *oros ginnid* (red rice), *gay* (sugar cane), and various other edible plants, both domesticated and wild, are among the primary plants used by the Kuna. In the nainu (cultivated area), one finds many useful species from fruit trees to edible plants to plants used for dyes for traditional ceremonies and cosmetics.

The Kuna inter-crop, sometimes with trees. The agricultural cycle generally starts with clearing trees during December and January, beginning with areas of primary forest and leaving the younger vegetation for March and April. This activity

**2.10. Boys net-fishing along
the beach.**
James Howe, Niatupu, 1975.

is considered to be hard labor and diverts attention from other activities such as
fishing (which is difficult during this season because of strong summer winds).

In general, summer (December to April) can be characterized as a period of
scarcity. Fires begin in March and planting follows a few days or weeks later after the
first rains in April or May. In some parts of the Comarca it is customary to plant a
second crop in October or November. In Kuna Yala, the *yoleb*, the job of planting
corn in very scarce fertile terrain along the shores of some of the bigger rivers, is still
practiced in November and December.

There are two elements that distinguish the practice of agriculture in Kuna Yala
from practices of campesinos on the Pacific Slope. The primary difference is that
there is no cattle ranching in the Comarca and no pasture land. Farmland is fallowed
from four to ten years before successive cultivation for a two- to three-year period.
In the Pacific sector, an agricultural cycle like this is practically impossible because
the practice of cattle ranching ensures that recently logged forest will end up as
permanent pasture land within a few years. The second important difference is that
the Asian grasses, *Saccharum spontaneum* and *Hyparrhenia rufa*, are absent in Kuna
Yala. These grasses impede natural regeneration of secondary forest once they become
established in a logged area. Therefore, extensive areas become useless. Not even
cattle can feed on these plants.

Thus the land that we see in the Comarca is primarily an expanse of tropical
jungle that runs down from the Cordillera de San Blas to the Caribbean coast, an
abrupt topographical change. Followed by a narrow strip of flat land, agricultural
areas here are mixed plots of crop plants, vegetation in different stages of regeneration,
and primary forest. Closer to the sea, the countryside is covered with coconut groves
and mangrove swamps.

In general, the people distinguish between the *neg serred* ("old place" or primary forest) and the *neg nuchukwa* ("young place" or secondary forest, known also as *nainu serred*, "old farmland"), while nainu is the name that is given to small farms or cultivated plots. Other local designations are also given. For example, in Gangandi the people refer to the *mergi serred* ("primary" jungle) that occurs in sites which were formerly banana plantations (established in this sector some seventy-five years ago). The Kuna call people from the United States and other similar people *mergi*.

It is uncommon for the Kuna to use measures of area. The first time that primary forest is cleared, rivers and streams are used as borders for agricultural plots, as are mountain ridges. When the owner divides the land—for example to pass it on as inheritance to his or her children—fruit trees are planted which serve as the future boundary lines of the *nainumar* (cultivated areas).

The land is inherited by both sons and daughters and the right to work on it may be commercialized, but only among dule, because by law no non-dule may own property in Kuna Yala. Some land, especially in secondary growth, may be inherited by brothers and sisters without being divided for years. In some regions, family coconut groves are harvested on a rotating basis by the people in a family group who have land-use rights. Because land may be inherited by women, there are many women who own large tracts of land, which is important in Kuna social structure.

The *ogob* (coconut) trade with Colombian traders has been the principle source of economic input for years. By the nineteenth century, many coconut groves had already been established in the Comarca. In 1967, the commercialization of coconuts represented seventy percent of the total economic input. This activity has occurred such that some islands, and extensive coastal zones, have been converted into coconut monocultures. On the other hand, Colombian traders bring products to sell on the

2.11. Meeting a Colombian *canoa* docked at Ailigandi.
Vernon Salvador, 1974.

2.12. Faustino Rodriguez brings home conchs gathered for food.
James Howe, 1975.

2.13. Fish smoking on a rack in the Western islands, Kuna Yala.
James Howe, 1979.

islands like oil, salt, gasoline, hammocks, canoes, coffee, rubber boots, and sugar—indispensable products for everyday living.

Subsistence labor continues to be the principal occupation of the majority of the population, but the sale of lobsters and turtle shells, salaried work on the islands, tourism, and the sale of molas are activities that have greatly expanded in the last twenty to thirty years, although some of these activities have taken place since the last century. It is important to make clear that for a long time the Kuna have been producing for a market outside of the Comarca. Their subsistence depends completely on tools and products which they do not make themselves, which must be imported.

The employment of Kuna who emigrate from Kuna Yala to the urban centers of Panama City, Colon, and the banana plantations of Changuinola, is, after the sale of coconuts, the primary source of economic input.

The land

The topography of the Comarca of Kuna Yala is varied and irregular. Its most outstanding features include the San Blas Range, the rolling hills from one hundred to two hundred meters in height that fall toward the coast, the plains near the shore, the islands, the Gulf of San Blas, and the continental shelf. The Dianmaiyala (or Cerro Brewster), 850 meters high, is the highest point in the Comarca.

All of the rivers of the Comarca flow into the Caribbean Sea. There are more than twenty large rivers in Kuna Yala that generally have beds less than twenty-five kilometers long and relatively small drainages, with certain exceptions in the western part of the Comarca (the Gangandi and Mandi basins).

2.14. Birds and fish mola panel. Black and white molas were particularly popular in the 1960s and 1970s.
37.5 x 48.5 cm. Private collection. 1968.

The rivers are full, dropping precipitously to the sea from the continental divide. As a consequence there are hundreds of falls, cataracts, and rapids in their upper courses. In the rainy season, even these small rivers may cause severe flooding. The waters are crystal clear except in a few areas where colonists have entered, as they have at the headwaters of the River Gangandi. The mountain waters are relatively cold (23°C). In low-lying areas, rivers flow slowly. Here the average temperature of the water is 25–27°C.

The Kuna obtain fresh water from the rivers. Each day, women (men also do this) cross in canoes to the mainland to obtain fresh water for their houses, also taking advantage of the trip to do their laundry and bathe. If they have an outboard motor, it is an obligation to turn it off when they enter the rivers. Furthermore, today there are aqueducts to the major islands so it is no longer necessary to go to the mainland for fresh water.

Rivers are also used for navigation between the coast and the agricultural plots. They are fished by Kuna who live on the mainland, especially when summer winds make ocean fishing difficult for the Kuna who live on the islands.

Due to the conservation of the natural forests and their watersheds, the rivers of Kuna Yala are among those with the best water quality in all of Central America.

In the sea and its environs, the Kuna conduct most of their day-to-day activities. They obtain the majority of their animal protein and materials for traditional medicines from the sea.

Further from the coast of the Comarca there are a variety of marine environments: open sea, coral reefs, islands, mangrove swamps, and sandy and rocky beaches.

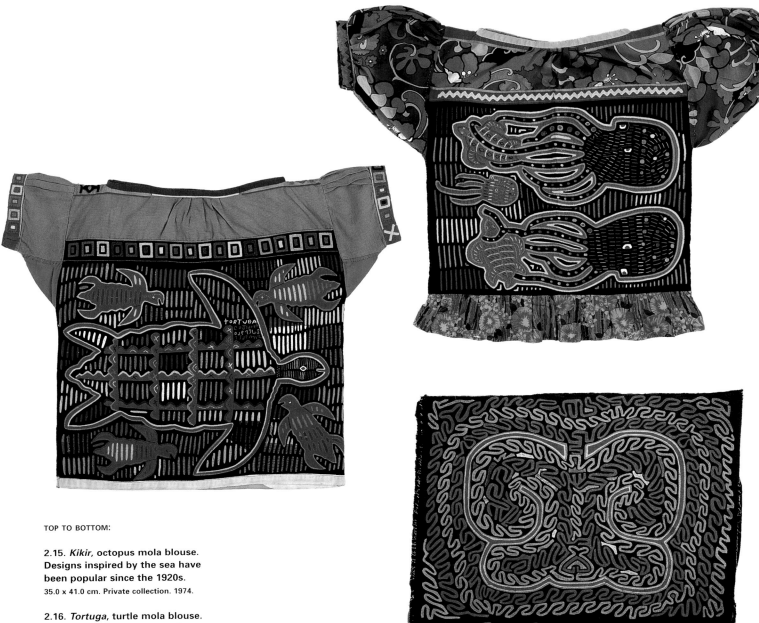

TOP TO BOTTOM:

2.15. *Kikir*, octopus mola blouse.
Designs inspired by the sea have
been popular since the 1920s.
35.0 x 41.0 cm. Private collection. 1974.

2.16. *Tortuga*, turtle mola blouse.
Lettering on the blouse reads *tortuga*
(turtle) and the date that the mola
was sewn.
55.5 x 68.5 cm. Private collection. 1968.

2.17. Brain coral mola panel.
22.0 x 41.0 cm. FMCH X83.454. Gift of Dorothy
M. Cordry in memory of Donald B. Cordry.

Along the coast of Kuna Yala the continental shelf is narrow, eight to seventeen
kilometers. Islands vary in size and are less than a meter above sea level in altitude.
The great majority of the islands are located within five kilometers of the coast, with
the exception of the islands Gaimau (Mauqui or Cayos Holandeses) located fifteen
kilometers offshore.

The estimated number of coral species in the region, according to marine biologists
at the Smithsonian Institute, is one of the highest in the Caribbean. Also, nearly sixty
species of marine sponges are reported from the western zone of the Comarca.

It appears that cultural adaptation to the marine environment has not had time
to fully develop. Cultural activities endanger the resource base of the sea in several
ways. Populations of species such as lobster (*dulub*), sea turtles, especially the carey
(*yaug*), certain shellfish, and even ocean fish have been under pressure due to over-
exploitation. This pillage of marine resources is motivated by a constant, injudicious
external demand, in addition to the eagerness of the Kuna to make money.

It has been discussed at length in General Congresses, that adequate internal rules and real protection for certain marine resources are essential. Certain practices, such as the use of trawling nets and nets that do not discriminate on the basis of the size of the fish that are taken, ought to be immediately controlled to stop the depletion of populations of marine organisms that sustain the Kuna people. The dule of today have the unavoidable task of caring for the sea and stopping the process of over-exploitation, moving quickly toward rational use.

Climate

Kuna Yala presents two types of climate: an extremely wet tropical climate in mountainous regions, and the humid tropical climate on the plains and parts of the coast. Average temperatures vary between 26 and 27°C in low-lying areas to roughly 20°C at higher elevations. The average annual precipitation is between twenty-six hundred millimeters to more than four thousand millimeters, and varies according to elevation.

During the year the wind blows from different directions and at different velocities. The Kuna name the directions in which the winds blow: *Sagir burwa* ("coming from the Chagres river"), *yoor burwa* (trade winds of the north, "winds of summer"), *dad nakue burwa* (winds of the northeast, "from where the sun rises"), *yala burwa* (winds of the south, "from the mountains"), *Mandi burwa* (winds of the west, "from the Mandi River"), *magad burwa* (gentle winds of the northeast, during the winter; when they blow, the people comment: "Today it is not going to rain"), and *dii burwa* ("winds of rain," that blow suddenly before it rains and then stop just as suddenly). The names for the winds also have local variations, depending, in part, on the direction in which the coast extends.

The names of the months of the year also make reference to events that occur in nature:

January	*Yola nii*	Month of summer, of the Sun.
February	*Ari nii*	Month of the iguana.
March	*Dilla nii*	Month of the flowering of the Dilla tree.
April	*Ollor nii*	Month when the cicadas sing.
May	*Yauk nii*	Month of the hawksbill turtle.
June	*Masar nii*	Month of the white cane.
July	*Bunur nii*	Month of Bunur, a medicinal plant.
August	*Gig nii*	Month of the seagulls.
September	*Api nii*	Month of Apin, a medicinal plant.
October	*Giblo nii*	Month when the hawks pass.
November	*Ina nii*	Month of medicine.
December	*Bardud nii*	Month of the salt flower, a medicinal plant.

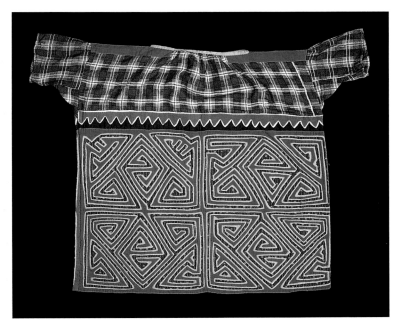

2.18A,B. Octopus mola (both sides shown). Elvira Torres and Balbina Denis pointed out that this design is an octopus shown from the underside with its tentacles curled back.
76.0 x 89.0 cm. NMAI 16/6367. Collected in 1922 and presented by Lady Richmond Brown and F.A. Mitchell Hedges.

Kuna Children's Art Workshop

A Smithsonian project on Cultural and Environmental Education among Indigenous Children in Panama

In Central America, forty-five indigenous cultures exist with an estimated, combined population of more than five million people. In this region, the indigenous peoples have direct influence over much of what is left of the tropical forest. As a result, both their knowledge and actions must be part of the ecological movement.

The Kuna are one of the most well-known indigenous groups in Panama. They live in a region called Kuna Yala that is approximately 320,600 hectares. They inhabit coral islands close to the land that is still covered tropical forest (ninety percent of the Kuna Yala region).

The well-being of the children is central to Kuna culture; however, the children do not have enough opportunity to express and expand their creativity. Outside the schools, there are no organizations promoting child creativity, Kuna cultural values, or the ecological importance of the region in which they live.

Since the beginning of 1993, several Kuna organizations that had worked on environmental education, particularly the Juventud Duiren (a grassroots organization of young Kuna) and the office of Education of the Smithsonian Tropical Research Institute, started a project called, "Red de Talleres de Arte Infantil Kuna." Today, workshops take place in four communities (Carti Suidupu, Mandiyala, Akuanusadup, Ukupseni). In the work-

2.19. Norelis Arias, age 10 years.

Vegetation

In comparison with the other nine provinces of Panama, the Comarca Kuna Yala has the greatest percentage of forested land. For the little dule children who have never left their territory, it would be difficult to imagine that the world is not green and leafy as they have always seen it.

The Comarca is of great interest to botanists due to its floristic relationship with the Chocó of Colombia, the mountains of Guyana and South America. That is to say, the vegetation of Kuna Yala is more related to that of South America than to that of western Central America. Some plants in Panama are only found in the San Blas Range.

Deforestation and ancestral rights

Latin America and the Caribbean are regions privileged by their high biological diversity, assembled in a great variety of different environments, and including the largest expanse of tropical forest on the planet, almost eight hundred million hectares.

More than two-thirds of the species of flora and fauna on earth are found in the tropics, which means that the biological diversity of the planet is located in large part in a group of "developing" countries. It has been calculated that the American tropics support twice the forested area of Asia and three times that of Africa.

Brazil, alone, contains twenty-two percent of the flowering plants in the world. Colombia and Peru each support more than seventeen hundred species of birds. In the entire tropical region of the American continent there are forty-one hundred species of birds. That is to say, they account for forty-five percent of the avifauna of the world. The abundance of life present in our region is a privilege and a responsibility, and ought to be protected and used rationally, not with the logic of a voracious market economy, rather with the logic of survival and support for present and future generations.

More than ninety percent of Kuna Yala is covered with forest. We still have many pristine and natural areas, but the destruction of tropical forests like these is a serious ecological problem, not only in Panama, but in all of the tropical regions of the world. Although to a lesser extent, deforestation problems also exist in Kuna Yala. On one hand, there are zones along the coast where the Kuna themselves have cut too much forest, for example, in wet areas where mangroves are cut to make drainage ditches for agricultural plots.

On the other hand, there are sites where non-Kuna colonists have entered and developed extensive range lands, for example, at the head of the rivers of Gangandi, near Nusagandi on the El Llano-Carti road and in lands bordering on Colombia.

At these sites, indiscriminate deforestation threatens the territorial and cultural integrity of Kuna Yala. It is urgent that an immediate solution to this problem be found via the legal mechanisms that defend the legitimacy of the Comarca. Even so, the situation is not nearly as serious as it is in the territories of indigenous peoples of the Amazon.

The Kuna people have a particularly advantageous situation due to their relationship with the Nation-State of Panama. They are owners of their land, the Comarca of San Blas (Kuna Yala). No one who is not of dule nationality may own land or resources in Kuna Yala.

To reaffirm these ancestral rights before the State of Panama has not been easy. It has required both a decided and sometimes violent struggle on the part of the native people, as well as the particularly logical and/or flexible stance of Panamanian political authorities. The Kuna keep these events in mind. Nearly all of the conflicts between Kuna and non-Kuna in the Comarca have been based on disputes over the possession or profit from natural resources.

From the beginning of the century, the Kuna have been changing politically from a system of autonomous communities grouped into one—or more than one— fragile confederation (united nominally by the Nation-State of Panama) into a more complete and formal regional structure, incorporated into a modern nation.

Terrestrial fauna

Since its formation, the Central American isthmus has been the scene of migration and convergence of the fauna of Abya Yala (American continent). Therefore, part of the animal life which we find in the region is of South American origin: *bero* (sloth), *gwigib* (anteater), *dede* (armadillo); and part is of northern origin: *sugachu* (raccoon), *moli* (tapir), *goe* (brocket deer). It is fitting to mention that in the jungles of Kuna Yala there are more species of birds, butterflies, and trees than are found in most European countries.

Here I present a description of seven native animals from the mainland that are especially important to the Kuna: those whose meat forms the basis of their diet. In addition to the natural history of each species, I will also discuss how these animals are hunted by the Kuna.

And here I pause to reflect upon a very important point: extensive and uncontrolled hunting (along with forest destruction) is the reason that many animal species in our country are seriously endangered. Hunting with dogs, in particular, has caused the disappearance of entire populations of game animals in many parts of the Panamanian interior.

2.20. Milciades Hernández, age 11 years.

shops, the children develop artistic expressions in drawings, poetry, painting, theater, puppetry, and singing.

The objectives of the workshops are as follows:

- contribute to the importance of Kuna childhood, so that in the Kuna Yala regions as well as outside, the adults focus their attention on children and their potential
- teach the children to appreciate their ecological surroundings
- encourage Kuna cultural values among the children

Communities participate fully in these workshops; the promoters are all young natives. The organizers believe this work supports the preservation of knowledge and respect toward nature, both of which Kuna focus on in their daily existence, but it is also a way to conserve and transmit the autochthonous culture of the Kuna people.

2.21. Samuel Ortiz, age 12 years.

2.22. *Manga,* **yucca leaves mola.**
70.0 x 84.0 cm. NMAI 16/6417. Collected in
1922 and presented by Lady Richmond Brown
and F.A. Mitchell Hedges.

Hunting dogs are foreign elements in the forest and have been trained to very successfully pursue wild animals, which have not developed instinctive defenses against them.

In Kuna Yala dogs are almost never used for hunting. If the use of hunting dogs becomes more generalized, and there are indications that this is beginning to happen in communities close to the borders which are being colonized, certain wild animals will not survive and the majority will become fearful, and disappear from areas near human settlements.

The following descriptions are both the result of literature research and of the testimony of Kuna hunters and farmers, who have always lived in contact with the fauna of their land. I have shared hunting trips with the community of Gangandi and long hours of conversation with them, experiences that contributed to the reformulation and enrichment of our knowledge of the natural history of the Comarca.

Wedar

Wedar (peccary, *Tayassu tajacu*) is of particular importance to the Kuna because it is the wild animal that supplies communities with the most meat. Peccaries travel in groups of two to eight individuals, being a very social species.

Their range and distribution is extensive, covering a series of different habitats. This very adaptable animal is found from Arizona in the United States to the Río de la Plata in Argentina. Its distribution in Panama includes forested sites and disturbed lowlands found in areas such as Kuna Yala.

In contrast to the northern race, which has been well studied, there is little information about the peccary of Central and South America. The animals which we have weighed in Kuna Yala averaged forty-seven pounds. In Costa Rica it is reported that litters are born in May, at the beginning of the rainy season. The wedar is diurnal, but may be active in the first hours of the night as well. In Gangandi, the wedar is more often captured in pasture land or in cultivated fields than in primary forest. The same is true in the Darién where the indigenous Emberá and Wounaan hunt them on their farms which are surrounded by forest.

The meat and hide of the peccary are commonly used in many parts of their extensive range of distribution. In the Comarca the meat is used, but not the hide. In some communities the meat of wedar is a requirement for the celebration of the *inna*, the *Chica* Festival.

Wedar is considered to be one of the pest animals that disturbs Kuna crops the most, principally the root crops such as yucca. In the opinion of some farmers in the Gardi area, there are now more wedar than there were before. They can be found all year in the *nainu* (farm), but in the summer, the land dries up and is harder to dig. Therefore, peccaries move to higher ground.

It is said that the fruit of *igwa* (*Dipteryx panamensis*), which appears between December and January, is "special food" for the wedar because only the peccary can break the tough outer seed coat.

One strange phenomenon is the hunting of peccaries in the sea! In June 1989, three peccaries were taken from the sea, two near the island of Pico Feo and one near San Ignacio de Dad Nakwe Dupir. People passing in canoes first spotted them. Some older Kuna say that such behavior is also observed among collared peccaries, white-lipped peccaries, and deer after an earthquake.

Yannu

The *yannu* (white-lipped peccary, *Tayassu pecari*) is similar in appearance to the wedar, but larger in size, usually weighing up to 110 pounds. It has whitish lips and lacks the collar of the wedar. White-lipped peccaries live in large groups that may have more than one hundred individuals. The groups roam constantly throughout the forest, covering long distances between sites which they periodically revisit.

The yannu are omnivorous (they eat nearly everything) and are often seen eating in areas where palms are abundant. They defend themselves aggressively and are considered to be dangerous animals. Their only natural enemies in Panama are the big forest cats such as the *achu barbad* (jaguar) and the *achu ginnid* (puma). It is said that the yannu is very sensitive to habitat disturbances of both high- and lowland humid forests and that, with the jaguar, they are the first large mammals to disappear when a road is opened into a virgin area.

Little is know about their mating season. The average weight of the yannu hunted in Gangandi was sixty-six pounds and the maximum weight reported for a female was one hundred pounds. Small yannu piglets have been seen in August and January.

The yannu is one of the most symbolic animals for the Kuna. It is this animal that the older people speak of most enthusiastically. A good Kuna hunter knows many details about the life of the yannu: where and what it eats, in which months it comes near their community, when it reproduces, and which individuals are dominant in the group.

It is said that the yannu has an odor of "burnt earth" and while the wedar has a stronger odor, the yannu has a better sense of smell. Therefore, you have to "play with the wind" in order to hunt it. The old Kuna people hunted yannu and *moli* (tapir) using pit traps. When they checked the traps, they did not get too close so as not to leave the smell of their body to frighten the animals.

According to some Kuna hunters there are two types of yannu bands which can be distinguished by their tracks: the *no bravos* (nonaggressive) take flat steps and leave three-toed tracks. The *bravos* (aggressive) step more strongly and directly. In addition, the bristles on their body are raised. These differences between "bravos" and "no bravos" may refer, in the case of the "bravos," to bands that have been frightened by a predator or by a hunting party.

2.23. *Wedar*, **peccaries raised in captivity in the community of Gangandi.**

2.24. **A herd of** *yannu*, **white-lipped peccaries.**

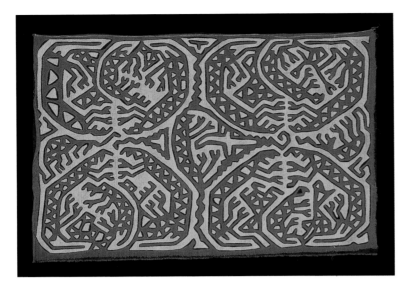

2.25A,B. *Usgwinni,* **squirrel mola. One side of this shows squirrels perched in trees, while the other side shows them in cages. 1922.**
52.0 x 69.0 cm. NMAI 19/8402. William W. Andrew Collection.

Some hunters claim to have seen males mount females as they run through the jungle without stopping, and they indicate that the young are born when the preferred food, the *isberula* (*Manilkara bidentata*) is in fruit. The yannu also likes to eat igwa (*Dipteryx panamensis*) and *nalub* (*Bactris gasipes*).

If a hunter puts the scent of his breath or his armpits on a young peccary, it will follow him like it would follow its mother. We have witnessed this situation in Gangandi.

Compared to its relative the wedar, the yannu spends more time in undisturbed forest and highlands, and is not as attracted to the cultivated lands of the Kuna. Nevertheless, we have seen quite a few tracks of this animal roughly three kilometers from the community of Gangandi, in an area of secondary growth. Seventy years ago, a banana company built houses there, and today the yannu come to eat the flowers of the *waa* palm (*Roystonia regia*) that were planted as ornamentals in front of the houses of the banana plantation.

The Kuna hunters consider the yannu an intelligent animal. According to them, three or four leaders run ahead and the others follow behind in several lines.

In general, when a hunter sights a band, he returns to the community to recruit more hunters. If he sights the animals early in the evening, the group of hunters will go to find them very early the following morning. To locate the band, after following the tracks they leave, the hunters make a decision to surround the animals, being careful to take note of which way the wind is blowing.

The Kuna hunter who is in charge of the hunting party will locate each hunter in succession (the first to be placed will be the one who notified the rest of the presence of the yannu). Finally, the person who is in charge sits with his back to the wind and whistles like an animal previously agreed upon and takes the first shot. The animals come together when they hear the shot and at the third scream of their leaders they bolt, running in stampede. They may continue to run for hours.

The yannu and the *ari* (iguana) are the only two animals which the Kuna hunt in groups. If the group does find game or even as much as sight a yannu, the men will feel embarrassed to return to the community empty-handed because they are subject to a lot of pressure: Everyone in the community will be hoping to eat fresh game when they return.

According to tradition, just as the lightning over the sea marks the coming of the *yauk* (sea turtle), lightning over the mountains means that the bands of yannu are approaching. The *bakaka* (*Daptrius americanus*) also may announce their coming with its song. If someone dreams about soldiers, it is said that he will find a band of yannu. On one occasion when I was accompanying a Kuna on a hunt, I told him that I had been dreaming of a yannu the night before, and he immediately asked about the place where I was in the dream.

According to the hunters of Gangandi, the populations of this wild pig on the Mandinga Plain dropped appreciably when the banana company came in the 1920s and cut the forest. In addition, their own agriculture has resulted in the elimination of food plants of the yannu. A hunter from Gardi Sugdup commented on one occasion that on his island they do not make as many hunting forays as they used to because now the people prefer to shoot white-lipped peccary as soon as they see them, rather than to return to announce their find to the other hunters of the island, perhaps also because there are fewer hunters than there once were.

In the area of Gangandi the yannu are attracted to the fruits of *nalub*, the flowers of the waa, and the isberula. Some hunters are of the opinion that the yannu come closer to the coast during the summer, when there is little water on the mainland. There are two groups of yannu that arrive in the hunting grounds of the people of Gangandi. One group comes along the coast, and the other group from the high mountains. The two groups originate from the two sides of Mandungandi, on the Pacific slope. Because Kuna are familiar with the routes that the peccaries follow, the hunters from one community often advise those of the neighboring community to prepare because the yannu are coming from their direction.

In many areas of Panama this wild species has been exterminated, whether directly through indiscriminate hunting, or by the destruction of its habitat. To be able to maintain populations of yannu in Kuna Yala, no more animals than necessary should be killed. Furthermore, when the forests are protected, the house of the yannu is protected.

2.26. Monkey mola panel.
47.0 x 34.0 cm. FMCH X83.181. Museum purchase in memory of Sidney S. Kallick.

Usu and *sule*

The *usu* (agouti, *Dasyprocta punctata*) is the forest animal that is seen most frequently in the lowland forests of Kuna Yala. The *sule* (paca, *Caniculus paca*) its nocturnal cousin, is larger, twice its weight, and can live at higher altitudes. Both animals are extremely timid and prefer to live in wooded areas near rivers and streams. The sule is also known as the *napanono* (Head of earth) in Kuna Yala. According to tradition one must bathe after eating its meat. If not, those who eat it will feel lazy on the following day.

Usu plays an important role in the forest because it has a habit of burying seeds when they are abundant, which it will feed upon later. It does not always dig up all of the seeds in a time of scarcity. Therefore, it allows some seeds to germinate and grow to become new trees. In regions where indiscriminate hunting has eliminated the usu, certain trees do not reproduce normally.

In the communities of Gangandi and Gardi Sugdup, four usu are required for the celebration of the *inna suid* (ceremony of female puberty). Sule are not required, but their meat is prized if it is available. Normally, the community of Gangandi offers meat of this animal to dignitaries who come to visit.

The sule is nocturnal and lives in areas similar to those of the usu. It seems that the usu feeds upon more agricultural corps than does the sule. In Gangandi we have seen sule giving birth at the end of September, and usu doing the same in February.

Both are very sought after by hunters and their natural behavior leads to their easy extermination when dogs are used, even without the use of firearms. This applies especially to the usu. One friend of mine, Heraclio Herrera, grabbed an usu in his hands during a botanical expedition. If a dog finds one, the usu begins to run in circles without leaving its territory, thus facilitating its own capture.

2.27. *Sule* entering a streambed in Kuna Yala.

2.28. *Goe* in a dense forest habitat.

Goe

Goe (red brocket deer, *Mazama americana*) is not as well known in Panama as the *wasar* or *goe bebe nikad* (white-tailed deer, *Odocoileus virginianus*). The goe usually inhabits dense forests where it lives alone or in pairs. Its distribution in Panama includes all undisturbed forested areas.

Goe is reported to be common in the western part of Kuna Yala, although there are no good estimates of populations in other parts of the Comarca. Goe have occasionally been seen eating crop plants. Some people in Gangandi maintain that the meat of younger animals is not as pleasing as that of the adults. One person from Gardi Sugdup told us that goe is an animal required for the celebration of the inna suid in this community, and that it could be replaced only by iguana.

Of all of the hunters who we have interviewed, only two report having seen white-tailed deer in the Comarca. It seems that this animal is uncommon in Kuna Yala, however, the hunters recognize it if one shows them a photograph. Some Panamanian campesinos say that the goe fights with the wasar and does not share the areas where it lives. It appears that the wasar finds disturbed or deforested areas more to its liking.

Moli

The largest forest animal in the Latin American tropics is the *moli* (tapir, *Tapirus bairdii*). An adult may weigh five hundred pounds or more. Moli has a solid, muscular body and short, fairly thin legs. Its overall coloration is dark brown, paler on the belly and lower parts of its body. Its skin is quite thick: on its back and rump it may be up to an inch thick. It has short, sparse hairs covering its entire body.

The moli lives in jungle areas near rivers and swamps. Despite its appearance, it can run and jump when the need arises, and it has no difficulty entering the water and swimming, which it does with great dexterity. Moli is a solitary animal, although the male may accompany the female while she is pregnant. The female gives birth once per year and usually has only one offspring which stays with her until it is one year old. The young (from four to eight months old) have a different coloration than the adults. That is, the skin is chestnut colored with white and tan spots and stripes. This coloration, similar to that of the paca and of fawns, provides camouflage when they are approached by a predator such as a jaguar. Their upper lip is flexible and long, somewhat reminiscent of that of an elephant. Nevertheless, in evolutionary terms, the moli is related to the horse and the rhinoceros.

2.29. *Moli,* the largest terrestrial inhabitant in Kuna Yala.

Moli is a completely vegetarian animal, feeding on leaves, fruit, buds, and some seeds. It is primarily nocturnal, although it is possible to find it during the day. It has the habit of loitering in the same places, cutting easily recognizable paths.

Moli has poor vision but it is credited with a tremendous sense of smell, and likewise, a great auditory capacity. On the coast, moli is often found in areas where mango trees (*Mangifera indica*) are in fruit. In areas further from the coast where mangoes are less common, for example, in Gangandi, hunters wait in *suu* trees (*Spondees mombin*) for the moli to come looking for fruit.

Moli is one of the animals most sought after by hunters. In most of its range of distribution it has been eliminated or is in serious danger of extinction, principally because it yields a lot of meat. In addition, among the Kuna, the best hunters are recognized by the number of moli that they have taken. It is very likely that another factor is related as well; formerly it was more common that the meat of forest animals was divided among the members of the community (always first among the children) that contributed to the fame of a hunter in his community. Communities still exist in which the meat of moli and other animals is shared. These Kuna villages are still farther from the market economy.

It is not uncommon for active hunters to know who has returned with the most moli in Kuna Yala. Thus a hunter from Niadup (Digankiki) told us that he only knows of four hunters who have taken more than a dozen of these animals. In reality, to have taken more than three moli already makes a hunter noteworthy in Kuna Yala.

Ari

Ari, the iguana (*Iguana iguana*), is a very important animal in the life of the Kuna. We see the iguana on the ground only when it comes down to lay its eggs or if it is escaping from an enemy. It eats the leaves, flowers, and fruit of forest trees. Its diet includes numerous plant species, but biologists do not know exactly how many. There are certainly trees whose leaves contain chemical substances that iguanas avoid.

As is the case with all of the reptiles, the temperature of the iguana depends upon the ambient temperature. Therefore, we see ari sunning itself in the treetops early in the morning and in the evening when the sun is setting.

Iguanas are up to 1.5 meters long. But despite their relatively large size, they prefer to hide rather than to fight. If grabbed by a hunter, they will definitely defend themselves by striking with their tail, biting, or scratching with their sharp nails. But, basically, ari is a nonaggressive animal that likes to live at peace in the branches that sway in the breeze. Ari cannot live where there are no trees and prefers, in any case, to be in trees on river banks, so that if startled, it can hide behind the vegetation or jump into the water.

2.30. The *ari*, ever present in the life and worldview of the Kuna.

Iguanas reproduce once per year. At the end of October they appear to be very restless and move about among tree branches. Males begin to establish and defend territories in the tops of trees where they copulate with females that come to accept their gallantries. Younger males wait in the corners of the adult males' territories to see if, by chance, they can also mate with the females.

Males defend their reproductive territories until the end of January. Later, in February, females put their eggs in holes that they excavate in the ground on sites with soft earth and without much vegetation, the famous *ponederos de iguana*. In the interior of the country, the ari is known by the nickname *Gallina de Palo* (branch hen).

Between April and June we find the little, green, recently-hatched iguanas. It is common in these months for Kuna parents who go to work in the field to bring back little iguanas to their island houses as gifts for their children.

Ari live not only in Kuna Yala but also in all other areas with the appropriate environment, from Mexico to Brazil. In many places natural populations of ari have fallen drastically due to uncontrolled hunting and deforestation. For our own good and the good of the iguanas we have to make sure that nothing like this happens in Kuna Yala.

The iguana is a very important animal in the life of the dule people. It is present in their popular songs, in legends that they tell at home, in the chants recited by the *gandule* (puberty rite chanter) in the ceremony of inna suid, and of course, as food.

The Artfulness of Everyday Life

Mari Lyn Salvador

The Kuna approach all aspects of their daily life with an interest in the appropriate use of nature's gifts and with a concern for beauty and form. For their homes, men weave baskets, make wooden implements for cooking, and create rattles and serving utensils out of gourds. Their houses are built with aesthetic discernment and symbolize the solidarity of family and community. Some families live in cement block houses with butane stoves and refrigerators, cassette players, and occasionally a television.

Kuna villages are made up of dozens of matrilocal households, each with an extended family group of two or three generations of women along with their husbands and children. Traditionally, marriages were arranged by older family members. The husband moved to the wife's home where he was expected to work for her parents. Although the senior man is often called the "owner of the house," the structure itself passes from mother to eldest resident daughter. Both men and women inherit fields and coconut groves, and though men predominate in the public spheres of politics and ritual, relations at home are based on balance and equilibrium.

Men are responsible for providing food and women for preparing it. Women in the household share daily tasks and allocate duties by age. While the men are off fishing or farming, women cook, wash clothes, sweep, haul water, and sew. Elder women often take on the smoky and time-consuming job of cooking, leaving girls and younger women time for hours of mola making. In the evening, when other work ends, women continue into the night, talking and sewing by lantern light.

Women often create designs for their molas based on household objects. Many of the geometric patterns seen on molas from the 1920s are easy to recognize, such as the basketry pattern in Figure Q or the clear shapes of rattles in Figure BB. Other are less apparent, such as the two large gourds in Figure FF or the row of cane houses along a street in Figure B. The names of the designs often indicate the subject.

A. Traditional house.
Mari Lyn Salvador, Ailigandi, 1974.

> Then Ibeorgun came, and he said, "We will sleep in houses. Everything has its home." Ibeorgun said, "We must have houses."
> — Cacique Carlos López, January 1997

B. *Nega mor*, house mola. Houses with cane walls made from masa *caña blanca* (cane), and thatch roofs are shown as if laid back along a street.
76.5 x 83.0 cm. NMAI 16/6470. Collected in 1922 and presented by Lady Richmond Brown and F.A. Mitchell Hedges.

House construction

> In the beginning they didn't know about house building. He was about to teach them. "First you get a centerpost (*buar*)," he said. "Get rafters (*maket*)," he said. "They are all kin to each other," he said.
>
> —Cacique Carlos López, January 1997

Traditional house building is a communal enterprise on many islands. Decisions are made in the gathering house, work parties are designated, and a construction date is selected. Men cut logs for the frame, gather cane or bamboo for the walls and palm leaves for thatch. The cane, lashed with a strong vine that grows in the forest, was the inspiration for the mola in Figure C. Palm leaves are lashed over the roof frame.

C. *Masar mor,* cane mola.
63.0 x 79.0 cm. EMG 1927.27.932.

D. Men comment and make suggestions as others work on building a traditional house.
James Howe, Niatupu, 1970.

E. Cane wall lashed with vine.
Vernon Salvador, Ailigandi, 1974.

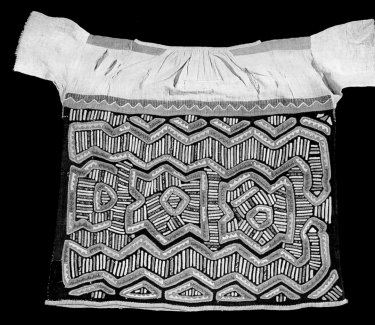

Household compound

Many people live in extended family compounds that include a large sleeping house, cooking house, and fenced open area. Sometimes quiet, sometimes a flurry of activity, the yard changes throughout the day. The space for washing clothes, preparing coconuts, and relaxing accommodates, on occasion, a table set for visitors. In the afternoon, children learn by watching and imitating adult activities or play with handmade wooden boats (Figs. G, H).

F (TOP LEFT). **Compound yard.**
David Mayo, Suitupu, 1997.

G (TOP RIGHT). **Toy wooden boats.**
Length of longest, 63 cm. Left to right:
FMCH X96.25.14; X97.5.65; X96.25.12; X96.25.15; X96.25.13; X97.5.61.

H (ABOVE LEFT). **Children's canoe.**
Wood. 134.0 cm. FMCH X96.25.11.

I (ABOVE RIGHT). **A toy truck hangs on the cane wall behind a hammock.**
David Mayo, Ubigandup, 1997.

J (RIGHT). **Children playing with a toy camera.**
Mari Lyn Salvador, Ailigandi, 1974.

K (ABOVE LEFT). **Preparing bananas for** *dule masi*, **a fish stew made with a base of grated coconut.**
Mari Lyn Salvador, Ailigandi, 1986.

L (ABOVE RIGHT). **Dishes and pans drying on a table.**
Mari Lyn Salvador, Ubigandup, 1997.

M (RIGHT). **Large aluminum pots of chocolate drink covered with carved wooden lids stand ready for family members and visitors.**
Vernon Salvador, Ailigandi, 1974.

N (BELOW RIGHT). *Inna okir mor*, **pot cover mola. Design illustrating a wooden pot cover (see Fig. M).**
72.0 x 85.0 cm. NMAI 22/4836. Presented by Elena Eritta. Opposite side shown in Cat. 28, p. 335.

Cooking house

The cooking house holds a variety of both store-bought and handmade implements. Women sit on low, carved stools and tend food that is cooking in large metal pots over an open fire. Coffee or a drink made of ground corn, bananas, and cocoa is served with bread in the morning. *Dule masi*, a fish stew, is served as the main meal. Avocados, pineapple, oranges, and mangoes are enjoyed in season. Baskets filled with eggs, sugar, and other perishables hang from the beams overhead.

O (TOP LEFT). *Ake,* hook. Hooks are used to hang cups, necklaces, and baskets from the cane walls or the ceiling.
Wood, twine, monofilament. 12.0 cm. FMCH X97.5.47

P (TOP RIGHT). *Ake mor,* hook mola. This pattern, with its descriptive name, was recognized throughout Kuna Yala as an old design based on a household hook.
52.0 x 43.5 cm. Private collection.

Q (ABOVE LEFT). *Garba mor,* basket mola. The treatment of the edge, called *dientes,* represents the stepped edge of the basketry design.
35.0 x 43.5 cm. Private collection.

R (ABOVE RIGHT). Basket with geometric pattern.
Plant fiber. 17.0 cm. FMCH X97.5.86.

Household objects

Men weave baskets and fire fans with geometric patterns that have inspired mola designs for decades. Baskets are used to carry coconuts and other agricultural products from the mainland, to store food, and to keep fabric, needles, scissors, and thread up off the ground. Hooks, used to hang mugs, necklaces, or bundles of rice, are represented in molas (see Fig. P). Imported objects, such as gas cans, inspire mola designs as well.

S (TOP). Baskets.
Plant fiber. Width of largest, 24.0 cm. Left to right: FMCH X97.5.2, X97.5.23, X97.5.26, X97.5.32, X97.5.21.

T (ABOVE LEFT). Gas canisters. Many families now have a gas stove in addition to the traditional hearth.
Vernon Salvador, Ailigandi, 1974.

U (ABOVE RIGHT). Gas can mola.
41.0 x 48.0 cm. Private collection.

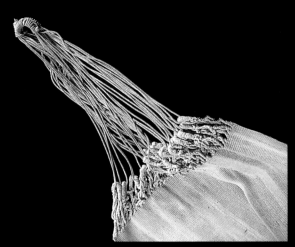

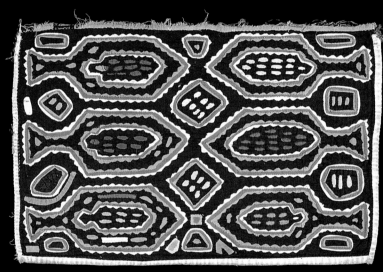

Sleeping house

A traditional sleeping house may hold anywhere from five to fifteen or more people depending on the size of the family and the number of visitors. People sleep in hammocks hanging from the beams overhead and pull them up out of the way during the day to open more space inside. Everyday hammocks are purchased from the Colombian trade boats. Traditional hammocks, now mainly used for girls' puberty ceremonies, are woven from cotton twine on an upright loom. The wooden batten in Figure Z is depicted in the mola in Figure Y.

Lullabies

Throughout the village, especially in the morning, singing is heard from almost every house. Women and young girls sing lullabies to babies to calm them or put them to sleep while swinging back and forth in the hammock and shaking a rattle.

V (TOP LEFT). Woman relaxing in the shade.
Mari Lyn Salvador, Ubigandup, 1997.

W (TOP RIGHT). Handwoven hammock (detail).
Cotton twine. Length, 269 cm. FMCH X97.5.59.

X (ABOVE LEFT). Warp threads on a loom.
Vernon Salvador, Ailigandi, 1974.

Y (ABOVE RIGHT). Hammock batten mola.
36.5 x 54.0 cm. Catalogue #420445, Department of Anthropology, Smithsonian Institution.

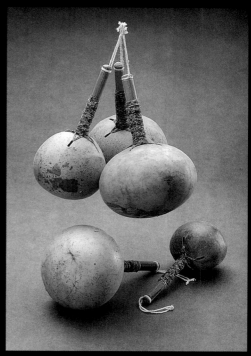

Z (OPPOSITE). **Wooden hammock batten.**
Wood. 41.0 cm. Private collection.

AA (TOP LEFT). ***Nasis mor*, rattle mola.**
47.5 x 68.0 cm. Private collection.

BB (TOP RIGHT). ***Nasis*, gourd rattles. Rattles used to accompany lulla-bies and dancing.**

CC (ABOVE LEFT). **Gourd canteen used to carry food to the mainland. Vines are used to make a handle, and a corncob serves as a stopper.**
Gourd, corncob, plant fiber. 23.5 cm. Private collection.

DD (ABOVE RIGHT). **Mola showing large gourd used to carry clothes.**
72.0 x 75.0 cm. NMAI 25/2497. Collected by Jane D. deTomasi. Presented by Dr. James

EE. Verrill gourd mola.

73.0 x 90.0 cm. NMAI 8/3627. Collected by A.H. Verrill.

FF. Gourds drying on a cane fence.

Mari Lyn Salvador, Ubigandup, 1997.

Gourds

The Kuna grow two species of gourds for a wide range of tasks. When they reach the proper size, the pulp is removed and they are dried in the sun. Larger gourds are used to carry water (Fig. GG) or cut open at the top to carry clothes to be washed in the river (Fig. DD). Medium sized gourds are dried, leaving the seeds inside for rattles (Fig. BB), or hollowed out to use as canteens (Fig. CC). Gourds are also cut in half and used to bail water from boats, or attached to wooden handles to make ladles for serving drinks.

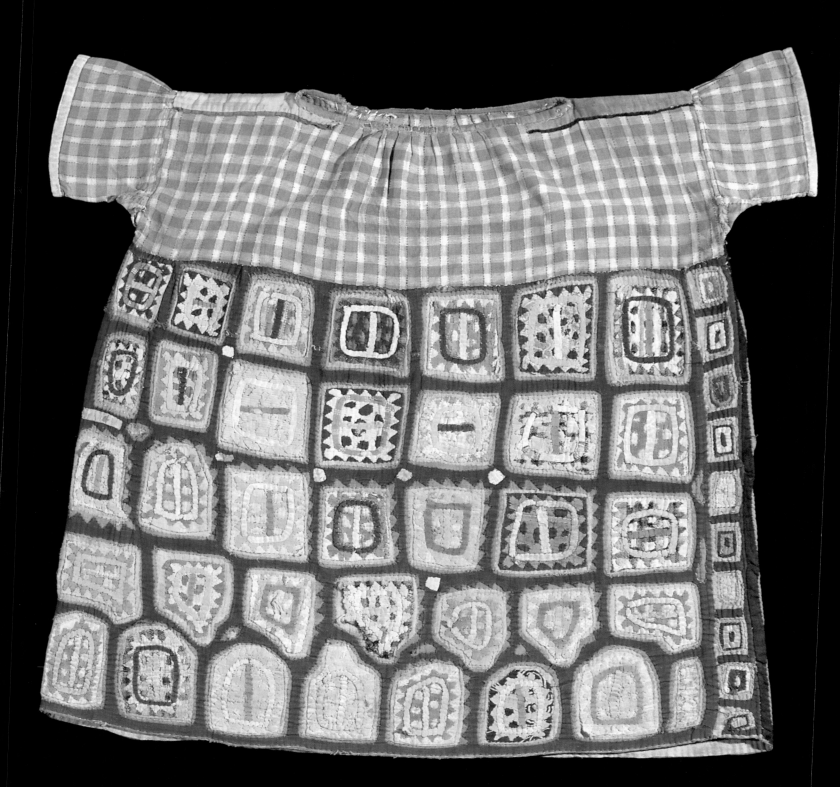

The Kuna and the World

Five Centuries of Struggle

James Howe

The Kuna of Panama have been dealing with intruders from the Old World since the beginning of the sixteenth century. Inhabiting a region of great strategic significance, a field of conflict between English-, French-, and Spanish-speaking powers, they have found themselves caught up in other people's schemes and other people's wars, attempting on their part to trade and ally themselves with one side or another without giving up their independence. Repeatedly missionized and subdued, they have each time rebelled and broken free, even in the twentieth century. Today, when no one is truly isolated or independent, they still struggle to preserve a measure of autonomy and cultural integrity.[1]

The Isthmian holocaust

The conquest of the American mainland began in 1510 when two failed Spanish expeditions came together at a village by the mouth of the Gulf of Urabá, where the Panamanian Isthmus meets the South American mainland. Parties setting out from the village, renamed Santa Maria la Antigua del Darién, explored south on the Atrato River and west onto the Isthmus, establishing an outpost called Aclá, and on one of these forays their leader, the famous Vasco Nuñez de Balboa, discovered the Pacific. In time, the whole eastern Isthmus came to be known to the Europeans as the Darién and the northern shore as the Coast of San Blas.

Balboa, while anything but gentle, did spare many of the local people, who were his only source of information, gold, and provisions. In 1514, however, he was superseded by Pedrarias Davila, who executed Balboa and embarked on a search for gold so brutal that within ten years he had exterminated most of the population of the region. In 1524 he moved his headquarters to a spot called Panama well to the west on the Pacific coast, and the open savannas and cultivated fields of the Darién region soon reverted to forest (Castillero Calvo 1995, Sauer 1966, Andagoya 1865).

The chiefdoms of the contact period, as sketchily described by Spanish chroniclers, seem very different from the Kuna as they have come to be known in later

3.1. Mola blouse. This design is likely to have been inspired by small cracker packages sold in stores in Kuna Yala. The fabric used for the yoke was popular in the 1920s. Collected by Baron Erland Nordenskiöld in 1927.
66.0 x 70.0 cm. EMG 1927.27.916.

Kuna Marriage
in the Late Seventeenth Century
As Described by a British Pirate

When a man disposes of his daughter, he invites all the Indians within 20 miles around, to a great feast, which he provides for them. The men who come to the wedding bring their axes along with them, to work with; the women bring about half a bushel of maize; the boys bring fruit and roots; the girls fowl and eggs; for none come empty-handed. They set their presents at the door of the house and go away again, til all the rest of the guests have brought theirs; which are all received in and disposed of by the people of the house.

Then the men return first to the wedding, and the bridegroom presents each man with a calabash of strong drink and conducts them through the house one by one, into some open place behind it. The women come next, who likewise receive a calabash of liquor and march through the house. Then come the boys, and last of all the girls, who all drink at the door and go after the rest.

Then come the fathers of the young couple, with their son and daughter: the father of the bridegroom leads his son, and the father of the bride leads his daughter. The former makes a speech to the company and then dances about, with many antic gestures, til he is all in a sweat. Then kneeling down, he gives his son to the bride, whose father is kneeling also and holds her, having danced himself into a sweat, as the other. Then the young couple take each other by the hand, and the bridegroom returns the bride to her father, and thus ends the ceremony.

Then all the men take up their axes, and run shouting and hollowing [*sic*] to the tract of woodland which is laid out for a plantation for the young couple. There they fall to work, cutting down the woods and clearing the ground as fast as they can. Thus they continue about seven days, working with the greatest vigor imaginable, and all the ground which they clear the women and children plant with maize, or whatever else is agreeable to the season. They also build a house for the new-married couple to live in.

The seven days being ended, and the young man settled with his wife in his new house, the company make merry there with *Chicha Copah*, the Corn drink before described, of which they are sure to provide good store. They also make provision for feasting, and the guests fall to very heartily.

Lionel Wafer
*A New Voyage and Description
of the Isthmus of America*

centuries. Most of the names and terms that were recorded in the early 1500s bear little resemblance to modern Kuna words, with a very few exceptions, notably *oba* for corn and *ulu* for canoe. It seems certain that Kuna speakers inhabited at least some of the region, but historians debate whether they were found on the Isthmus during this period or migrated out of the Atrato basin after Pedrarias' holocaust. A hundred years later at the beginning of the seventeenth century, on the other hand, they can be identified with near certainty all the way from the Atrato across the Darién (Howe 1978, Helms 1979, Romoli 1987).

Missionaries, war, and pirates

After 1524 the Darién provided some refuge to its indigenous inhabitants. The Panamanian Isthmus as a whole played a crucial but very restricted role in Spain's New World empire, as the point where silver from Peru crossed overland by mule train from the Pacific to the Atlantic. On the Pacific side, the small city of Panama, with a population of only about five thousand, was fed by a cattle-raising hinterland stretching off to the southwest, in the opposite direction from the Darién. The northern, Caribbean coast was occupied only by a fort at the mouth of the Chagres River and two small ports, Nombre de Dios and Portobelo, which were little better than

Tom. I.II. N.° 68

MARIAGE des INDIENS du PANAMA.

3.2. French illustration of seventeenth-century Kuna marriage, probably based on Wafer's account.

villages except during the trade fairs that took place when the silver fleet was in.
The lands further east between Panama and Cartagena held such marginal interest
for imperial Spain that they might have escaped serious attempts at control had it not
been for the Dutch, French, and English pirates preying on the Spanish Main, who
visited the Isthmus with alarming frequency (Rojas y Arrieta 1929, Severino 1956).

The pirates found the northern shore of the Darién, in particular, almost ideal for
their purposes; close but not too close to the route of the silver fleet and to stationary
targets at Portobelo and Cartagena, the Coast of San Blas offered sea turtles for provi-
sioning, islands and coves for hiding ships and careening weed-infested hulls, and
native inhabitants for guides and auxiliaries. Although the earliest raiders, such as
Francis Drake, found local support more among runaway slaves than among the
Indians, by the end of the sixteenth century Spain had succeeded in neutralizing the
rebel Blacks, and at the beginning of the seventeenth the Kuna made their presence
known by attacking Panama's eastern frontier. Thereafter, Spanish authorities worried
not just about Indians but about Indians in league with pirates.

With military resources stretched thin by the demands of imperial defense,
Spain depended on missionaries for help in pacifying hostile frontier peoples. In the
1630s, authorities gained entrée to the Kuna through a young man named Julio
Carrisolio who had been shipwrecked on the coast and accepted by the Indians.
Assisted by Carrisolio, a Dominican, Father Adrián de Santo Tomas, succeeded in
founding four missions encompassing about fourteen hundred Kuna, for which a
grateful crown rewarded the two men with titles and honors and renamed the region
Santo Domingo del Darién. Their charges, however, stubbornly resisted conversion,
and the rest of the Kuna remained outside imperial control. Equally bad from a
Dominican perspective, within a few years rival Capuchins started to poach on their
territory. In 1651, after the retirement of Father Adrián, civil authorities tried to station
troops in the region, provoking the Kuna to revolt and drive out the soldiers and
Capuchins, along with the miners and colonists who had come in on their coattails
(Castillero Calvo 1995, Rojas y Arrieta 1929, Severino 1956, Stout 1947, Ward 1993).

Throughout the second half of the seventeenth century, the Kuna successfully resisted Spanish reconquest except at a few Dominican missions, and the pirates, who had established a strong Caribbean base on Jamaica, attacked the Isthmus repeatedly. Henry Morgan took Portobelo in 1668 and returned to sack Panama in 1671, fighting a battle on the plains before the city in which unpacified Kuna on his side were opposed by mission Indians on the other. Spanish gold mines recently opened in the eastern Darién at Cana were attacked in 1684, 1702, 1712, 1724, and 1734, and through the 1680s parties of pirates were guided by the Indians across the Isthmus to raid on the Pacific side. The Kuna exercised caution towards these lawless men, some of whom were not above enslaving unwary Indians, and unlike the Miskitu of the Nicaraguan coast, the Darién Indians did not become professional slave raiders or mercenaries. They did cooperate regularly with parties of buccaneers, to the extent that some Kuna on the north slope began raising crops to provision foreign ships.

A number of pirates published accounts of their adventures, the best of them written by a ship's surgeon named Lionel Wafer who was left behind in the Darién for several months in 1681. Based on his observations and the few words of the Kuna language he learned, Wafer described the Indians in some detail. He found them living in hamlets scattered up and down river valleys, each cluster of hamlets centered on a fortified meeting house. Despite the hostility of the unpacified Kuna toward colonial rule, several spoke a little Spanish and one had escaped from service to the Bishop of Panama (Wafer 1970).

Wafer's narrative, even before it appeared in print, helped inspire interest in the Darién, and in 1698 a company of Scots established a colony in eastern San Blas near the site of Aclá. The local Kuna received them warmly, but the effort collapsed within a few months, and by the time a relief force arrived, the first contingent had already departed. The disastrous colony, having lost seventeen hundred out of twenty-five hundred members, mostly to disease and malnutrition, was evicted in 1700 by a Spanish expeditionary force that included two hundred mission Indians led by Carrisolio's son (Prebble 1968).

By this time the imperial system of silver fleets and trade fairs had all but collapsed, and along with them the great age of piracy (Ward 1993). Even as Panama slipped into economic depression and obscurity, however, the Spanish Crown, badly frightened by the Scots, worried more rather than less about the Darién. Pirates and privateers returned periodically to loot the Cana gold mines, and a number of Frenchmen took up residence on the coasts of San Blas and Urabá, joining with the Kuna in raids on Spanish settlements. Over the course of the eighteenth century, moreover, European powers fought a series of West Indian wars, which bestowed considerable strategic value on the Darién as a potential military base, site for colonization, and interoceanic crossing route. Although Spain succeeded in recolonizing and missionizing parts of the region, it failed to consolidate control, and in 1728 a mestizo named Garcia led the Indians in another massive revolt. Garcia was eventually defeated and killed, but Kuna resistance continued (Severino 1956).

The Frenchmen on the north coast eventually gave up piracy in favor of raising cacao for sale and taking Indian wives, and in the late 1730s they petitioned the Spanish Crown for pardon and permission to settle permanently. Spanish authorities, eager for a buffer against growing English incursions, readily agreed. The British, who bombarded Portobelo in 1739 during the War of Jenkin's Ear and tried to take Cartagena two years later, actively courted the Kuna, and some strategists even dreamed of instigating a massive Indian uprising against Spain all across Central America.

The Kuna, however, felt such pressure from Spanish attacks that in 1740 they sued for peace and agreed to accept new missionaries, this time Jesuits. Over the following decade, missionized Indians, who continued to resist conversion, were ravaged by European infectious diseases. In 1750 they rose again, expelling settlers from the Darién and even menacing Panama City. In the same rebellion, they attacked the French colonists and drove the survivors off the Isthmus, refusing thereafter to marry outsiders or allow them to live among them.

In the years after the insurrection of the mid-eighteenth century, Spanish authorities regained control of the southern Darién and brought a few hundred Kuna into mission settlements. They also built a small fort at the town of Yaviza on the lower Chucunaque, effectively blocking a key military passage and cutting off the pacified Kuna on the lower Tuira from their rebel kin. The latter, however, kept up hostilities for more than three decades, assisted by the British in Jamaica, who provided them with muskets, letters of alliance, canes of office, and even military advisors.

In 1785, Spanish authorities elaborated a plan to defeat the Kuna once and for all. To cut the Indians off from their English allies, they built four small forts along the San Blas coast, as well as three more in the southern Darién. The garrisons held on despite fierce attacks and losses to disease, and the Kuna, having been abandoned by Britain, came to terms with Spanish authorities and once again signed a peace treaty. Two years later, however, a new colonial administration concluded that costs of the campaign should not be sustained, and by 1792, all of the forts had been abandoned (Luengo Muñoz, 1959, 1961).

After nearly three hundred years, peace finally came to the Darién. As foreign powers and freelance raiders lost interest in the eastern Isthmus, so did the Spanish Crown and the Church, and the Kuna were left alone to lick their wounds. During just the last half of the eighteenth century, war and epidemic disease had cut the indigenous population in half, to an estimated five thousand, and except for a few hundred "tame" Indians on the Tuira watershed, the Kuna had been driven from the southern Darién. They left their names behind on rivers and towns occupied thereafter by Black freemen and slaves, and increasingly, by an indigenous people called Emberá or Chocó, traditional enemies of the Kuna, who were in the process of migrating onto the Isthmus from South America.

Trade and expansion

At the beginning of the nineteenth century, some of the Kuna lived upstream in the Bayano and Chucunaque Valleys and others on the Gulf of Urabá, but the greatest number were found in San Blas, north of the mountain spine of the Isthmus, on the small rivers flowing into the Caribbean. Living a few miles upstream, they could exploit marine resources and continue to trade with foreign vessels but keep some distance from outside threats and influences. After 1812, the rest of Latin America was in any case too caught up in the wars of independence and the creation of new states to give much attention to a backwater like the Darién.

Toward the middle of the century, the Kuna began moving down to the coast, first to sites near river mouths, and then out onto inshore islands, a gradual process that continued for more than eighty years. In this new niche they gained increased access to trading boats, along with relief from snakes, mosquitoes, and endemic diseases, though at the cost of increased exposure to smallpox and other epidemics. The tiny coral islands, laboriously reclaimed from thorny brush and mangrove swamps, functioned as dormitory communities, supported by agriculture and hunting on the mainland, as well as by fishing and gathering in the coastal waters.

The sea turtles with which the pirates had provisioned their ships now provided "tortoiseshell," in great demand on the world market, as were products gathered in the forest such as ivory nuts, medicinal plants, wild rubber, and other latexes. As the century progressed, however, the Kuna increasingly specialized in selling coconuts, industriously planting palms on uninhabited islands and the mainland shore. In 1874, a British consul noted that the Kuna accounted for a quite significant portion of the trade in and out of Colombia, which then included the Isthmus, and in 1890, the Consul in Panama estimated (undoubtedly with some exaggeration) that in the previous year fifty tons of turtle shell, seven hundred tons of ivory nut, and five million coconuts had come out of San Blas. The Kuna traded and sold these products for cloth, firearms, steel tools, and other manufactures imported by merchant captains, many of whom left goods to be retailed by Kuna trading partners and took young Indian men to sea with them.

The move to the islands and the growth of the cash economy encouraged a fundamental change in the gender division of labor. As in many lowland South American societies, women had carried out all agricultural tasks other than felling and burning the forest. Now, however, with the increased distance between fields and village, with the great weight of the staples, bananas and coconuts, and with the expansion of cash-cropping, men shouldered more of the burden. Women continued to fetch drinking water from mainland rivers and do a little light agricultural work but otherwise mostly stayed at home.

The system of land use also changed. Previously, fields reverted to forest and communal ownership after fallowing, but now men who cleared land alienated it permanently, and a system of private property and inheritance rapidly developed, one especially important for coconut groves and the beaches on which sea turtles came to lay their eggs.

Their enthusiastic participation in the world economy notwithstanding, the Kuna kept outsiders at arm's length, refusing to allow merchants or anyone else to settle in their villages or use debt to control them. After Isthmian independence from Spain in 1821, national and provincial governments in Panama and Colombia were too distant and too weak to exert more than intermittent influence on the Indians. Throughout the century, Colombia was isolated from the outside world, internally fragmented by geography and a primitive communication system, and periodically racked by political strife. The national government passed laws to end communal land tenure and integrate Indians into national society, but San Blas lay well outside the highland zone in which such laws could be enforced. Kuna leaders periodically traveled to Cartagena, Panama, and even to Bogota, but for the most part they managed to live their lives without much outside interference.

Panama, part of Colombia except during brief interludes as a secessionist state, was still oriented towards the Isthmian crossing and a southwestern hinterland. Its capitol, less a city than a decrepit provincial town that burned down every few years for lack of an adequate water supply, had been caught in a depression for more than a century, and the two moribund ports on the Atlantic side had negligible effect on the Kuna.

This isolation could not last, however. At mid-century, gold miners began traveling to California via Panama, and in 1855 a railroad was completed across the Isthmus. At the line's northern terminus a new port called Colon sprang up, giving Panama an effective presence on the Caribbean only a hundred miles west of San Blas. Intrusions into Indian territory increased, impelled by economic demand from the growing economies of Europe and North America: coastal peoples, the descendants of rebel slaves who had lived to the west of the Kuna since the sixteenth century, increasingly competed in San Blas for forest products and sea turtles. Over the mountains to the south, in the valleys of the Bayano and Chucunaque, mestizos and Blacks in search of wild castilloa rubber provoked a conflict, known as "the Rubber War," with the riverine Kuna in the early 1870s.

Worse intrusions threatened. The construction of canals in Europe, North America, and the Middle East inspired serious thought about a link between the Atlantic and Pacific, and among the various routes considered— which included Tehuantepec, Nicaragua, central Panama, and the Atrato—a possible Darién canal figured prominently. Attention focused particularly on a place called Caledonia in eastern San Blas, once a favorite of pirates and site of Aclá and the Scots Colony. A British doctor, Edward Cullen, claimed in 1850 to have crossed repeatedly from one side to the other through a pass at Caledonia that he insisted never exceeded 150 feet above sea level. A disastrous expedition in 1854, during which a U.S. naval party was lost for more than a month on the Pacific side, found no pass under a thousand feet, but interest in the Darién route persisted (McCullough 1977).

In 1870 another North American expedition led by Commander Thomas Selfridge crossed at Caledonia to an affluent of the Chucunaque. In the course of a few highly uncomfortable weeks, during which unwilling Kuna guides led them through swamps and thickets, the surveyors determined that the Caledonia pass was far too high for a canal. Several years later, two French officers, Lieutenants Wyse and Réclus, investigated the Darién route once again, but the best they could suggest was a tunnel through the cordillera. Ultimately, when a French company attempted unsuccessfully to build a canal (1880–1889), it chose the line of the traditional Isthmian crossing in Central Panama.

Although the Kuna escaped the disaster of a major waterway forced through the heart of their territory, the world was pressing them more closely in other ways. In about 1890, Colombia moved to regulate trade with the Indians, insisting that vessels on their way to San Blas from Jamaica, the United States, Curaçao, and other parts of the Caribbean pay duty at Colon or Cartagena. By the end of the century, most of the sloops and schooners trading with the Kuna sailed out of the two ports, even if quite a few of those based in Colon were still owned by English-speaking foreigners.

At the turn of the twentieth century, the Kuna were still keeping their distance, still holding to some of their time-honored practices and strategies. They continued to favor English-speakers, if now only in trade and cultural preference rather than war, but they realized that they must deal with Hispanic political powers, and in the last analysis, they rightly suspected all outsiders. In their own ranks, divisions had started to open, differences between men who had worked as sailors or in Panama and those who had always stayed at home, between families interested in having their children educated if the opportunity arose and others adamantly opposed to all schools, and between those who most feared Panama and others more afraid of Colombia.

A Letter Delivered by Several Kuna Men
to the British Consul in Colon in 1893,
along with a Gift of a Rooster and Hen
Decorated with Red, White, and Blue Beads

Rio Diablio
San Blas Coast
May 16th 1893

To Her Majesty Queen Victoria

We William Thomson, Lewis Breakman, Emanueleta Yarso, Joseph Harvey, James Leverage, Chiefs of River Diablio do hereby beseech you to listen to our troubles and help us. We as Indian Chiefs have our families here and live in the land that God has given us, and now they intend driving us from our homes, and we have no where to make a home.

Miguel Nunis the President of Cartagena and Miguel Antonia Caro Vice President of Bogota are trying to Sell our Country to the Americans. Our people have lived here for centuries. We have our plantations, our Cocoanuts, we get our living by hard work. They wish to take our Cocoanuts, our rubber and everything God has given us, and drive us and our children into the mountains. We being under the Colombian flag was satisfied and well treated when Panama was a Souvereign State, but Since Bogota and become So; we are not treated well and they wish to Sell us for the gold and rubber, Even now we are well treated by Panama. The wish to keep our country to ourselves and for them to keep theirs. God gave us our wives and we do not wish to mix with other nations.

Now Most gracious Queen Victoria we beseech the[e] not to allow the Colombians to take our land and homes And drives us to the mountains to die of starvation, and we sign ourselves your most humble Subjects.

Public Record Office (FO 135, 1893)

3.3. Kuna boys sent to school with Christian brothers in 1906.
Archivos Estanislao López.

New missions

In November of 1903, Panama rebelled against Colombia, and the United States, which had been unsuccessfully negotiating with the government in Bogota to build an Isthmian canal, prevented Colombian troops from suppressing the rebellion. Panamanian delegates were forced to sign a treaty ceding extensive long-term rights to the United States, and in 1904 construction began on a new Panama Canal (Conniff 1992, Major 1993, McCullough 1977).

In these early months, the Kuna were courted by both Colombia and Panama. Several Indian leaders, including the recently retired paramount chief Abisua of Narganá, visited Panama City and accepted flags of the new republic. The current high chief, however, Inanaginya of Sasardi, stayed with Colombia, comparing the choice between the two states to a husband who keeps to his tried and true old wife despite temptation by a younger woman.

Panama was eager to secure its eastern border and to bring San Blas into the nation, but with a weak police force and an army that had been disbanded to forestall coups, it lacked the means to overcome Kuna resistance. The government thus adopted an initial policy of making contact with the more compliant and friendly indigenous leaders, most of all with Charly Robinson, the twentieth-century equivalent of Julio Carrisolio. Robinson had been taken as a young boy by a ship's captain to be raised and educated on the island of Providencia. After spending a few early adult years as a sailor, he returned home to his natal village of Narganá in about 1902. Active in village politics and favored by the retired high chief Abisua, Robinson was himself elected first village chief following Abisua's death in 1904.

In 1905, Robinson arranged with Miguel Amador Guerrero, the first president of Panama, to bring sixteen young Kuna boys to be educated by Christian brothers, which he did the following year, and in 1907 he welcomed to Narganá a Jesuit missionary sent by the President and Bishop of Panama, Father Leonardo Gassó. Over the next two years, Gassó gained a foothold on Narganá and its nearby sister island, Nusatupu, which he renamed Corazón de Jesús. In addition to baptizing large numbers of young children, he attracted many boys and some adults to teaching sessions in which they were catechized in the rudiments of the Catholic faith (Gassó 1911–1914, Howe 1990, 1992).

Gassó's presence and his aggressive proselytizing provoked immediate conflict. On Narganá and Corazón, he was opposed by a large segment of the community,

in which ritualists and conservative chiefs played leading roles, and support for
the mission waxed and waned, diminishing especially during the long periods that the
priest spent outside San Blas. Gassó, who distrusted what he saw as the corrupting
effects of literacy, resisted lending much time or resources to schooling, which was
what many mission supporters most wanted. He did succeed, however, in having
Charly Robinson named governor of the coast and in securing a small shipment of
rifles, which in late 1908 his supporters used to repel an attack on Narganá by Kuna
enemies of missionization.

Except in their opposition to Gassó, those enemies were divided. The high chief
Inanaginya died on a trip to Bogota during 1907, and when representatives of the
thirty or so villages in San Blas met to choose his successor, the contentious issue of
national affiliation split them into two confederacies, the pro-Colombian group led
by the late chief's nephew, Inabaginya, and the other by another ex-sailor, Cimral
Colman of Ailigandi. Colman, though much less sanguine about Panama and the
modern world than Charly Robinson, recognized that the Kuna would eventually
have to come to terms with the national government.

Over the next few years, Father Gassó managed to build churches and residences
on Narganá and Corazón, create a boarding school for Kuna boys, and gain admittance
for several more priests and brothers. Support on the two islands lacked depth or
constancy, however, and other Kuna continued to oppose and threaten the mission.
Government backing was also fragile. The Conservative Party, which initially held
power, favored strong church-state ties, but many in the government backed the
missions only as a temporary expedient and expressed dissatisfaction with their results
even in official publications. It was unlikely that the anti-clerical Liberals, who enjoyed
a majority of popular support, would continue sponsorship of Gassó when they came
to power, or that any government would leave San Blas solely to the Church for
much longer.

In 1909, when Gassó attempted to establish a new mission on the island of Tupile
to the east of Narganá, pagan Kuna attacked the village and tore down the cross he
had erected. In the aftermath of the incident, the government established a police
post at the Colombian border, though with little success in overawing the Kuna. In
1910, a prominent Liberal named Carlos Mendoza made an official visit to the coast
during a few months as acting President of the Republic. Welcomed at Narganá as
well as the islands controlled by Cimral Colman's confederacy, Mendoza was abruptly
turned away by Inabaginya's group, an affront he lacked the means to punish. Two
years later the Liberals came fully to power with the election of Belisario Porras, the
leading political figure of the era. Among other initiatives, President Porras began
mapping out plans for secular control of San Blas.

In this altered political climate, the fortunes of the Catholic mission rapidly
declined. Narganá had not yielded as Gassó hoped, still less the rest of the Kuna.
With the death of Gassó's mentor, the Bishop of Panama, and the change to a Liberal
administration, the missionary departed for his native Spain. Other priests and brothers
carried on for a while, but resources were diverted to distant mission fields.

As had happened before in the seventeenth century, competitors also intruded,
this time Protestants. An evangelical missionary, Anna Coope, who had tried unsuccessfully to enter San Blas in 1910, was invited to Narganá by Charly Robinson in 1913
after Gassó's departure, provoking a new round of dissension and turmoil. Catholics
protested, and in November of that year, pagan Kuna returned to attack Narganá, again
without success. The following year, when Coope and Robinson imposed prohibition
on the island, they stirred up further agitation. On issues other than liquor, however,
Coope showed more patience. She did not attack Kuna religion as directly as had

Gassó, and her warm, motherly manner won friends and supporters. The government, if not actively supportive, was willing to tolerate her mission, and an especially sympathetic visiting official encouraged her to take over the Catholic buildings on Narganá (Coope 1917, Howe 1990, 1992).

The Porras administration, meanwhile, pushed ahead on plans for secular control, soliciting memos and reports on the project, and in 1912 and 1915 it passed laws authorizing colonies, plantations, and an official administration for the coast. The President gained consent to a government presence from Cimral Colman, leader of one Kuna confederacy, who was anxious for help in delimiting Kuna lands and keeping the intruders out of San Blas.

The conquest of San Blas

In May of 1915 Porras set out on an official visit to the coast. The presidential party stopped at the border post, Narganá, and several other villages, and like his predecessor Mendoza, Porras was rudely turned away by Inabaginya's pro-Colombian villages. Undeterred, he established a new territorial unit, the Circumscription of San Blas, with a governor or intendente and a headquarters on an island at the western end of the region, which was renamed El Porvenir, The Future. Within a few months schools were opened and a handful of government police stationed on Narganá, Corazón de Jesús, and two other islands.

A North American company was also granted sixty thousand tax-free acres at Mandinga in western San Blas, in return for which it was to sponsor an agricultural colony to be called Nicuesa. Nothing came of the colony, but the company mined manganese in Mandinga from 1916 to 1919, and it began developing coconut and banana plantations. Worst of all from the Kuna point of view, the government, rather than excluding poor Afro-Panamanians from the forests of San Blas, encouraged them to gather ivory nut and the latex of a tree called *Níspero*, reserving only the sea turtles for the Kuna themselves.

Despite all this commercial activity, from 1916 through 1918 and the end of World War I, the government devoted minimal resources or attention to the region. This neglect ended in October 1918, with the inauguration of Belisario Porras to another term as President. Porras appointed a new intendente, a choleric individual named Humberto Vaglio, and together the two made plans to subdue the Kuna and erase their culture, turning them into "civilized" Panamanians.

In his first few months in office, Vaglio induced Inabaginya to renounce allegiance to Colombia, while on Narganá the intendente suppressed Anna Coope and Charly Robinson. Robinson, by now middle-aged, had been contending with an assertive group of young men led by a few graduates of urban Catholic and government schools, notably a firebrand named Claudio Iglesias. Iglesias's group was backed by the local Panamanian teachers and police, who resented competition from Coope's English-language school and the pro-American sentiments she fostered. President Porras ordered that schoolgirls should give up the nose rings and bead limb-bindings traditionally worn by Kuna females, and Vaglio closed down Coope's school. In reaction, Robinson and his supporters rose up in June of 1919, only to be put down by Vaglio a few days later and decisively supplanted in favor of the youth faction.

During the same months, Vaglio prohibited Kuna consumption of alcohol, which formed an essential part of female puberty ceremonies, and he extended to several other villages the ban on traditional female dress, all this as the opening of a general campaign against Kuna culture. Cimral Colman, who up to the beginning of 1919 had hoped to continue cooperating with the government, ended up in strong opposition to Vaglio, leading to a propaganda war in which each incessantly protested and criticized the other's actions and character. So personal and vitriolic were Vaglio's attacks on Colman that in late 1920, during a brief period in which President Porras stepped down, an acting President decided that the intendente was needlessly inflaming the situation and removed him from office. His replacement, however, proved just as eager to subdue and transform the Kuna.

Small-scale confrontations between Indians and outsiders occurred repeatedly over the five years from 1919 to 1924, including the burning of a rebellious village by police, a Kuna ambush of forest workers, a raid on a police post, and most notoriously, the killing of the young modernist Claudio Iglesias and five others during an attempt to arrest a Kuna dissident. The police extended their grasp from the four islands where they were first stationed to about half of San Blas. In each pacified village they repeated the pattern first established on Narganá, suppressing Kuna dress, religion, curing, and most of the rest of traditional culture, imposing Panamanian equivalents in their place. They quelled resistance with stocks, jail, and beatings—though they did not subject the Kuna to the kinds of torture typical in some parts of the Americas—and they tried to cut off the villages under their control both from the unpacified Kuna and the outside world (Howe 1991).

Kuna well-being was also menaced by accelerating economic encroachment. The government continued to encourage extraction of forest products, and, yielding to political pressure, it opened up turtling to non-Indians. Outsiders with police backing imposed stores on pacified islands, replacing shops run by the Kuna themselves, and policemen rigidly controlled subsistence labor. In the mid-1920s, as the banana plantations at Mandinga began large-scale production, they brought in large numbers of non-Indian workers, while a second operation got underway in eastern San Blas, with plans to build a railroad over the Caledonia Pass.

Kuna leaders resisted these encroachments in different ways. Inabaginya and his followers actively confronted non-Indian turtlers and forest workers, and he refused to allow police or teachers to be stationed on his islands. Otherwise, however, he played a mixed role, lending little support to Kuna under police domination and informing regularly on his rival Colman. For his part, Colman kept up contact with resisters on captive islands, when possible paying lightning visits to whip up opposition, and he persisted in his campaign of criticism and complaint. Having despaired of government help in obtaining legal guarantees for Kuna lands, in 1919 Colman hired a lawyer named José de la Rosa in what proved to be an expensive and fruitless campaign to secure land titles for his followers. De la Rosa did, however, act as the chief's advocate for three years, defending dissidents accused of attacking policemen, freeing Colman and other leaders from arbitrary detention, and representing the Kuna resistance to newspapers and the government. In October 1922, President Porras declared de la Rosa persona non grata in San Blas, effectively muting Colman's protests.

Colman and his heir apparent, Nele Kantule of Ustupu, broadened their search for outside supporters and advocates. In early 1924, an American employee of the Panama Railway named William Markham, who had visited San Blas the previous year, wrote President Porras a long but friendly critique of government actions in San Blas. Porras, already disturbed by recent events there, decided to go investigate personally. He never made the trip, however, and in October a new president took office.

By this time the Kuna had found another English-speaking ally. Richard Marsh, a consulting engineer who had briefly been chargé d'affaires in the U.S. Legation in 1910, returned to Panama in 1923 in search of lands suitable for planting rubber. After a brief visit to Yaviza in the Darién, in which Marsh encountered several light-skinned individuals, he convinced himself that a tribe of white Indians lived at the headwaters of the Chucunaque. Back in the United States, he organized an expedition

3.4, 3.5. Kuna delegates at the Smithsonian in Washington, 1924.
National Anthropology Archives, Smithsonian Institution.

to search for white Indians as well as rubber lands, and in early 1924 he returned to Panama with a large party, including representatives from the Smithsonian, the American Museum of Natural History, and Pathé News. At the end of two months at Yaviza, Marsh and his followers ascended the Chucunaque and crossed the Caledonia Pass into San Blas, losing two members of the group to disease, without finding any white Indians (Marsh 1934).

Once in San Blas, Marsh learned of the Kuna plight during long talks with Inabaginya, and when at last he encountered white Indians—an albino minority found throughout the Kuna population rather than a separate people—he hatched a plan to take a delegation of Indians, white and otherwise, to the United States. The Panamanian government prevented Inabaginya from going on the trip, but representatives of Colman and Nele Kantule accompanied Marsh and three albino children to New York, Canada, and Washington, D.C., generating considerable public notoriety. The delegates were studied at the Smithsonian, and Marsh tried, with little success, to lobby the U.S. government on behalf of the Indians.

The last rebellion

Marsh and the Kuna delegates returned to Panama in January 1925. His small party, which included a biologist chosen to study the white Indians, slipped into San Blas and joined Colman's forces on Ailigandi. Marsh's presence inflamed an already tense situation, and although the Kuna would almost certainly have rebelled in any case, Marsh helped precipitate and organize the uprising. He wrote a long "Declaration of Independence and Human Rights," supposedly dictated by the Kuna, proclaiming an independent republic, copies of which reached the city at the end of February.

On Sunday, 22 February 1925, the first day of Carnival, the Kuna in villages under Panamanian domination revolted, supported by forces sent by Colman and Nele

Kantule. The police who escaped the killing fled the region, abandoning even Narganá and the government headquarters on Porvenir to rebel control. Marsh, who did not take part in the violence, was by this time at Carti in western San Blas, where a large Kuna force awaited the Panamanian response. The government moved on two fronts. Impelled by angry public demonstrations against the Indians, it assembled a volunteer force of 160 policemen, who set out on the evening of 26 February in a vessel loaned by one of the fruit companies. At the same time, however, Panamanian officials asked the U.S. Legation for help in dealing with the situation.

North American support had not followed from Marsh's proclamation of an independent republic as he had hoped, but the alarm he inspired in both Panama and the Legation as a foreigner involved in an Indian uprising did lead to U.S. intervention. The U.S. Minister to the Republic, John Glover South, took a party of Panamanian and American officials to San Blas on a cruiser, the U.S.S. Cleveland, arriving at Porvenir on the morning of 27 February, just ahead of the police boat.

The Cleveland proceeded across the Gulf of San Blas to Carti, where Marsh and the Kuna were barricaded behind a stone wall. Among the group on board the Cleveland was William Markham, the North American who had written President Porras on behalf of the Kuna the year before. Sent ashore to make contact, Markham acted as impresario for a meeting at which Kuna leaders recited their grievances, winning over Minister South with their eloquence and sincerity. South began pressuring the Panamanians as well as his superiors in Washington in favor of a negotiated settlement and expulsion of Marsh without the scandal and difficulties of a trial. Panamanian officials on board the Cleveland resisted, so South flew back to the city in a seaplane and persuaded the Minister of Foreign Affairs, Horacio Alfaro, to go along with the plan. Back in San Blas, he arranged a meeting on Porvenir between Panamanian officials and Kuna leaders, at which he brokered a settlement. In return for a cessation of hostilities and declaration of allegiance to Panama, the Kuna were allowed to live as they wished without coercion. The settlement did not, however, offer explicit guarantees for Indian lands.

After the revolution

In the following months, apart from arresting a few Kuna and firing into two or three villages, the police refrained from retaliation, and to almost everyone's surprise,

3.6. Kuna giving testimony on board the U.S. warship Cleveland, March 1925.
Courtesy of Richard Marsh, Jr.

3.7. Chief Nele Kantule (third from the left) and other Kuna delegates with General Preston Brown, 1930.
Archivos Estanislao López.

the peace held. Within a few weeks, the government recaptured Narganá and Corazón, and it imposed an embargo cutting off rebel islands from trading boats, but it did not try to reimpose schools or Panamanian custom on other communities. The tense stalemate with the rebels, which left unresolved the legal status of indigenous lands and the relationship of the Kuna with national society, continued for five years.

The stalemate ended in 1930, when Colman's successor, Nele Kantule, took a delegation to Panama, where he was warmly received by President Florencio Arosemena. A comprehensive settlement was arranged guaranteeing civil rights to the Kuna and recognition for their land, and in the following days, Nele also negotiated an agreement with North American military authorities by which Kuna men would be hired for kitchen duty on Canal Zone military bases. Although Inabaginya at first opposed Nele's initiative, Arosemena persuaded him to join in the settlement, and by the end of the year a bill protecting Kuna lands was passed by the National Assembly.

By this time the banana plantations in San Blas were also on their way out. By 1929, an endemic blight had forced the Mandinga operation to close down, and in 1934 its lands were returned to the government. Over the same period the plantation in eastern San Blas succumbed to the blight and to the worldwide depression.

Catholic missionaries returned to Narganá in 1928 to take charge of public schools in San Blas. Foreign Protestant missionaries had been excluded since 1925 from San Blas, but in 1932 Anna Coope's most important Kuna convert, Alcibiades Iglesias, returned from schooling in the United States, bringing with him an American wife. The couple set up a nondenominational school and mission on Ailigandi.

The two Kuna confederacies continued on the courses set before the rebellion. Inabaginya and his followers supported the government on some issues, while holding strong against schools and change. Nele Kantule followed a middle course, resisting government control but promoting private village-run schools, retail cooperatives, communal planting and coconut-cropping, and new forms of village task organization. Narganá and Corazón de Jesús, where women gave up wearing molas altogether soon after the rebellion, continued their adherence to Panamanian civilization, schools, and salaried employment.

In 1938 Panama increased the security of Kuna lands by reconstituting San Blas as a special Comarca or district, and in 1945, after the deaths of Nele and Inabaginya, an especially sympathetic intendente named Felix Oller worked with Alcibiades Iglesias and a number of Kuna leaders to engineer a reorganization of San Blas, which was codified in a constitution known as the Carta Orgánica and ratified by Panamanian law in 1953. The constitution created a legislative body, the Congreso General, which meets at least twice a year, and a hierarchy of three ranked high chiefs or caciques. In the initial choice of these chiefs, the political heirs of Inabaginya and Nele Kantule filled the first and second positions, while the third position went to a Narganá man, Estanislao López, who in the 1920s had led the modernist youth.

Beginning in the 1930s, schools and government offices slowly expanded in San Blas, as did Catholic and Protestant missions, though most teachers, policemen, and Protestant missionaries were Kuna. In the mid-1950s, when the ban on foreign missions was lifted, Kuna Protestants affiliated with the Southern Baptists. Aggressive proselytizing by both faiths in the 1950s and 1960s, combined with generational tensions and electoral competition, sparked conflict and political schism on a number of islands.

Cash-cropping of coconuts continued as the mainstay of the Kuna economy, increasingly supplemented by tourism and migrant labor. Colombian merchant vessels took over the trade after World War II, buying up the entire output of San Blas, a situation that Panamanian officials disliked but usually tolerated. During and after World War II, migrant labor increased greatly, as Kuna men took restaurant jobs in the city or traveled to western Panama to work in the banana plantations of Bocas del Toro. Tourism and a market in reverse-appliqué mola blouses, which had begun on a small scale as early as the 1920s, also expanded in the post-war years.

Kuna relations with the government, which had shifted with each intendente and presidential administration, altered significantly after a National Guard coup in 1968 brought General Omar Torrijos to power. San Blas shared in the expansion of schools,

3.8. Dr. Máximo Carrizo mola. Likely to have been inspired by a political poster, the letters indicate that the candidate is from the "Partido Repúblicano" and that Dr. Máximo Carrizo was running as a representative for Colon in 1964. The party's emblem, a deer head, is written in both Kuna (*koenono*) and Spanish (*el venado*).
40.5 x 51.0 cm. FMCH X82.612. Museum purchase in memory of Sidney S. Kallick.

health clinics, and other populist programs sponsored by the Torrijos government, and the suppression of political parties and electoral politics brought some calm to Kuna public life. A major generational change in regional politics occurred in 1971 with the retirement and death of the first and second caciques and the elevation of the third, Estanislao López, to the first position—the government, which had always favored López, later named him cacique of all the Indians in Panama. In 1972 a new national constitution granted San Blas its first representatives on a National Assembly, and in the late 1970s political parties were once again legalized.

In recent decades the integration of the Kuna into national life has continued and accelerated. Migrant labor keeps growing, and several thousand Kuna, including women in mola and their families, live in Panama City and Colon. In addition to primary schooling, now almost universal, many young people attend secondary school and the university. Newspapers include articles almost daily on Kuna Yala, as the Comarca is now officially called; political parties actively court Kuna votes; and government ministries maintain an active presence.

At the same time, however, conflicts with the government and outside economic interests keep surfacing, especially when the integrity of Kuna Yala is threatened. In 1977, during the ratification of the Torrijos-Carter canal treaties, a majority of the Kuna voted "No" on the canal plebiscite, exacerbating anti-Indian sentiment in Panama. In the Noriega years, plans to build a military base in Kuna Yala led to a protracted standoff, and in the mid-1990s, mineral concessions totaling three-quarters of the reserve's surface area have inspired heated opposition.

Threats to Kuna lands by impoverished outsiders have also recurred. Landless peasants from western Panama have flooded into the Darién in recent decades, felling the forest and pasturing cattle, and some have crossed the cordillera into Kuna Yala. The government, which often favors peasant and landlord interests, has offered little help, but the Kuna have enjoyed considerable success in obtaining international funding for a forest reserve, as well as in ejecting peasants and cutting boundary trails around Kuna Yala (see Ventocilla, in this volume). Gold miners and other intruders from Colombia have so far proved harder to dislodge.

Tourism, a perennial source of trouble, has sparked internal schism as well as external conflict. In the mid-1970s, a large majority opposing a hotel and jet airport proposed by the government tried to dismiss the three Kuna representatives on the National Assembly, who supported the project. The government responded by suppressing the General Congress and partitioning the reserve into three districts, each run by a representative and cacique. Protracted negotiations finally healed the schism and reunited Kuna Yala, but another crisis soon erupted, when Kuna frustration with an unauthorized hotel ended in violence against the hotel owner and the death of two Kuna National Guardsmen. In 1995, the General Congress censured the supposed Kuna owners of several new inns as figureheads for outside interests, and Panamanian entrepreneurs proposed to exploit ethnic tourism by building a resort just outside the limits of Kuna Yala.

Over the course of these many crises, the Kuna have grown increasingly disenchanted with the clumsiness, inefficiency, and unresponsiveness of their own political

3.9. National Liberation Movement mola. This mola depicts a worker breaking free from the chains that enslave him.
44.0 x 50.0 cm. Private collection.

system. The General Congress, which meets two or three times a year, has a tiny budget and little ability to implement its decisions or take action between sessions. The caciques, despite severely limited authority to take independent action, are repeatedly subjected to pressure by outsiders seeking authorization or help. Intendentes have since the early 1980s all been Kuna, nominated by the General Congress and chosen by the government, but turnover has been rapid, preventing administrative continuity, and the government has rejected efforts by the General Congress to dismiss unsatisfactory appointees. For many years, indigenous leaders have been lobbying for a comprehensive revision of the enabling law of 1953, so far without success.

More generally, many thoughtful Kuna feel that they have reached another crucial juncture in their history, one in which their relationship to Panamanian society, to the natural environment, and to their own culture are all in question. As frequently as orators invoke the example of 1925, everyone recognizes that the era of successful rebellions has passed, that they must instead find the will for a fundamental rethinking and reorganization comparable to the one carried out a half-century ago in 1945.

A Kuna Leader Speaks to His Followers
Concerning the Quincentennial Celebrations of Columbus's Discovery of America

Now then, we are sitting together here. We sit listening. We sit here feeling our pain. We sit here knowing our sorrows. This five hundredth anniversary that is coming, this great day that is coming, it is our pain. Why is it our pain?

When the Europeans came here, they abused us, you see. They beat our grandfathers, they killed our grandfathers, they cut open our grandmothers, you hear. They came here and killed our wise men, you see. So now they say, "Celebrate the day," you see, "We discovered this land." But we say, "They didn't discover this land at all, they didn't discover it." Well, we've always been here....

Therefore this day that is coming, they're coming to celebrate the day of our grandmothers' and grandfathers' death. Our pain, you see. As for them, they feel happy....

Cacique Leonidas Valdéz
February 1992

Kuna Language and Literature

Joel Sherzer

Introduction

The Kuna have a rich and dynamic verbal life. Like most tropical forest and lowland South American Indian societies, the Kuna's world is permeated by and in fact organized by means of verbal expression, which I call discourse, following current anthropological and linguistic usage. Any visitor to a Kuna village cannot but be impressed by the prominent place of speaking and chanting in Kuna life; the myths and counsels of chiefs; the histories, legends, and stories of traditional leaders; the long magical chants and secret charms of curing specialists; the laments chanted for the dying and the dead; the lullabies sung by mothers and sisters to little babies; the speeches and reports of personal experiences of all men and women; the colorful tellings and retellings of humorous anecdotes; and the greetings, leave-takings, conversations, narrations, and joking of everyday life. All of this is oral—spoken, chanted, sung, shouted, whispered, and listened to.

In each form of Kuna discourse, there is a remarkable verbal artistry that is essential to successful Kuna oral performance. This rich and elaborate system of oral discourse can be viewed in relation to Kuna politics, religion, curing, and puberty practices. But it can also be studied in and for itself, in terms of its textual, poetic and literary, and musical properties. One striking aspect of Kuna discourse is the existence of a great many linguistic varieties, styles, and genres. Each of the ritual styles and genres has associated with it its own grammatical properties and distinct vocabulary, as well as its own particular intonational pattern and form of musical expression.

While to a certain degree all Kuna discourse, including everyday conversations and joking, is verbally artistic,

4.1 (OPPOSITE, DETAIL), **4.2** (BELOW). **This mola illustrates a story about a spirit being that holds the earth on his head—his slightest movement causes earthquakes. The words *nega pandur* mean "shake the place" and refer to an earthquake in Kuna Yala in 1951.** 57.5 x 106.0 cm. **Private collection.**

it is especially in formal and ritual contexts that the Kuna most consider themselves to be verbally "on stage" and "on display," attempt to heighten the quality of their own verbal artistry, and critically evaluate the artistry of others.

Kuna verbal expression can be characterized in a number of ways. One way is in terms of three distinct languages, musical patterns, settings, sets of actors, and communicative events:

1. *The gathering house tradition*, in which chiefs address their villages in chants and speeches, recounting myths, history, and personal experience; political leaders counsel, debate, and report in long and eloquent speeches; and expert storytellers unfold their humorous and moralistic tales, told for both amusement and edification.

2. *The curing-magical tradition*, in which specialists address many different kinds of spirits in chants, labeled "ways" by the Kuna. This communication, whose purpose is magical and curative, is in the form of long chants, usually performed in the home of the performer or his or her patient.

3. *The puberty rites tradition*, in which a specialist, called a *gandule* (flute man), addresses a long chant to a single spirit, that of a long flute, in order to ensure the proper carrying out of this important ritual.

Associated with the three ritual verbal traditions are two general, basic patterns in the organization and performance of discourse, each of which is widespread in the world:

1. A *fixed or relatively fixed text* that must be memorized in line-by-line fashion, the pattern found in curing, magical, and puberty rites discourse, that is, human-to-spirit communication.

2. A *flexible text*, in which a general idea, theme, or set of metaphors is adapted to fit a particular situation, the pattern characteristic of gathering house discourse, that is, human-to-human communication.

Given the fact that Kuna literature is oral, many of its properties derive from the expressive use of the voice, indeed dramatization of the voice in performance. These include especially the creation of poetic units such as lines and verses by means of pause, intonational, and melodic patterning of the voice, as well as modulating and modifying the tempo, volume, and manner of delivery. In addition, there are features of Kuna literature that are found in all literature throughout the world, oral as well as written, of course expressed in the Kuna way. These are patterned repetitions of sounds, words, grammatical forms, and meanings, including assonance and rhyme, figurative and symbolic language, rhetorical and metaphorical devices, storytelling and humor, and the manipulation of grammar for poetic effect.

One important aspect of our cultural and linguistic competence as members of the contemporary Western world is to be able to listen to or read instances of discourse—whether a story, a political speech, or a newspaper article—and understand and interpret it. This means comprehending a totality of elements, from pronunciation, through grammar, to narrative logic. The same is true for the Kuna, whose literature is my focus here. I consider my task in transcribing and translating Kuna literature to be twofold: first, to reflect the Kuna ways of experiencing this literature; and, second, to render the Kuna experience meaningful for a non-Kuna audience, in particular for an English-reading audience.

Any appreciation of Kuna literature must begin with an understanding of the basic principles of Kuna grammar, since this grammar contains within it an inherent poetic imagination which is carried further in literary performances. The diversity

4.3. Men chatting on the pier.
James Howe, Niatupu, 1971.

and vitality of Kuna literature, as well as the complex principles and processes involved in producing it orally, constitute a poetics of performance. This literature can be appreciated both for its form, when listened to by Kuna individuals and even by others who can attend to the musicality and vibrancy of the performing voices, and for its content as well as form, when transcribed and presented on the printed page in a Kuna orthography and in translation, as is done here. Attention to details of transcription, representation, and translation enable us to display this poetics in action. Presenting an oral performance in written form reveals the Kuna conception and perception of the performance, as well as making it available to a wider audience.

Kuna is a Chibchan language, one of the many Chibchan languages that were and are still spoken in Central America. Distinct from the Mayan languages of Mexico and Guatemala, the Chibchan languages form a linguistic bridge into South America. Kuna and languages like Kuna were spoken in Panama at the time of the arrival of the Spaniards five hundred years ago.

Kuna literature

General features

By Kuna literature I mean certain verbal forms which Kuna people themselves, through their performances of these oral forms and their appreciation of them, indicate that they consider to be verbally artistic. This oral literature occurs within and is a crucial aspect of important Kuna sociocultural contexts—ritual, ceremonial, life-cycle, and recreational. They include the various events that occur in the central gathering house: chanting of ritual greetings, myths, legends, and Kuna history by chiefs; and speeches by village leaders and others explaining and interpreting chiefs, giving counsel, documenting experiences, and telling humorous but moralistic folktales.

There are also many chants, used in curing rituals, addressed to spirits by men usually but sometimes women, in order to cure certain ailments, such as high fever and headaches, snake bites and epilepsy, as well as to aid in the performance of important tasks, such as hunting and learning ritual. Long chants are also central to the puberty rites of young girls and are performed by a ritual specialist, the *gandule*, to the spirit of a long flute which controls these rites. Lullabies and laments are performed mainly by women and are essential aspects of the two endpoints of human life, childhood and death.

Kuna literature displays many features that are found in literature throughout the world, both written and oral: manipulation and stretching of the grammatical possibilities of the Kuna language; figurative and metaphorical language; patterned repetitions and parallelisms in sound, form, and meaning; definable line and verse structures; narrative creativity; and play and humor. In addition, because Kuna literature is oral, it has features created and expressed through modulations of the voice—speeding up, slowing down, increasing volume, decreasing volume, pausing, imitating sounds, and—in chanting and singing—producing melodies. I begin with a discussion of each of these features and then provide illustrative textual examples.

Grammar and literature

The complex grammatical potential of the Kuna language, especially the many distinct meaningful forms and possibilities of combination, are drawn on creatively in the production of literary forms. The long forms with final vowels which are typically deleted in everyday speech are used in chanting and singing to express the melodies of songs and chants. Here are some examples from a chant by a chief in the gathering house. (A portion of this chant, in translation, appears in the last section of this paper.) I have placed parentheses around the vowels which occur as part of the melody and which would usually be deleted in rapid, everyday speech:

> *we yal(a)s(e) bab(a) an barmial(i)marye*
> Father sent us to this mountain
>
> *bab(a) us(u) dul(a)gwa urbis(a) dayle soge*
> Father left living agouti see it is said

As in many literatures throughout the world, Kuna literature makes use of a poetic license according to which the grammar of everyday speech is manipulated, stretched, and creatively reworked in literature. An example is verbal suffix *-ye*, which in colloquial Kuna is used with a meaning quite like the optative or subjunctive of European languages ("would that something might happen"). Its function changes in literary language. It occurs especially, with great frequency, in magical and curing chants, perhaps stressing the optative mood of these chants, but also as a place filler, giving the performer time to remember the next line of these memorized chants. It is especially noticeable as a verbally artistic embellisher, frequently occurring at the ends of lines, and thus serving, along with other devices to be discussed later on, as a poetic line marker. Another example involves the positional suffixes on verbs (see "Guide to Kuna Pronunciation and Grammar," pp. 131–134). These, like *-ye*, are used much more in magical and curing chants than in everyday speech, no doubt in part because of the role close attention to body position plays in these chants, but also for verbal artistry, in and for itself. These positionals are furthermore used metaphorically, to capture and express a particular quality of an individual or object. They are also sometimes alternated in adjacent lines of a chant, for purely poetic effect. This will be illustrated later in this chapter.

Metaphor

Imaginative, figurative, and metaphorical language, as well as esoteric and secretive vocabulary, are central to all Kuna ways of speaking. Metaphors are a basic aspect of all Kuna aesthetics and expressive culture and are especially characteristic of ritual

4.4-6. Men converse during the daytime in the village gathering house.
James Howe, Niatupu, 1971.

speech. They are the hallmark of the gathering house, where chiefs, village leaders, and all men and women express their opinions and try to convince others of particular points of view. From the Kuna perspective, one of the most characteristic markers of a good gathering house speaker is the use of metaphorical speech. Good examples have to do with the nature of politics itself. In gathering house speeches and chants, chiefs are represented as trees, birds, and other animals, and as steering a boat or lying in a hammock. Creative speakers select certain trees to represent chiefs. They compare chiefs to *sabkwa sis* or *igwa* trees, hard, strong, long-lived trees found far away in the jungle. Other speakers prefer comparing chiefs to *isber* trees, which are more generous with their fruit, even if they do not last as long. Bad chiefs are compared with unpleasant animals, such as scorpions, spiders, or cockroaches.

A different set of metaphors represents Kuna political organization in terms of the structure of a Kuna house. The central pole represents the chief, secondary poles represent the chief's spokespersons, and smaller poles and side walls represent other officials and people present. This symbolism can be further developed, creatively and individually, so that a central pole which is rotten represents a bad chief who must be removed from office or a pole which had its rotten part cut away represents a chief who has been reinstated. In general, the ecology of the Kuna world, its plants and animals, is drawn on in the metaphorical representation of people and their characteristics.

In addition to their metaphors, esoteric and secretive language is particularly characteristic of curing chants addressed to representatives of the spirit world who understand this language, whereas most humans do not. It is only humans who know curing chants or have studied them who understand the chants' secretive language.

Repetition and parallelism

Repetition is in many ways the basis of poetry. Patterns of repetition are found in sounds, groups of sounds, words, groups of words, sentences, groups of sentences, and meanings of various kinds. Repetition is usually pleasant to hear and is incantatory, a very important aspect of all literature and especially oral literature. Repetitions of sounds create alliteration, assonance, and rhyme. Rhyme does not occur in Kuna in regular, named schemes the way it does in European languages, but it does exist. Nor does Kuna exhibit the regularity of stress pattern which creates meter in European poetry. As I will show here, however, Kuna poetic literature does have lines and verses, which are created by the regular patterned repetition of certain words and phrases, as well as patterns of volume and pause.

Paying attention to repetition leads us to a central feature of Kuna literature, grammatical and semantic parallelism, that is also extremely common in oral and written ritual and poetic language around the world. Parallelism involves the interplay of invariants and variants, of recurrences and differences. There are many kinds of parallelism in Kuna literature, involving words, groups of words, meanings, and sentences. Extensive and pervasive parallelism is especially characteristic of ritual speaking and chanting, an important aspect of the poetry of ritual performance.

Parallelism is closely tied to the poetic organization of lines in that it sets up correspondences based on and cutting across lines and units composed of lines, such as verses. Sometimes adjacent lines are identical, except for the deletion of a single word. Sometimes adjacent lines differ only slightly, in nonmeaningful ways. Sometimes a series of lines differs only in that a single word is replaced by others with slightly different meaning within the same general field of meaning. Sometimes the pattern underlying the parallel structure is not a single line, but rather an entire set of lines, a verse, or a stanza, a frame which is repeated over and over with changes in one or more words. The result of all these types of parallelism is a slow moving narration, advancing by slight changes in content, added to repeated information. Extreme attention is paid to minute and precise detail. The parallelistic structure of curing and magical chants in particular involves many levels, from the most minute—repetition of sounds, grammatical forms, and words—to the most general—repetition of whole verses and stanzas. The result is an overlapping and integration of various parallelistic patterns, a verbal polyphony composed of a tenacious array of cohesive and contrapuntal forms and meanings.

In addition to poetic function, these various types of parallelism have other functions as well. It is important for Kuna ritual chants to be long, length being an aspect of their magical power as well as their aesthetic quality. Parallelism slows and lengthens the performance of the text. Performers' knowledge, especially of such matters as taxonomic classification, is displayed through the parallel listing of items. The repetition involved in parallelism contributes to the incantatory aura of chanting. And, finally, parallelism seems to be a mnemonic aid to the retention and performance of memorized chants.

Poetic organization: lines and verses

In addition to its special, sometimes esoteric language, its metaphors, its parallelism, and its narrative structure, Kuna literature is organized in terms of poetic lines. In fact, the poetic line is at the heart of Kuna literature. The line is in many ways the most basic unit of all forms of Kuna discourse, from the most informal and colloquial to the most formal and ritual. It is independent of and yet related to grammatical units such as phonemes, morphemes, and sentences and is the most overtly marked discourse unit linguistically and, in chanting, musically.

Discovery of Kuna lines requires attention to very different features than those traditionally associated with the European poetic tradition, especially rhyme and meter. Kuna line structure and organization incorporates and integrates all of the features of Kuna poetics that I have just discussed, especially phonological and morphological patterning, parallelism, and features of the dramatization of the voice such as pause, intonation, and musical melody, as well as aspects of the social organization

4.7. Village leader Vicente Arosemena in a gathering house discussion. James Howe, Niatupu, 1971.

of speech such as turn taking. It is furthermore extremely useful for a diagnostic comparison and typological classification of Kuna verbal genres.

In each of the Kuna verbal styles and genres, it is possible to recognize the existence of lines. These lines are marked by a set of distinct devices. Not all of the devices are operative in every case. In addition, the devices have other functions besides marking lines. As a result there is not always congruence among them. In fact, a most interesting aspect of the various line-marking devices in Kuna is the ways in which speakers play them off against each other, creating contrasts and tensions among them. The four principal line-marking devices are:

1. Lines are marked grammatically by means of *an elaborate set of initial and final words and forms*. Among the various other functions of these elements is metacommunication; they signify such notions as "say," "see," "hear," and "truly." They are furthermore simultaneously sociolinguistic markers in that different verbal styles and genres have distinct sets of these elements.
2. Especially in more formal and ritual styles, lines are marked by *extensive syntactic and semantic parallelism*. This parallelism is organized in terms of line structure and in turn contributes to this structure.
3. Lines are marked by *intonation patterns*, in particular in spoken speech by the structuring of pauses and the rising and falling of pitch, as well as tempo, and in chanting by melodic shapes involving volume, duration, and tempo, along with pauses and, in some genres, the structured use of coughs or coughlike noises.
4. Lines are marked according to a *coparticipant dialogic interactional structure* in which an addressee responds with one of a set of ratifiers after each line. This pattern is common in many styles of speaking; it is formalized in certain forms of ritual chanting.

Gathering house chanting

In the most ritual styles and genres of Kuna that are frequently chanted, there is the greatest tendency for there to be a combined, cooperating, congruent, and

4.8 (ABOVE LEFT). **A visiting chief performs a chant to Mulatupu Chief Mantiweginya in the Mulatupu gathering house.**
Joel Sherzer, 1971.

4.9 (ABOVE RIGHT). **Mulatupu Chiefs Muristo and Dionysio perform a ritual greeting with visiting chiefs in the Mulatupu gathering house.**
Joel Sherzer, 1978.

reinforcing use of all the line-marking devices. In gathering house chanting, myths, legends, and personal experiences are performed to an audience in the form of a ritual dialogue between two chiefs, the second chief responding to the chanted utterances of the first. Lines are often grouped together into clearly marked verses. The responding chief chants *degi* (indeed) after each verse, thus quite clearly marking verse endings. Verses typically consist of two lines. Lines and especially verses drop in pitch at the end and final vowels are lengthened. There is a decrease in volume and tempo at the ends of lines and verses. The responding chief begins to chant during the lengthened final vowel of the principal chanting chief, who in turn begins his next line during the lengthened i of degi. There is thus never silence, since each chanter begins his turn by overlapping the long, held vowel of the previous voice.

This combination of falling pitch, vowel lengthening, decreasing volume and tempo, and alternation of chanters clearly marks lines and verses in gathering house chanting. In addition, verses often begin with the word *sunna* (truly) or the phrase *al inso* (thus) and end with the word *soge* (say, it is said), *obarye* (mention, it is mentioned), or *dayleye* (see). The first line of a verse often ends with the phrase, sometimes combined into a single word, *dayle soge l itole* (see it is said, it is heard). Syntactic and semantic parallelism also contributes to the structuring of lines and verses. Performers can create poetic counterpoint by playing off the line-initial and line-final words and phrases and the parallelistic patterns against the intonational, musical, and interactional markers of lines.

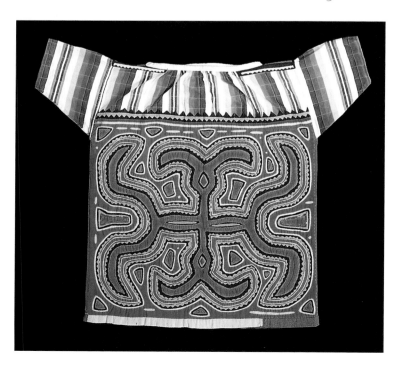

Curing and magical chanting

Curing and magical chanting, performed by specialists to representatives of the spirit world, is in a linguistic variety quite distinct from chiefs' chanting. In addition to

falling pitch, final vowel lengthening, and decreasing volume and tempo, lines in this genre are marked primarily by the suffix -ye. There is a notable pause between lines and for some performers a slight cough or coughlike noise between structured groups of lines, which constitute verses. There is extensive line parallelism, involving a layering of phonological, morphological, syntactic, and semantic features, resulting in an incantatory regularity. At times, however, performers introduce some contrast and counterpoint, especially between verbal and musical parallelism, still against the backdrop of considerable regularity.

Formal speech making

The most formal of speaking styles is that of the chief's spokesperson, who follows a chief's chant, retells the chant, and interprets it for the gathered audience. In spokespersons' speeches, there are short but clearly audible pauses between lines, coupled with a falling pitch contour and a slowing of tempo. Longer pauses set off verses, units of several lines. The words *deg* (well), *inso* (thus), and *daylegudi* (indeed) are common line openers of spokespersons' speeches and are often bunched together. A very common line-final marker in this style is *bitosursoge* "don't you hear it is said," often coming at the ends of verses. Spokesmen introduce various contrasts and tensions among the different line and verse-marking devices.

Puberty rites

In puberty rites performances, a third distinct ritual genre of chanting (as opposed to gathering house chanting, curing, and magical chanting) which the Kuna call shouting to distinguish it from other ritual performances, lines are marked by syntactic and semantic parallelism, lengthened final vowels, and a particular, unique melodic shape, involving extremely regular lineal repetition. Of the three ritual genres, puberty rites performances display the most regular, congruent, isomorphic stacking of line-marking devices. It is interesting that the Kuna consider the puberty rites tradition to be their most archaic and immutable.

4.11 (ABOVE LEFT). **Lanni, a curing specialist from Mulatupu, with a sick child in a hammock.**
Joel Sherzer, 1979.

4.12 (ABOVE RIGHT). **Mulatupu medicinal specialist Olowibiginya discusses medicinally valuable plants with his wife and son at their home.**
Joel Sherzer, 1974.

4.10 (OPPOSITE). *Bab igar* (Father's Way) **mola blouse, c. 1940. This design represents the journey taken by souls on their way to heaven.**
65.0 72.5 cm. NMAI 25/0194. Gift of Dorothy H. Roedder

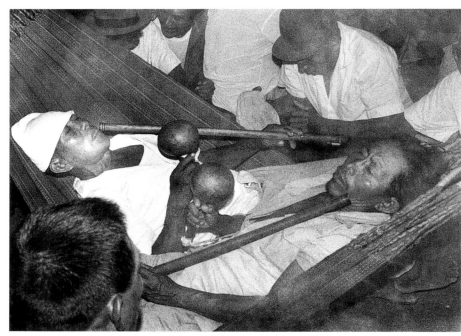

4.13 (ABOVE LEFT). **Chief's spokesperson Pedro Arias in Mulatupu gathering house.**
Joel Sherzer, 1978.

4.14 (ABOVE RIGHT). **Gandule Ernesto Linares and his assistant Andrew lying in a hammock while performing at puberty rites.**
Joel Sherzer, Mulatupu, 1970.

Storytelling

Stories, both serious and humorous, are told publicly in a less formal style than that of the speeches of chief's spokespersons. Typical line openers are *degi* (well), *dakargu* (so), and *emide* (now); the line-final markers are *soge* (say, it is said), *nabir soge* (it is true), and *soysundo* (he, she said in truth). There is even less congruence, that is, there is even more contrast, among the various line markers than in the more formal spokespersons' speeches. In particular, pause structure and grammatical elements and words, both resources for the marking of lines, are often used contrapuntally in order to create a rhythm of performance characteristic of storytelling involving dramatic interplay of long and short, slow and fast lines as the narration proceeds.

Characteristics of Kuna narrative

Narrative is the verbal reformulation of a set of events, real or fictional. Kuna narratives are told in either the first person or the third person, that is, they recount either personal experiences or those of others. In either case, they may be descriptions of new events, not known to the audience, or descriptions of known events which are retold. One striking aspect of Kuna discourse and verbal art, which is shared with other native lowland South American groups, is the constant retelling of the same narrative, in different contexts and in different ways, for different purposes. This includes the incorporation of narratives within narratives, tellings within tellings.

Whether first person or third person, fact or fiction, myth or history, spoken or chanted, ritual or everyday, Kuna narratives are appreciated for their length. Length is achieved by various poetic devices, including repetition and parallelism. Narrative length is also created by means of extreme attention to fine detail, including such matters as waking up, going to sleep, travel to and from places, and reported conversations.

Humor

Humor, always a feature of Kuna narration, is omnipresent in Kuna verbal life. Humor is notoriously difficult to translate from one language and culture to another. Kuna humor is intimately dependent on and integrated with actual verbal performance, in conjunction with knowledge, assumptions, and experiences shared by narrators and audiences. The manipulation of the voice in performance is crucial, especially the stereotyped imitation of various noises and the mocking imitation and quotation of the speech of others. Surprising juxtapositions of events, humorous in themselves, are made even funnier through being expressed by means of juxtapositions in the dramatization of the voice—fast versus slow, loud versus soft, high versus low pitch, and staccato versus fluid. Humor is also highlighted by describing experiences in great and exaggerated detail and by considerable repetition.

Verbal power

The Kuna believe that in verbal performance there is power and that different kinds of verbal activities produce different kinds of power. In magical chants, narratives have the power to activate the audience of spirits that listens to them. Upon hearing a chant and because of hearing and understanding it, the spirits do, detail by detail, everything that the narrative contained within the chant describes. Narratives addressed to humans involve other kinds of power. A narrative report, especially a public one in the gathering house, is a validation of one's experience for the immediate audience and for the entire community. The detailed report of the experience of learning ritual knowledge concretizes this knowledge and grants the performer the right to exercise the role of ritual specialist. Chiefs display and exercise their power through their chanting and telling of myths, personal experiences, and counsels to the community. Gathering house discourse more generally often expresses exemplary, moral lessons, a crucial feature of the exhortative nature and the power of this discourse. It is important to stress that Kuna power as I have described it here is verbal and aesthetic and, in the context of the Kuna orientation to egalitarian democracy, never authoritarian.

Before turning to examples, it is important to stress once again that Kuna literature is oral and that the oral properties of Kuna voices are crucial to an appreciation of it. These include all the ways a voice can organize and express sound, including silence, creating intonation and melody, rhythm, balance, suspense, and tension, imitating other voices and sounds, and generally ornamenting a performance. It is impossible to appreciate these qualities in the full sense without being present at actual performances or listening to tape recordings of them. But certain aspects of these performances can be represented here, for example, pause, intonation, and melodic patterns, loudness, softness, fast and slow speech, and line and verse structure—this is what I will do in the remainder of this chapter through the presentation, in textual form, of actual performances of Kuna literature.

Kuna literature: illustrative examples

My first examples will be presented in both Kuna and English, so that readers can read aloud and thus appreciate for themselves the sounds and rhythms of the Kuna language. In addition to transcribing the actual sounds of spoken and chanted Kuna, I will demonstrate the intonations, musical shapes, patterns of loudness and softness, and interplay of sound and silence that are so crucial to Kuna verbal aesthetics. I will do this by means of visual representations made by computer analyses of the voices in each of the performances I discuss here. These computer analyzed displays focus on the orality of the voice.

"The Way of the Basil Plant"

The first example is *Biseb Igar*, "The Way of the Basil Plant," performed by Pranki Pilos from the San Blas island of Mulatupu on 2 March 1971. This magical chant, addressed to the spirit of the basil plant, named *inabisebdili* in Kuna magical, ritual language, is used to ensure success in the hunting of wild animals in the jungle. The hunter bathes in a potion made from the fragrant basil plant and has this chant performed for him by a specialist. The opening portion of the chant, which is my focus here, deals with the birth, symbolically described, of the basil plant.

In this performance, there is considerable melodic, as well as grammatical and semantic parallelism. There is also considerable assonance and alliteration, created by the repetition of sounds and forms. Pairs of lines constitute verses. There is a short pause after the first line of a verse, a laryngeal tightening followed by a long pause after the second line of a verse. Here is a transcription/representation and translation which highlights the extreme repetition and parallelism of words and grammatical affixes, by lining them up, stacking them under one another.

inabisebdili	*olouludi*	*dulalemaiye*
	olouludi	*dulallemaiye*
inabisebdili	*olouludi*	*sikirmakemaiye*
	olouludi	*sikirmagmamaiye*
inabisebdili	*olouludi*	*wawanmakemaiye*
	olouludi	*wawanmagmainaye*
inabisebdili	*olouludi*	*akdudumakemaiye*
	olouludi	*akdudulemainaye*
inabisebdili	*olouludi*	*gollomakemaiye*
	olouludi	*gollomagmainaye*
inabisebdili	*olouludi*	*mummurmakemaiye*
	olouludi	*mummurmagmainaye*

Inabisebdili	in the golden box	is moving
	In the golden box	is moving
Inabisebdili	in the golden box	is swinging from side to side
	In the golden box	is swinging from side to side
Inabisebdili	in the golden box	is trembling
	In the golden box	is trembling
Inabisebdili	in the golden box	is palpitating
	In the golden box	is palpitating
Inabisebdili	in the golden box	is making a noise
	In the golden box	is making a noise
Inabisebdili	in the golden box	is shooting out
	In the golden box	is shooting out

The first two verses of this performance were analyzed on Sound Edit, a computer program which displays sound in terms of amplitude and pause pattern. Figure 4.15 shows the Sound Edit display with the verses labeled as follows: 1a (first line of first

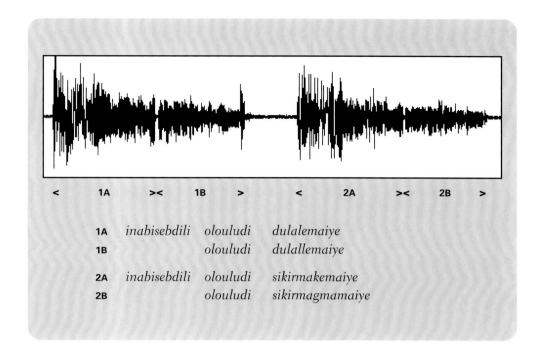

1A	*inabisebdili*	*olouludi*	*dulalemaiye*
1B		*olouludi*	*dulallemaiye*
2A	*inabisebdili*	*olouludi*	*sikirmakemaiye*
2B		*olouludi*	*sikirmagmamaiye*

4.15. Representation of the first two verses of "The Way of the Basil Plant."

verse), 1b (second line of first verse), 2a (first line of second verse), 2b (second line of second verse).

This representational display shows the parallelism of the two verses in terms of amplitude, from high to low. The sharp burst of amplitude at the end of the first verse is a loud laryngeal tightening which sounds very much like a cough. Notice the long pause between verses, the very short pause between lines within a verse.

Still another transcription is a more conventional linguistic representation and specifies the grammatical divisions of the text as well as its most literal meaning. This representation is multilinear. Line 1 of each row is a transcription of the tape recording of the performance. In line 2, words are divided into morphemes (minimal meaningful and grammatical units). Morpheme boundaries are indicated by dashes. The morphemes are presented in their fullest, most underlying and abstract form. Parentheses ( ) surround vowels which are potentially deletable according to Kuna rules of grammar and pronunciation. In line 3, the grammatical categories of morphemes are labeled as follows:

RP = ritual prefix, a nominal prefix used in magical chants
NOUN = noun stem
RS = ritual suffix, a nominal suffix used in magical chants
ADJ = adjectival stem
PAS = passive suffix
POS = one of four verbal suffixes that indicate the position of the subject
    of a sentence in ongoing movement
OPT = optative mood
VERB = verb stem
V FORM = verb formative suffix
DIR = one of verbal suffixes that indicate the direction of the subject of a
    sentence

Line 4 provides a literal translation of morphemes. Line 5 is a freer translation.

inabisebdili
ina-biseb-dili
RP-NOUN-RS
medicinal-basil-nominal
Inabisebdili

olouludi
olo-ulu-di
RP-NOUN-RS
golden-box-nominal
in the golden box

dulalemaiye
dula-le(g(e))-ma(i)-ye
ADJ-PAS-POS-OPT
alive-is-horiz-hopefully
is moving

olouludi
olo-ulu-di
RP-NOUN-RS
golden-box-nominal
In the golden box

dulallemaiye
dula-le(g(e))-ma(i)-ye
ADJ-PAS-POS-OPT
alive-is-horiz-hopefully
is moving

inabisebdili
ina-biseb-dili
RP-NOUN-RS
medicinal-basil-nominal
Inabisebdili

olouludi
olo-ulu-di
RP-NOUN-RS
golden-box-nominal
in the golden box

sikirmakemaiye
sikir-mak(e)-ma(i)-ye
VERB-V FORM-POS-OPT
swing-verbal-horiz-hopefully
is swinging from side to side

olouludi
olo-ulu-di
RP-NOUN-RS
golden-box-nominal
In the golden box

sikirmagmamaiye
sikir-mak(e)-ma(i)-ma(i)-ye
VERB-V FORM-POS-POS-OPT
swing-verbal-horiz-horiz-hopefully
is swinging from side to side

inabisebdili
ina-biseb-dili
RP-NOUN-RS
medicinal-basil-nominal
Inabisebdili

olouludi
olo-ulu-di
RP-NOUN-RS
golden-box-nominal
in the golden box

wawanmakemaiye
wawan-mak(e)-ma(i)-ye
VERB-V FORM-POS-OPT
tremble-verbal-horiz-hopefully
is trembling

olouludi
olo-ulu-di
RP-NOUN-RS
golden-box-nominal
In the golden box

wawanmagmainaye
wawan-mak(e)-ma(i)-na(e)-ye
VERB-V FORM-POS-DIR-OPT
tremble-verbal-horiz-go-hopefully
is trembling

inabisebdili
ina-biseb-dili
RP-NOUN-RS
medicinal-basil-nominal
Inabisebdili

olouludi
olo-ulu-di
RP-NOUN-RS
golden-box-nominal
in the golden box

agdudumakemaiye
agdudu-mak(e)-ma(i)-ye
VERB-V FORM-POS-OPT
palpitate-verbal-horiz-hopefully
is palpitating

olouludi
olo-ulu-di
RP-NOUN-RS
golden-box-nominal
In the golden box

agdudulemainaye
agdudu-le(g(e))-ma(i)-na(e)-ye
VERB-PAS-POS-DIR-OPT
palpitate-verbal-horiz-go-hopefully
is palpitating

inabisebdili	*olouludi*	*kollomakemaiye*
ina-biseb-dili	olo-ulu-di	kollo-mak(e)-ma(i)-ye
RP-NOUN-RS	RP-NOUN-RS	VERB-V FORM-POS-OPT
medicinal-basil-nominal	golden-box-nominal	make noise-verbal-horiz-hopefully
Inabisebdili	in the golden box	is making a noise

olouludi	*kollomagmainaye*
olo-ulu-di	kollo-mak(e)-ma(i)-na(e)-ye
RP-NOUN-RS	VERB-V FORM-POS-DIR-OPT
golden-box-nominal	make noise-verbal-horiz-go-hopefully
in the golden box	is making a noise

inabisebdili	*olouludi*	*mummurmagmainaye*
ina-biseb-dili	olo-ulu-di	mummur-mak(e)-ma(i)-ye
RP-NOUN-RS	RP-NOUN-RS	VERB-V FORM-POS-OPT
medicinal-basil-nominal	golden-box-nominal	make noise-verbal-horiz-hopefully
Inabisebdili	in the golden box	is shooting out

olouludi	*mummurmakemaiye*
olo-ulu-di	mummur-mak(e)-ma(i)-ye
RP-NOUN-RS	VERB-V FORM-POS-DIR-OPT
golden-box-nominal	shoot out-verbal-horiz-go-hopefully
in the golden box	is shooting out

A close examination of the multilinear representation reveals a certain degree of play, manipulation, and, apparently, experimentation on the part of the performer, Pranki Pilos, with the basic structure of this memorized chant. One of the invariables of the text is the syntactic structure of the lines and verses, the first line of each verse consisting of two nominals followed by the verb and second line of each verse paralleling the first without the initial nominal. Another invariable is the inclusion of the positional verbal suffix and the final verbal suffix, the modal *ye*.

The variable aspects of the text draw on the potential provided by the polysynthetic structure of this language, in which many suffixes are potentially strung along, especially after verb stems. Here are some examples. The most abstract, underlying form of the verb formative suffix is *make*, represented as *mak(e)* on line 2 of the multilinear representation. This is also the usual ritual form this morpheme takes, its more everyday variant being *mag*. Interestingly, Pranki Pilos alternates *make* and *mag*, the ritual and everyday forms, in lines 1 and 2 of verses 2, 3, 5, and 6 of this performance.

A related manipulation involves an alternation between the verb formative suffix and the passive suffix. The passive suffix is used in both lines of verse 1 and in this sense contrasts with all other verses. The two lines of verse 4 exploit this contrast as well. Line 1 of this verse has the verb formative suffix; line 2 has the passive suffix. Both of these examples involve breaking with an overall pattern of repetition and parallelism and creating another within it. The *make/mag* alternation is particularly striking, in that it inserts an everyday, colloquial form into a ritual performance, a possibly dangerous move, but one that provides one more level of poetic tension and which in itself provides still another pattern of repetition and parallelism.

Another performance manipulation is the reduplication of the positional suffix *mai*, which occurs only in line 2 of verse 2. In lines 2 of verses 3 through 6 *mai* is followed by the directional suffix *nae*, thus creating another pattern of parallelism. From the point of view of ordinary Kuna grammar, this sequence is ungrammatical and illogical. In addition, since *nae* appears in its short, everyday form *na*, it is perhaps ambiguous with *nai*, a positional suffix with the meaning hanging or perched, thereby providing even more tension in the text.

What this seemingly and at first glance purely linguistic representation captures is individual creativity, play, and manipulation against the backdrop of a highly ritual, repetitive, parallelistic, memorized chant. In all of this, grammatical, semantic, sociolinguistic, and logical rules and structures are played down and poeticized, in the service of Pranki Pilos's performance, in which formal patterning competes with referential meaning.

This leads to still another representation of this performance, a most abstract one, which highlights the formal patterning of repetition and parallelism, of variants and invariants. In this representation, a and b stand for the nominals *inabisebdili*, the name of the basil plant, and *olouludi*, the golden box; c, d, e, f, g, and h stand for the various verb stems; p stands for the passive suffix; W and w stand for the verb formative suffix, W in its ritual form and w in its everyday form; x stands for the positional suffix; y stands for the directional suffix; and z stands for the optative suffix. This representation shows the incredible repetition, reduplication, and parallelism involved in this performance—of sounds, grammatical forms, phrases, and sentences. It is this patterning that causes the assonance, alliteration, and overall hauntingly incantatory feel of the performance. It is furthermore fascinating to compare this patterning with the visual repetitions and parallelisms which characterize Kuna visual art, especially molas.

a	b	c	p	x		z
	b	c	p	x		z
a	b	d	W	x		z
	b	d	w	x	x	z
a	b	e	W	x		z
	b	e	w	x	y	z
a	b	f	W	x		z
	b	f	p	x	y	z
a	b	g	W	x		z
	b	g	w	x	y	z
a	b	h	W	x		z
	b	h	w	x	y	z

Each of the representations of Pranki Pilos's performance of "The Way of the Basil Plant" that I have presented here reveals different aspects of the poetic structuring of the actual performance. A comparison of all of them brings out the dynamic intersection of all of the resources that Kuna performers draw on—grammatical, lexical, intonational, paralinguistic, and musical—and demonstrates quite clearly the interplay of congruences, isomorphisms, repetitions, and parallelisms—as well as tensions, contrasts, and counterpoints—so characteristic of the dynamics of Kuna verbal art. In this particular performance we have an excellent illustration as well of the interplay of memorization and creative improvisation, which is also clearly evident in a comparison of the different representations.

"The Way of the Hat"

The next example is the opening portion of *Gurgin Igar*, "The Way of the Hat," performed by Olowidinapi of Mulatupu on 23 February 1970. *Gurgin* means "hat" and, metaphorically, "brain." This is a magical, curing chant used for headaches.

As in "The Way of the Basil Plant," lines are paired into verses. This representation reveals the grammatical and semantic parallelism characteristic of this chant and this performance.

> *gurgin ibegandinaye.*
> *olobillise bubawalagan akuegwichiye.*
>
> *gurgin ipekandinaye.*
> *olobillise be maliwasgagan uboegwichiye.*
>
> *gurgin ibegandinaye.*
> *olobillise be maliwasgagana bioglegegwichiye.*
>
> *gurgin ibegandinaye.*
> *olobillibiiye   abigaegwichiye gurgin ibegandinaye.*
>
> *olobilli aytikimakegwichi gurgin ibegandinaye.*
>
> *olobilli gwamakegwichi gurgin ibegandinaye.*
>
> *olobilli aydidimakegwagwichiye gurgin ibegandinaye.*

> Owners of gurgin.
> Your roots reach to the level of gold.
>
> Owners of gurgin.
> Your small roots are placed into the level of gold.
>
> Owners of gurgin.
> Your small roots are nailed into the level of gold.
>
> Owners of gurgin.
> You are resisting   within the very level of gold owners of gurgin.
>
> You weigh a great deal in the level of gold owners of gurgin.
>
> You are firmly placed in the level of gold owners of gurgin.
>
> You are moving in the level of gold owners of gurgin.

Figure 4.16 shows the Sound Edit representation of the amplitude and pause pattern of the first two verses, followed by an intonational or pitch tracking, also done on Sound Edit. Notice that the pitch tracking has the amplitude and pause pattern display beneath it, for comparison. The pitch tracking shows the intonational-melodic patterning of the performance, the rises and falls of the voice.

The Sound Edit display clearly shows the falling pitch and volume characteristic of lines and verses in this genre, as well as the long pauses between lines.

A comparison of the different representations of "The Way of the Hat" reveals Olowidinapi's creativity in this performance. In the first three verses, there is an isomorphic congruence in the use of grammatical affixes and words, musical and grammatical parallelism, and pauses. Each verse begins with a vocative line and ends in the optative suffix *-ye*. The second line of each verse begins with *olobillise* and ends with a verb with the following sequence of suffixes: *-gwichi* (in a vertical position) *-ye*. Final vowels are lengthened. In the fourth verse, while continuing to use the same musical and pausal structure, except for a pause after the first word of the second line, Olowidinapi introduces a new model, creating a moment of nonparallelistic contrast. In this new model, *gurgin ibegandinaye*, which was in the first position of lines and

4.16. Representation of the first two verses of "The Way of the Hat."

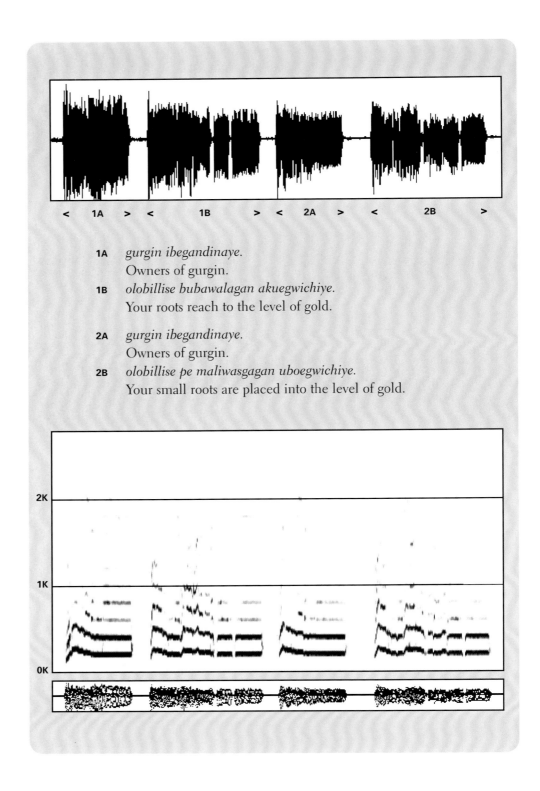

1A   *gurgin ibegandinaye.*
Owners of gurgin.
1B   *olobillise bubawalagan akuegwichiye.*
Your roots reach to the level of gold.

2A   *gurgin ibegandinaye.*
Owners of gurgin.
2B   *olobillise pe maliwasgagan uboegwichiye.*
Your small roots are placed into the level of gold.

verses, is now in final position in lines and verses, and *-gwichi-ye* now no longer marks the end of lines. The new model is used to create a new system of parallelism in which each verse consists of only a single line. Thus Olowidinapi, in this contrastive interplay between grammatical and musical parallelism, like Pranki Pilos in his performance of "The Way of the Basil Plant," demonstrates individual creativity in the performance of a chant that he has memorized word for word.

Gathering house chanting

The next example is of gathering house chanting, which is performed in the form of a ritual dialogue between two chiefs. The second chief, called the responder, chants *degi* (indeed) after each verse. The responder begins to chant during the lengthened final vowel of the principal chanting chief, who in turn begins his next verse during the lengthened i of *degi*. In gathering house chanting there is thus never silence, since each chanter begins his turn by overlapping the long, held vowel of the previous voice. This central aesthetic feature of the event is clearly shown in the

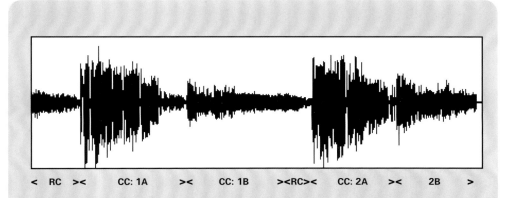

4.17. Representation of gathering house chanting.

| < | RC | >< | CC: 1A | >< | CC: 1B | ><RC>< | CC: 2A | >< | 2B | > |

CC: 1A *sunna sukun galuse dayle soge l itole girmar pato l an abindakegwichi ibidi.*
Indeed I got to Sukunya I say and the brothers were already waiting for me.

1B *sunna dar gu dayleye.*
Indeed it is thus see.

RC: *degi.*
Indeed.

CC: 2A *girmarde l anga soymargu "muisdaragi be idu nadmarmo" dayle sog ito.*
The brothers said to me "a little while before you they left" it is said it is heard.

2B *"bito diwar mos ebinso" soyye.*
"They have already arrived at the river I think" it is said.

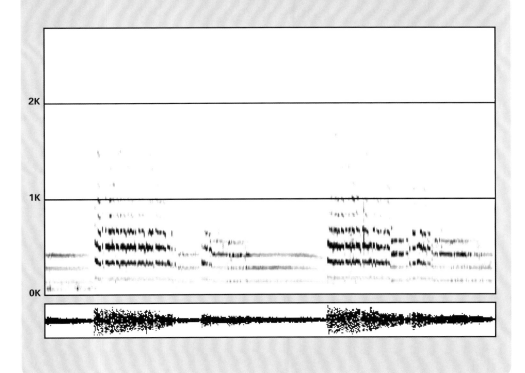

Sound Edit display of two verses from a chant by Muristo Pérez of Mulatupu on 29 June 1970 (Fig. 4.17). Chief Muristo's verses are labeled CC (for chanting chief), those of the responder RC (for responding chief). Two verses are represented here. Each verse consists of two lines. The lines and verses are represented as 1A, 1B, 2A, and 2B. The Sound Edit representation and translation is followed by a pitch tracking that shows the intonational and melodic pattern of the chanted performance.

Chief's spokesperson

Chief's chants are followed by a spoken reformulation, translation, and recasting by a chief's spokesperson. There is a clear delimitation of lines and verses by means of a pause pattern, which involves long rhetorical/poetic pauses between lines and especially verses. The spokesperson's monologic performance constitutes a quite different aesthetic from the overlapping voices of the dialogic performance of chanting chiefs. Figure 4.18 shows a Sound Edit display of three verses from one such interpretation, performed by spokesman Armando of Mulatupu on 9 April 1970. The Sound Edit display is followed by a transcription/representation. The first verse consists of two lines labeled 1A and 1B. The second verse consists of one line, with three phrases marked by short pauses, which are represented here by commas. The phrases are labeled 2X, 2Y, and 2Z. The third verse consists of one line, with two phrases, labeled 3X and 3Y. Sound Edit clearly shows the remarkably long pauses between verses.

Kuna literature in translation

Now I will present a set of examples in English translation. Since English is so different from Kuna, some of the Kuna grammatical and vocabulary subtleties and

4.18. Representation of three verses from a performance by a chief's spokesperson.

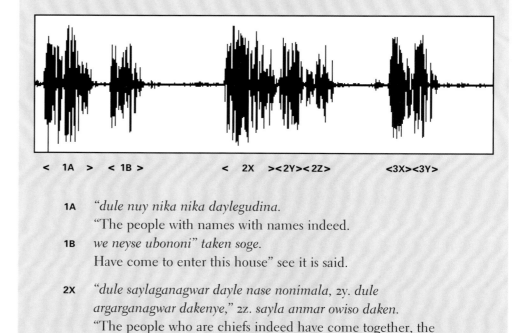

1A *"dule nuy nika nika daylegudina.*
"The people with names with names indeed.
1B *we neyse ubononi" taken soge.*
Have come to enter this house" see it is said.

2X *"dule saylaganagwar dayle nase nonimala, 2y. dule argarganagwar dakenye," 2z. sayla anmar owiso daken.*
"The people who are chiefs indeed have come together, the people who are spokespersons see," the chief informs us see.

3X *"dule daylegudi bolisiaganagwar," 3y. taken soge.*
"The people indeed who are policemen," see it is said.

poetic devices are of necessity lost in these translations. I maintain the line and pause patterning of the original Kuna performance in the translation, as well as the manipulations of volume and other expressive uses of the voice. I try to express in English the poetic and metaphorical vocabulary so characteristic of Kuna literature. Hopefully readers of these translations are able to appreciate, in their own language, the beauty, creativity, expressivity, and imagination of Kuna literature.

Gathering house chant

My first example is a portion of a chant performed by Chief Mastaledad of the village of Mulatupu on 20 February 1971. It is a religious origin myth, depicting the animals and plants which Father (the Kuna way of saying God) left for the Kuna people in this mountain (one of the Kuna metaphors for world) and how the Kuna people, true to their ecological orientation, must care for them. The animals and plants are listed in the parallel lines and verses so characteristic of Kuna ritual chanting. As in my earlier representation of a chief chanting in the gathering house, the chanting chief is labeled CC and the responding chief is labeled RC.

> CC: Father sent us to this mountain it is said it is heard.
> In order to care for banana roots for him I mention.

> RC: Indeed.

> CC: In order thus to care for taro roots for him it is said it is heard.
> In truth I mention.

> RC: Indeed.

> CC: Thus in order to care for living yams for him it is said it is heard.
> I mention.

> RC: Indeed.

> CC: Thus in order to care for living squash for him it is said it is heard.
> I mention.

> RC: Indeed.

> CC: Thus in order to care for pineapple roots for him it is said it is heard.
> Father gave us this world.

> RC: Indeed.

> CC: "Here together you will all go about" it is said.
> Father said he did I mention.

> RC: Indeed.

> CC: Father left white-lipped peccary strongholds it is said.
> We came in order to care for them it is said.

> RC: Indeed.

> CC: Father left tapir strongholds it is seen it is said.
> We came in order to care for them it is said.

> RC: Indeed.

> CC: Father left living collared peccary it is seen it is said.
> We came in order to care for them it is said.

RC: Indeed.

CC: Father left living agouti it is seen it is said.
    We came in order to care for them it is said.

RC: Indeed.

A curing chant: "The Way of Cocoa"

"The Way of Cocoa" is addressed to the spirit of the cocoa tree in order to cure a child whose soul has been taken away by an evil spirit, thus causing such symptoms as high fever and fainting. In the chant, the spirit of the cocoa is counseled to get the soul back from the evil spirit which has abducted it and return it to the body of the child. Here is the opening portion of this chant, performed by Mulatupu curing specialist Anselmo Urrutia in 1993. In this translation, words which are esoteric for the Kuna are highlighted in bold. Poetic, especially metaphorical, allusions are explained in brackets. Blank spaces within lines indicate pauses in the performance.

Sister Kelilikkwa White-faced One [White Cocoa]   you are being counseled.
In the beginning Sacred God transformed to his liking your live being.
In the beginning Sacred God to his liking.
Gave form to your trunks.
In order to protect again.
Here the **little ones** [children], of the owners of **tobacco** [the Kuna people]
    against the angry people [evil spirits=sicknesses] those who **abduct**   [take
    away].
In the beginning Sacred God transformed your live being.
Here the **little ones** [children] of the owners of **tobacco** [the Kuna people].
If the sacred uncles the owners of the long canoes [pirogues=caimans=evil
    spirits=sicknesses].
At times want to **abduct** [take away] the sacred soul.
If you want to go and recover again the sacred soul.
In the beginning Sacred God gave form to your **body** [trunks].
As far as the **tiny** [distant] **mountain levels** [peaks] in the beginning Sacred
    God left no empty space.
He left your **bodies** [trunks].
The prophets of Sister Kelilikkwa the White-faced One [White Cocoa] you
    are being counseled.
All around your **body** [trunk] your beads [seeds] are **floating up and down**
    [hanging].
All around your **body** [trunk] your beads [seeds] are **extending themselves.**
The branches of the **body** [trunk] are full your beads [seeds] are **extending**
    themselves.
The **tiny** [small] branches of the **body** [trunk] are full your beads [seeds] are
    extending themselves.
Every kind of **winged creature** [insect=evil spirit], is entering up to your bead
    [seed].
The **hummingbirds** are **imbibing** [drinking] the very **liquid** of the body
    [juice] of your beads [seeds].
Hummingbirds of various kinds are **imbibing** [drinking] the very **liquid** of
    the body [juice] of your beads [seeds].
Their wings are making sounds.

The wings are extended as far as they can go.
Every kind of **winged creature** [insect=evil spirit].
As if it were feeling the **breeze** [wind] for you.
The **breeze** [wind] is causing your branches to make sounds for you.
The **breeze** [wind] is causing your branches to **swing** [**move**] **back and forth**
    for you.
With the **breeze** [wind] your mola [leaves] is **floating upward** [rising].
Up to the lap of the **earth** [middle of the ground] your molas [leaves] are
    accumulating [being gathered].

Where the cosmos [day=sun] rises [in the east] the chiefs [leaders] are truly
    called.
At the very place where the cosmos [day=sun] rises [in the east] the chiefs
    [leaders] truly are coming to know.
Where the cosmos [day=sun] rises [in the east] Sister Kelilikkwa White-faced
    One [White Cocoa] truly calls the spirit shamans.
The chiefs [leaders] surely are coming to know.
The **breezes** [winds] sway you the **breezes** [winds] come carrying you away.
The chiefs [leaders] come entering.
The chiefs [leaders] come anchoring.
With their **low** [short] **sticks** [canes] the chiefs [leaders] arrived.
Your beard [fur] seems pale around.
The chiefs [leaders] are coming to meet.
In order to recover again the sacred soul of the little one [child] of the owner
    of tobacco [the Kuna people].
The chiefs [leaders] are coming to meet.
Because of the sacred souls of the **little one** [child] of the owner of **tobacco**
    [the Kuna people] the chiefs [leaders] are coming to meet.
Beneath the sacred hammock of the **little one** [child] of the owner of **tobacco**
    [the Kuna people].

Puberty rites

Puberty rites chants are performed by the master of ceremonies of these rites,
the gandule. They are narratives which describe in detail the various actions which
occur during the rites and are necessary in order for them to occur. While performed
in a secretive language, these chants are extremely realistic, describing in minute
detail every aspect of the puberty rites, from the preparations of the participants, to
the cutting of the young girl's hair, to the eating of a special meal, to the drinking
of *inna*, the fermented drink. The following selections were performed by Gandule
Ernesto Linares of Mulatupu in 1970. Here is a description of the young girl going
to the jungle river in order to bathe in preparation for the ritual.

> The girl goes quietly.
> Along the path of the river.
> Walking along the path of the river.
> She arrives at the river.
> She stands up in the river.
> She bathes in the river.
>
> The young girl undresses and bathes.
>
> She carries her *garba* basket.

She carries her *sile* basket.
The girl takes off her belt.
The girl takes off her underwear.
The girl takes off her coin necklace.
The girl takes off her bead necklace.
The girl takes off her beads.
The girl takes off her mola.
The girl quietly bathes.

Here is a description of some of the utensils used for the tasting and drinking of the fermented drink.

There is the strainer.
There is the large inna drinking cup.
There is the small *siki* cup.
There is the *nogmur* drinking cup.
There is the mouth rinsing cup.

Here is a description of the carrying into the young girl's enclosure of the cosmetics and utensils used in the ritual haircutting.

The women carry in the *mageb* dye.
The women carry in the *nisar* dye.
The women carry in the comb.
The women carry in the scissors.

Here is a description of the ritual haircutter drinking the fermented inna.

They take the cover off the inna jar.
They scoop up inna.
The haircutter begins to drink.
The haircutter greets people as she drinks.
The haircutter swallows.
Her throat makes a loud noise.
The inna makes her burp.

Here are descriptions of the cutting of the girl's hair.

They arrange her hair.
They comb her hair.
The hair is all arranged.
They open the hair.
They raise the hair.
The cutting of the hair makes noise.
It can be heard far away.
The hair doubles over.
The hair piles up.

Folktale: The agouti story

My next example is the telling of a humorous folktale, "The Agouti Story," by Chief Muristo Pérez of Mulatupu, on 21 April 1970. This story, about the renowned

trickster Agouti and his victim Jaguar, was told in the Mulatupu gathering house
to a group of men and women. Chief Muristo is known as a great storyteller, able to
pull his story out of his fantastic memory and tell it dramatically, with suspense and
humor, at times relating it to current or recent events in the village. His performances
are greatly appreciated by Kuna audiences. I have used a set of conventions so that
readers can read aloud, dramatizing their voices the way Muristo did in his performance. Lines are determined by a combination of falling pitch and long pause. Long
pauses without accompanying falling pitch are represented by a large space between
words. Extra loud speech is indicated by means of capital letters. Dashes between
syllables indicate stretched-out speech. Dashes between letters indicate that the voice
is vibrating. Expressive lengthening of sounds is indicated by the doubling of letters.
Faster speech is indicated by a dotted underline under the words which are spoken
faster. Slow speech is indicated by stretching out the letters of the words affected.
When part of a line is higher in pitch, this is indicated by raising the words. When
a whole line is higher in pitch, this is indicated by ^ placed before the line. The
translation is relatively literal, but accessible enough to readers of English to be able
to appreciate the flavor and the humor of Kuna trickster tales. I use brackets to fill in
anaphoric references not overtly expressed in the Kuna text but needed in English.
Here are the first two episodes of the eight Chief Muristo told on that day. While he
told them to an audience, he did so by dialoguing with his spokesperson, Armando.

First episode

Well listen Armando.

So let's listen to a bit of a story now.

A story.

It's the Agouti story.

So   and   Agouti Jaguar the two of them   they were about to compete with each other.

And Jaguar   Agouti the two of them Agouti   Agouti is a trickster ah.

Jaguar is a hunter.

He got there and saw him ah.

So Agouti is sit-ting-up-straight.

Uncle saw him Jaguar did.

He started chasing him.

When he started chasing him   over there say, it's true it is said.

So Agouti is sitting eating.

So "I'm sitting eating ikwa fruit" he says.

On top of a hill   seated.

Sitting on top of a hill, sitting eating, there to Uncle   Agouti says to
Uncle.

"Now   you are going to eat too" he says it is said.

"<u>He is going along chasing him ah, he is going to eat</u>" he says "<u>he is going to eat his head</u>."

(Armando interjects: its true his head is going to be caught I think.)

"<u>In point of fact</u>" he says, "<u>what are you sitting eating it's true I am going to eat some too</u>" he says.

It's true it is said.

"How did you split it open ah?" he said.

^ "How were you able to split it open?"

"In point of fact" he says "I split it open with my balls" see it is said.

^ "With my balls I split it open.

You watch" he says ah.

He got a rock a rock a rock   he got.

Agouti ooopened up his balls his balls he op he set them <u>against the side of the hill</u>. TAK the ikwa fruit TAK AK.

(Armando interjects: Wow what pain!)

"You see" it is said ah.

It's true it is said.

Ah Jaguar is astounded ah.

"<u>Here you're going to do it like that too</u>" he said to him.

Well he got a rock for him too.

But the other one placed the ikwa fruit right on top of his balls ah.

Did you hear?

This Agouti he tricked him for the fun of it.

This one he smashed against the stone the stone he didn't do it on his balls.

But Jaguar is going to place it right on his balls.

Then he diiid it   TAK.

So he smashed him in the banana.

(Audience laughs uproariously.)

(Armando interjects something unintelligible.)

It's true it is said.

(Armando interjects something unintelligible.)

Well   so   he diiid it he finished off his balls it is said.

That big boy Agouti knocked him out he-sure-made-him-jump-a-round.

Ah.

Poor Jaguar.

He passed out   he fainted.

And Agouti took off again started running again.

<u>Running running running run</u> laugh-ing a-long down the path ah.

Second episode

Uncle came to Jaguar did.

When Jaguar came to again   it's true it is said.

"Where did that guy go?

He's making fun of me" he says then he started chasing him again, catch-ing-him-a-gain.

When he got there he saw him again   he got there and reached him again.

So he was standing on a hill here on a hill ah.

It-was-fal-ling-straight-down.

It's true it is said.

When he got there he says to him "Friend how can you be standing there like that"

he [Jaguar] says to him "come help Uncle," he [Agouti] says.

"Now indeed, a big wind is coming see the rock is going to fall on us therefore help

me   a-g-a-i-n-s-t i-t" he said to him ah.

(Laughter from gathered audience.)

Jaguar is ready   then he went there and held against it ah.

"Against it here   you hold" he said to him "and I'll go and cut a stick for you did you hear.

With the stick we'll hold it tight" he said "well if it's not done we would die."

Jaguar heeeld-on and Agouti slowly slowly left <u>he ran on again</u>.

But the stick was well in place   truly how was it going to fall?

(Laughter from gathered audience.)

"This guy tricked you for the fun of it."

Mm and Agouti took off again.

He heard Agouti go-ing-a-long-laugh-ing he stood listening "he tricked me" he left <u>slowly slowly</u>   how could it fall? it was in place.

(Laughter from gathered audience.)

Lullaby

My final example is a lullaby performed by Donalda García of Mulatupu on 15 March 1978. If you walk through a Kuna village, especially in the morning when men are at work, you hear singing coming from almost every house. These are women, from young girls to quite old grandmothers, singing to little babies to keep them calm and put them to sleep. In the performance of lullabies, the singer holds the baby in her lap in a hammock or sits next to it, moving the hammock back and forth and shaking a rattle. Lullabies have certain basic themes. The baby is told not to cry, that it will soon grow up and perform adult tasks and that its father is off working in the jungle or fishing. In addition, there is improvisation to fit the actual situation of the baby and its family, whether the singer is a mother, sister, or aunt; whether the baby is a boy or a girl; whether those off at work are fathers, uncles, or brothers; whether they are farming in the jungle, fishing, or working in Panama City. The language of lullabies is that of everyday Kuna, with particular stylistic features. Final vowels are typically not deleted and are used in the expression of the melody. The suffix *-ye* is often used to mark the ends of lines. Stanza-like units are terminated with a long *mmmmm*.

> Little baby.
> Your mother is sitting with you in your hammock.
> Little baby she is sorry to see you cry.
> mmmmm.
>
> Little girl.
> You can now walk.
> You can run as well.
> Your aunts are sorry to see you (cry).
> My little baby girl can now walk.
> mmmmm.
>
> Father is not here I see.
> He went to the jungle.
> "I am going to clear out the coconut farms."
> Father said as he left.
> mmmmm.
>
> Little girl.
> You will stay in the house.
> You will make a little mola.
> You will also sit beside your mother.
> You will wash clothes.
> You will go to the river.
> With your relatives.
> You will wash small clothes.
> Your mother is raising you alone.
> You have already grown up a bit mother sees also.
> mmmmm.
>
> When your uncles return.
> You will serve beverages to your uncles.
> You will serve them food.
> When your uncles return.
> mmmmm.
>
> Your relatives will call to you.
> "Bring me a beverage."
> mmmmm.

Little baby girl.
My little girl lying here.
Little baby.
mmmmm.

The examples I have presented here constitute Kuna traditional oral literature. They have existed for a long time and continue right up to the present. At the same time, in Kuna Yala and in the increasingly large Kuna population in Panama City, new forms of discourse and literature are emerging. These new forms share some of the features of Kuna traditional literature I have described here, but are adapted in fascinating and creative ways to the new situations the Kuna encounter today as well. They include theatrical productions; oral letters and reports recorded on cassette tapes and mailed to family, friends, and village leaders; performances on the radio; and new ways of telling stories. Today as always Kuna language and literature are intimately and dynamically related to Kuna culture and society and dependent on the vitality of this culture and society for their continuing existence.[1]

Guide to Kuna Pronunciation and Grammar

An orthography for Kuna

This orthography is adapted from the writing systems that have been used by the many people who have studied the Kuna language and written about it and in it. It is important for readers to realize that there is no official Kuna writing system and for this reason the language has been written in different ways by different individuals. The way it is written here should make it relatively easy to pronounce, and accessible to both English and Spanish speakers and readers, as well as Kuna individuals.

I. Vowels: There are five vowels in Kuna, *a, e, i, o, u.* These can be pronounced either short or long (written single or double).

II. Consonants: The consonant sounds of Kuna are *p, b, t, d, k, g, kw, gw, s, ch, m, n, l, r, w,* and *y. l, m, n,* and *y* can be pronounced either short or long (written single or double). The voiceless consonants, *p, t, k, kw,* occur only between vowels in the middle of words. The voiced consonants, *b, d, g, gw,* when they occur at the beginnings or ends of words, sound at times almost like their voiceless counterparts and in fact in these positions *b* is pronounced somewhere between *p* and *b, d* somewhere between *t* and *d, g* somewhere between *k* and *g,* and *gw* somewhere between *kw* and *gw.* Here are some examples, which also constitute a glossary for many of the basic elements and concepts of Kuna life discussed in this volume.

Kuna grammar

Kuna, like many American Indian languages in both North and South America, is polysynthetic, that is, a language in which long words are constructed out of many separate forms which have distinct meanings and functions, forms that linguists call morphemes. The result is that what in European languages is expressed as a sentence containing several or even many words is often expressed in Kuna in one quite complicated word. The Kuna verb especially is characterized by adding several forms to it. Most of these are suffixed, that is, added on at the end of the verb. This aspect of Kuna provides still another interesting challenge of writing Kuna, namely where to place word boundaries. As an English speaker might pronounce the words "He is going" as "he's going" or "We do not like them" as "We don't like them," Kuna speakers also often combine words and sounds. The question of where to place word boundaries in a Kuna orthography, like the question of what letters to use to represent sounds, is complicated by the fact that there is no established tradition of writing Kuna, which is essentially a spoken or oral language. Here are some examples of how separate words and forms come together to combine into words. In these examples, hyphens are placed between separate meaningful elements which combine into single words. These are first translated literally, element by element, and then more freely.

Kuna / English

nuu dove

dii water

boogwa quiet

gae grab, catch

sui husband

goe deer, baby

ua fish

waa smoke

dake see

dage come

oba corn

yapa don't feel like

nade he/she left

sate no, none, nothing

ome woman, wife

mimmi child

gorogwa yellow, ripe

sina pig

sinna kingfisher

gwalu sweet potato

gwallu oil, light

ari iguana

asu nose

achu dog

wisi know

wagwa grandchild

sayla chief

argar chief's spokesman

nele seer, shaman

suar ibed "owner of stick" (native policeman)

ina duled "medicine person" (medicinal specialist)

gandule ritual specialist at girl's puberty rites

sapur jungle

daniki is coming

warbo two oblong objects

wargwen one oblong object

igar path, way

soysa he/she said

be you

nega house

neyse to the house

dummad big

bane tomorrow

ginnid red

diwar river

gadi much

binye transform

uysa he/she gave

gwaysa he/she/it changed

ogob coconut

wara tobacco

wala pole

ina medicine

inna chicha

mola woman's blouse or cloth panel from blouse

ommaked nega gathering house

dule person, Kuna person

waga Panamanian

mergi North American

ulu canoe

demar sea

diwar river

burba spirit

gurgin hat, brain

sunmake speak

namake chant, sing

gormake shout

boe cry, lament

dodoe dance

naybe snake

gabur hot pepper

nia devil

suar nuchu stick doll

garba basket

---

wisi - sa - suli - moga > wichurmo
know - past time - not - also
he/she did not know either

Notice that in this and the following examples, the pronoun he/she is not expressed, but is rather understood, much like it is in Spanish dice "he/she says."

gabe - mai > gammai
sleep - ongoing
he/she is sleeping

soge - sa > soysa
say - past time
he/she said

In general, most Kuna morphemes have both a long form and a short form, the long form having a final vowel which is deleted in the short form. Examples (with the deletable vowel in parentheses) are *neg(a)* "house," *dak(e)* "see," *an(i)* "I, me," and *s(a)* "past tense." When these forms come together to form words, the final vowel is often deleted, especially in rapid speech, as distinct from chanting or singing. This brings consonants together which undergo changes according to rules of Kuna pronunciation. Here are some further examples, now written with the parentheses:

gach(i) - gin(e) > gasgi
hammock - in
in the hammock

neg(a) - se > neyse
house - toward
toward the house

bangu(e) - s(a) - mal(a) - mog(a) - ye > bangusmar-
   moye
leave - past tense - plural - also - indeed
I indeed left all of you also

As a result of this way of combining distinct forms with distinct meanings into large words, the Kuna language is a finely tuned instrument or lens for expressing and focusing attention on details and subtleties of form, shape, motion, position, direction, time, and the way in which things are conceived of as occurring. Words all by themselves often seem to be poetry in action. Here are some examples of some particularly expressive, indeed, poetic forms and combinations of forms in Kuna.

There are four suffixes which, when used with verbs, indicate the position of the actor or the doer of the verb. These are *gwichi* "standing, in a vertical position," *mai* "lying, in a horizontal position," *nai* "perched, in a hanging position," and *sii* "seated, in a sitting position." Here are the different meanings these suffixes produce when used with the verb *ogabe* "to put to sleep" as in *nana mimmi ogabe* "the mother puts the baby to sleep." (Notice that the most common word order in Kuna is subject followed by object followed by verb, as in the following example.)

nana mimmi ogab - gwichi
The mother is putting the baby to sleep by standing
   next to the hammock and swinging it.

nana mimmi ogab - mai
The mother is putting the baby to sleep by lying in
   the hammock with the baby.

nana mimmi ogab - nai
The mother is putting the baby to sleep by straddling
   the hammock with the baby beside her or on her
   lap.

nana mimmi ogab - sii
The mother is putting the baby to sleep by sitting
   in the hammock with the baby beside her or on
   her lap.

Notice how imaginative these forms are because of the concise and precise way in which they express the position of the mother in relation to the baby.

Another set of verbal suffixes describes in fine detail the interplay of time, motion, direction, movement, and the ways in which an action is conceived as occurring.

Here are some examples with the verb *masgunne* "eat."

mas - gunsokali "about to eat"
masgunn - ali "beginning to eat"
masgu - te "at that moment ate"
masgun - binne "just ate"
masgun - nadapi "goes about eating"
masgun - dapi "went there to eat"
masgun - api "went there to eat and came back"
masgun - daniki "is coming to eat"
masgun - noniki "came to eat"
masgun - tae "always eats"
masgun - tii "was eating"

Also poetic and imaginative are the forms, used along with numerals, which classify objects according to their form and shape. Here are a few of the many, illustrated with the numeral *gwen* (one).

war - gwen "one oblong object," used for human
   beings, poles, trees, and large animals
gwa - gwen "one round object," used for fruit, small
   animals, and Kuna houses
ga - gwen "one long, thin object," used for single
   hairs, teeth, pencils, and cigarettes
mata - gwen "one flat object," used for leaves,
   books, and pieces of paper
tar - bo "two objects stuck together," used for any
   objects that are stuck together

Another interesting feature of Kuna grammar, which reveals Kuna attention to form, shape, texture, and the way things happen, as well as humor, is reduplication, the partial or total repetition of a form. Many American Indian languages use reduplication in their grammars, but Kuna does so in its own unique, imaginative, and poetic way. Some forms are reduplicated in order to indicate that actors are distributed here and there in space. The verbal positional suffixes are used this way. Thus,

sayla namay - nai "the chief is chanting"
sayla namay - nanai "the chiefs are distributed here
   and there chanting"

Certain adjectives and adverbs are reduplicated, somewhat playfully, to stress their meaning, or to change it somewhat, often indicating form, shape, movement, and texture, with a remarkable attention to detail.

bane "tomorrow"
bane bane "every day"

mata "stained"
mata mata "stained all over"

gwae "fast"
gwae gwae "very fast"

sinni "curl"
sinni sinni "all curled up"

murru "hill, bump"
murru murru "bumpy, like the skin of a caiman"

yamo dae "imitate"
yamo yamo dae "imitate in a playful mocking way"

burwi "small"
burwi burwi sunmake "talk a little"

mete "throw away"
suar mete mete gamaidii "go about throwing a stick
    this way and that," said playfully and poetically of
    the way Kuna "police officers" (*suar ibed*) walk
    around

In addition to the particular salient characteristics of
the Kuna language I have illustrated here, it is useful to
mention some general properties of grammatical structure. The most common or basic word order in Kuna is,
for transitive verbs, subject followed by object followed by
verb, and, for intransitive verbs, subject followed by verb:

dule sapi dake "The man sees the tree" (literally,
    man tree see)
mimmi gabe "The baby is sleeping" (literally, baby
    sleep)

Adjectives follow the noun they modify:

sapi dummad "big tree" (literally, tree big)

Possessors precede the object or person possessed:

Julio ome "Julio's wife" (literally, Julio wife)
an nega "my house" (literally, I/me house)

Postpositions follow nouns and relate to nouns the way
in which prepositions do in English, indicating such
notions as location and direction. They are often suffixed
to nouns in actual speech:

neki "in the house" (<*neg(a)* "house" - *gi* "in")
neg urba "under the house"
babse "toward father" (= toward father's place;
    < *bab(a)* "father" - *se* "toward")
mesa birgi "on the table"

The many suffixes that can occur with verbs express
such notions as tense, aspect (the way an action is conceived of as occurring), position, movement, direction,
negative, also, and again:

dake "see"
daysa "he/she saw"
daynadapi "he/she sees as he/she goes along"
dakwichi "he/she is seeing in a standing position"
daysuli "he/she does not see"
daymoga "he/she sees also"
daybali "he/she sees again"
daydapi "he/she went there to see"

The Kuna language has a grammar which is imaginative and poetic in and of itself, and remarkably attentive
to form, shape, texture, motion, and direction, thus
providing a rich set of possibilities for individual and
literary creativity. Kuna grammar and vocabulary provide
the imagery, metaphors, and humor that are actualized
in Kuna literature.

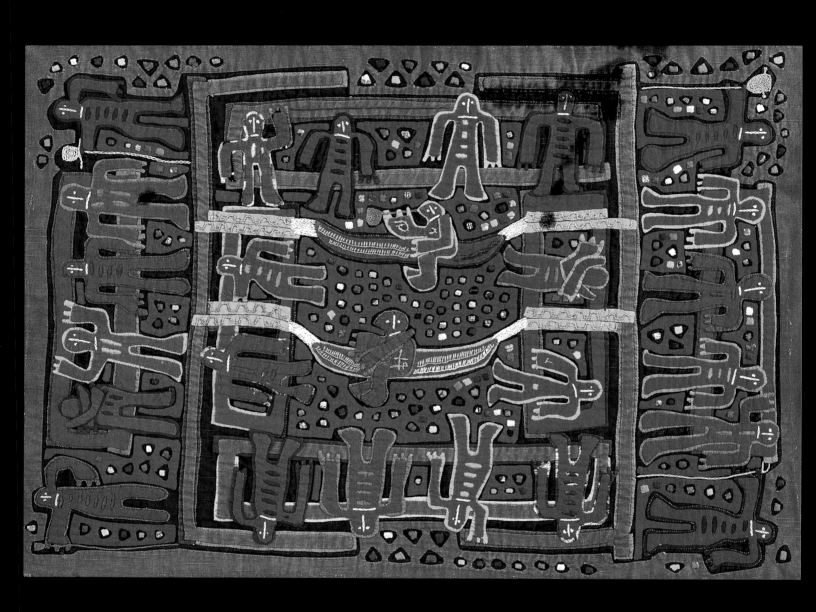

The Gathering House
Heart of a Kuna Community

James Howe

When the pirate Lionel Wafer lived with the Kuna for a few months in the late seventeenth century, he noted that each Kuna community clustered around a large building, which served as both military stronghold and council house. In the three hundred years since Wafer's visit, Kuna culture has changed in many ways, but a community building, called *onmaked nega*, "gathering house," or in Spanish, *casa de congreso*, is still found in every village. This massive rectangular structure is essentially an enlarged version of a Kuna house: its heavy posts and beams, lashed together with vines, support a thatch roof and walls of cane or split bamboo. Typically, the dirt floor of the building is entirely taken up by rows of wooden benches, except for an open space in the center, in which several hammocks are strung. Photographs and drawings of past leaders hang from the roof overhead, along with banners and historical symbols; sports trophies sit on a shelf; and calendars and circulars hang near the bench used by village secretaries. This building is the heart of a Kuna community, the place where it organizes village labor, makes decisions, resolves disputes, teaches Kuna values, deals with the outside world, and assembles before its God (Howe 1986, Sherzer 1983, Prestán 1991).

Calling to Father

Kuna villages organize events in the gathering house on different patterns and schedules, but all of them "hear issues" (*igal itoe*) that affect community life, and all of them "call to Father" (*babse golle*). Traditionally, sacred gatherings occur several nights a week, bringing all the members of the community together to hear a chief sing. Many villages also hold occasional singing gatherings in the morning just for women, and today on some islands, as populations have outgrown their gathering houses, men and women meet separately.

In the late afternoon of the day that a singing gathering is scheduled, a line of village constables called "masters of the staffs" (*suar ibgana*) file through the streets, calling out to announce the gathering. At sunset, men and women enter the gathering

5.1. Gathering house mola panel (detail). Chiefs in hammocks, one with a pipe, listen as several of the men sitting on benches gesture and speak.
42.5 x 59.5 cm. FMCH X83.440. Gift of Dorothy M. Cordry in memory of Donald B. Cordry.

**5.2. Men keeping a visiting chief
company in the gathering house.**
James Howe, Niatupu, 1970.

house and take their seats, women throughout the hall, ordinary men on the benches
around the outside. Village leaders sit on benches on the open space in the center,
or in the case of two or three chiefs, lie in hammocks in their midst. As night falls
and the hall fills, two of the chiefs sit up, shake hands, and then almost inaudibly
begin to sing.

The chant is a dialog, a sung conversation between the two men. One of the
pair, the lead performer for the evening, sings a long line of verse, and when he stops
to take a breath, the other man answers with "Yes," "Thus it is," or a hummed tone,
holding the note until the first man is ready to begin again. They continue in this
way for several hundred verses, slowly building volume and speed; depending on
the endurance, knowledge, and ambition of the lead singer and how he assesses his
audience's patience, his chant may last anywhere from forty-five minutes to well over
an hour.

The audience sits quietly throughout, except for a few murmured conversations
and scattered games of marbles and other amusements played by young boys, who are
mostly ignored by the adults. Women sew molas by the light of small smoky lamps
that they bring with them, and a few men weave baskets. Traditionally, both sexes

smoked pipes, and today cigarette smoking is almost universal among the men. As the evening wears on, background noise subsides as children lie down to sleep on benches and pieces of cloth spread on the ground. Many men seem to be dozing behind the caps and hats that shade their eyes, as do women inside the headcloths pulled around them. Real sleep is impossible, however, for every few minutes the village policemen let out an ear-splitting cry, "Don't sleep! Listen well!" (*Gabidamalarye, nue balitomarye*).

Eventually the first chief sings several verses signaling the approaching end of his chant, in some cases even offering excuses for not continuing longer in terms of the presumed infirmities of his oldest listeners.

5.3. Chiefs chant to assembled villagers. The foot of a child sleeping in the chief's lap protrudes from the hammock.
James Howe, Niatupu, 1970.

The police let out one huge cry in unison, the chanting ends, and another village leader, called an *argar* or *vocero* stands and begins speaking. He goes through the content of the chief's chant, repeating its most important points, and if it is a narrative, he retells the story. The Kuna sometimes justify this interpretation in terms of the chant's supposed unintelligibility, noting that chiefs often use esoteric vocabulary and opaque metaphors. In fact, the language of gathering chants is much closer to colloquial speech than are the languages of curing and puberty chants (see Sherzer, "Kuna Language and Literature," in this volume), and the audience usually understands most of what the chief is saying. Rather than decoding the chant, the *argar* explicates it, making obscure points clear, and he develops its meaning and implications, in the same way that a Christian preacher turns a biblical text into a sermon.

Each time a chief chants, he creates a new text, improvised on the basis of a body of traditional knowledge and wisdom called "Father's Way" (*Bab Igar*). Chiefs and argars acquire this lore from each other, some apprenticing themselves with famous traditionalists and trying to acquire from them their whole fund of knowledge, but most play the field as they learn from peers and senior colleagues all over Kuna Yala. Each element in Father's Way, each story or set of metaphors, can be learned in a few

5.4. Women at a singing gathering.
James Howe, Niatupu, 1970.

late nights spent with a teacher after the gathering house has shut. Unambitious chiefs content themselves with acquiring a repertoire of ten to twenty stories, which they perform with only small variations from one occasion to the next. Those who wish to make a name for themselves go on to master several dozen narratives, and the greatest leaders and teachers of this century have learned everything they could, not just from teachers of Father's Way, but also from anyone who had learned something useful about the outside world and the challenges facing their people.

Father's Way consists first and foremost of the sacred history of the Kuna, the *Olotule* or "Golden People," and their unciv-

ilized predecessors, the "animal peoples" (*immar dulegana*). As Chapin (in this volume) notes, this history holds a great many episodes describing how the deities, Great Father and Great Mother, created and populated the world, how Father repeatedly sent seers and prophets to rid the world of demons and reform the animal people, how those peoples willfully rebelled and backslid, provoking the repeated destruction of the world, and how eventually the Spaniards arrived, bringing war and destruction (see Chapin). The greatest of the civilizing heroes, named Ibeorgun, established the basic institutions of Kuna society, and the gathering house is often called Ibeorgun's House in his honor.

Father's Way also encompasses cosmology—the eight levels of the universe, their spirit inhabitants, the soul's journey through the layers to Father's Place above, and the punishments it may receive on the way—as well as elaborate metaphors, extended descriptions of trees, animals, and other features of the world, each of them an allegory for a virtue or vice. Since history and cosmology are in theory unchangeable, metaphor offers the widest scope for creativity, and the great leaders of this century are known for their poetry as well as for their actions.

Inanaginya, for instance, the chief of all the Kuna at the turn of the century, is best remembered for warning his followers against switching their allegiances from Colombia to Panama in terms of a choice between a young and beautiful but unreliable charmer and an old and dependable wife. Cimral Colman, who led Kuna resistance to Panamanian domination through the 1920s, warned his followers against the national police and invading rubber-gatherers through vivid descriptions of monsters he had seen in dreams. Those who remember his chants render them today in spoken prose, as in this oral history by Jimmy Solis:

> Now then…in truth, the singing would start again, from time to time. A frog would truly be heard singing underground. The frog, toorr, toorr, a great frog came rising up, through the levels of the underworld. "What might the frog be saying to me, I thought," he said. "What does it say to me? I lay listening. When I listened well again, I dreamt," he said, "and towards the land something else could be heard. A devil was shouting," he said. "A devil came shouting. 'You Kuna, I will be surrounding-surrounding.' I lay thinking that it would surround us all."

In the same way, after the successful rebellion of 1925, Colman's successor Nele Kantule counseled his followers about the situation that confronted them, representing the work of reorganizing their society in terms of clearing the weeds from a farm, and the task of helping young girls who had been forced to wear Western dress to return to molas as letting cacao plants show their flowers. The following comments by Nele are from an oral history by Cacique Carlos López:

> "I was working with my brothers-in-law…. The dry season arrived, and I began to think of clearing land," he said…. "The farm was a terrible tangle…. I was ready to cut the great trees…. In the burning sun, I began to burn off the place…. I was ready to plant great things…," Nele was singing, so they say. "I planted everything, all the good things. The great cacao began to flower. The great cacao began to give fruit."

Nele also urged his followers to be self-reliant, to manage their own destinies without outside interference.

> "Young men, I hope you go around in your own canoe," he sang, so they say. "I want to be cutting with my own axe," he said…. "I want to be paddling

5.5. Authority staffs, carried by village policemen and curers.
All are carved wood, some with pigment. Longest, 116 cm.
A,B,C. Private collection.
D. FMCH X84.648. Promised gift of Dorothy M. Cordry in memory of Donald B. Cordry.
E,F. Collection of Ann and Monroe Morgan.

with my own paddle," he said. This means, "Would that I care for the land myself.… That's what I put the place in order for, to carry the land myself."

Chiefs may also counsel people directly in their chants, instructing men about working in the forest literally rather than figuratively and reminding women about caring for their homes. They seldom sing directly about the present, however, except in very circumscribed ways: they may devote a few verses to telling how they arrived at the island where they are singing or enumerating the kinds of people who have come to the gathering house, but they seldom mention specific recent events or problems.

Nonetheless, everything the chiefs sing, however removed in time or space, bears on the present. A chant about the soul's journey in the afterlife through the levels of the universe or the landscape of heaven informs people of the consequences of their actions; a chant about the quarrels of the peccary people or rivalries between ancient leaders warns them against doing the same. The Kuna say that people today carry the *burba*, the soul or essence of past times, and it is the function of the argar to lay bare that soul, to exhort his listeners to face foreign threats like the great solar hero, Dad Ibe, or to mourn properly as they were taught by the Star-woman Inanadili. Even in history and metaphor, however, chiefs tend to be general and circumspect, warning their followers against slovenliness or anger, but seldom singling out angry or slovenly individuals, even by implication.

At the same time that chiefs are communicating with their followers, the gathering as a whole communicates with the deities, a relationship often metaphorized as a golden cord stretching from the building to heaven. In the gathering house, the Kuna express their devotion and their dependence on Great Father and Great Mother, who have given them the land to care for and use, and as they "call to Father," they reconstitute their villages as religious congregations. Great Father is a jealous god, and traditional Kuna worry that he will punish or destroy the world as he has before if they misbehave, particularly if they neglect his house. These millennial fears resurge periodically, especially in times of crisis, as they have in recent years among the Kuna of the Bayano Valley, whose lands and culture are threatened by outsiders.

5.6. A village chief, Luis Ortiz, listens while one of his followers speaks.
James Howe, Niatupu, 1975.

The talking gathering

The gathering house is also the site for secular politics, for all the public tasks that Kuna villages undertake. Any evening or portion of an evening devoted to talking rather than singing typically consists of a string, often a very long string, of *igar*, a word that in this context means "cases" or "issues." As hard as it may be to predict which igar will be discussed on a given evening, the kinds of events and the kinds of speech that will be used fall into a limited number of types.

Frequently, a secretary or task leader will read a long list connected with some form of communal labor or obligation—who participated the day before in repairing a village wharf or clearing a communal field, who contributed fish or sugarcane for a puberty ceremony, who is supposed to help build a house tomorrow, or the fines that men have accumulated for work sessions they have missed. While such list-reading is not fascinating in itself—except to men who feel a mistake has been made—it plays a crucial function in organizing labor in a society where most people are literate but communication is still largely oral. Secretaries also read aloud any communications that come into the village from the government, private agencies, individuals, or other islands, translating the letters and circulars from Spanish into Kuna, thus ensuring that all the people have the same information at their command.

Clearly, the gathering house plays a crucial role in processing information, information it also collects from visitors and returning community members. A chief back from singing on another island or the members of a task force returning from a mission to a government ministry will give detailed accounts of what they did and who they saw, as will a curer who returns from learning medicine in the Bayano or a migrant laborer home on vacation from work on a United States army base. In addition, anyone who has an event to announce, for instance, a government representative, a teacher offering a night of performances in the school, or a young man come to work on the island, is expected to present himself to the gathering. As a result of this very active form of information-processing, not only can the Kuna respond to threats, opportunities, and needs in the short term, but over much longer periods they have had remarkable success in understanding the organizations, individuals, and societies that impinge on their lives and in surviving as a people with their lands, culture, and political autonomy largely intact.

In addition to informing each other, villagers in the gathering house "give each other the way" (*naga igal uke*). Chiefs and argars are expected to admonish their followers regularly in speech as well as chants. Young men leaving for a basketball tournament should be counseled, as should newlyweds and recently elected chiefs and argars; and traditionally, village members of every sort—curers, midwives, village policemen, agriculturalists, young girls, women in general, even, and especially, chiefs—should be reminded of their duties from time to time. During the dry season, which is the time for clearing, burning, and planting, almost every gathering includes an exhortation urging men to work hard and provide for their families. The following brief excerpt (Salcedo 1979) comes from the admonishment of a newly married couple:

> Well, now then, young man, yesterday you were given a house. And a companion was given to you. And in truth you have come to this place to become the master of a house, in accordance with the destiny fixed on you by Great Father.... Before, when you were younger, you did things according to your own desires. But now you have been given work. From now on, when the village works, you will be here to work too....

5.7. A Kuna General Congress.
James Howe, Ustupu, 1981.

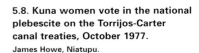

5.8. Kuna women vote in the national plebescite on the Torrijos-Carter canal treaties, October 1977.
James Howe, Niatupu.

5.9. A secretary takes attendance at a communal work session.
James Howe, Urgandi (Rio Sidra), 1978.

5.10. Adjudication in a schoolroom.
James Howe, Niatupu, 1975.

You were given a woman, but not to be angry with her, not so that you and she should have quarrels....

Disputes and trouble cases are also handled collectively, though some villages do so outside the gathering house, in a home or schoolroom, especially if it is feared that the adjudication of a dispute will prove rancorous and thus profane "Father's house." Some villages have specialized judicial officers and regular tribunals, but their proceedings sound remarkably like traditional adjudications in the gathering house. The men hearing a case not only decide between the rival claims of disputants, for instance concerning a contested boundary between farms on the mainland, but they also fine people or exact punishments in labor for misbehavior. (Serious crimes are usually sent to a regional court presided over by a Kuna judge.) Whatever the outcome to a case, the adjudicators always admonish the culprits or disputants, and in many instances they decide that a harsh tongue-lashing, delivered by several chiefs, argars, and other leaders in a row, is by itself sufficient punishment.

Perhaps the most important function of the talking gathering is to debate public issues and make decisions. Points for discussion come up frequently during the course of an evening, for instance when the reading of a list of workers provokes a debate about how to best organize communal labor, or a letter from a Kuna-run conservation project prompts discussion of intrusions into Kuna Yala by non-Indian peasants and a decision to send the young men of the village to help cut a boundary path around the Comarca. Other issues are brought up by a chief or anyone else who has something on his mind.

Debates and decision making are democratic, though with oligarchical tendencies. For an issue of even moderate importance, a number of speeches follow each other, and quite a few men participate. Given this wide participation, it is often not apparent that many other men, usually a majority, speak seldom or not at all, which, given the devotion of the Kuna to all forms of speech, is somewhat surprising. Among the young men of a village, typically a few speak regularly, especially secretaries to the gathering, but most lack the confidence and experience to do so often, and even among middle-aged men, many do not enjoy orating. Similarly, although feminism has reached Kuna Yala, and a few villages have elected female chiefs or argars or instituted women's gatherings, so far males dominate village politics. Even in this strikingly participatory, democratic society, some exert more influence than others.

The first chief of a village often introduces issues that have been brought to his attention and sums up at the end of discussion, and he may or may not give his thoughts during debate, but he is expected to avoid becoming entangled in heated argument. Secondary chiefs seldom manage issues as the first chief does, and overall, argars and rising middle-aged men often speak more often and more forcefully. In private consultations, on the other hand, chiefs do have frequent opportunities to influence outcomes. Some routine decisions, moreover, are left to their discretion, and their followers must let them have some scope for independent decisions when they act on the village's behalf in Panama City. But the Kuna are very suspicious of their leaders, and they scrutinize them to keep them from accumulating too much power or acting arbitrarily. Even Father's Way, which chiefs themselves carry on and perform, warns against the ambitions of power-hungry men. If the village objects strongly to a chief's actions or they find he has misbehaved, they may throw him out unceremoniously, and many villages replace and reshuffle their leaders fairly frequently.

Fortunately, villages have to make major policy decisions only once in a while, and even when they do, they often have time to discuss the issue repeatedly and at great length, letting consensus emerge over a period of weeks or months, in contrast with New England town meetings and government committees in many societies, which typically must resolve questions in a very short period of time. Some Kuna islands have been racked by conflict and even split into two villages over a contentious issue, such as whether to allow a mission on the island or, early in this century, which country deserved their allegiance, but by and large, their members recognize that they depend on the gathering for their welfare and their identity as a people, and they would rather lose an argument than endanger a crucial institution. In the 1980s and 1990s, as attendance has flagged at singing gatherings and many Kuna have moved to the city, far from their gathering houses, the role of this institution is now in doubt. Even today, however, most Kuna recognize how well the gathering house has served them and the support it deserves.

5.11A,B. Mola panels of the Democratic Revolutionary Party from elections in 1984 support the presidential candidiate Nicolas Ardito Barleta and evoke the late Omar Torrijos.
Both, 32.5 x 39 cm. FMCH X96.25.3A,B.

The Kuna Portray
Their Own Revolutionary History

James Howe

The greatest event of twentieth-century Kuna history was a rebellion carried out in 1925, known as the Tule or Kuna Revolution. This revolt followed years of encroachment on Kuna lands by banana plantations, rubber-tappers, and turtle-fishermen, as well as a decade of police oppression. By the mid-1920s, police and bureaucrats had pacified about half the islands on the coast, suppressing native curing, puberty ceremonies, the gathering house, and women's dress, while quashing resistance through stocks, jail, and guns.

The Kuna, goaded past endurance, finally rose up in late February 1925 during the Carnival celebrations imposed on them by the police, killing some of their oppressors and putting the rest to flight. Panamanian authorities appealed for North American assistance, and within a few days the United States Minister to Panama brought the two sides together, brokering a peace agreement that has provided the basis for Kuna autonomy ever since.

Each year in February, the islands that threw off police rule commemorate the Kuna Revolution with speeches, parades, banners, and street dramas recreating the events of 1925. Actors portray the abuses of the police, the traditional practices they suppressed, the dancing and Carnival merriment they imposed, and finally the revolt itself. Through these dramas, the Kuna speak to themselves not only of continuing threats to their autonomy and the need for vigilance, but also of the value of traditional ways, now threatened less by government policy than by changes they themselves are making.

A. Banner for festival commemorating the Kuna rebellion of 1925.

B. Police stationed in Kuna villages during the 1920s forcibly suppressed many customs they considered uncivilized, including the traditional practice of bathing outdoors.

C. Traditional medicine, in this case a curer counseling his medicines, was also suppressed.

D. Female puberty ceremonies were a specia target of the police program. Here, actors portray the formal drinking characteristic of the ceremonies

E. In a light-hearted re-enactment of the social dancing imposed on Kuna villages in the 1920s, a policeman enforces attendance at a dance.

F. Young boys have tremendous fun playing the devils associated with Carnival, one of the elements of Panamanian culture forced on the Kuna in the 1920s.

G. The rebellion against police tyranny breaks out.

H. Spectators of the drama.

I. Rebels hunt down and kill their oppressors.

6

Looking Back
Contemporary Kuna Women's Arts

Mari Lyn Salvador

Introduction

Kuna women take pride in the way they look and have developed a distinctive style unlike that of their neighbors or visitors now or at any time in the past. Beauty and fastidiousness, attributes the Kuna associate with being a woman, are common topics of discussion in the gathering house as well as in the home. Family wealth is often expressed through the women's dress and jewelry. Beautiful women bring prestige to the whole family and exemplify what Joel Sherzer refers to as Cunaité, "Kunaness," an aspect of their identity (Sherzer 1983). Contemporary women use clothing as a mode of personal expression, taking great care with decisions about combinations of skirts and scarves, as well as with the creation of their mola blouses. Although mola panels are often framed or made into pillows by outsiders, they are actually the front and back panels of a traditional mola blouse.

Narratives told again and again in Kuna Yala associate two female mythological figures with bringing the traditional arts to Kuna women. They describe a time in the distant past when women wore animal skins decorated with feathers until Kikkatiriyai taught them to make long dresses, weave hammocks, and make pottery. Nagagiriyai, a female teacher (*nele*), discovered designs in her dreams in Kalu Duibus, a mythological dwelling only women can enter. She memorized the designs along with their names and taught them

6.1 (OPPOSITE). **Mola panel. Kuna woman sitting with children in a hammock sewing a mola. The hammock is attached to the house beams with rope and the cane walls are shown around the edge. The two figures on the top are sitting on traditional wooden stools. 1997. Cooperativa Productores de Mola.** 35.0 x 38.5 cm. FMCH X97.18.1.

6.2. **Ana Julisa standing in the doorway with fancy nose paint, Tupile. A teenager at the time this photograph was taken, she chose to draw attention to her nose by painting designs along the traditional line. Over the years, women have expanded the arm bands until they now reach from the wrist almost to the elbow.** Mari Lyn Salvador, 1986.

6.3. Young girls learn to make molas by watching women in the family sew.
Mari Lyn Salvador, 1994.

to the women, who began incorporating them into their hammocks, body painting, underskirts, and eventually molas (Tice 1995, 58).

In the late nineteenth century, Kuna women started experimenting with ways to transfer body painting designs onto handwoven cloth. The new process eventually developed into the creation of designs that were cut out and sewn onto imported fabric. This innovation combined the creative use of new materials—manufactured trade cloth, scissors, and needles—and new processes—cutting and sewing (Fig. 6.4). Over the years, the women have intensified the process and have developed hundreds of mola designs, as well as more creative ways of executing them. At this time, the art form is going in the direction of heightened complexity, refined designs, smaller and smaller filler elements, and an increasingly elaborate system of aesthetic judgment. These women have created an art form that is uniquely Kuna and have established corresponding criteria for artistic criticism.

In studying Kuna aesthetics and concepts of beauty, it is clear that the Kuna value talent, learning, competence, and productivity, and have an interest in both continuity and change. Kuna criteria for fine-quality molas are based on the skillful manipulation of the technical process, proper organization, design visibility, appropriate subject matter, and the use of acceptable color combinations.

At this time, when the women have so mastered this process that they are able to execute almost any contemporary design they wish, many are looking to molas from the past for inspiration. They experiment with old designs by combining various types of mola work and techniques, adding elements and changing color combinations to create blouses that conform to contemporary standards of taste (Figs. 6.5-10).

Kuna dress

The women's extraordinary clothing style figures prominently in Kuna narratives and has captured the attention of explorers, visitors, and photographers for centuries. Early descriptions of the Kuna, written by European visitors, focus mainly on the environment, trade, and men's activities and appearance, with only brief reference to the women.

Lionel Wafer, a seventeenth-century buccaneer doctor, wrote a vivid account of the native people he lived with while stranded in the Darién jungle in 1681. Illustrations in his book, published in 1699, show men with loincloths, necklaces, and feather headpieces and the women with wraparound skirts, nose rings, and beads. He writes enthusiastically about body painting and jewelry (Fig. 6.11).

By the mid-1800s, some Kuna men had begun to change their style, donning nontraditional clothing that had been introduced by outsiders. Captain Jacob Dunham, an American adventurer, writes, "They dress in check or flannel shirts, with linen trowsers [sic]. The young men are not allowed to wear their shirt flaps inside of the waist-bands [sic] of their trowsers until they are about forty years old, when they assume the character of old men" (Dunham 1850, 147).[1] However, traditional men's dress was not totally replaced by imported clothing styles. In 1867, Fessenden Otis notes in his book about the Panama Railroad, "Their usual dress consists of a simple fold of cloth tied about the loins, though they are not infrequently seen clad…in a loose shirt and loose cotton or hempen trowsers" (Otis 1867, 77).

Commander Thomas Selfridge, who led an exploration to Darién in 1874, mentions that outsiders saw few women and were allowed little contact with them (Selfridge 1884). Although his report is richly illustrated with line drawings, it does not include recognizable images of Kuna women. Others mention the Kuna's caution about outsiders, pointing out that they "have cherished such a jealousy of their independence that, to the present day, no white man has been permitted to land" (Otis 1876, 77).

6.4. Celina Porras begins a mola panel in Suitupu. She is wearing a small crab necklace and arm bands made with maroon, gray, and green beads, a color combination popular in the 1990s.
Mari Lyn Salvador, 1994. Courtesy of the Smithsonian Institution.

6.5. *Gole igar*, path of the hermit
crab mola, collected by Pérez
Kantule, c. 1931. A *sergan* mola
with a red *obogaled* (interlocking)
line on top and a black background.
This example of the old fashioned
blouse shape with short tight sleeves
and loose bodice represents the style
in the 1930s.
67.0 x 79.0 cm. EMG 1931.19.3.

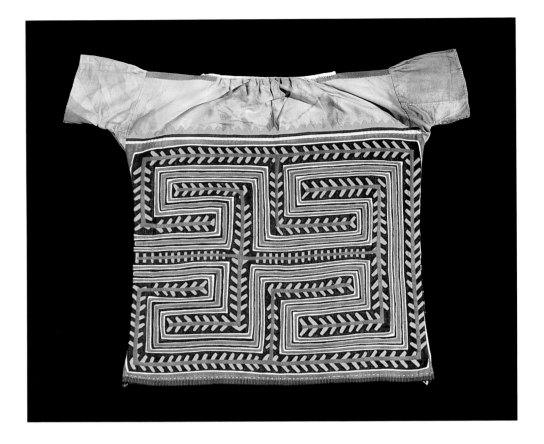

6.6. Scarf (*muswe*), collected in 1969,
made from imported trade fabric.
"They have recently allowed one or
two small trading schooners twice
or thrice a year to anchor near their
shores and traffic with them, receiving
calicoes, beads, and other ornaments,
machetes, etc., in exchange for
tortoise-shell, ivory-nuts, and gold
dust but every attempt to explore
their country has been uniformly
resisted" (Otis 1867, 77-78).
Cotton cloth. 74.5 x 129.5 cm. FMCH X83.509.
Gift of Dorothy M. Cordry in memory of
Donald B. Cordry.

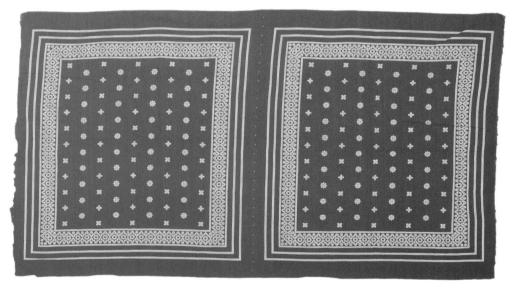

6.7. Skirt (*sabured*), collected in 1969,
made from imported fabric. At the
end of the eighteenth century, two
Scottish ships, the *Caledonia* and the
Saint Andrew, carried large and varied
cargoes to the Darién colony: "There
was 'cloth in great bulk,' bales and
bolts of ticking, canvas, linen, serge,
muslin, glazed calico, tartan plaiding,
hadden-grey and harn" (Prebble
1968, 98).
Cotton cloth. 271.5 x 79.0 cm. FMCH X84.656.
Gift of Dorothy M. Cordry in memory of
Donald B. Cordry.

6.8. *Gole igar,* path of the hermit crab mola, by Onelia Gonzalez, Suitupu, 1993. Similar to the mola in 6.5, this design with crosshatch patterns below the top layers, rarely seen in the 1960 and 1970s, is popular now as it was in the 1920s and 1930s.
59.0 x 80.0 cm. Private collection.

6.9. Scarf (*muswe*), c. 1980s.
Cotton cloth. 124.0 x 73.0 cm FMCH X84.654. Gift of Dorothy M. Cordry in memory of Donald B. Cordry.

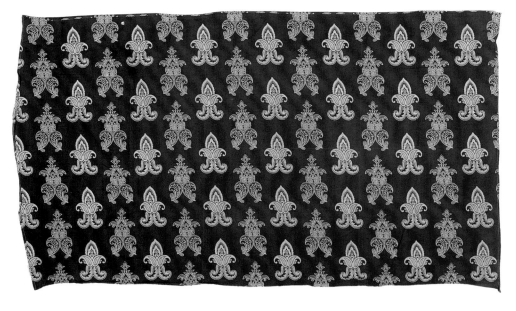

6.10. Skirt (*sabured*), c. 1980s.
Cotton cloth. 126.0 x 76.0 cm. FMCH X83.161. Gift of Susan Masuoka.

6.11. A seventeenth-century illustration of a group of Kuna men and women. The women are wearing wraparound skirts. The one in the back is shown carrying two baskets on a pole, a system used to this day. "Both Men and Women when painted, and set out with all these Fineries, make no ordinary Figure" (Wafer 1699, 89).

By the late 1800s, we begin to find descriptions of women wearing skirts and head coverings, as they do to this day. Orlando Roberts, a British merchant marine and trader who traveled along the eastern coast of Central America in 1872, describes the dress of Kuna women thus, "They were clothed in wrappers of blue *baftas*, or stripped [*sic*] cotton of their own manufacture, reaching from the breast to a little lower than the calf of the leg." He goes on to write, "Over the head was thrown a piece of blue *bafta* or *sahempore*, completely covering the back, breasts, and one side of the face" (Roberts 1827, 43).

In 1868, Lucien De Puydt described the women in "short sleeved chemises extending to the knees" (De Puydt 1868). Armando Reclus, writing around 1881, portrays them in blue skirts that go to their knees and specifically mentions a band of red and yellow (Reclus 1958/1881).

Mugana: the grandmothers

The early 1900s bring more detailed descriptions of the women and their extraordinary dress style, accompanied by photographic images as early as 1912 (Figs. 6.12, 6.13). Women at this time were wearing long chemiselike blouses with a large yoke and small, short sleeves made of plain or print fabric. Some blouses have mola work as a border along the bottom of the blouse, while others have broad panels of mola work that hang from the wide yoke. During this period, women began wearing wraparound skirts of printed trade cloth that reached almost to the ankle and covered a shorter underskirt that had painted designs. As in the past, they wore large nose rings, necklaces, and strands of beads wrapped around their arms and legs.

Reporting to the Smithsonian Institution about her visit to Kuna Yala in 1909, Eleanor Bell offers a brief description of the mola work: "Their garments consist of a short skirt and sort of chemise of colored cotton, composed of various layers of appliqué work neatly sewed together forming very curious designs" (Bell 1909, 630).

In his report to the Heye Foundation, A. Hyatt Verrill (1918) writes:

> The women wear a costume consisting of a trunk-like short skirt worn like bloomers, and, over this, a strip of cloth wrapped about the limbs and tucked in at the waist like a sarong. The upper part of the body is covered with the typical San Blas smock or blouse of richly decorated cloth. This article of apparel is the most striking feature of the San Blas women's costumes. The yoke and short sleeves are of solid color, while the body of the smock is worked into intricate and beautiful designs….

The writings of a tourist and adventurer give information about traditional women's appearance in 1922. Lady Richmond Brown, an adventurous British woman who visited the Darién area with her companion, Mr. Frederick Mitchell Hedges, wrote about their experiences and described the women and their molas: "The woman had her head and most of her face covered with a brilliant figured scarf, while her dress consisted of a remarkable-looking top, rather like a jumper, with another piece of cloth wrapped around her waist" (Brown 1925, 56).

Over the next fifty years the overall dress style changed gradually, becoming more form fitting. The large blouses and long loose skirts of the 1920s and 1930s were replaced by smaller blouses and shorter, more tightly wrapped skirts.

The mid-1920s was a time of transition in Kuna women's dress. While some women chose to change to Panamanian style clothing, the general response to efforts

6.12. Two women with gold nose rings and earrings and elaborate coin necklaces. "The necks of the women are loaded with necklaces made of red, white, or blue beads to which are added old Colombian silver coins. They also wear, occasionally, in their ears gold rings or disks... and in their noses always another ring of the same metal..." (Henry Pittier 1912, 637).
Fredrick Oliver, c. 1902-1906. Courtesy of the National Anthropological Archive, Smithsonian Institution. 55,584-587.

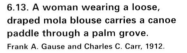

6.13. A woman wearing a loose, draped mola blouse carries a canoe paddle through a palm grove.
Frank A. Gause and Charles C. Carr, 1912.

6.14. A group of Kuna girls and young women. "The costumes of the women and girls are unique and pretty. They lay several squares of brightly colored cloth, one upon the other and by cutting away the material, show the various colors beneath in curious and intricate designs. These squares are used for the lower parts of children's dresses and for the fronts and back of their own blouses" (Core 1925, 176).
Photograph by Richard Marsh, 1924.

by the Panamanian police to suppress traditional dress and force women to change was intensely negative. Tension rose to the breaking point as descriptions of police ripping out nose rings, tearing molas, and obliging women to dance with them spread throughout Kuna Yala, and in 1925 a group of Kuna rebelled (see Howe, "The Kuna Portray Their Revolutionary History," in this volume). To this day, men as well as women refer to the beauty of traditional women's dress as an important aspect of Kuna identity.

6.15. Woman with a nose ring that hangs to her mouth and a large coin necklace. Luis Hurtado, a Spanish photographer, took hundreds of photographs of Kuna for their Panamanian identification cards. Luis Hurtado, 1942. Courtesy of Magdelena Hurtado.

6.16. Marina laughing, Tigantiki. Lionel Wafer described the massive necklaces worn by Kuna women: "She is a poor Woman who has not fifteen or twenty Pound weight upon her; some have thirty or more.... And the Women, besides these Chains, have sometimes Bracelets about their Arms, of a small quantity and of the same Materials twisted several times about" (Wafer 1699, 88-89). Mari Lyn Salvador, 1967.

Omegana yer dailege: beautiful women

Kuna women feel that they are more beautiful now than at any time in the past. Contemporary women put a great deal of effort into being attractive and indicate, in a general way, their interest in increased options and flexibility. Changes in dress style reflect changes in Kuna women's concepts of beauty. Traditional dress now, as in the past, is structurally much like a uniform in that, until recently, all women wore the same general outfit—mola blouse with skirt, scarf, distinctive jewelry, and short haircut. The elements of the outfit have stayed the same since the early 1900s, but the shape and style of each component have been altered significantly.

The mola blouses themselves have been modified over time. In the 1920s, they were large and loose fitting with tight sleeves. Through the years, they have become smaller and more tightly fitted, with the mola work filling all but the yoke and sleeves. In the early 1980s several significant changes were made that heightened emphasis on individuality and personal style within the acceptable boundaries of tradition. All the pieces are there and the dress is still distinctly Kuna, nevertheless there are several subtle, new options. Women began to wear fitted mola blouses with huge, puffy sleeves. Women speak enthusiastically about these refinements, explaining that the new top draws attention to the face. They continue to experiment with fancy new fabrics and with the size and shape of the blouse, adding more and more elaborate trim on the seam between the bodice and the yoke and on the sleeves.

Skirts (*sabured*) and scarves (*muswe*) made of imported print fabrics have been popular since the 1800s. While the skirt has changed very little, it is now being

6.17. Although the women dress in the same style, there are subtle variations. The printed patterns of the skirts and scarves vary and choices are made with care. Designing a mola blouse offers the women a great deal of freedom for self-expression. The young man playing a panpipe is an albino.
Mari Lyn Salvador, 1967.

6.18. Jacaline wears a traditional mola blouse and skirt, but unlike her mother, Rebecca, she does not use a nose ring nor does she wear arm and leg bands. Rebecca participated in Salvador's ethnoaesthetic research in 1974, and again in 1984.
Mari Lyn Salvador, Ailigandi, 1986.

6.19. Skirts and scarves hanging over the cross beams in the house.
Mari Lyn Salvador, Suitupu, 1992.

6.20. Woman holding a child. She uses her scarf to shade her from the sun.
Mari Lyn Salvador, 1986.

6.21. A cluster of safety pins becomes part of this woman's jewelry. "These are several Strings or Chains of Teeth, Shells, Beads, or the like, hanging from the Neck down upon the Breast, and to the pit of the Stomach…. Whatever Bugles or other such Toys they get, they find a place for them among their Chains…" (Wafer 1699, 87-88).
Mari Lyn Salvador, Ailigandi, 1986.

6.22. Beatriz Oller with nose ring and paint and daughter Belgiz in Panamanian dress. Both have decorative lines on their noses.
James Howe, Niatupu, 1975.

6.23. Ana Lopéz applies nose paint. "They temper them (body paints) with some kind of oil, and keep them in calabashes for use; and ordinarily lay them on the surface of the skin with pencils of wood, gnaw'd at the end to the softness of a brush. So laid on, they will last some weeks, and are renewed constantly" (Wafer 1699, 83).
Mari Lyn Salvador, Tigre, 1997.

6.24 (FAR LEFT). Gold nose rings. Diameter of largest, 2.0 cm. Clockwise from top: FMCH X97.5.13, X97.5.11, X97.5.14, X97.5.12.

6.25 (LEFT). Gold rings. In the 1960s, most women wore several rings on both hands. In the late 1970s and 1980s, many women sold them but by the 1990s they were popular again.
Diameter of largest, 2.5 cm. Left to right: FMCH X97.5.8, X97.5.9, X97.6.14, X97.5.7.

wrapped more tightly. For decades, the women used the head scarves to protect themselves from the sun and as an expressive device to hide or accentuate the face. Some women still use them when they travel or when they are dressed up, but no longer wear them everyday (Fig. 6.20). The scarf is now worn less often by young women, or worn in nontraditional ways—twisted behind the neck, or rolled and wrapped around the head.

Recent changes in personal adornment have centered on the upper portion of the body. The large gold nose rings of the past are no longer widespread, although having a long, striking nose is considered to be beautiful. Many women still feel that it is important to highlight the nose. Some have chosen to wear smaller and less noticeable rings, while others no longer wear them at all (Figs. 6.21, 6.22). Nose painting—a cosmetic option that does not permanently alter the body—continues to flourish (Fig. 6.23).

The huge gold earrings, breastplates, and coin necklaces seen in the photographs from the 1940s-1960s continue to be used for fancy occasions. In Figure 6.26, changes

6.26. Lelia, Dolecita, and Jesse Linares, three generations of women from the island of Ailigandi.
Mari Lyn Salvador, 1984.

6.27 (BELOW). **Gold necklace and earrings.**
Length of necklace, 27.5 cm. FMCH X97.510A,B,C.

6.28 (ABOVE RIGHT). **Gold chest plate.**
Gold, brass, glass beads, nylon monofilament. Length, 46.5 cm. FMCH X83.481. Gift of Dorothy M. Cordry in memory of Donald B. Cordry.

6.29. Gold earrings.
Height, 12.0 cm. FMCH X83.480A,B. Gift of Dorothy M. Cordry in memory of Donald B. Cordry.

6.30 (LEFT). **Beaded necklace.**
Beads, string. 24.0 cm. Private collection.

6.31 (BELOW). **Ornament.**
Beads, coins, string. 19.5 cm. Private collection.

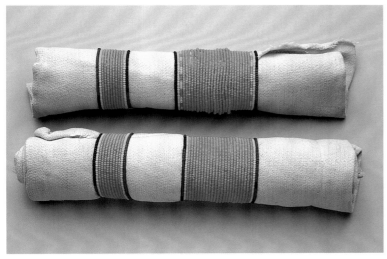

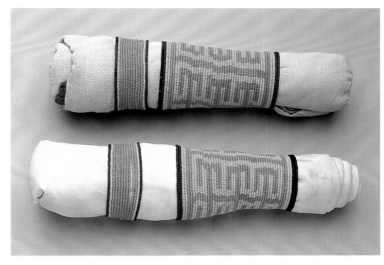

in dress and adornment over three generations are illustrated: Lelia, the grandmother, wears a large nose ring and coin necklace; her daughter, Dolicita, has a smaller nose ring and wears the gold breastplate her parents gave her; and Jessie has a mola sundress but no nose ring. Many women now wear small gold necklaces, even for everyday adornment.

The beaded arm and leg bands (*wini*) described in the early literature remain popular and have, in fact, become larger with more complicated patterns created in a wide range of colors. Now they cover the arms from the elbow to the wrist and the legs from just below the knee to the ankle. These elaborate bands are made by winding a single strand of colored beads in a planned manner so the borders and geometric bands appear as the strand is being wound around the limb (Figs. 6.32, 6.33).

6.32, 6.33 (ABOVE, LEFT AND RIGHT).
Wini, arm bands (left) and leg bands (right), wrapped around cloth.
Beads, thread, cloth. Private collection.

6.34. Leañi stands in the doorway just after her *inna.* **Her hair was cut short and her head is wrapped in a scarf.**
Mari Lyn Salvador, Tupile, 1984.

6.35. Schoolgirl with white ribbons in her hair.
Mari Lyn Salvador, Tupile, 1984.

Until the 1970s, women either wore the complete traditional outfit or had abandoned it entirely. By 1974, some women who had previously worn Panamanian dress began to wear mola blouses with skirts or pants, and many young girls now alternate between the two styles. At this time, there is more flexibility which allows for both continuity and change. Some women wear Panamanian-style dress in the daytime and traditional dress at night. Other women use Panamanian clothing for everyday wear and traditional dress when visiting, attending meetings in the gathering house, or representing the Kuna in the city or abroad. Schoolgirls shift with ease, wearing sundresses or shorts one day, and traditional dress the next (Figs. 6.34, 6.35). Regardless of which type of clothing they choose to wear, they maintain the same sense of finesse and personal style.

Molas over time

Although the origins of dress and the designs women used for body painting, and later used for their molas, are richly represented in traditional Kuna narratives, creating these patterns in trade fabric is a relatively new art form. In his book, Lionel Wafer (1699, 83) describes body painting:

> They make figures of Birds, Beasts, Men, Trees, or the like, up and down every part of the Body, more especially the Face, but the Figures are not extraordinarily like what they represent, and are of differing Dimensions, as their Fancies lead them. The Women are the Painters, and take a great delight in it. The Colours they like and use most are Red, Yellow and Blue, very bright and lovely.

These designs, first painted onto the body, then onto cloth, were later sewn onto the borders of the blouses. Women to this day make molas using birds, beasts, people, and other figures as designs, and still prefer the same basic color combinations: red, yellow, and dark blue or black.

Underskirts made of heavy cotton and painted with repeated patterns like those on baskets and leg bands were worn at least through the 1920s (Fig. 6.36). Some

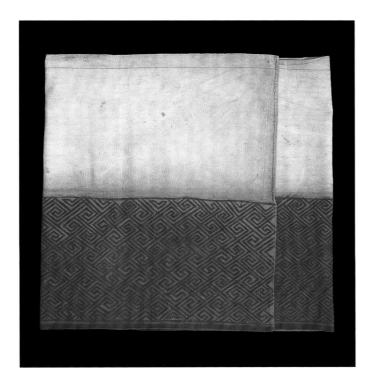

women still wear underskirts, but they are made from commercial fabric and are no longer painted. Many molas from the 1920s have designs similar to those used on the underskirts (Fig. 6.36). Some of these early mola blouses were long and had mola work only along the bottom like those described in the late 1800s. These tend to have simple, repeated geometric patterns like the one shown in Figure 6.37. The blouse in Figure 6.41, collected in 1918, has a similar design but was made using a sewing machine. By this time, women were using machines for putting the blouse together, and sometimes even experimented with machine stitching for the actual mola panels. To this day some women use sewing machines for the mola work; however, most women find it inefficient and consider it unacceptable because the stitches show.

Some examples from the 1920s have the entire bodice made from a single piece of cloth rather than a yoke with a mola panel attached below. The piece shown in Figure 6.41 has blue fabric for the blouse with a geometric pattern sewn on top of it, forming an appliquélike band along the bottom. The small sleeves are made from separate pieces of fabric and attached at the shoulder.

As early as 1906, some women were creating complex integrated designs with thin, even lines as seen in Figure 6.42. This example, with intense color on one side and pastels on the other, illustrates that although the women choose bright, colorfast fabrics and take great care with washing and drying their molas to preserve their color, exposure to light causes the cotton to fade, as is seen in many early molas (Fig. 6.43)

By the late 1920s women were making all of the types of molas that remain popular today. The style, complexity, and quality of the mola work varied greatly in the past, as it does in the present. These early molas often had abstract designs that were inspired by nature or were based on household objects. Women created these molas by reducing an object to its basic lines to make a geometric pattern and then replicating it. These designs often have specific names that identify the original source. The guava mola, for example, shows the fruit pod from the side, split open to reveal the seeds inside (Fig. 6.44). Wooden plates, seen from the bottom to expose

6.36 (ABOVE, LEFT). *Bicha*, underskirt, c. 1941. Patterns on the woven underskirts were originally painted onto the body and later transferred onto fabric.
51.0 x 128.0 cm. NMAI 20/4531. Collected by David B. Stout.

6.37 (ABOVE, RIGHT). Geometric mola blouse, collected by Erland Nordenskiöld, c. 1927. Designs similar to those on the underskirts were cut out and sewn onto the bottoms of early mola blouses.
83.0 x 85.0 cm. EMG 1927.27.876.

6.38. Woven hat bands hanging from house beam. Women have used similar geometric patterns in their molas for decades.
Mari Lyn Salvador, Tupile, 1974.

6.39. Mola blouse, collected by Erland Nordenskiöld, c. 1927. A wide border with geometric patterns is sewn along the bottom portion of this long, full blouse.
83.5 x 86.0. EMG 1927.27.875.

6.40. The geometric design carved on this gourd is similar to the patterns in early mola panels. This type of design continues to be popular to this day on some islands.
Mari Lyn Salvador, 1974.

6.41. Mola blouse with geometric design. Collected by A. Hyatt Verrill in 1918. In this early example, the mola work was sewn on a machine.
91.0 x 86.0 cm. NMAI 8/2613.

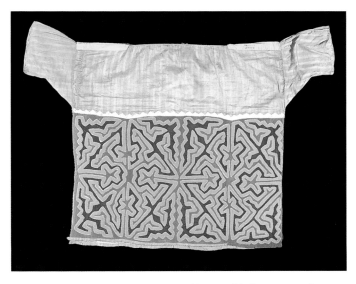
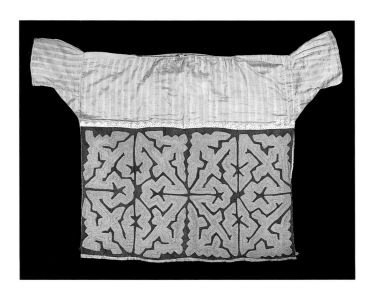

6.42, 6.43 (ABOVE LEFT AND RIGHT). **Mola blouse with fine geometric pattern (front and back shown). Collected by Eleanor Yorke Bell in 1906.**
68.0 x 69.0 cm. Smithsonian Institution. 26.33.59.

6.44. *Marya,* guava mola. **Women often illustrate objects from more than one perspective in the same design. The pod, although shown from the side, reveals the seeds as they would be seen through the split in the top. Yokes made from plaid fabric were popular in the 1920s.**
78.0 x 88.0 cm. NMAI 16/6456. Collected in 1922 and presented by Lady Richmond Brown and F. A. Mitchell Hedges.

6.45. *Batesor,* wooden plates mola. **Here the mola maker chose to depict these household plates from the bottom, revealing the carved wooden bases that create an X on the underside.**
65.0 x 83.0 cm. NMAI 16/6390. Collected in 1922 and presented by Lady Richmond Brown and F. A. Mitchell Hedges.

the carved geometric pattern on the base, served as inspiration for many early mola designs, as shown in Figure 6.45.

Blouses with more obvious figurative designs from outside Kuna culture are seen in collections from the 1920s as well. Molas based on foreign objects, package labels, books and cards, the type of molas that most people associate with the Kuna, became very popular by the 1940s and flourish to this day. The pair of umbrellas in Figure 6.46 is an early example of such a design. At this time, women began to create central, representational designs in the foreground with repeated geometric filler patterns in the background.

By the 1940s, women were representing a wide range of visual images that interested them, often based on new products in stores in Kuna Yala or things they might

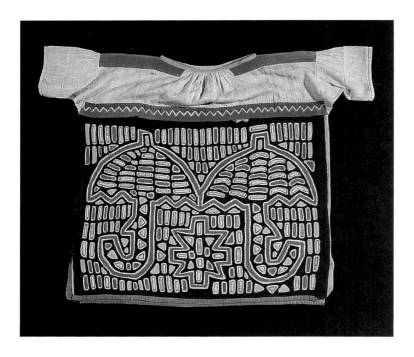

6.46 (ABOVE, LEFT). **Two umbrellas, collected by Erland Nordenskiöld, c. 1927. Women sometimes use umbrellas to protect them from the sun while traveling between islands.**
67.0 x 81.0 cm. EMG 1927.27.913.

6.47 (ABOVE, RIGHT). **Mola blouse inspired by Parrot Safety Matches box.**
66.5 x 57.0 cm. FMCH X83.182.

6.48. Moon with stars mola by Doralinda Denis, Suitupu, 1997. This traditional pattern has been created with particularly fine lines and small filler elements. The panel on the other side has an image of Dad Ibe, the sun.
63.0 x 108 cm. Private collection.

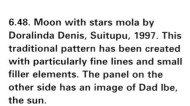

have seen in Panama City or Colon. As they copied labels and product trademarks, they began to use letters in their designs, as in Figure 6.47 which was copied from a Parrot Safety Match box. The artist even included the Swedish design element from the original image.

In the early 1980s, there was renewed interest in creating contemporary molas based on past designs. Figure 6.48, Stars and Moon, is an example of an old idea updated in the present style.

6.49. Ana Lopéz sits on a bench outside of her house attaching the yoke to the mola panels to make a blouse.
Mari Lyn Salvador, Tigre, 1997.

6.50. Lelia tends a large pot cooking over an open fire in the cooking house.
Mari Lyn Salvador, Ailigandi, 1984.

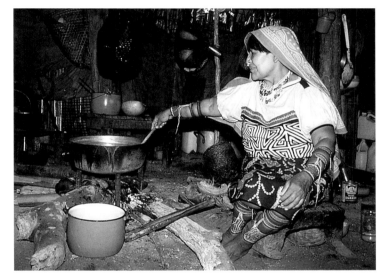

Mor maynamaloe: "Go make molas"

Despite its relatively recent development, the Kuna consider the art of making molas to be an integral part of their culture and important to their ethnic identity. They live in matrilocal, extended family groups. When a woman marries, her husband usually moves into the home of her mother and lives with her female relatives and their families. Women in the family share household responsibilities by allocating duties according to age. The oldest women take care of most of the heavy work, including cooking, a smoky and time-consuming job. Younger women spend some time taking care of the children, hauling water, washing clothes, and hulling rice. Women of this age may also take turns working in small stores. Young girls assume much of the responsibility for the care of the younger children in the household. This arrangement—the combination of matrilocality and the division of responsibilities by age—enables women from their late teenage years through middle age to spend many hours each day making molas.

6.51. Women often sit in the doorway, sew molas and visit.
Mari Lyn Salvador, Suitupu, 1994.

6.53. Drawing a mola pattern is the first step in the process. Here the woman is creating the outline for a mola figure for the co-op.
Mari Lyn Salvador, Suitupu, 1994.

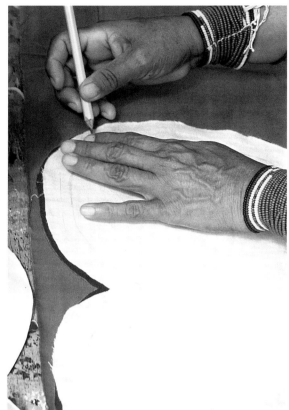

6.52. In the dim lamplight of the gathering house, women sit together listening to the chanting and sew.
Mari Lyn Salvador, Playón Chico, 1974.

6.54. Luisa Peréz finishing a mola with a bat design. With the tip of her scissors she opens small holes to reveal the fabric below.
Mari Lyn Salvador, Suitupu, 1997.

For women's meetings, village constables walk through the streets shouting, "*Mor maynamaloe*" (go make molas), to encourage the women to come to the gathering house (Sherzer 1976). Groups of women sit together sewing while listening to a visiting *sayla* (chief) chant about the history of mola making or to a discussion centered on some aspect of the women and their arts (Fig. 6.52).

Women sew while visiting, traveling, participating in village meetings, or sitting by themselves. Young girls are encouraged to learn to sew as early as they seem interested, which may be at the age of three or four; by the time they are five they usually play at sewing each day. They begin by sewing small scraps of material together or by cutting pieces of cloth to place in molas that women in the household are working on. By the time they are seven or eight, they may sew small designs on a piece of cloth for practice or even begin to do some stitching in small areas on "real" molas.

Mola making

The process of mola making, often described as appliqué, is actually a distinct technique in its own right. The basic sequence is draw, baste, cut, and sew.

To make a mola, the woman draws the design onto the top layer. Next she bastes carefully along the line and cuts about ⅛ of an inch on both sides of the basted line. She then folds under about ¹⁄₁₆ inch along the cut edge of the top layer and sews the folded edge to the base layer with fine, hidden stitches using matching thread. For a mola with more overall layers the process is repeated. Molas with "lots of colors,"

6.56. Animal mola. *Mor gwinagwad,* **one color.**
40.0 x 32.0 cm. FMCH X87.141.

6.55. Spools of thread. During the late eighteenth century, two Scottish ships brought a wide range of goods including, "Fourteen thousand needles, balls of twine and thread in black and grey and white" (Prebble 1968, 98).
Mari Lyn Salvador, Suitupu, 1994.

6.57A, B. Blue and black geometric *mor gwinagwad* mola in progress. The design was drawn, basted down, and then cut evenly along each side of the line. Little by little the edges are creased with the point of the needle and sewn down with tiny, hidden stitches.
37.5 x 31.0 cm. FMCH X97.5.109A,B.

6.58. Rubiela González, a Co-op member sews a geometric pattern that has been basted down.
Mari Lyn Salvador, Suitupu, 1997.

and complicated filler motifs require additional steps, including a wide range of finishing touches.

Women name molas in a number of ways. They use classificatory terms that identify the type of mola based on the number of layers or how it was made, such as *mor gwinagwad* (one color) and *obogaled* (two interlocking colors) and *mor gonikat* (many colors). They also identify certain kinds of design elements like *suigandamakaled* (long lines with teeth), or identify the content of the design, such as *sikwi mor* (bird mola). The subtleties of the mola-making process can be most easily understood in the context of each mola type.

Mor gwinagwad

Mor gwinagwad are called "one color" because Kuna women only count the color above the base layer. This earliest type of mola, also called grandmother style (*mugan*), continues to be popular today. These generally have repeated, abstract geometric patterns or pictorial designs with an integrated geometric filler (Fig. 6.57).

Obogaled

Obogaled molas are those that have two interlocking colors in one layer over the base. This complicated technique requires careful planning before the first cut. The artist starts with two panels. If there is a different design on the front and back panels, the woman draws and cuts the layer that she wants to go to the seam, which in this case is red. She removes the excess fabric, leaving an open space, and then folds over the edges and stitches them to the base. She then places the orange design into the space and stitches it to the base as well. In this case, the base layer, which is actually a print fabric, forms a very thin outline around the two interlocking designs. If the design is the same on both sides, the design is drawn, basted, and cut out of the top layer of each panel. The cloth in the spaces around the cut design is removed and transferred to the space opened by the same process on the other panel (Figs. 6.59, 6.60).

6.59. Gricelda Morris and Rubiela González working on *obogaled* mola panels. They have cut out a geometric pattern, removed it, and switched it to the panel of the opposite color. At this point they are organizing the design and will then baste it down and proceed with the stitching. Co-op house.

Mari Lyn Salvador, Suitupu, 1997.

6.60. Purple and green *obogaled* mola in progress. *Obogaled* means "changing, changing." Here a leaf design is cut out of the green fabric and the blue fabric. These are then removed and switched and put into the open spaces in the opposite color. Green leaves are placed into the space in the blue material and the blue leaves are placed into the space in the green. The edges will be stitched onto the pink base layer.

36.5 x 45.0 cm. FMCH X97.5.110A,B.

6.61. Lizards mola. *Obogaled*. The red outline fabric is placed directly on the base layer.

38.5 x 48.5 cm. Private collection.

6.62A, B. (ABOVE). *Mor gonikat,*
multicolored mola with intricate
design that was probably copied
from a book. Front and back shown.
34.5 x 42.0 cm. FMCH X97.3.1A,B.

**6.63. Two fish molas in various
stages of production.**
Largest panel, 33.5 x 37.0 cm.
FMCH X97.5.111A-F.

6.64. The needle is used to fold under the top layer of fabric, revealing multicolored mola work below. Mari Lyn Salvador, Suitupu, 1997.

6.65. Yoke trim from *ulu* **canoe mola by Doralinda Denis. Women were enthusiastic about the very fine trim on the seam on the bodice and on the sleeves of this blouse. The full blouse is shown in 6.79.** Mari Lyn Salvador, 1994.

Mor gonikat

Mor gonikat, "many colors," are the most complex and currently the most popular type of mola. The basic process is the same as previously described, merely repeated. The principal difference is in the treatment of filler areas and finishing details. Mor gonikat usually have at least two full layers above the base, but also have small areas of color placed under the top layer with small areas cut out to reveal the color below. These may also have embroidery, small areas of built-up motifs, or other kinds of surface decoration (Figs. 6.62-64).

Making a mola blouse

When the panels are completed they are sewn onto the piece of fabric that will form the front and back of the yoke. The seams are covered with a strip of material which is often decorated with rickrack, *dientes* (a handmade sawtooth outline), or other embellishments. A slit is made in the center of the yoke for the neck opening and the edge is finished with a contrasting color (Figs. 6.65, 6.66). The sleeves are gathered or pleated and attached at the shoulder. The sleeve opening is bound with a different color fabric and may be decorated with mola work, rickrack, or other fancy trim. Even though many women use sewing machines to put their blouses together, it is not common to use the machine for stitching the actual mola panels (Fig. 6.67).

6.66. Sleeve trim from *ulu* **canoe mola by Doralinda Denis.** Mari Lyn Salvador, 1994.

Kuna aesthetics

6.67. Benita Garcia assembles a blouse on a sewing machine. Mari Lyn Salvador, Suitupu, 1994.

Although there is an explicit emphasis on egalitarian principles and relative sameness, the Kuna have developed an implicit system of subtle differentiation. Prestige is generated by high-level performance and is evaluated, at least in part, using aesthetic criteria. Generally, the arena for women's performance is visual art—mola making—while the arena for the men is verbal art—chanting and political oratory.

Ethnoaesthetics, the study of artistic criticism from the perspective of the artist, offers an opportunity to understand Kuna expressive culture and leads to a better understanding of the ideology behind it. Through the analysis of their arts, it has become clear that the Kuna value talent, learning, competence, productivity, and eclecticism. Further, there are similarities in the structural principles that guide the verbal and performance arts as well as the visual arts. Parallelism and repetition with minor variation, subtle asymmetry, filled space, embellishment, and appropriate content—basic criteria for evaluating molas— are similar to those documented for Kuna speech, chants, lullabies, and flute music (see Kramer 1970, Sherzer and Sherzer 1976, Smith in this volume).

Basic to Kuna ideology is the concept of *gurgin*, which can be roughly translated as intelligence, natural aptitude, talent, and the ability to excel in artistic endeavors. Kuna believe that gurgin is distributed in varying degrees to all people by Muu, the spirit grandmother midwife (see Chapin, in this volume). One can have gurgin for any skill: hunting, political oratory, learning a foreign language, or making beautiful molas.

Kuna context for evaluation

Evaluation is a part of everyday life in Kuna Yala. Subtle judgments are made on the basis of a person's skill and finesse. Chanting and verbal abilities are taken into consideration in the selection and evaluation of traditional political leaders. The quality of the music and costumes as well as the dance performance is considered in evaluating dance groups in inter-island festivals. Women distinguish themselves through their dress; talented mola makers are esteemed and bring prestige to their families and communities.

The home is the primary context for evaluating as well as creating molas. Conversation and mola making go together, and friends often sit and sew and talk. Most of their commentary focuses on the subtleties of technical process in their own work as well as the work of others. Mola making represents a series of carefully considered decisions that reflect what women are thinking about, and provides access to a better understanding of Kuna thought and concepts of beauty. Which type to make? What style? What subject? Which designs to use: traditional or new? What fabric? Which colors? All have to be thought out before investing time, energy, and money in a new mola. Discussion about these decisions, commentary regarding how the molas the women are working on are progressing, evaluating the work of the young girls in the family, and sharing opinions about other women's molas are a part of everyday conversation. Visiting from house to house on one's own island, as well as visiting other islands, Panama City, Colon, or even the National Museum of the

Artistic criteria

The concept of rank ordering is not foreign to the Kuna. Women make molas of varying quality for themselves for different occasions and designate some as better than others. They compare their molas to those of their peers. For sale purposes, the Kuna have a consistent system of ranking molas by quality into price classes ranging from five to two hundred dollars (Salvador 1978).

The sophistication of the Kuna women's aesthetic system and the fact that Kuna women are very articulate about artistic criteria and indeed enjoy talking about molas became clear in 1966 when I was in Panama in the Peace Corps. Kuna women taught me to buy molas for Artesania Panameña, the co-op's retail store in Panama City, because they felt it was essential that I learn to pay the "proper" price for the appropriate quality mola and they insisted that I grasp the smallest details of evaluation.

In 1974, as part of dissertation research, I began a long-term study of the natural setting for performance and evaluation, using an aesthetic preference set of eleven molas to elicit specific information about artistic criticism and aesthetic preference. After discussion about type, design, content, sewing, and color, as well as the general impressions of overall qualities and draw-backs of a standard set of eleven molas, the women ranked them, often hanging them on a clothesline or on the edge of a boat.

Research in 1986 centered on changes in artistic criteria, and three molas were added to the standard set. Photographs of molas collected in 1927 by Baron Erland Nordenskiöld as well as those from the collections of the National Museum of the American

Indian, and the Smithsonian Institution were used to learn more about the names, sources, and interpretation of *sergan* (old) designs and to gain an understanding of contemporary Kuna women's views about the history of the art form. In 1994, Kuna representatives Cacique Leonidas Cantule Valdéz, Nicanor González, Serafina López, and Rodolfina Andreve visited the collection of the Smithsonian in Washington, D.C. In 1996, four Kuna who were knowledgeable about sergan designs visited the National Museum of the American Indian in New York: Cacique Carlos López, Balbina Denis, Elvira Torres, and Nicanor González traveled from Kuna Yala to see the original molas and document the collections. It is their interpretation that informs and guides the material presented in this chapter.

6.68. Cacique Carlos López, Balbina Denis, and Elvira Torres visit the National Museum of the American Indian.
Pam Dewey, 1996.

American Indian in New York, provides intensified contexts for presenting one's own molas and for scrutinizing other women's molas.

Artistic criteria

The Kuna aesthetic system is based on the skillful manipulation of the technical process and the amount of work involved, together with design considerations which include filled space, repetition with subtle variation, subtle asymmetry, visibility, complexity, and interesting subject matter.

6.69. Mola panels with four dancers. These were the front and back panels of a blouse before the yoke and sleeves were removed. The mola type, subject matter, basic organization, and color combination are the same. Nevertheless there are subtle differences. On the left, the figures have their hands on their headresses, the skirts are shown in front of the legs, and the eight subordinate motifs have pointed tips. On the right, the hands are on the hips, skirts are behind the legs, and there are nine subordinate motifs including the one between the figures.
43.0 x 103.0 cm. Private collection.

Visual organization

Kuna concepts of visual organization prescribe that designs should be generally balanced bilaterally and that all space should be filled. Both the right and left sides of a mola panel are more or less symmetrical. Main figures tend to be centered and balanced, and the filler elements in the background create a unified pattern. Molas with separate sections are usually divided bilaterally along the vertical axis or into quarters. Panel motifs occur in clusters of fours or eights, which are ritual numbers for the Kuna. Even though molas at first glance often appear to be symmetrical, the women actually emphasize subtle asymmetry in either the shape of the pattern, the color of the outlines, or the variation in the filler motifs.

Repetition is an important element of mola design. Abstract patterns and space fillers—geometric designs, slits, triangles, or circles—are repeated over and over. However, the repetition is consciously varied: either the shapes, the colors, or both differ. Front and back panels are always the same type, having similar color combinations and related subject matter, but are rarely exact duplicates (Fig 6.69).

Artistry

The women mention the importance of careful cutting and sewing as essential to creating fine molas. "Good" molas meet the basic rules of cutting and sewing. "Beautiful" molas are well cut and sewn, involve a great deal of work, are difficult to make, and are pleasing to the eye.

Skilled cutting creates a good design. Molas are considered to be most beautiful if the lines are straight and have distinct, clear-cut edges, parallel sides, and even spacing throughout. The line on the top layer should be about ¼ inch; the layer below even thinner, forming an even outline. The space on the base is usually a bit wider. The width of the line and the spaces between them should be even (Fig. 6.70). Each time the fabric is cut, it must be sewn down. The molas in Figures 6.71 and 6.72 are the same type and have very similar geometric designs. Women consistently mentioned the broad, uneven lines in the example from 1927 and pointed out that the new example was better because the lines were thin and even.

6.70. *Sikwi* bird mola, 1968. This *mor gwinawad* (one color) mola is an example of fine, even lines and an integrated design.
35.5 x 44.5 cm. Private collection.

Careful sewing is essential. Large, uneven stitches using unmatched thread evoke strong criticism. The stitches should be small, evenly spaced, as hidden as possible, and made with thread that matches the top layer. Stitches that show because the thread has faded create problems, so only colorfast brands are used. If stitches show because of inferior thread quality, however, the thread, and not the woman, is criticized.

Figure 6.73, a bird mola for tourists, breaks with most of the criteria for good quality, and therefore it helps to define the range of Kuna aesthetics. The stitches, though generally good, are too large and uneven, and made with unmatched thread in some areas. The lines are too thick and the spacing is too wide. Wide areas of the red top layer are left unfilled, most notably between the birds.

Women mentioned the unevenness of the spacing and the variation in the width of the lines. The wide spacing and lack of care in cutting and sewing were

6.71 (ABOVE LEFT). Geometric *mor gwinagwad* (one color) mola, collected by Erland Nordenskiöld, c. 1927. Spacing is broad and uneven, and there is little trim on the bodice and sleeves.
59.0 x 66.5 cm. EMG 1927.27.917.

6.72 (ABOVE RIGHT). Child's blouse with geometric design, c. 1968. This blouse, made for a young girl, shows care with every detail and was often praised by Kuna women who pointed to the fine, thin lines and tight points at the corners as well as the hand-made sawtooth trim on the sleeves and neck. Ailigandi.
35.0 x 41.0 cm. Private collection.

6.73. *Turista* **(tourist) bird mola, 1974. Although an excellent tourist mola, it was highly criticized. Ailigandi.** 35.5 x 44.5 cm. Private collection.

6.74. Angel mola, 1968. Suitupu. 59.0 x 79.0 cm. Collection of Nelson and Katherine Graburn.

described as time- and work-saving devices and were highly criticized. They agreed that it did not represent very much work, and explained that it was made just to sell. Although there was much criticism, it was also noted to be of a better quality than most tourist molas.

The worst fault of all is the lack of clarity or visibility. The design does not stand out—partly because of the variation in spacing and the widths of the outline, but mainly because of the colors used. All of the women said that the colors were *feo* (ugly) because they are far too *suave* (soft), or *pálido* (pale). The effects of combining unsaturated colors that show little tonal difference are diminished contrast and visibility. The women consistently laughed at and made fun of this example.

Visibility

What the Kuna refer to as seeing the design or visibility has mainly to do with contrast and color. Women explain that designs should stand out and that it does little good to go to the trouble of cutting and sewing several layers together if you cannot see the design. Several factors contribute to the sense of contrast, including hard edges between colors, regular spacing, and the use of closed figures such as circles. The edges between the layers are as sharp as possible given the cloth medium. Women select fabric carefully to get a hard edge and choose cotton poplin with a tight, even weave that will hold a crease rather than choose loosely woven materials that would produce a diffuse edge. Fine, close stitches contribute to the relative sharpness of the edge as well. The sense of contrast is further enhanced by the use of saturated colors and the combination of light and dark tones. Kuna women's preference for bright colors has been documented for decades. They do not like pastel shades at all, and although women in the co-op may use these shades in mola products made for sale, pastels have not been integrated into their own mola blouses.

The angel mola in Figure 6.74 was often ranked first in the 1974 research mainly on the basis of the amount of work involved, but was ranked much lower in 1984. Most women said that it was *mucho trabajo*, a lot of work. Several women mentioned the fine sewing, pointing out the small holes and filled triangles. Although many women ranked it first, saying that it was a great deal of work, they went on to criticize it on several points. They claimed that the design was too spread out and hard to see. Some women said that it was *demasiado*, too much. A common complaint was that there were too many small areas of color, and that there was no overall outline color in the middle layer. This design generated the most conversation over the years, with the most interest occurring in the 1970s. Women looked at it carefully and talked about it, and they argued about how it should be ranked. Yet, despite the great interest, no one copied it.

Filler elements

In order for a design to be acceptable to mola makers, space must be filled. There are several ways to accomplish this. Most methods involve cutting through the top layer, opening holes to expose a variety of colors below, or appliquéing bits of colored cloth onto the top layer. Some filler motifs are more difficult to execute than others. Molas that reflect obvious control of technique, in that their design elements are difficult to execute, are greatly appreciated. Designs with long, thin lines on the top layer are especially admired. These pieces are hard to cut evenly and difficult to hold in place while sewing them down.

Short parallel slits called *das das* can be made in the top layer and stitched open to expose small patches of different colors, which have been placed between the two layers. Das das, a simple yet popular way to fill space to this day, raises criticism if the slits are too large or uneven. Figure 6.69 is an example of good das das. Tiny circles (*gwini gwini*) and inset triangles (*wawanaled*) require patience as well as skill and the smaller the motif or filler element, the more work involved. Women demonstrate technical abilities and finesse by executing difficult filler elements, such as *ada ada* or *dientes*, a handmade rickrack used for the trim on sleeves or between the mola panel and the yoke, as well as for drawing attention to the outline of central figures. Embroidery, an easier and faster way to fill space, is generally only acceptable on most islands for decorative details, especially on a figure's face or for their hair. Above all, small even stitches made with fine thread are preferred.

Yet another way of filling space is to create an integrated design that minimizes the distinction between the central figure and background filler. The bird design in Figure 6.70 is a good example of fine, even spacing in which the subordinate space is filled with connected geometric patterns called *bisu-bisu*, a difficult and prestigious type of filler.

Women say explicitly that they make better molas today than their grandmothers did in the past. They go on to explain that the grandmothers figured out how to make molas, experimenting little by little as they went, and that women now are improving the technique. Contemporary women who are fine mola makers have such command of the process that they can make whatever they please.

As an example of the subtleties of technical refinement, compare Figures 6.75 and 6.76. The mola from 1974 was included in the original aesthetic preference set and the mola from 1986 was added the year it was made. These are the same design,

6.75 (LEFT). *Gwallu*, lantern mola, **1974. Ailigandi.**
31.0 x 45.0 cm. Private collection.

6.76 (BELOW). *Gwallu*, lantern mola, **1986. Ailigandi.**
54.5 x 64.5 cm. Private collection.

6.77. *Ua*, fish mola, by Leorbigilda Martinez, Ailigandi, 1986.
52.0 x 82.0 cm. Private collection.

6.78. *Yala*, mountains mola by Delia Méndez, Ailigandi, 1986.
60.0 x 98.0 cm. Private collection.

described by the women as sergan (an old design) and called *gwalla mor*. The name, "lantern mola," is based on the double mirror images of the outline of a lamp.

The 1974 version generated extensive discussion in the early research. Although most women agreed that it represented a great deal of work because it had several full layers and very fine sewing, it was ranked in the lower end of the top group because they felt the design was too simple. Principles of Kuna aesthetics dictate that outlines be thin and even throughout, which draws attention to shape and increases contrast. Women in both studies commented on the thin, even lines. In 1986, women used these two molas to demonstrate the primary difference between contemporary molas and those of the past. They pointed out that the design elements in the newer molas are thinner, straighter, and finer, and the stitches even smaller than in the earlier versions. All these aspects represent considerable refinement of the system.

Mountains

Beginning in the 1980s, women throughout Kuna Yala began to take a greater interest in grandmother (mugan) molas. They enjoy sergan designs from the 1920s and 1930s, and express a keen interest in "copying" the photographs of this type of design. Nevertheless, they made it very clear that they would modify the motifs by refining the spacing and using different colors if they so desired. These changes reflect contemporary aesthetic taste. At a more general level, the interest in the sergan designs demonstrates a widespread interest in the ways that the Kuna have lived in the past, at a time of introspection and rapid change in Kuna Yala.

The mola in Figure 6.78 was added to the standard set in 1986. The mountain design is based on a popular one from the 1930s created in contemporary colors. The style of filler elements, the very thin outline layer, and the tiny dientes line make this an outstanding mola.

Ua *(Fish)*

As an example of "looking back," the polka dot fabrics so important in early molas and almost totally absent in molas in the 1960s and 1970s are once again fashionable. Women are experimenting with the use of patterned fabric for the bottom layer, sometimes extending it to the sleeves and top of the blouse.

On some islands, the current trend is to make mola blouses that combine two previously discrete types of molas: one-color molas (mor gwinagwad), the oldest type of designs, with multicolored molas (mor gonikat). This provides an opportunity to maintain elements of a style they like from the past while managing contemporary stylistic changes. In Figure 6.77, a fish design, Leorbigilda Martinez has created a blouse that is ultramodern while also drawing on the past. She kept the style appropriate for each type discrete. For example, the background one-color (mor gwinagwad) area has geometric filler while the multicolor (mor gonikat) central figure has a pictorial design with repeated das das elements. The overall shape of this blouse is modern in that it has a tight bodice with large, flowing sleeves. In this way, Kuna women create a new style by combining modern and traditional elements in an innovative fashion.

Ulu *(Canoe)*

The mola in Figure 6.79, a canoe design, was considered to be beautiful in all regards. The blouse has elaborate trim which is widely appreciated by mola makers. The design is from a sergan mola and is an abstraction based on the side view of a boat combined with the outline of the view of the prow from the inside of the canoe (Figs. 6.79-81). This is an example of a sergan design done in a contemporary style. In Figure 6.12, a photograph taken between 1903 and 1916, the woman on the right is wearing a mola with the same design. Note the differences in the spacing and the evenness and width of the design elements, as well as the overall shape and size of the blouse.

Obogaled molas tend to have this preciseness and are particularly prestigious. Most of the obogaled molas the author has seen have been well made, perhaps because they require such a high level of skill that only women who are experts attempt to make them. Similarly, designs with thin lines that change direction radically, particularly at forty-five degree angles, are difficult to cut and sew.

Mola designs

Molas in collections from the 1920s to the present show innovative ways to create designs in fabric and a remarkable range of motifs from the simplest geometric patterns to complex pictorial designs with a concern for movement, realism, and perspective. Although all of the types of molas made today are also represented in the early collections, there are more one-color and obogaled molas in the 1920s-1940s, for example, and more mor gonikat, multicolored pictorial motifs that illustrate foreign objects or events, from the 1940s-1980s. Starting in the 1980s women also began to focus attention on the sergan designs from the past and to create new molas based on old motifs.

6.79. *Ulu*, canoe mola, by Doralinda Denis, 1994. Kuna women took great interest in this blouse, using it to explain what they meant by "Yer dailege!" and to show just how designs from the grandmothers have been refined. They particularly liked the choice of intense green, satinlike fabric for the yoke and sleeves, and the beautiful trim.
67.5 x 112.0 cm. Private collection.

6.80. View of a canoe prow as seen from the inside.
Vernon Salvador, 1974.

6.81. Canoe at the edge of the island.
Mari Lyn Salvador, 1997.

Sergan designs

The answer to the question "What is this design?" is often simply "sergan" or "mugan." Sergan refers to the pattern and means old or from the past, while mugan means grandmother and seems to refer more to the overall style and to carry the connotation of old-fashioned in a general sense (Fig. 6.82). There are very few really old molas in Kuna Yala in part because cotton fabric deteriorates quickly in the tropics and because a woman's molas are usually buried with her. Further, women have been selling their blouses to outsiders since the 1920s.

Young women do look to the grandmothers and their molas for inspiration. Muu Elena, a woman in her seventies, has always made sergan designs but now changes

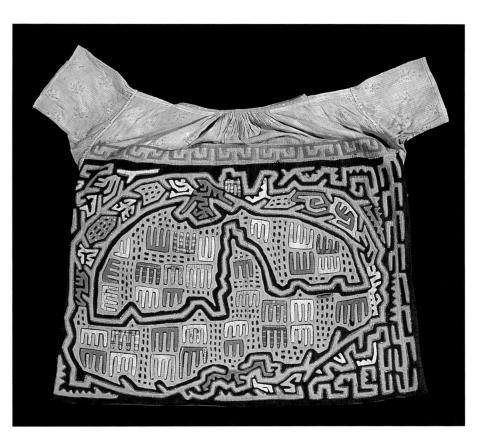

them to a more contemporary style. She likes the new shape of the yokes and sleeves and has her granddaughter change her mola panels into stylish blouses with big sleeves and fancy trim (Fig. 6.83).

Abstract designs

Some sergan designs are simply geometric patterns, while others are taken from basketry, beaded leg bands, and body painting, or from abstract designs based on images in nature or common household objects. This type of motif often has a descriptive name that identifies its source such as *nusu mor* (worm mola), *naa mor* (gourd mola), and *ake mor* (hook mola). Some retain qualities of the original object and are easy to recognize while others are so abstract that they must be explained.

To create this type of abstract design, women scrutinize an object, often turning it to observe it from all angles, and reduce it to what they consider to be the basic components of its form. Balbina Denis and Elvira Torres used this same technique to interpret the molas they saw at the National Museum of the American Indian. They rotated the blouse to see it from all angles and focused on tiny details as well as the overall image in order to discern what the design was. In some cases they figured out the design after exploring the mola carefully, tracing small areas with their fingers and discussing the possibilities. They quickly discovered that the design in Figure 6.84, for example, was based on frog's legs and explained that frogs are used for medicinal purposes in Kuna Yala. Often, Kuna women depict only selected parts of animals, not the entire body. Here only the stylized back legs are repeated four times in a design that presents them in opposing pairs. The mola panel is balanced bilaterally with the space divided into quarters, which is a common technique. Balbina and Elvira pointed out that this is a clear example of *suidamakaled*. *Suigan* means long elements, and *suidamakaled* refers to long elements with dientes (teethlike edges). Dientes are considered a difficult and prestigious technique because

6.82. Nonrepresentational mola blouse, collected by Erland Nordenskiöld, c. 1927. This blouse shows early experimentation with a central figure, small circular openings as filler elements and integrated geometric patterns in the background.
69.0 x 78.0 cm. EMG 1927.27.922.

6.83. Muu Elena from Ailigandi. Many older women maintain their interest in fashion, fastidiousness, and self-expression and continue to make molas as long as their health permits.
Mari Lyn Salvador, 1984.

6.84. *Nogi mali suid,* frog legs mola. *Nogi* is one type of frog or toad, *mali* means leg, and *suid* means long. This design is based on a particular kind of frog with long legs.

70.0 x 82.0 cm. NMAI 16/6408. Collected in 1922 and presented by Lady Richmond Brown and F. A. Mitchell Hedges.

of the complexity involved in cutting and sewing these multiple, small points. This mola is a fine example of attention to detail in both content and technique.

Some molas elicited enthusiastic and complimentary responses from the Kuna visitors. They exclaimed, "*Nued!*" and "*Yer dailege!*" (beautiful), as molas were brought out. Other molas did not evoke much interest or generated critical commentary. In one case of extremely poor quality, Balbina took one look at the panel and rubbed her eyes, humorously indicating her displeasure. In most cases, they handled the molas, turning them over, looking at the stitching on the backs of the panels, pointing to details in the design. One of the molas that drew an enthusiastic response was an *ake* (hook) mola panel shown in Figure 6.85. Kuna women make several kinds of hook molas and are quick to distinguish between them (see Figure P, p. 78, for an example of a different hook motif). This mola is based on a long vine with natural hooks that grows in the forest. It is a relatively realistic design and looks much like what it represents. The ake motif appears in the yellow vines that are "growing" vertically up the panel, with pairs of hooks facing one another. The overall pattern, created by repeating the paired motif, enhances the vinelike impression (Fig. 6.86).

Another example of natural forms that inspired a mola is the *diba mor* (spider) mola shown in Figure 6.87. This mola shows spiders and their webs. It is a relatively symmetrical design in red and blue layers that are placed on top of a base layer of print fabric. In these older mola panels, very little of the base layers shows. The calico of the yoke and sleeves is repeated as part of the ruffle on the bottom of the blouse, combined with red and white striped cloth.

Although women do make many designs that are simply repeated patterns, the content of some geometric designs becomes clear once it has been pointed out. Figure 6.89 shows spines from a forest plant. Within the panel there are eight groups of spines. The image emerges most clearly in the black layer of the two sections on the lower left side. The principles of spatial organization that guide mola making

6.85. *Akebandup aibinnit,* hook mola, c. 1967.

51.0 x 39.0 cm. NMAI 24/0701. Collected by Eva and Neville A. Harte. Presented by Dr. and Mrs. Arthur M. Sackler. Purchase from Mr. Harte.

6.86. *Akebandup,* vines with natural hooks that face each other.

17.0 cm. FMCH X97.5.48.

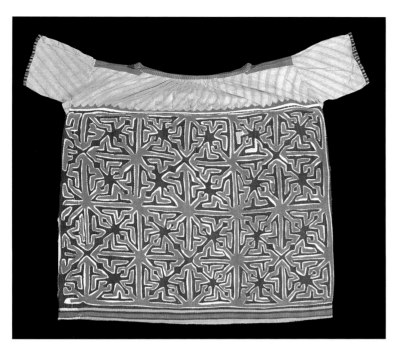

6.87. *Diba*, spider mola.
72.0 x 75.0 cm. NMAI 16/6357. Collected in 1922and presented by Lady Richmond Brown and F. A. Mitchell Hedges.

6.88. A spider in its web.
Mari Lyn Salvador, Ubigandup, 1997.

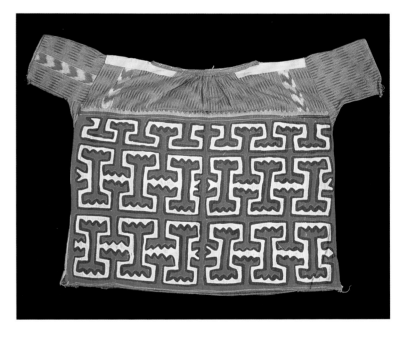

are similar to those that occur in other aspects in Kuna culture. For example, motifs in Kuna narratives are presented in units of four and ritual activities are repeated four or eight times. Here, the spine panel can be seen as two sets of four when the panel is divided in half vertically. Note that the elements are similar but not exactly the same.

Kuna interest in pairs, balance, and equilibrium is reflected in mola designs as well as in the verbal and performance arts (discussed by Joel Sherzer and Sandra Smith in this volume). Figure 6.90 is an example of balance achieved when opposing designs create a kind of equilibrium. The name of the mola is *sagiko abinned* (opposing forks), and this visual sense of opposition is created by depicting a specific kind of fork that has a set of prongs at each end. Not only are the forks themselves balanced by the prongs at both ends but the overall symmetry of the panel is maintained by the placement of each fork "against" another.

6.89 (ABOVE LEFT). *Ikomoro*, spines from a forest plant mola.
74.0 x 80.5 cm. NMAI 16/6490. Collected in 1922 and presented by Lady Richmond Brown and F. A. Mitchell Hedges.

6.90 (ABOVE RIGHT). Opposing forks mola.
69.0 x 89.0 cm. NMAI 16/6424. Collected in 1922 and presented by Lady Richmond Brown and F. A. Mitchell Hedges.

Animals play an important role in Kuna culture, and many of the molas illustrated in the introduction and Jorge Ventocilla's chapter show molas with animals that are presented in a recognizable way. The Kuna also depict the internal organs of animals, giving an indication of the Kuna interest in form and detail, and in presenting elements from more than one perspective. Figure 6.91 is a *gwage mor* (hearts) showing a pair of animal hearts that have been opened up from the center. Figure 6.92 illustrates the liver of a mountain pig. The outline of the design in the hearts mola is dientes; the design that encircles the liver design is *idi idi* (little radiating lines).

Kuna women, well known for their pictorial molas based on trade goods, were creating abstract designs based on foreign objects by the 1920s. Figure 6.93 is called *akwanan* (rock's mother) mola and the name most likely refers to the large grinding

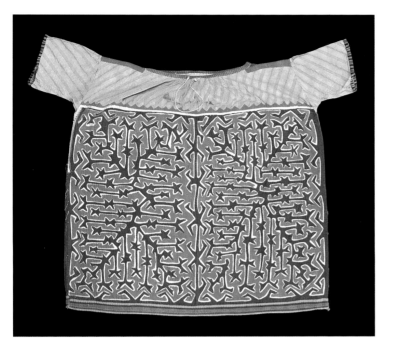

stone from a kind of corn mill that may have come from Germany and was sold by traders in Kuna Yala during the earlier part of this century. Cacique Carlos López remembered this brand of corn mill from his childhood. In the center of the image are four openings where the corn was dropped in to be ground. Figure 6.94, a well known design in Kuna Yala, is the steering wheel from a boat. Men as well as women on several islands remembered the kind of boat that had this type of steering wheel. The soft, muted colors are the result of fading.

Old and new

Copying designs is a favorite pastime for Kuna women. They trace their friends' molas and often draw designs they see while traveling. This leads to the proliferation of designs made over and over throughout the comarca for decades and illustrates some of the ways in which molas have changed and developed.

Over the past ten years women have shown more interest in copying or creating molas based on designs from the past. They copy old molas or photographs of older pieces by either tracing or making sketches which they use as a basis for making new versions of old designs that reflect contemporary aesthetic sensibilities. They are interested in the older molas, but are very clear about the fact that they have refined the technical processes and improved these designs over time. The *gannirgo mor* (chicken feet) mola (Fig. 6.95) shows a series of chicken feet, including legs and claws. These claws are an example of *nasi*, a kind of design element where projecting parts of an object cross, in this case these are the claws which are seen from above or below, creating an X-like shape. A new version of the chicken feet mola, collected in 1983, is shown in Figure 6.96. The old and new *nusu dummad* (big worm) molas are shown in Figures 6.97 and 6.98. The spots on the worm are described by the Kuna term *gwagwanaled* (piece and piece), referring to the little squares of fabric sewn along the body of the worm. Figures 6.99 and 6.100 are old and new *butalar* (sea urchin) molas.

Print fabric

In the early 1920s, beyond experimenting with the new mola-making process, women were trying out various ways to incorporate imported trade cloth into their

OPPOSITE PAGE:

6.91 (UPPER LEFT). *Gwage*, hearts mola.
71.0 x 77.0 cm. NMAI 16/6422. Collected in 1922 and presented by Lady Richmond Brown and F. A. Mitchell Hedges.

6.92 (UPPER RIGHT). *Yambina*, liver of a mountain pig mola, 1996.
36.5 x 41.5 cm. Private collection.

6.93 (LOWER LEFT). *Akwanan*, rock's mother mola (corn mill).
75.0 x 89.0 cm. NMAI 16/6449. Collected in 1922 and presented by Lady Richmond Brown and F. A. Mitchell Hedges.

6.94 (LOWER RIGHT). Steering wheel from a boat mola.
52.0 x 55.0 cm. Catalogue 42.56.35, Department of Anthropology, Smithsonian Institution.

THIS PAGE:

6.95 (ABOVE LEFT). *Gannirgo mor*, chicken legs mola.
72.0 x 75.0 cm. NMAI 16/6357. Collected in 1922 and presented by Lady Richmond Brown and F. A. Mitchell Hedges.

6.96 (ABOVE RIGHT). *Gannirgo mor*, chicken legs mola, 1983.
43.0 x 38.0 cm. FMCH X83.456.

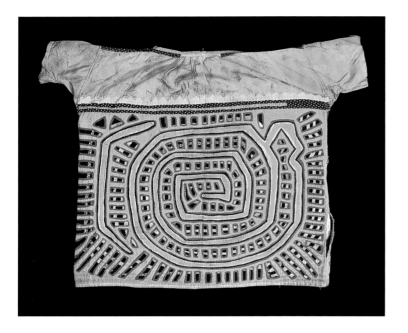

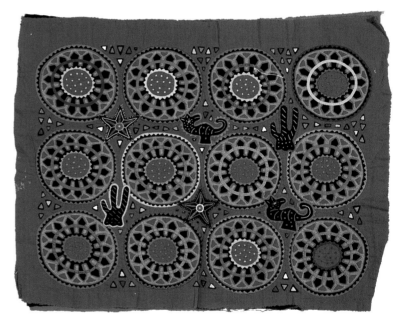

6.97 (UPPER LEFT). *Nusu mor,* worm mola, c. 1924.

85.0 x 80.0 cm. NMAI 12/7646. Collected by A. Hyatt Verrill.

6.98 (UPPER RIGHT). *Nusu mor,* worm mola, 1997.

39.0 x 49.5 cm. Private collection.

6.99 (LOWER LEFT). *Butalar,* sea urchin mola.

67.0 x 75.0 cm. NMAI 16/6372. Collected in 1922 and presented by Lady Richmond Brown and F. A. Mitchell Hedges.

6.100 (LOWER RIGHT). *Butalar,* sea urchin mola, 1997.

34.5 x 42.0 cm. FMCH X96.35.1.

blouses. We see many blouses with a wide range of prints used for the yoke and sleeves. During this time, polka dots, checks, plaids, and prints with small repeated floral or geometric patterns were widespread.

Throughout the 1920s and 1930s, and again starting in the 1980s, the same print is used for both the yoke and sleeves and as the base layer of the mola panels, creating a unusual look with less emphasis on contrast between the mola panel and the rest of the blouse (Fig. 6.101). The red and white print fabric as the base layer softens the geometric design of the black layer.

Using plaid as the base layer also produces a distinct look that was fashionable in the early years but has not been popular since. Women consistently criticized this type of mola saying specifically that the grandmothers made these molas but that they did not like them. Balbina Denis criticized the mola in Figure 6.102, which has a base layer made from print fabric, saying that she did not like the use of the plaid because she found it distracting. She explained that this kind of patterned cloth was not meant for the panels themselves, but only for the yoke and sleeves. This blouse is an example of *ogwagaled*, which means "changing, changing"; the front and back panels are the reverse of one another. Here the interlocking patterns, one in red and the other in orange, are stitched over a plaid base.

As indicated by photographs of Kuna women over the past eighty years, the imported material they use for scarves and skirts has made them familiar with hundreds of patterns. Women especially enjoy looking at printed fabric and make a pastime of visiting the stores in Kuna Yala. It is likely that many of the geometric patterns that do not have traditional names were inspired by patterns on commercial textiles.[2] Figure 6.103, collected in 1993, has a bat design inspired by the skirt material shown in Figure 6.104.

Inspiration

Women illustrate things that interest them, and almost anything a woman sees or hears about may become the inspiration for a pictorial mola. Designs are based on elements common in Kuna Yala, are drawn from Kuna culture, or may be from outside. Any Kuna woman can create a new design but they most often copy designs from existing molas. These may be from their female relatives or friends, or from the innovative molas that circulate throughout whole villages. As women visit they copy molas they like and fads spread throughout the comarca. They also freely copy designs from photographs. For specific events, such as dance performances or puberty ceremonies, several women may decide to wear the "same" mola. Often one woman creates a design and the other women in the group copy it for their own blouses. Nevertheless copies are rarely the same as each woman makes subtle changes for her own blouse. Some women are noted as being especially good at designing new molas.

Motifs based on elements from the local environment are things the women see again and again, while objects or experiences foreign to Kuna Yala which have been seen briefly but are not available at the time the mola is made also serve as inspiration. Women scrutinize labels from the foreign products that fill the shelves in stores in Kuna Yala for designs, often copying minute details such as trademark symbols and logos. Sometimes Kuna living in the city buy cards or magazines, or even sketch subjects they think their friends or family members might like, and send them to Kuna Yala.

There is a difference in the creative process between the designs based on objects the women have in front of them, like plants, fish, or animals, or the redesign of a pattern based on a drawing or an existing mola, as compared with those based on something that the woman might have actually seen but may not have access to while she designs a mola. Women create designs from objects they see or events they participate in, such as the girls' puberty ceremony, but that are not available to refer to while working on the mola. They listen to narratives in the gathering house and illustrate the primary characters and activities in their molas.

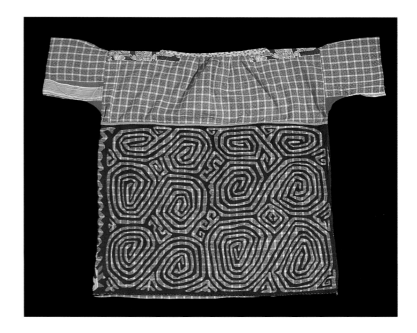

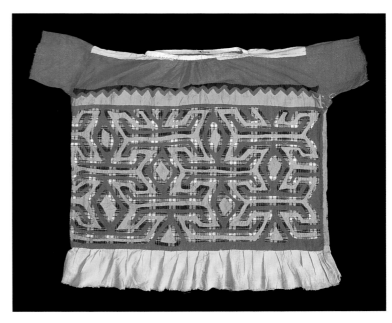

6.101. Mola blouse with black geometric design over print fabric, collected by Henry Wassén, c.1935. 66.0 x 85.0 cm. EMG 1935.15.21.

6.102. Mola blouse with red and orange geometric design over plaid fabric. This is an example of ogwagaled in that the red and orange designs are all interlocking and both are sewn onto the plaid base. The cut out section of the design is placed in the space left in the overall orange layer and the orange cut-out goes into the overall red layer. 67.5 x 81.5 cm. NMAI 16/6366. Collected in 1922 and presented by Lady Richmond Brown and F. A. Mitchell Hedges.

**6.103. Blouse with a bat design, 1994.
Women in Carti were particularly
enthusiastic about this blouse. They
liked the design and the small circle
fillers with varying colors under-
neath.**
59.5 x 95.0 cm. Private collection.

**6.104. *Sabured*, skirt made from
printed fabric (detail) with a bat
design likely to have inspired the
mola in Figure 6.103.**
136.5 x 84.0 cm. Private collection.

**6.105. Interior of a Kuna store in
Wichubwala. Beyond sodas, canned
food, and household goods, these
stores stock bolts of brightly colored
fabric the women use to make molas.**
Mari Lyn Salvador, 1997.

Designs can also be based on things they have only heard about during conversations about life outside of Kuna Yala, including spaceships or events such as boxing,
as people return from travel to the city or abroad. Women make keen observations
and discuss what they like. Although they do sometimes make sketches, they always
make mental notes, enabling them to remember elements of a design.

Motifs from the outside

The Kuna are protective of their traditional lifestyle, showing exceptional cultural
resilience and continuity. Nevertheless their tastes are eclectic and they are not
opposed to incorporating foreign elements into their expressive arts as long as they
can be made to fit comfortably within their cultural criteria. Missionaries, anthropologists, doctors, military personnel, Peace Corps volunteers, and, more recently,
shiploads of tourists have brought a wide range of new ideas and material goods to
Kuna Yala. For the Kuna themselves, travel outside the Comarca and long stays in
urban centers have become common among many families. Elements such as scissors,
elevators, and swivel chairs, have been included in
narratives; helicopters, Santa Claus, Mickey Mouse,
and product labels often appear as designs in molas.
Nevertheless, these outside elements are integrated in
"Kuna ways."

Foreign products

Boats loaded with trade goods have been coming
to Kuna Yala for decades. Colombian boats bring
hammocks, household goods, coffee, sugar, cookies,
and so on to trade for coconuts. Kuna cargo boats travel
from Colon through Kuna Yala carrying clothing,
canned foods, soft drinks, and sometimes even ice
cream. Lots of Panamanian and imported products
fill the stores and serve as a popular source of designs
(Fig. 6.105). Labels on cereal boxes, milk cartons, or

6.106. Anheuser Busch trademark mola.
49.0 x 56.0 cm. FMCH X82.606.

6.107. Design based on a box of Super X shotgun shells.
32.0 x 40.0 cm. Private collection.

6.108 (ABOVE AND RIGHT). **Side 1: Clock mola.** This design seems to be from an alarm clock or a pocket watch with engraved floral designs. **Side 2: Cuckoo clock mola.** Leaves, birds, and other elements from the clock are spread over the design. The clock is shown upside down.
46.5 x 60.0 cm. FMCH X82.872. Museum purchase in memory of Sidney S. Kallick.

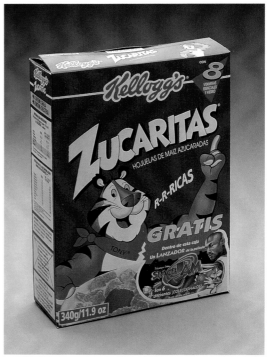

6.109. Tony the Tiger is shown with his characteristic broad smile and whiskers. Women in the Mola Co-op now make Tony the Tiger masks.
47.0 x 50.0 cm. FMCH X82.613. Museum purchase in memory of Sidney S. Kallick.

6.110. *Zucaritas* (Kellogg's Frosted Flakes) cereal box.
33.5 cm. Private collection.

matchboxes, and graphics from soft drink bottles and tobacco cans are copied, and appear as themes in molas.

Kuna women's interest in representing elements from outside their environment is evident in 1920s molas in museum collections. For example, Figure 6.46, collected in 1924, shows two umbrellas, and Figure 1.44 (p. 50) illustrates the Arabia, a commercial boat that traveled to Kuna Yala in the 1920s. The Anheuser Busch trademark that appears on beer cans, bottle tops, and shipping cartons provides inspiration for one mola (Fig. 6.106), while the label of a box of Super X shotgun shells inspires another (Fig. 6.107). Figure 6.108 shows a cuckoo clock with the doors open and a bird on top. This panel was put onto the yoke of the blouse upside down. The reverse side shows what appears to be an alarm clock.

One complicated and intriguing blouse depicts the design on a package of Army and Navy embroidery needles: a gunboat and plane with an eagle on top on one side (Fig. 6.112) and planes and birds with people in their claws on the other (Fig. 6.111)

Transportation, the Canal Zone, and the U.S. military

Travel in Kuna Yala is mainly by sea, and a wide range of boats and dugout canoes are represented in molas. Commercial planes that fly daily between Kuna Yala and Panama City or Colon are common themes and women also depict helicopters and even the occasional spaceship. Military planes and helicopters carry Panamanian and American doctors as well as political and military personnel to and from Kuna Yala. A four-engine air force transport plane is shown in Figure 6.114; a helicopter with the name "Sikorsky" on the fuselage is illustrated in Figure 6.115.

Kuna men have been working in the Canal Zone for years and have sent pictures of machines and technology to the women in their families, providing yet another source of imagery for mola designs. Figure 6.121 is based on an American military insignia. Another mola shows a radar station with men and women inside and others on a top level, running the unit (Fig. 6.116). The splashdown and rescue operation of the Gemini 5 Titan Rocket in 1965 is illustrated in Figure 6.117. As the men return

home, women listen to their accounts of life in the Canal Zone, rich with descriptions of experiences and events. In the spaceship mola (Fig. 6.118), the artist has combined men parachuting, which she may have actually seen, with the insectlike shape of a spacecraft she had heard about. This ingenious mola became a fad in the late 1960s.

Entertainment and humor

Women draw on a combination of their personal experiences and the representations of pictorial materials for their designs. Although televisions are rare in Kuna Yala, women do enjoy watching TV while in the city, inspiring molas such as the logo for Channel 2 (Figs. 6.123). Boxing is a popular event in Panama; the mola in Figure 6.119 is likely to be a combination of an event the woman has heard about and perhaps a poster advertising the fight. The boxers are inside the ring and the ropes are behind them. One of the upright man's legs is actually placed in front of the fighter who is falling. Spectators and bells are stylized.

Humor is expressed in the verbal as well as the visual arts. Women joke and tease playfully as they go about their daily routine and enjoy molas with humorous motifs. During the 1974 research project women commented on the hilariousness of the Mosquito Evangelita mola (Fig. 6.120), often mentioning that it must be from an ad for insect repellent. An army re-enlistment poster is presented with a lighthearted image in Figure 6.122. Women thought it was funny to wear a mola with a somewhat realistic illustration of a bra—complete with fasteners—on one side and matching panties on the other (Figs. 6.125, 6.126).

6.111 (ABOVE LEFT). **Planes and birds mola. This mola raises several questions. Why are the people falling out of the planes and what are the birds doing? Are they attacking or are they carrying the people to safety?**
58.5 x 55.0 cm. FMCH X80.169 (SIDE 1). Donated by Alice Jean Minkus in memory of Robert Minkus.

6.112 (ABOVE RIGHT). **Needle book mola. Gunboat with a flag and drifting smoke and a plane with an eagle on top on one side, from a needle book.**
58.5 x 55.0 cm. FMCH X80.169 (SIDE 2). Donated by Alice Jean Minkus in memory of Robert Minkus.

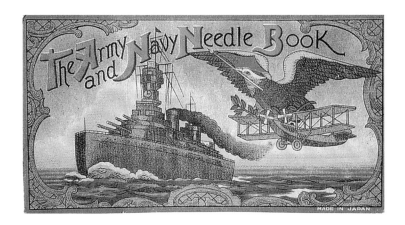

6.113. The cover of a needle box, illustrated on the mola in Figure 6.114.
Ann Parker and Avon Neal, 1977.

6.114. Transport plane mola. The plane has "US AIR FORCE 495" on the side, the registration number on the tail and personnel in the windows. The artist filled the background with whimsical images. 40.0 x 52.5 cm. FMCH X82.598A. Museum purchase in memory of Sidney S. Kallick.

6.115. Helicopter mola. Sikorsky is the name of the manufacturer. On this side the artist included a submarine with a man catching a turtle with a fishing line. 42.5 x 54.0 cm. FMCH X82.598B. Museum purchase in memory of Sidney S. Kallick.

6.116. Radar listening station mola. Here the operators seem to be wired to the listening device that is attached to the parabolic reflectors. Subordinate figures could be planes seen from above and the two figures standing behind the cars are waving to the men and women inside.
61.0 x 57.0 cm. FMCH X82.873. Museum purchase in memory of Sidney S. Kallick.

6.117. Titan Rocket mola. Here the splashdown and rescue of a space capsule is illustrated. The side has been cut away to show the astronauts inside and a frogman holds a line from the tip of the space craft to the waiting helicopter. The letters identify "El Astronaut Norteamerican Gordon Cooper" who was aboard the Gemini 5 Titan Rocket when it took off on 21 August 1965.
41.5 x 49.0 cm. FMCH X82.603. Museum purchase in memory of Sidney S. Kallick.

6.118. Spaceship mola. Parachutists fill the space around the insectlike spacecraft. 1967.
58.5 x 75.0 cm. Private collection.

6.119. Boxing mola, 1968. On side one, a spiritlike figure hovers over the body of the falling boxer, and the legs of the two men are actually crossed.
52.5 x 66.5 cm. Private collection.

6.120. Mosquito mola, 1968. The letters say "mosquito evangelita." The filler elements are particularly fine and the sleeves are in the style of the 1960s.
60.0 x 72.0 cm. Private collection.

6.121 (BELOW LEFT). **Military emblem mola. The lettering indicates that this is probably an emblem from Fort Sherman in the Canal Zone.**
42.0 x 54.5 cm. FMCH X82.616. Museum purchase in memory of Sidney S. Kallick.

6.122 (BELOW RIGHT). **Army re-enlistment poster mola.**
66.5 x 57.0 cm. FMCH X82.882. Museum purchase in memory of Sidney S. Kallick.

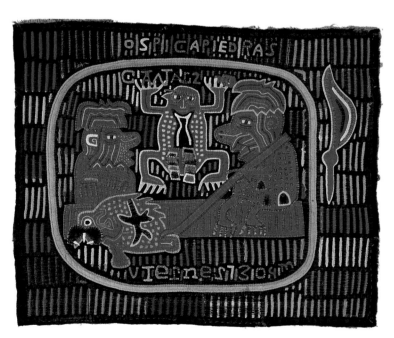

6.123 (ABOVE LEFT). **Logo for television station Channel 2.**
52.0 x 38.5 cm. FMCH X82.878. Museum purchase in memory of Sidney S. Kallick.

6.124 (ABOVE RIGHT). **"The Flintstones" mola, showing Fred Flintstone and Barney Rubble framed inside the shape of a TV set with lettering that notes that the show can be seen on Friday nights at 7:30 on Channel 2.**
44.0 x 37.0 cm. FMCH X82.601. Museum purchase in memory of Sidney S. Kallick.

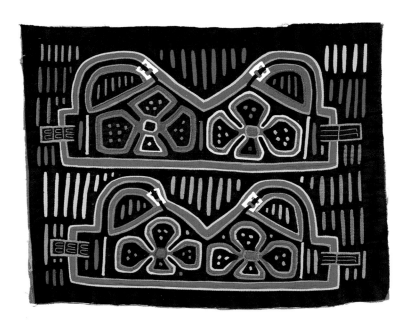

6.125. Two bras mola, 1967. The hooks and fasteners are treated in a realistic fashion; the filler in the background is called *das das*.
33.5 x 41.5 cm. Private collection.

6.126. Four pairs of panties mola, 1967. In the mid 1960s, women on the island of Nargana asked one of the women in the Peace Corps to teach them to make dresses and lingerie. Searching for a large amount of light, silky material, the innovative volunteer talked someone from the Canal Zone into giving them a parachute for the project. Such sewing experiments eventually led to the development of the Mola Co-op.
35.0 x 42.0 cm. Private collection.

6.127. John F. Kennedy memorial mola, 1967. One of the posters or memorial images of President Kennedy, abundant in Latin America in the late 1960s, was likely to have been the inspiration for these panels.
44.5 x 99.0 cm. Private collection.

Posters and books

The abundant supply of books, magazines, comic books, and posters in Kuna Yala serves as inspiration as well. There are small libraries on several islands; the missions have bibles, catechism books, and religious pictures; a few people get newspapers or magazines, and around election time political posters abound.

Although Kuna Yala is an autonomous region, the Kuna vote in Panamanian national elections. Mainland politicians come with flags and posters to campaign, and Kuna women use these images and the symbols of the political parties in their molas. Movimiento Nacional Liberación (Fig. 3.9, p. 100) shows a worker breaking the chains that enslave him. The main figure is translated quite realistically; his muscles are bulging, his hands are strong, his eyes are cast upward. The chains are circles of fabric actually linked together, with the last one broken. The details from the poster on which it was based are realistic, but the subordinate figures are quite stylized. Dr. Máximo Carrizo, a Panamanian Republican Party candidate, is depicted surrounded by flags and party emblems (Fig. 3.8, p. 99).

Images of President John F. Kennedy, a popular American figure in Latin America in the 1960s, have been integrated into molas as well. Figure 6.127 is likely to have been based on a commemorative poster. It has the U.S. Presidential insignia, rocking chair, and "P.T. 109 boat," symbols often associated with JFK. Jackie Kennedy, daughter Caroline at her side, is shown with her signature hairstyle and purse, as well as being depicted wearing a necktie, a marker the Kuna use to indicate an important person or someone acting in an official capacity.

Catholic and Baptist missionaries have been in Kuna Yala since the early 1900s; in the 1960s, bible molas were very popular. These were often copied from catechism books or religious cards. Many designs interpret bible stories, including Noah and the Ark, Adam and Eve, and the Crucifixion. Molas with biblical themes seem to come and go. Figure 6.128, collected in the 1970s, shows the Crucifixion with a soldier bearing a lance, Mary mourning at the foot of the cross, and a man on the right reaching for the ladder. An earlier version of the same design collected in 1938 includes the symbols of the passion (Fig. 6.129).

6.128 (ABOVE LEFT). *Cristo*, Christ mola, by Rebecca Harris, Ailigandi, 1968. On side one, the soldier pierces Christ's chest with his lance, as mourners kneel at the base of the cross. The phrase *"pap machi purkwisa"* means "the Son of God died."
51.0 x 75.5 cm. Private collection.

6.129 (ABOVE RIGHT). *Cristo* mola, c. 1938. Christ is shown in black in both of these molas to indicate that he is dead. The passion images at the left include the rooster, the veil of Veronica with the face of Christ, and a jar of oil. On the right side are the lances, the ladder, and other implements of the Crucifixion.
55.0 x 54.0 cm. Catalogue 38.56.41, Department of Anthropology, Smithsonian Institution.

6.130. "R" mola.
34.0 x 46.0 cm. FMCH X97.3.12A.

6.131. "S" mola.
33.0 x 40.0 cm. FMCH X97.3.12B.

6.132. La Cucharita Martina mola. Martina puts a nice Christmas treat of almonds, rice, and raisins on to cook for Perez and goes outside to sweep her patio. Perez smells the delicious dish, leans over to taste it, and falls in.
39.5 x 42.5 cm. FMCH X82.605. Museum purchase in memory of Sidney S. Kallick.

Letters have been popular in molas since the 1940s. Embroidered or cut out of fabric, they can identify the artists, the occasion for which the mola was made, or the subject of the design. Women take letters from the images they copy. Beyond the intention to communicate information, they use letters as decorative features and playfully fit them into the overall design, sometimes turning the cut-out forms upside down or backwards. Figures 6.130 and 6.131, probably taken from a child's book about the ABCs, show raccoons peeking out from behind the letter R and squirrels climbing on the letter S. In some mola designs, a double S represents sea cucumbers, while in other instances a similar design has been modeled from the Singer sewing machine logo. The mola of La Cucarachita Martina (The Little Cockroach Martina) illustrates "Perez and Martina," a popular Puerto Rican folktale that tells the story of a refined Spanish cockroach who falls in love with a mouse (Fig. 6.132).

Molas that depict comic book characters have been popular since the 1960s. Hawkman struggles with fantastic creatures, and Tarzan rides with Cheetah on the back of an elephant while accompanied by a lion and birds (Figs. 6.135, 6.133). Leonardo, Donatello, Raphael, and Michelangelo (the Teenage Mutant Ninja Turtles) are shown in action, while another panel depicts Leonardo relaxing in a hammock under coconut trees (Figs. 6.134, 1.45, p. 51).

Women and the economy

Over the past thirty years, the Kuna economy has shifted from a system based mainly on exchange to one based, at least in part, on cash. Well into the 1970s coconuts were used for trade. Products from the Colombian boats were traded for coconuts which could also be used to purchase things in the Kuna stores. Although they are still used as a mode of exchange the emphasis is now on cash.[3]

6.133. Tarzan mola. Edgar Rice Burroughs's lord of the jungle is portrayed with his animal friends. Letters are cut out as separate pieces and are often turned around or re-ordered in the way the woman thinks they look best. In this case, she left off the "T" but the image is easily recognized.
31.5 x 37.5 cm. FMCH X96.25.9.

6.134. Teenage Mutant Ninja Turtles mola, Carti, 1996. These cheerful Ninjas are portrayed with their initials on their belts, their names along side each one, and their weapons poised and ready to fight injustice.
36.0 x 42.0 cm. FMCH X96.25.4.

6.135. Hawkman™ mola. Based on a 1960s comic book this mola shows Hawkman in his "old style" helmet fighting gallantly against evil. The artist has captured his hovering stance but has chosen to depict him without his traditional wings.
45.0 x 44.0 cm. FMCH X82.608A. Museum purchase in memory of Sidney S. Kallick.

6.136. Hawkman comic book.
Courtesy DC Comics Inc.

6.137. Young girls and women selling molas on the steps of the Baptist church on the island of Ailigandi.
Mari Lyn Salvador, 1974.

Men generate cash by diving for lobsters and working for wages, mainly in Colon and Panama City. Over the past twenty years women have developed a strong business in the sale of molas and mola artwork, and play an ever intensifying role in the economy. Beyond purchasing jewelry and fabric to make mola blouses, these women now provide cash to purchase food and household commodities, to support family members living outside Kuna Yala, to send their children to school, and to travel. More and more emphasis has been placed on selling molas and creating mola products for sale. Given their contributions to the economy, many Kuna women are currently raising issues regarding their participation in the decision-making process, and have clearly expressed their interest in gaining a stronger voice in the gathering house.

Making molas for sale

To this day, women mainly create traditional mola blouses for themselves to wear. Although they sew blouses for their young daughters and nieces and occasionally make a blouse for another woman who might not be able to sew her own, only

rarely does a woman sell a mola to another Kuna woman. They have, however, for decades sold used blouses that are out of style, faded, or those they have lost interest in to tourists. If they need the money, some women sell blouses that they like and are still using. Blouses are sometimes taken apart and the mola panels sold separately. Lady Richmond Brown mentions in her book that she bought sixteen hundred mola blouses during her travels in 1924.

Scientists, missionaries, researchers, commercial buyers, and more recently hundreds of tourists have over the years bought thousands of molas and taken them back to their countries throughout the world. When small numbers of tourists arrive on an island, women often deal with visitors themselves, although some do prefer to send the younger children in the household to sell their molas (Fig. 6.137).

January brings crystal blue skies, relatively calm seas, and cruise ships with thousands of tourists to the Carti area. Tours range from huge luxury liners that dock just outside the reef and send hundreds of tourists zipping around in speed boats, to smaller vessels that pull right up to the islands. As word spreads that a ship is due to arrive, women from nearby islands take molas, dresses, T-shirts, and a wide range of toys, beads, and small items to hang, in open market style, along the street or clustered in an open space designated for the purpose. Visitors stroll through the streets, buying products and taking pictures. Most transactions require cash except on some islands with high tourist activity like Porvenir, where credit cards can be used (Figs. 6.138-140).[4]

For decades, Kuna women have been sending molas to the city with the men in their families, who sell them to the doctors and military personnel, or market them to retail stores. Men often carry a few molas to sell when they travel abroad as well. Recently, with so many women living outside Kuna Yala, they market their own molas at street fairs or to retail stores. The mola co-op and other Kuna owned mola production enterprises market a wide range of mola products locally and

6.138. Shopping on the island of Yandup. Tourists walk around where women have set up marketlike stands with molas, mola products, and sometimes even live lizards. Mari Lyn Salvador, 1997.

6.139. The Mayan Prince docked at Yandup. Mari Lyn Salvador, 1997.

6.140. "Mayan Prince" mola. 1997. This tourist mola, made by a man, is more like an appliqué picture than a mola. These are sold to tourists as they visit Yandup. 34.5 x 38.5 cm. Private collection.

6.141. Tourist frog mola, 1994, from the Mola Co-op.
34.0 x 43.0 cm. Private collection.

6.142. Black vest with geometric design, 1997. Many Kuna women, like Adella López, are designing and making fine quality, nontraditional mola clothing for sale. Here, Adella has chosen to use an atypical color combination to execute a popular geometric pattern with the aesthetic taste of the clients in mind.
64.5 x 53.0 cm. Private collection.

internationally. Over the past thirty years, a small group of Kuna women have become brokers or intermediaries. Some work for the mola co-op while others have developed independent commercial businesses. These women travel between Kuna Yala and the city buying molas, commissioning products, and bringing information regarding the marketing process to the islands. As mola makers themselves, they are familiar with the process; they make an effort to understand what the consumers like and to communicate to the producers a sense of the current taste of outsiders. They design products they think will be appealing and marketable.

Over the decades, a vibrant commercial line of mola products, often made in nontraditional forms, has been developed to sell to outsiders. Rectangular panels reminiscent of those taken from traditional mola blouses are made with simple figures and simple background filler. Called turista molas, these are made especially to sell and sometimes are made rapidly, with simple designs and wide spacing, at the expense of good quality. Figure 6.141, a well-made tourist mola with fine stitching, looks more like a traditional mola, except for the slightly more open space and pastel colors.

T-shirts with all kinds of mola designs or mola trim are available for tourists as are mola headbands, purses, jackets, vests, dresses, and patches to put on one's carefully tattered jeans (Fig. 6.142). The pastels and distinct color combinations found in these products have not been integrated into women's own mola blouses. Some women who wear Panamanian style clothing put mola pockets or trim on their dresses and sometimes make sundresses with mola work for young girls, but they do not use the mola products that they make for tourists.

Kuna women have been copying package labels, insignias, and commercial logos as special orders for years. In the 1980s the Texaco Corporation had a contest to design graphics for an advertising campaign and sent images to the Kuna to be turned into molas (Fig. 6.144). Oversize molas have been commissioned by businesses in Panama City and the United States. The large banner (7 x 2.5 ft.) in Figure 6.143 was ordered by the Dairy Queen in Panama City. The franchise provided the images, but by the time the panel was completed, the fish sandwich had been discontinued and the panel was returned for revision.

The Mola Co-op

Clothing, pillows, stuffed animals, Christmas ornaments, and many other novelties using mola work, designed and made by members of the Mola Co-op, are marketed in Latin America, Canada, and the United States, as well as in Panama. *La Cooperativa Productores De Molas, R.L.*, which started as a Peace Corps project in 1966 now has twelve hundred members in Kuna Yala and in Panama City.[5] They have fourteen "co-op houses" in Kuna Yala and own two stores in the comarca and a workshop and retail store in Panama City. Co-op officers are elected from among the members and there is also a general manager and staff in Panama City.

The workshop is always a flurry of activity. Women cut up bolts of brightly colored fabric and trim stacks of material with an electric cutter into the shapes of birds, fish, turtles, and lions. These will be sent to Kuna Yala where the members select the pieces they want to work on, create the mola work, attach a tag with their name and co-op number on it, and return the pieces to the co-op house where the products are checked for quality, placed in the inventory, packed, and sent back to the workshop to be made into stuffed animals. Sewing machines are used to sew the seams of dresses, handbags and many other objects, but the mola work itself is always done by hand. Mola work with machine stitching is not accepted. The staff takes and fulfills wholesale orders, maintains inventory, and travels abroad to represent Kuna women and market co-op products.

The Mola Co-op now has stores on the islands of Porvenir and Suitupu that are open during tourist season. It has become a significant economic institution and a unifying social context for Kuna women living in the city, as well as for those living in Kuna Yala. The administrative staff works with international development specialists to create seminars on the principles of cooperativism, leadership, production, quality control, management, and

6.143. Dairy Queen banner, 1967.
Mari Lyn Salvador, 1968.

6.144. Donanciano with "Texaco" mola. Tupile. Donanciano, referred to as *omekit* (a womanlike man), makes beautiful traditional molas as well as making picturelike panels for sale. He has been part of the Mola Co-op for many years and worked with Salvador as a research assistant in 1984.
Mari Lyn Salvador, 1984.

6.145. The co-op store and many other shops have been clustered in an artisan center in Panama Viejo.
Mari Lyn Salvador, 1997.

6.146. *Socias*, members, in front of their new co-op house on Suitupu.
Mari Lyn Salvador, 1997.

6.147. Co-op mola blouse. As a celebration at the Mola Co-op, many women made this blouse. They wanted to use the official colors—yellow and green—but though it wouldn't look right so they added a red *obogaled* line.
59.5 x 70.0 cm. Private collection.

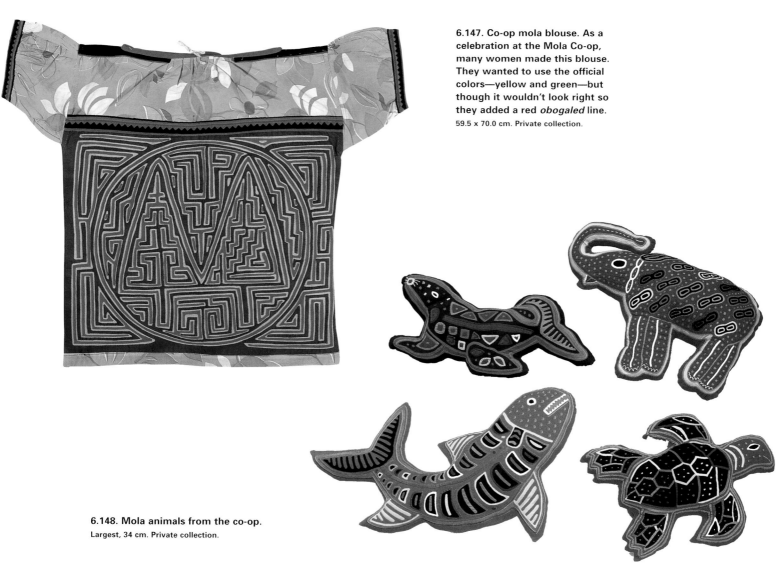

6.148. Mola animals from the co-op.
Largest, 34 cm. Private collection.

6.149. Eneira Gonzalez, the manager
in January 1997, and her daughter
in the window of the co-op store,
Porvenir.
Mari Lyn Salvador, 1997.

6.150. Enilda Martinez sews a mola at
the Panama City workshop.
David Mayo, 1997.

6.151. Newly opened co-op store
on the island of Porvenir. Women
from the Mola Co-op take turns
managing the store which is only
open during the tourist season.
Mari Lyn Salvador, 1997.

accounting. Women in the co-op stress the value of the companionship between members and are clear about the importance of the institution. Rosa Angela Martinez, the staff accountant, speaking of the importance of the co-op, explains, "Cooperativisim—you need to understand the term, what it means…to teach and to help one another. You help me and I help you. If you don't know how to do this I'll teach you…."

While the Kuna emphasize conservatism and tradition, they have a deep appreciation for innovation. Today, at a time when Kuna women are pushing the boundaries of their art form, making mola blouses with ever smaller and smaller elements and finer and finer lines, they create molas that reflect continuity and change. Some choose to look back to the molas of the grandmothers for inspiration as in Figure 6.152, which show a design based on the ritual braziers used for girls' puberty ceremonies. Others look outside their own culture and make molas with themes such as the Nativity and Santa Claus (Fig. 6.153). Many women do both. Integral to their aesthetic system are tradition—rules, repetition, and balance—and innovation—pushing beyond the rules, subtle variation, and asymmetry. It is this tension which produces a dynamic field for the continuing growth of this vital and unique art form.[6]

6.152. Brazier mola blouse by Doralinda Denis, Suitupu, 1997.
62.5 x 105.5 cm. FMCH X97.5.37.

6.153A,B. Christmas mola blouse, Río Sidra, 1994.
Side A: sequins. 58.5 x 113.0 cm. FMCH X97.3.2.

The Spirit of the Flute

Mari Lyn Salvador

When a girl reaches puberty, her father informs the men and her mother tells the women. Each man brings four large leaves from the mainland to build an enclosure inside her house where she is cloistered. Women bring sea water in calabashes and bathe the girl for four days. Her hair is cut off, and she is painted with *sabdur*, a natural black dye, to protect her from evil spirits.

Later, the community celebrates the girl's transition into womanhood with lavish ceremonies called *inna*. These are multisensory events—rhythmic assemblages of chanting, dancing, feasting, and drinking—that last from one to several nights. A festive atmosphere radiates from the chicha house.

The ritual is orchestrated by the *gandule* (flute man), a ritual specialist. Chanting to the spirit of his long cane flute, he guides parallel activities in the spirit world and describes every step of the ceremony in ritualized, formal language. Amid the ritual smoking, drinking, and toasting, women sing to each other of kinship and friendship, while men play panpipes and flutes or perform excerpts from curing chants. From time to time, men and women stand up and join in vigorous stomping dances called *gwile*. During this event—a time for playful speech, artful expression, and performance—there is a sense of letting go that contrasts with everyday Kuna etiquette.

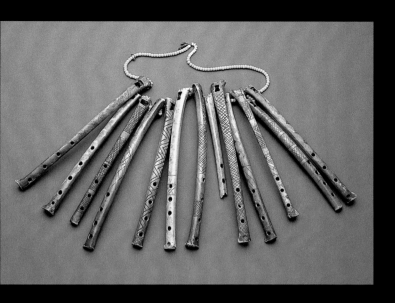

A (OPPOSITE TOP). *Inna, chicha* mola panels.
46.5 x 104.0 cm. Private collection.

B (OPPOSITE BOTTOM). **The mother of the pubescent girl invites the haircutter and her assistant to the *inna*.**
Mari Lyn Salvador, Tigre, 1997.

C (TOP LEFT). *Gorgi gala,* pelican bone necklace.
Pelican bone with incised designs, beads, cotton string. 56.5 cm. Private collection.

D (TOP RIGHT). *Gandule gurgin,* gandule's hat. **The gandule wears a hat with woven patterns and feathers. Other men and women can wear such hats during puberty ceremonies.**
Plant fiber, feathers, cotton fabric, cotton string. 52.0 cm. Private collection.

E (ABOVE LEFT). *Sianala,* brazier. **Braziers are used for burning cocoa bean incense during curing and puberty rituals. In the mola there are eight beans in each brazier and eight subordinate figures on each panel, four on each side when divided vertically or horizontally. Four and eight are ritual numbers.**
Ceramic, plant fiber. 33.0 cm. FMCH X97.5.27.

F (ABOVE RIGHT). *Nasis,* rattles. **Rattles used for chanting and dancing. The one with the bone handle is made at the beginning of the ceremony especially for the *inna*.**
Gourds, wood, bone, cotton cord, seeds. Longest rattle, 20.0 cm. FMCH X84.635.
Gift of Dorothy M. Cordry in memory of Donald B. Cordry.

Figure A is a mola panel showing the "keeper of the braziers," who wears a feather hat like the one shown in Figure D. He also holds two ceramic braziers used for burning cocoa bean incense (Fig. E). In the background two of the dancers play panpipes and two play gourd rattles. The "tobacco doers," wearing feather hats, are smoking in the traditional way (Figs. J, L). Behind the smokers, men with single cane flutes and rattles represent the gandule, the director of the ritual, and his assistant, and the other figures are dancers.

G (RIGHT). *Chicha* **pots mola blouse. A repeated mola pattern based on ceramic jars used to store chicha.**
61.0 x 74.0 cm. NMAI 16/6412. Collected in 1922 and presented by Lady Richmond Brown and F. A. Mitchell Hedges.

H (BELOW RIGHT). **Several sizes of drinking cups in a variety of shapes are used throughout the ceremony. Special toasts are made with pairs of tiny gourds called** *siki* **that are joined with coarse thread.**
Gourds, string. Height of tallest, 17.0 cm. Clockwise from left: FMCH X97.5.40, X97.5.41, X97.5.52, X97.5.74, X97.5.53, X97.5.38.

> *There is the strainer.*
> *There is a large inna drinking cup.*
> *There is a small* siki *cup.*
> *There is the* nogmur *drinking cup.*
> *There is the mouth rinsing cup.*
>
> — **Gandule Ernesto Linares, Muladupu, 1970**

I (BOTTOM RIGHT). **Ceramic jars for fermenting chicha.**
Levon Mardikyan, Playón Chico, 1996.

> *The inna-making specialist says to the owners of the inna,*
> *"Bring me sugarcane juice (inna)."*
> *He tastes the sugarcane juice.*
> *He tastes it.*
> *The inna-making specialist lines up the jars in order of strength.*
> *The jars are lined up in order of strength.*
> *The jars are in a straight line.*
> *The inna-making specialist says to the owners of the inna.*
> *"In three days you will have the festivities."*
>
> —**Mastaletat, Muladupu, 1970**

Toasting and drinking

Puberty ceremonies are called inna, the name for the fermented drink prepared for these occasions. Men gather sugarcane and families extract the juice using a large wooden press. The chicha specialist directs the preparations—mixing the ingredients, cooking the drink, and fermenting it in large ceramic jars. He chants the "way of making inna" to guide activities in the spirit world.

After the drink has fermented for ten to fourteen days, the chicha maker comes to taste the brew and when it is ready he toasts the girl's father and announces that the festivities can begin. Formal toasting, ritualized drinking, and dancing follow for hours.

Ritual smoking and drinking

When the chicha is ready, the guests bathe, enter the chicha house, and seat themselves in their proper places on benches. After a series of toasts, the smoking ceremony begins. Moving in short dance steps, the "tobacco doer" smokes a hand-rolled cigar with the lit end in his mouth and blows smoke in the men's faces as has been done for centuries. At times, the ritual haircutter and her assistant simultaneously carry out the smoking ritual, moving in synch with their male counterparts.

J (RIGHT). "Tobacco doer," wearing a bird bone necklace, blows smoke for a guest who is holding a gourd drinking cup.
Mari Lyn Salvador, Tigre, 1997.

K (BELOW). Ritual cigar and brand.
Above: Brand, used to light the cigar. Wood. 26.5 cm. Private collection.
Below: Hand-rolled cigar. Tobacco, 31.5.cm. Private collection.

L (ABOVE RIGHT). Dalia Roldán, who assists the haircutter, lights a ritual cigar. The smoke protects the participants from evil spirits.
Levon Mardikyan, Playón Chico, 1996.

M (RIGHT). Seventeenth-century illustration.

"Their way of smoking when they are in Company together is thus: a Boy lights one end of a Roll and burns it to a Coal, wetting the part next to it to keep it from wasting too fast. The End so lighted he puts into his Mouth, and blows smoake through the whole length of the Roll into the Face of everyone of the Company..."
Lionel Wafer, 1699

N. During the celebration there is continuous activity in the communal kitchen of the chicha house. Women cook huge quantities of food each day for feasting.
evon Mardikyan, Playón Chico, 1991.

D. The pubescent girl, painted black, erves chicha to the guests during one-night *inna*. Dancers wear bird one necklaces that clatter, giving a ercussive quality to the movements.
Mari Lyn Salvador, Tigre, 1997.

The chicha house, a large structure much like the gathering house capable of holding the entire community, is opened only for girls' puberty ceremonies, when the space is reorganized and divided by long benches. The women's and men's areas are separated by an open space

P. Double chicha mola panel. Sometimes the chicha is stored in canoes. Four canoes are shown in this mola panel.
70.0 x 52.0 cm. NMAI 16/6558. Collected in 1922 and presented by Lady Richmond Brown and F. A. Mitchell Hedges.

> *The inna-making specialist opens the door of the inna house.*
> *He enters the door of the inna house.*
> *There are many golden benches in place.*
> *There are many silver benches in place.*
> *On his golden bench.*
> *The inna-making specialist sits down.*
> *On their silver benches.*
> *The inna tasters sit down.*
>
> —**Gandule Ernesto Linares, Muladupu, 1970**

Q. The *ied* (ritual haircutter) and her assistant.
Mari Lyn Salvador, Tigre, 1997.

The World of Spirit, Disease, and Curing

Mac Chapin

Introduction

While many of the indigenous peoples of Central America have seen their cultures erode away and disappear in the face of increased cultural contact and domination by Western society, the Kuna have managed thus far to maintain their way of life relatively intact. In this context of strong cultural identity—which is sustained through the language, a variety of traditional institutions and rituals, and the insularity of the Kuna Yala region—the curing system has endured into the present day as the most highly valued and sacred corner of their culture. While some cracks have formed on the surface with the incursion of Western systems of thought, the core of the traditional Kuna worldview remains intact and vital.

That worldview is grounded in the belief that the tangible world we perceive with our waking senses is dependent on and secondary to the world of spirit, which underlies it and animates it with its life force. Well-being is present when the spiritual nature of the Earth is healthy and robust; individual well-being is likewise dependent upon the health of the soul (*burba*) of the person who possesses it. Whenever the spiritual nature of the Earth is damaged, corrupted, or depleted, its inhabitants lose their moral bearings, natural calamities occur, and life becomes a dangerous enterprise. By the same token, disease occurs when a person's soul is injured or disfigured. The physical symptoms of illness—a broken leg, an infection, skin rash, fever—are simply mirror images of the real damage that has been sustained by the spirit residing inside the body. Consequently, to cure illness the specialists must perform rites that establish contact with the world of spirit and confront and overcome the spirits that have caused the problem.

At the same time, the field of Kuna curing encompasses a good deal more than strategies for healing illness. It also serves to enhance desirable qualities and to serve as a prophylactic against disease. The Kuna utilize numerous medicines and chants to improve physical strength, dexterity, intelligence, creativity, work ethic, and sexual appeal. Men drink red, bitter potions to strengthen their *niga* (inner force) and their

7.1. The patient lies in the hammock while the *igarwisid*, curing specialist, with a hat and a pipe in his mouth, stirs dried cocoa beans in a clay brazier. He chants to the spirits to cure the patient. The women in the family help care for the patient as well. 37.0 x 49.0 cm. Private Collection.

burba (spirit); and students subject themselves to lengthy treatments to "open up," "firm up," and give a healthy, reddish color to their *gurgin* (spiritual brain). Preventative measures are performed regularly for those who find themselves vulnerable—young children (whose spirits are not yet "firmed up"), pregnant women, those debilitated by illness, older people (whose inner force is on the wane), or the entire village if a generalized threat such as an epidemic has been perceived.

Among the Kuna there are two primary ways in which the spirit may be adversely affected. First, a person may lose a piece of his burba. When this occurs, the Kuna say that "his burba has been taken" or "his burba has been grabbed" by an evil spirit and held captive, a process that depletes the victim's strength and causes fevers, weakness, and dizziness. If the burba is not found and restored to the body, the victim will continue to decline and eventually die. The second way in which illness can occur is through the attack of a spirit that gets inside the victim's burba and corrupts it. This may cause a wide variety of illnesses, such as numbness, pain, bleeding, infection, and dizziness.

To combat these illnesses, the Kuna employ a varied repertoire of strategies that combine medicines and chants. Medicines may be fresh plants gathered in the forests of the adjacent mainland, freshly killed animals, or objects "that do not rot," such as stones, animals skulls, dried roots and pieces of wood, light bulbs, and marbles. These are gathered and prepared for administration together with short chants that "counsel" the spirits of the medicines to perform their duties. These medicines are frequently used in conjunction with any one of a number of fixed-form chants designed for specific tasks, such as curing fever, effecting childbirth, and ensuring success in hunting.

The Kuna have three broad categories of curing specialists: the *nele* (shaman), who uses his supernatural powers to diagnose illness; the *ina duled* (medicine man), who collects, "counsels," and prepares medicines for use by the patient; and the *igar wisid* (knower of chants), who effects cures by performing any of a number of fixed-form chants over his patients. While women are specialists in only rare cases, they are always the ones in charge of administering medicines and physically handling the patients.

The world of spirit

The earth as it exists today has a dual nature: it is composed of "the world of spirit" (*neg burbaled*) and the "world of substance" (*neg sanaled*) The world of spirit is invisible to a person's waking senses, yet surrounds that person on all sides and resides inside every material object. Human beings, plants, animals, rocks, rivers, and villages all have invisible "souls" (*burbagana*), which are spiritual copies of the physical bodies they inhabit. Thus, the soul of a human being is, in form and appearance, a representation of the body in which it lives. It is the spirit that provides the material world with its vital force.

The world of spirit, then, is a replica of the world we experience about us. Yet it is a good deal more than that: it extends out in all directions from the surface of the earth through a series of eight levels that have no material counterparts. A person dropping down a mine shaft would not pass through a series of material levels paralleling the spiritual levels; and by the same token, passengers in an airplane are no closer to the higher levels than a person standing on the surface of the earth. The transition from the world of substance to the world of spirit is somewhat analogous to crossing over into a fourth dimension, for the spiritual levels exist in, and are part of, a completely different order of reality. It is into this realm that Kuna specialists journey when they go about the task of curing illness.

7.2. Mateo Brenes gathering medicinal plants by the Tigandiki River.
James Howe, 1970.

This order of reality is often not what it appears to be. It is full of distortions and embellishments that make it both magnificent and dangerous to those who would venture into it. Objects and people are of gold and silver and at the same time of different colors that are constantly changing into distinct shapes and hues. Smells are exaggerated, either pungently fragrant or violently disagreeable. Dangerous phenomena are far more common in the spiritual landscape, and they are more active—they are alive. Whirlpools of different colors swirl up into the air like flutes, rush down into the depths of the cosmos, spin furiously and throw off spume and mist, transforming the rivers into perilous obstacle courses. On the fourth level there are "water barrels"

7.3. A group of balsa wood figures, *urkurwala*, carved for a mass exorcism ritual.
James Howe, Niatupu, 1975.

of all colors that pulsate, groan, shuffle back and forth, and vibrate wildly as liquid "all like blood" spurts and oozes from long tubes attached to them.

This parallel world is populated with numerous human, nonhuman, and semi-human inhabitants. The most powerful spirits wear eight hats, eight suits, eight ties, eight pairs of shoes—all of which are gold and silver, of mutating colors, and continuously throwing off sparks and shining brilliantly. Many of the spirits were placed by Great Father and Great Mother among the levels when the earth was created, to guard sacred places and maintain the workings of the universe on a daily basis. They perform vital functions such as the birth of all fish and sea creatures at the "grandmother's umbilical cord" at the fourth level, and the regeneration of plants on earth at the domain of the trees; indeed, the fourth level is the reproductive level of the Kuna universe. Other spirits were banished to the levels for their immoral acts, and remain to perform penance of one sort or another. There are entire villages of spiritual animals who live along the rivers of the different levels, much like the Kuna when they all inhabited the mainland.

Within the realm of disease and curing, there are two major types of spiritual beings that figure prominently: *bonigana* and *nuchugana*.

The spirits that cause illness are called bonigana (singular: *boni*). While the Kuna often translate boni into Spanish as *espíritu malo* (evil spirit), in fact bonigana are not inherently malevolent. They take many forms and are found throughout the spirit world, moving freely through the levels and about the surface of the earth. There are crocodile bonigana, monkey bonigana, rock bonigana, and wind bonigana. The most virulent form of boni is the *nia*, which the Kuna usually translate as "devil" or "demon." In contrast to all of the other bonigana, the nia is not associated with any particular animal, plant, inanimate object, or natural force; it is variously pictured as

a humanoid creature with black skin and lights shining out of its back, or a hairy monster riding a giant tapir or a jaguar. *Niagana* (plural of nia) often disguise themselves as alluring men or women and try to seduce Kuna persons of the opposite sex.

Nuchugana (singular: nuchu) are carved wooden figures, most of them fashioned in the form of human beings, usually men (Figs. 7.5-7). They are used to combat bonigana; and all traditional Kuna households have boxes of them to guard against the incursion of spirits causing illness. Curing specialists enlist their spirits to journey into the levels of the cosmos and overcome disease. Nuchugana are usually about thirty centimeters tall and are almost invariably carved to look like non-Indians: they have large noses, wear suits and sometimes military uniforms or religious outfits, and often have hats with serrated tops perched on their heads. The magical properties they possess come from the type of wood they are carved from rather than their form. Balsawood, for example, is one of the leaders among the nuchugana because he is made of soft wood (the Kuna say that someone with a "soft head" is intelligent); the nuchu made of "drunk tree" (*Hura polyandra*) is constantly in a state of intoxication, possesses tremendous strength, and is frequently on the verge of breaking loose with uncontrollable violence. There are as many as twenty types of wood used to make nuchugana. Curing specialists refer to the nuchugana as their "helpers," for they figure prominently in both medicinal curing and chants.

The spirit realm constantly breaks into the lives of the Kuna as they go about their daily routine. Spirits periodically attack the weak and defenseless, causing illness, deformity, and death. Some of these attacks are random—as when a seemingly healthy man or woman is suddenly stricken—but to a significant extent life is benevolent to those who behave themselves in a moral fashion. The spirits generally respect those who follow the rules, which are recorded in and reinforced by Kuna tradition. The

7.4. Collection of medicines and *nuchugana* beneath the hammock of a patient. The buckets have liquids for bathing and the sticks are for keeping evil spirits away.
Mac Chapin, Usdupu, 1975.

7.5. Nuchugana.

All are wood, some with pigment. Tallest, 28.5 cm.

Left to right: FMCH X96.25.17; X97.3.3; X84.645, Gift of Dorothy M. Cordry in memory of Donald B. Cordry; X84.639, Gift of Dorothy M. Cordry in memory of Donald B. Cordry; X83.484, Gift of Dorothy M. Cordry in memory of Donald B. Cordry; X97.3.4.

7.6. Nuchugana stored together in a wooden box, as they are in Kuna homes.
Mari Lyn Salvador, Ailigandi, 1974.

7.7. Nuchugana.

All are wood, some with pigment. Tallest, 25.0 cm.

Third from left: Collection of Jim and Jean Piper. All others: Private collection.

Kuna strengthen themselves against spirit attack by administering a variety of medicines to fortify their burba and their niga.

Because the burba is a spiritual copy of the material self, a person with one leg, for example, has a burba that also lacks a leg. Each individual burba is in turn a composite of as many as eight burbagana. Thus, when a spirit abducts a person's burba it is carrying off one, or perhaps two (in more serious cases), of the composite spirits. When a person dies, his burba leaves the material remains and journeys into the levels of the cosmos.

The burba, like the niga, can be strengthened with medicines; the Kuna frequently refer to a healthy soul as a *nigaburba*. Niga is a spiritual element residing in the blood; the word translates roughly as "fortitude" or "strength." Children are born with a small supply of niga that increases with age, reaching a peak during youth and early middle age before declining in the twilight years. Both men and women take "niga-strengthening medicines" to build up their energy and provide a protective armor against disease. Those with strong niga emit a growling noise audible in the world of spirit.

How illness occurs

All forms of illness occur on the level of spirit and are caused by bonigana. Disease is not caused by physical agents that invade the flesh and organs of the victim. Physical manifestations of illness, such as swollen and infected wounds, fevers, weakness, broken bones, rashes, headaches, dizziness, and the like are merely visible symptoms reflecting a deeper damage that has been sustained by a person's soul.

A person may become ill in one of two major ways: soul loss or soul corruption. Soul loss occurs when one or more parts of his composite soul are abducted by a boni and carried off to the boni's domain. When this occurs, the person's spirit is depleted, a state that brings on fever and weakness. It is sometimes the case that a soul is abducted without the victim's realization; only later, when the victim returns home, he is struck with a sense of listlessness and nausea.

It often occurs, however, that a person is aware that his soul has been abducted at the moment it occurs. In the jungle, a man may be abruptly surprised by a wild animal or a loud noise; he may slip and fall from his canoe as he navigates the inland rivers or coastal reefs; or he may suddenly experience a strange sensation of weakness and break into a cold sweat. At these times, one or more pieces of the soul have been jarred loose and fallen to the ground, where they become disoriented, confused, and unable to find their way back to the owner's body. If steps are not taken immediately to recover the errant souls, they will be left behind to be picked up, sooner or later, by bonigana that are ubiquitous and constantly out scavenging the neighborhood.

Corruption of the soul takes place when one or more bonigana launch an attack on a person's burba, taking up residence inside it and tainting it. At times, bonigana will attack clothed in substance, as when a snake sinks its fangs into the leg of a man clearing brush on the mainland, or when a stingray strikes the leg of a man wading in shallow water along the coast. But bonigana most often strike as pure spirit, invisibly, and it is only after the victim is beset with physical symptoms of illness that he realizes what has happened and which spirit has attacked. For example, the snake spirit, unaccompanied by a material body, can cause the flesh to become cold and clammy, devoid of all sensation; it may dig burrows in a person's soul, creating rotten holes that will not heal; it may cause a person's soul to be covered with blotches, like the designs on a snake's body; it may cause sharp pains by sinking its fangs into a person's soul; or it may trigger rotting gums and loose teeth.

Kuna curing specialists

Among the Kuna, there are three types of ritual specialists concerned with curing: the nele (plural: nergan), or shaman; the ina duled (plural: ina durgan), which translates directly as "medicine man;" and the igar wisid (plural: igar wisidmalad), or "knower of chants." The nele is the only specialist who is born with innate powers, and both men and women may fill this profession. Women may study to become ina durgan and igar wisidmalad only if they are nergan.

7.8. *Urkuwala,* **balsa figures.**
Vernon Salvador, Ailigandi, 1974.

The nergan stand apart from all other ritualists by virtue of their possession of supernatural power, a condition that confers upon them an ability to peer into the world of spirit. Most nergan are born with the fetal caul covering part or all of the face, a sign that marks them as seers. Evidence of supernatural powers is observed in children who learn to speak at an unusually early age, who demonstrate intelligence beyond their years, or who in any way display clairvoyance or telepathy. Definitive judgment as to whether or not a child is a true nele, however, is made by already

7.9. Urkuwala, balsa figures.
Wood. Height of taller, 144 cm. FMCH X84.159,
X84.158. Gift of Dorothy M. Cordry in memory
of Donald B. Cordry.

7.10. Keli, medicine man from Ustupu, standing next to "medicines which do not rot"—dried roots, animal skulls, dried "coagulated medicine," stone axes, and polished rocks.
Mac Chapin, 1972.

7.11. Albertino Arias, medicine man from the community of Ogob Sukun ("Coconut Bay"), with his wife. His orange bead necklace marks him as a medicine man; the multicolored necklace is the sign of a "snake medicine" specialist.
Mac Chapin, 1972.

established nergan, who are able to scan the burba and detect real powers. Once the status of nele is detected, his or her powers must be nurtured, channeled, and disciplined so that they will develop along a healthy and effective course.

The most adept nergan have the ability to send their burbagana on journeys into the world of spirit and to communicate freely with its inhabitants. The nergan are master diagnosticians of illness, for they are equipped with supernatural "lenses" that enable them to peer directly into the spiritual makeup of their fellow human beings. The shaman is further distinguished from other specialists in that the shamanistic abilities are innate, having been formed spiritually inside the mother's womb.

In contradistinction to the nele, neither the ina duled nor the igar wisid is born with innate powers; both must learn their professions through years of arduous training from already established specialists. These two professions are not mutually exclusive, and indeed it is often the case that an ina duled is also an igar wisid; and nergan, while not curers per se, frequently train to become either ina durgan or igar wisidmalad. At the same time, each profession is conceived of as discrete and the different roles are kept separate. The Kuna say that a person with several professions is wearing a number of different hats.

Ina durgan specialize in gathering and preparing medicines, which are either fresh plants, dead animals or pieces of animals, or what are termed "old medicines" such as rocks, pieces of wood, and animal skulls. The best ina durgan are superb botanists, with a vast knowledge of the plants of the mainland forest. A key part of the medicine man's skill consists of knowing a series of "medicine counseling chants" that address the spirits of the medicines directly and bring them to life. The chants, which differ according to the type of medicine and the illness for which its assistance is being sought, characteristically describe the origin of the plants, paint a picture of how they grow and what they look like, provide details of the patient's illness, instruct the spirits of the medicines in the ways they should apply their healing powers, and finally exhort the spirits of the medicines to do their best work.

Igar wisidmalad go through a training similar to that of the ina durgan, yet they do not deal with medicines. Instead, they learn any number of a series of long, more or less fixed-form chants (*igar*) that serve to marshal a host of curing spirits for the purpose of combating illness. The shortest of these chants, "The Way of Cacao" (Sia Igar), generally lasts for half an hour to forty-five minutes, and is used to lower mild fevers. The longest and most complex, "The Way of Conversing" (Absoged Igar), runs over a period of eight days and is employed to stem assaults that hordes of malevolent spirits have made against the entire community. Other chants are used to combat dizziness and epilepsy ("The Way of Wind," Burwa Igar), facilitate childbirth ("The Way of Muu," Muu Igar), expel demons who have taken possession of a person's spirit ("The Way of the Demon," Nia Igar), and to cure chronic headaches ("The Way of Gurgin," Gurgin Igar).

These named specialists—virtually all of whom are men—are backed up in the curing process by the families surrounding the patients, and especially the women. The nergan, ina durgan, and igar wisidmalad work almost exclusively to establish a line of communication with the world of spirit. While the nele sits before the patient, smoking a pipe and peering with his "lens" through the smoke of burning cacao seeds, he is peering into the spirit. The igar wisid, by the same token, takes up his post at the head of the patient, but he addresses a host of spirits with his chants, which are performed in the language of the spirit world. The ina duled gathers medicines, counsels their spirits, and turns them over to the patient's family for administration. It is the women of the patient's immediate family that tend to the patient's every need: they feed, bathe, administer medicines, question the patient about his or her condition, and accompany the patient during long hours of repose.

The language of the spirit world

Both the medicine counseling chants and the longer curing chants are performed in the language of the spirit world, which is distinct from colloquial Kuna (see Sherzer, "Kuna Language and Literature," in this volume) and unintelligible to the nonspecialist. The purpose of the

Kuna Oral History

According to Kuna tradition, the Earth is the body of Great Mother (Nan Dummad). Great Father (Bab Dummad) joined in sexual union with Great Mother and she gave birth to all of the plants, animals, and humans. Together they were thinking of the future—"There was no end to what they were thinking"—and their plan was to prepare the world for the arrival, centuries distant, of the "Golden People," the Kuna. Everything at "the beginning of time" was pure spirit, and all of the creatures that issued forth from the womb of the Mother were given names and informed of their duties. The medicinal plants were advised about their role in curing illness; certain animals—peccaries, tapirs, armadillos, etc.— were told that they would be used by the Kuna as food; and a number of hardwood trees were given instructions for their use as construction materials in house building. All of this was done in preparation for the eventual arrival of the Kuna.

Great Mother then gave birth to a deity named Muu (midwife), who would carry on the task of producing the animals and human beings of the Earth. In similar fashion, she created a spirit couple, Olobengikiler and Olokekebyai, to propagate the Earth's plants, as well as a host of other deities who ensured the proper functioning of the Earth's life processes. The Mother had arrived naked and had soon thereafter become clothed with vegetation, her "green clothes." Her body was as soft as that of a newborn baby. She lived alone and took care of all of her creations, and the Earth was a paradise. There was no misery, no suffering, no illness. There were no noxious insects, nor were there poisonous animals. Plants were without thorns, and those with edible fruits produced every four days. Whenever the Mother desired game, she had merely to say "I wish to eat peccary" or "I want to eat agouti," and the animal in question would walk into her patio, where she would dispatch it with a machete, clean it, and roast it over a fire. The spirits causing illness were absent from the Earth, and death was unknown. The sun shone benignly over all, its beams as gentle as the rays of the moon.

It was into this idyllic setting that the first humans—a man named Biler and his wife,

Bursobi—made their appearance. They produced five sons, each of whom was a powerful shaman, and they in turn sired a host of offspring that were neither fully human nor fully animal, but intermediate beings that possessed physical and behavioral traits linking them to particular animals of the forest. Among those who came into being at this time were Tapir-man (who had a big belly and slept in pools of mud he found in the forest), Jaguar-man (who was ferocious and stealthy of step), and Red Howler Monkey-man (who had red hair and was a

7.12. *Galu* (spiritual domain) of the kigi hawk. Located high in the mountains, these galus periodically open their gates and send out hawks to replenish the world's supply.
Taken from the notebook of Enrique Guerrero, Ogopsukun, 1975.

7.13. A medicinalist, Francis Smith, admonishes a basket of *sigu* (arrow) medicine, which spiritually attacks bonigawa that are causing illness. James Howe, Niatupu, 1977.

womanizer). One of the sons of Biler and Bursobi was the father of a series of virulent spirits that caused crippling diseases, including paralysis, tumors and boils, "rotten vomiting," and "yellow sickness." Another of the sons was the father of Cold, while yet another produced violent winds.

As the animal-men spread across the Earth, corruption and vice became prevalent. The animal-men often staged drunken feasts where they brawled and caused havoc with their chaotic magic. Tapir-man delighted in crazed wrestling matches with Manatee-man, during which they would plunge through the walls of houses and snap trees in half.

The corruption brought about a fundamental change in the character of the things. The body of the Mother grew hard, like the heart of a tree. Plants became tough and fibrous, their sap ran bitter and stung the skin, and the forests were laced with foul

chants is to establish communication with inhabitants of the world of spirit and, in doing so, direct the course of events in that realm toward a positive curative outcome. While the spirits are fully capable of understanding and conversing in not just Kuna but any and all human languages, specialists maintain that for their cures to be effective the chants must be performed in the language of the spirit world.

Whereas colloquial Kuna is employed to refer to things existing in the world of the waking senses, the language of the spirit world refers to objects, beings, and events that are spiritual. It is essential to an understanding of Kuna curing that the referents of words in the two languages are different. For example, while the word *iawala* (in the language of the spirit world) and *diwar* (in colloquial Kuna) both mean "river," the former term refers to an invisible river in the world of spirit and the latter to a physical body of water. By the same token, the words *abisua* and *gana* refer to a "spiritual chanter" (or the burba of the chanter), while igar wisid refers to a flesh-and-blood "knower of chants." Thus, when a chanter performs a medicine counseling chant or a curing chant, his burba is the sender of the chant and everything his words describe exists on the level of spirit.

The language of the spirit world is characterized by its wealth of metaphor and lavish verbal imagery. According to the Kuna, the spirits are never satisfied with a mere listing of their names and matter-of-fact accounts of their history and behavioral characteristics. Instead, they bask in intricate and colorful descriptions of their existence that are replete with complex tapestries of metaphor, poetic expression, and elaborate pictures. In the chants, for example, butterfly becomes "the owner of the pieces of cloth"; the estuary bird broadbill ("flat mouth" in colloquial Kuna) becomes "the owner of the silver spoon"; and the crocodile becomes "he who holds his breath underwater." Colors are likened to natural phenomena: red is "like blood," "like macaw feathers," and "like fire;" yellow is "like a macaw's stomach"; green is "like a frog." Sounds are "like a machete" hitting a tree, "like bells," "like dogs growling," and so forth.

The most effective specialists are those who can converse with the spirits in their own tongue and, in doing so, delight them by weaving complex tapestries of metaphor, poetry, and elaborate descriptions. The spirits appreciate this talent for intricate description. It "makes them feel good" and bends them to the curative tasks they are being asked to perform.

Diagnosis of illness

When someone falls ill, those around the person take immediate steps to establish the identity of the spirit that has initiated the attack. This initial investigation into causation is crucial, for it will determine the curative strategy and dictate how it will be put into operation. Diagnosis is generally carried out during the first stages by older members of the family of the sick person, then taken over by curing specialists, always in consultation with family members, as the list of potential spirit culprits is narrowed. Simpler cases are generally resolved by examination of the physical symptoms (e.g., an infected finger or skin rash) or the circumstances that brought about the problem (e.g., stepping on a sea urchin). With the more complex illnesses, however, diagnosis is a process of inference that demands a thorough understanding of established theories of disease causation and an ability to isolate and assess all of the relevant facts of any given case. When a diagnosis proves elusive, a shaman is called in to search for clues by peering directly into the patient's soul, or conversing with guardian spirits that live in the patient's household.

smells and stinging insects. Thorns appeared, and edible plants became more stingy with their fruits. The animals of the jungle were transformed into wild and dangerous beasts. Rivers became swift torrents when it rained, the sun's rays burned the skin, and nature in general shifted from its benevolent and protective stance to become unpredictable and treacherous. It was during this time that the spiritual Earth became overlaid with substance, as it is today.

Great Father became concerned over this turn of events. He sent successive waves of "good men" to Earth with instructions to counsel the wrongdoers and bring them back to the moral path. These missionaries traveled far and wide, speaking and chanting in the communities across the Earth, warning of impending punishments from Great Father if they refused to correct their profligate behavior. But the inhabitants of the Earth refused to pay heed. They stopped attending the evening gathering sessions and replied simply that since they had arrived on Earth before the missionaries, and knew what they were doing. After repeated attempts to no avail, Great Father concluded that the tide of corruption and disrespect could not be turned through persuasion, and he sent cyclones and earthquakes to castigate the people. He caused the surface of the Earth to turn over, and everything and everybody was banished to the fourth level of the cosmos, where they still reside as spirits to the present day.

The Earth's population again began to increase, and with this trend came renewed depravation and disorder. Great Father sent a man named Mago to Earth to teach "The Way of Father" and he, like his predecessors, wandered the land to instill a sense of morality in the people. Mago took a woman and had three children, two of whom were twins, a boy named Olonitalibipilele and a girl named Kabayai. They had incestuous relations and from their union came Dad Ibe, the Sun, and six brothers and a sister, all of whom were stars.

The Earth at the time was a perilous, disease-ridden place. Snakes had merely to look at a person to bring on paralysis and death; bats the size of pelicans flew through the forests; and there were no medicines to combat the virulent spirits that roamed abroad at all hour of day and night. Dad Ibe and his siblings took it upon themselves to diminish the terrible power of the disease-causing spirits (*bonigana*). Great Father aided them by sending chants and medicinal lore through the medium of dreams. They also learned from the spirits of the medicines themselves; and at times they went directly to the spirits that were causing illness, and coaxed potent knowledge from them. Dad Ibe would stand before the spirit of the snake and say: "My Friend Snake, I would like to talk to you a bit...." And Snake would tell him what medicines were good for illness resulting from snake attacks.

At times Dad Ibe paid the spirits for their information, giving them what they valued most highly: a toxic beverage made of chile peppers, tobacco, and barbasco. On other occasions, he would trick them into revealing their secrets, and he even went so far as to court their daughters to gain access to their fathers' store of knowledge. All of the principal curing chants and medicines were discovered and learned by Dad Ibe and his siblings; and armed with these weapons they were able to reduce the terrible power of the evil spirits to a pale shadow of what they had been.

Their mission accomplished, Dad Ibe and his brothers and sister retired to the heavens and life continued to evolve. Four times the Earth was populated and destroyed when corruption took root and ran unchecked: first by wind, next by fire, then by darkness, and finally by a massive flood. When the waters of the flood had subsided, people similar to the Kuna of today appeared. But they did not have culture: they knew no history and lived like animals; they went about semi-naked, practiced no ceremonies, were ignorant of kinship ties, and left their dead to rot on the ground near their villages.

Shortly thereafter, a man named Ibeorgun and his sister Olokikadiryai arrived to live among these people and teach them how to live. Much of what they taught the Kuna consisted of knowledge that had been discovered by Dad Ibe and his siblings in the distant past, and then lost. Ibeorgun was a *gandule* (puberty rite chanter); he was dressed in golden clothes and adorned with eagle and macaw feathers. He taught the people the ceremonies for puberty, birth, and death; he instructed them in the

Diagnosis is often made on the basis of several types of evidence. First, the physical symptoms of the patient are examined (e.g., vomiting blood, sharp pain); second, attention is paid to any recent actions he, or a close member of his family, might have taken that would leave him vulnerable to spirit attack (e.g., visit to a dangerous place, contact with a taboo animal); third, the medical history of the patient and his family is discussed (e.g., recurrent dizzy spells, heart ailments); and fourth, an examination of the patient's moral character is made.

Curing

Curing is effected by the application of a wide repertoire of medicines, ritual observance, and the performance of long, fixed-form chants. In the more serious illnesses, the Kuna use a variety of these strategies in combination: several types of medicines are administered, while chants for different aspects of the illnesses are concurrently performed; and in recent years, with the arrival of government hospitals and public health personnel, Western medicines and practices are often enlisted as well.

It is significant that curing specialists deal with the world of spirit, not with the patient. While they are generally involved in the initial diagnosis of the patient's ailment, their main task is to establish contact with the spirits. Medicine men gather medicines in the forest or assemble them from among the items in their homes. Then they chant to them, instructing them as to the task before them.

Medicines

A brief examination of the contents of a medicine man's house shows that practically anything can be used as medicine (*ina*). Boxes of odd-shaped sticks and vines, animal skulls, carved wooden figures, shells, and numerous other items line the walls; baskets, gourds, and cloth packets stuffed with dried leaves, seeds, and coagulated pastes hang from the beams and walls; and if the specialist has just returned from a medicine gathering trip to the mainland, several baskets of freshly cut stems, vines, leaves, and bark will be found sitting in a corner awaiting preparation (Fig. 7.14).

When used by patients, medicines are counseled as to the task at hand and then administered either in a bath, ingested, anointed as a paste, or burned to produce smoke. It is not the physical substance of the medicine that effects the cure. The spirit of the medicines seeps into the spirit of the patient, much in the same manner as sweat oozes from the human body. In this way, the spiritual properties of the medicines leave the physical body in which they are housed (the "medicine husk") and are transferred to the spirit of the patient, becoming part of it.

Kuna medicine is used for a variety of broad purposes. First, there are curative medicines to treat all manner of illnesses. Some medicines are employed to eliminate boni-gana that have attacked and to restore the patient to a normal state of health. But many medicines are used when there is no disorder present, to add desirable qualities to the patient's spirit, such as strength, intelligence, muscular coordination, and fluency in speaking or chanting. Still other medicines are employed as protective measures, to block the arrival of bonigana by "confusing the road" they might take; for example, pregnant women are often painted black to "darken the road" so that attacking spirits will lose their way. In actual practice, treatment of a particular illness often involves a variety of medicines that serve all of these different functions at the same time.

Gurgin medicine

A prominent type of medicine used for enhancing intellectual capacity is gurgin medicine. In the past, men anxious to learn ritual chants frequently took gurgin medicine. ("Gurgin" means "hat" in colloquial Kuna and in the spirit language means something akin to "spiritual brain.") Today, many school children take it to improve their learning capacity. They often suffer from headaches, light-headedness, and poor concentration in the face of study. It is said that their gurgin is simply too small and undeveloped to incorporate all of the new things they are learning, and it needs to be "enlarged" and "opened up." The headaches come from the pressure of the knowledge pushing against the constrictive walls of the gurgin; and their dizziness is a result of the gurgin being forced to "rise up."

To prepare for treatment, a medicine man first gathers a selection of medicines, the bulk of which are sweet-smelling herbs, and counsels them. The patient is then isolated in a corner of the medicine man's house or his or her own home where, over a period of eight, sixteen, or thirty-two days, the patient bathes at regular intervals with the medicines. The patient's days are tightly controlled while the spiritual gurgin is being reformed. His or her food is brought either by prepubescent girls or older women past reproductive age; the spirits of the medicines, who guard the patient closely during treatment, are young women and they do not tolerate human competition. Only bland, unspiced food is consumed, few visitors are allowed, and radios and tape recorders are strictly forbidden. When venturing outside to urinate, the patient must wrap a towel around the head or wave a thin stick before the face to clear away any spiritual cobwebs that might foul his or her soft new gurgin. Both students and teachers at Kuna schools attest to the effectiveness of this treatment.

names of the parts of the body, all of the kinship terms, and words used in different types of communication; and he journeyed from community to community building gathering houses and teaching the people how to chant and conduct their daily business.

Olokikadiryai came fully dressed, with a gold ring in her nose, gold and silver necklaces, yellow beads encircling her arms and legs, skirts, a scarf for her head, and intricate mola blouses. She taught the women how to make their clothes and how to wear them. She taught them to make hammocks and clay pots; she taught them how to prepare food and drink; and she taught them how to take care of their children.

Ibeorgun and Olokikadiryai spent many years visiting the communities of the people of the earth. When their mission was completed, they disappeared and nine powerful shamans appeared to continue their teachings. It was during this time that the white-skinned foreigners came from a land across the seas called Yurub (Europe), and landed on the coast of Kuna Yala.

7.14. Store of "medicines that do not rot," including nuchugana, roots, vines, coagulated medicine, stone axes, and animal skulls, in the home of medicine man Domingo López.
Mac Chapin, Ustupu, 1972.

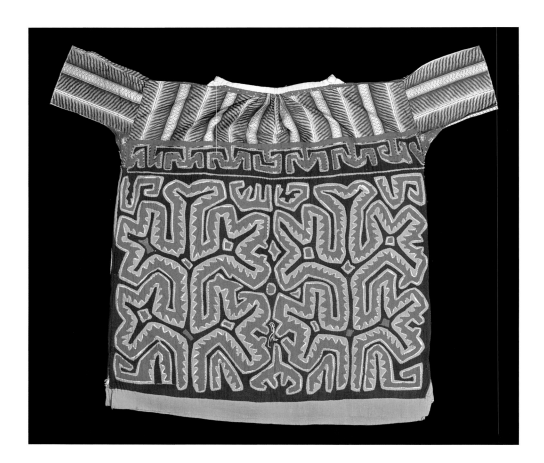

7.15. *Ina gaa mola,* **medicinal leaves mola. The Kuna visitors to the National Museum of the American Indian in New York recognized this design immediately and explained that it was an "old design." These are leaves used in medicine.**

80.0 x 81.0 cm. NMAI 16/6384. Collected in 1922 and presented by Lady Richmond Brown and F. A. Mitchell Hedges.

Snakebite medicine

When someone is bitten by a snake on the mainland, he must remain as inactive as possible while at the same time summoning help. If the bite is minor, he is generally treated on the spot and then carried home, where his treatment continues. If it is a more serious wound, however, he is taken to a small thatched hut located some distance from the community, either on a nearby uninhabited island or on the mainland. At this point, a specialist in snake medicine takes charge of the case. The only people allowed near the hut are the specialist, his assistants, and older members of the patient's family; the spirits of young people are too strong and will harm the patient's debilitated spirit. Women in the patient's immediate family strip the beads from around their necks, arms and legs, and wear their blouses inside-out, for their colorful, snakelike designs might attract snake bonigana.

The patient rests in the hut and is bathed with sweet-smelling plants to soothe his spirit. He eats bland foods and drinks medicinal concoctions made largely from bitter vines and bark to drive the snake boni from his system. Medicines such as chile peppers, tobacco, foul-smelling bark and vines, and barbasco are burned inside the hut to "confuse the road" that other dangerous bonigana might take to attack the patient: toad bonigana, which would cause the wound to swell; the squirrel fish boni, the morning star boni, and the fishhook boni, which would cause sharp pains; and various red animal bonigana, which would cause hemorrhaging. This is often accompanied by a chant called "The Way of the Rattlesnake," which strengthens the power of the medicines.

In serious cases, no one is allowed to journey to the mainland during the four days following the snakebite, for the snakes are said to be abroad in great numbers; and indeed, the snake spirit is menacing the entire community. A mildly toxic brew is prepared and everyone in the village is given a swallow. Its primary purpose is to

7.16. *Gabeewa*, **plant-that-closes-when-you-touch-it mola. This plant is used as an anesthetic and to aid in sleep.**
68.5 x 83.0 cm. NMAI 16/6363. Collected in 1922 and presented by Lady Richmond Brown and F. A. Mitchell Hedges.

"confuse the road" of the snake spirits, but it also serves to lower the strength of the villagers' spirits so they will not be a threat to the patient. Today, the Kuna often take the victim to the local government hospital for treatment with anti-venom, which serves to stem the infection; but they always follow this up with traditional medicines, for Western medicine is ineffectual at dislodging the snake boni from the patient's spirit.

Curing chants

There are ten major chant traditions, which can be divided into two types according to function and structure. The largest group might be termed "expedition" chants, in which a team of shaman spirits, accompanied by their spirit women, is sent to confront bonigana that have caused (or are threatening to cause) illness. Among these chants are Absoged Igar ("The Way of Conversing"), to combat epidemics; Muu Igar ("The Way of Muu"), for difficult childbirth; Gabur Igar ("The Way of Spanish Pepper"), to cure fevers and weakness; and Nia Igar ("The Way of the Demon"), to drive demons from the spirit of a person. The second category is that of chants that are similar to medicine counseling chants in structure and content, although they tend to be considerably longer. Examples of this category are Odammiboed Igar ("The Way of Cooling"), to reduce fevers; and Gurgin Igar ("The Way of Gurgin"), to alleviate headaches.

The chants are like scripts in which the events being described take place simultaneously in the world of spirit as the words come out of the chanter's mouth. Thus, when he calls his shaman spirits and assembles them around him, the spirits are understood to actually arrive at that moment, "like winds," and line up for action. And when the chanter details the steps of their journey into the realm of spirit, the shamans and women are, in fact, making their way to all of the places mentioned.

But he is doing much more than advising his spirit helpers. He is also manipulating all of the actors, good and evil, protagonists and antagonists, as well as sketching in the landscape in which the entire drama unfolds. In this way, the chants direct events in the world of spirit toward a successful conclusion, and bring about equilibrium and health.

Absoged Igar ("The Way of Conversing") is the most important and longest of all curing chants. It is generally performed to combat spiritual epidemics that have attacked or are menacing the community. The ceremony takes place over a period of eight consecutive days, during which the community is sealed off from the outside world. No loud sounds are permitted, children are kept from playing in the streets, and sex is forbidden. To assure that these rules are kept, a nele maintains spiritual vigil over the community. All of the adult men unite in the village gathering house, which is renamed the "tobacco smoking house," to assist in the preparation of a spiritual drink brewed from a selection of noxious herbs, including tobacco, which everyone smokes continuously over the eight-day period.

7.17. The birth house on Ustupu. Note that the roof goes down to the ground to keep those on the outside from peeking in on the birth ceremony. Mac Chapin, 1975.

Fifty large (roughly two meters) figures carved of balsawood are set in a line along the inner wall of the tobacco smoking house and surrounded by large quantities of nuchugana brought from houses throughout the community. With preparations in place, the chanter begins "The Way of Conversing," which he performs in the afternoon of each day for the duration of the eight-day ceremony. During the first day his chant describes the problem facing the community. The next four days summon the spirits of the balsawood figures and the nuchugana and prepare them for a journey to the fourth level of the cosmos, where they will confront the spirits causing the epidemic. The intoxicating drink is prepared amid much ceremony, growing in strength through the four days. On the sixth day the shaman spirits and their women (who carry the drink) travel down through the levels and arrive at the domain of the bonigana. The shaman spirits induce the bonigana to drink; they become comatose and the shaman spirits round them up with hooks, vines, nets, and baskets. They are then locked inside their domain with a surplus of drink; the shamans confuse the road the bonigana have taken to the community, and they return home.

At this point the chant ends. The shaman spirits stand vigil in the community for several days before the balsawood figures are taken to the mainland, where they leave for their homes in the world of spirit. The Kuna wrap up the ceremony by returning their nuchugana to their homes. Life gradually returns to normal; the villagers are allowed to move in and out of the community, and work on the mainland is resumed. If the ceremony has been successful, the epidemic will be eliminated.

Muu Igar (The Way of Muu)

Conception occurs when the "white burba" (the white spirit, or semen) of the male mixes with the "red burba" (the red spirit, or menstrual blood) of the female inside the uterus. Once this has occurred, the danger that the fetus' healthy development will be upset is great, and, in fact, this is potentially the most critical period in the entire birth cycle. Not only the pregnant women but her entire family must observe a large number of prohibitions such as:

killing or eating sea turtles; this will cause hemorrhaging;

touching, killing, or eating octopus, whose spirit will wrap its tentacles
around the fetus and keep it in the womb;

eating iguana, whose spirit will cause the woman's body to twist and
contort during childbirth;

handling needles, spear points, or other sharp objects, for their spirits will
cause sharp pains;

During pregnancy, the woman holds to a strict diet and takes medicines to
"obscure the road" that bonigana might take to attack the fetus, as well as to cool
the woman's spirit, reduce the size of the fetus so that birth will be easy, and bathe
the woman's spirit in sweet-smelling medicines to give it an agreeable fragrance.
Women with histories of miscarriages are given medicines to "fortify the hammock"
(the spiritual manifestation of the womb) and keep the "door" to the womb shut tight.
When time for birth approaches, the spirit of the woman's vagina is made slippery
through the ingestion of the meat of green moray eels, the slimy pulp of the cacao
fruit, and water steeped in plants with slippery sap.

At the level of spirit, the fetus is being taken care of during pregnancy in the
house of Muu, which is located on the fourth level of the cosmos and simultaneously
inside the womb of the pregnant woman. Muu is the deity responsible for the spiritual
development of the fetuses of all land animals and human beings born on Earth. She
is aided in this vast enterprise by numerous daughters and granddaughters (collectively
called *muugana*), each of whom specializes in the care and education of a particular
animal or type of human being. With respect to humans, for example, there are
muugana in charge of the formation of chiefs, shamans, albinos, weaklings, hard
workers, troublemakers, and so forth. Under normal circumstances, the spiritual fetuses
of such individuals are released from Muu's house at the end of the gestation period
to be born to mortal mothers on earth.

From time to time, however, difficulties occur and the baby cannot make its
way from the womb. This may be due to a spirit, offended by the violation of a taboo,
that has attacked the fetus and will not let it go. But it sometimes happens that Muu
herself is the responsible party. She and her assistants, in their role as prenatal mothers,
occasionally become overly attached to their "children" and refuse to give them up
at the appointed time. Muu is not considered by the Kuna to be evil in any sense;
yet she, like humans, sometimes lets her emotions overrun her behavior, leading to
life-threatening situations.

When complications of this sort arise, a chanter skilled in "The Way of Muu"
is summoned to the birth house, a specially constructed building sealed off from
the prying eyes of villagers (Fig. 7.17). As soon as he arrives, he consults with the
midwives and the nele (if present) about the expectant woman's condition. This
information is crucial, for it will orient his chant toward the particular boni that is
most likely responsible. While the midwives take care of the woman, the chanter
positions himself on a small wooden stool at the head of her hammock, places some
dried chile peppers on the coals of a clay brazier to keep the bonigana at bay, and
begins to intone his chant.

The chanter describes the village, the birth house, the woman, and her family.
Then he summons his spirit helpers from their homes in the direction of the
rising sun and assembles them beneath the hammock. The leader is Shaman
Balsawood, noted for his intelligence and levelheadedness. He is assisted by an array
of nuchugana and plant and animal shamans: armadillo shamans that will dig

tunnels, bee shamans that will entangle themselves in Muu's hair, vine shamans that will tie Muu's door shut. They are accompanied by women who will carry an intoxicating drink to Muu's house. When they are all gathered, the chanter warns them of the dangers that lie ahead and counsels them to behave well and with courage.

The armadillo shamans dig holes through the surface of the earth. The shamans then all travel to the first level, where they canoe up Muu's river. They next strike out overland, traversing the next three levels by climbing a series of hills. All along the path, they see blood gushing from the ground and spreading out like mist, dripping from the backs of animals; they move past a giant rock in the shape of a human skull and cross a field of "river barrels" that are shuffling back and forth, shooting off sparks, and spouting blood from long tubes. They pass through a grove of trees that have jaguars crouching in their branches. Finally they arrive at Muu's house on the fourth level. Fragrant flowers of gold and silver are climbing up the walls of the house.

The shamans enter and take stock of the house. It is full of animals of all types: peccaries, tapirs, monkeys, parrots, toucans, pacas, iguanas. They are scratching at the ground, growling, climbing up the walls, hanging from the beams, defecating, ruffling their feathers, and raising the hackles on their backs. The shamans walk past the animals and approach Muu, who is sitting in her hammock.

A long exchange takes place in which the shamans ask the whereabouts of the fetus and Muu says she has no idea. Muu tries to find out the identity of the chanter so she can stop the chant and drive the shamans out, but they will not tell her. Muu is offered the drink, which she swallows eagerly, and becomes intoxicated. The chile pepper shaman lifts off his hat and pepper smoke billows out, filling the house with a thick cloud. The muugana begin to cough and fall down and the shamans rush about the house looking for the fetus. They find it in a corner, lift it onto their hip as if it were a child, cover it with cool leaves, and begin to leave the house.

They seal Muu's door shut with sealing wax and sap, and set off down through the levels, traveling "like winds." They come to Muu's river and paddle down to its mouth, then move swiftly through the tunnels dug by the armadillo shamans to the surface of the earth, finally emerging in the birth house. They see the midwives taking care of the woman. They approach the woman and lift up her fetus, placing it in her lap, her knees, her body, her veins, her head, her eyes, her hair, and her hair lice. Then Shaman Balsawood stands back and says to his followers: "We will stand vigil. We will stand vigil to the east, the west, the north, and the south."

Muu Igar may last for as long as four or five hours, and is repeated over several days or until the mother gives birth. It rarely happens that the baby is born at the precise moment that the shamans bring the spirit of the fetus down Muu's river and emerge through Muu's door into the birth house. Rather, performed in conjunction with medicines and the ritual manipulations of a team of midwives, the chant exerts a powerful coercive force which hangs in the air and pressures the physical world to conform to the course of events charted in the world of spirit. With order restored to the world of spirit, the road is cleared so that childbirth can follow along it.

In real life, all of the different strategies—medicines, chants, and ritual practices—fit together in a wider context of curing as the Kuna utilize the resources they have available to overcome illness and restore patients to health.

The Story of Magiryai

In 1975, in the community of Ustupu ("Agouti Island"), a four-year-old girl named Magiryai became sick. Her lungs were congested, she had a hacking cough, she was seriously constipated, and she was losing strength. Despite medicinal baths aimed at cooling her spirit, her fever rose, she lost her appetite, and she cried often because of persistent headaches. At this point, her parents summoned a nele to make a diagnosis and suggest the best course of treatment. This decision was based on the fact that Magiryai's condition was becoming progressively worse, and she had suffered since infancy from chronic fevers (Fig. 7.18).

The nele, a woman who lived nearby and was a close friend of Magiryai's maternal grandmother and great-grandmother, took her position on a small wooden stool before Magiryai, puffed on a pipe given her by one of the women, and gazed intently through a shifting funnel of smoke rising from cacao seeds burning in a clay brazier at her feet. After several minutes of silence she turned to the assembled women and announced that when Magiryai had been vaccinated several days earlier in the village clinic she had been frightened by the needle. Her burba had been jolted loose, fallen to the ground, and been carried off by the spirit of the "water dog" that lived in a deep pool called "the hole of the dog" just off the beach behind

the clinic. She recommended that "The Way of Cacao" (Sia Igar), a short chant to recover errant spirits and reduce fevers, be performed. At the same time, she recommended additional medicines to relieve the congestion that made it hard for her to breathe.

That evening, "The Way of Cacao" was chanted, and the nele returned the next morning to evaluate the situation. She said that the missing burba had indeed been recovered, but during the night another "dog" spirit, a relative of the water dog, had appeared from directly under the house, shaken the burba loose again, and escaped with it. This had occurred because Magiryai's father, himself an igar wisid, had failed to protect her with a chant to "confuse the road" that the water dog spirit had opened up, and the new dog had taken this path.

At this point, Magiryai's paternal grandmother summoned another nele, also a woman, for a second opinion. After facing the patient and smoking her pipe she turned to the women and said in a staccato monologue that the first nele had been correct in her assessment of Magiryai's illness, that "The Way of Cacao" had restored the burba, that it had been shaken loose again by the "dog" spirit, and this was because the father had failed to "confuse the road." Then she went on to say that she had detected a "yellow worm" lodged in the abdominal region of

7.18. Women taking care of Magiryai. Note pots of different types of medicines on the floor beneath the hammock, and the wooden stool for chanters near Magiryai's head.
Mac Chapin, Ustupu, 1975.

7.19. Nuchugana beneath the hammock of Magiryai with a bucket of liquid medicine and a clay incense burner with burned cacao seeds inside it. Note the African carving among the nuchugana, which was given to the specialist by a visiting tourist. Mac Chapin, Ustupu, 1975.

Magiryai's burba, and this was causing the constipation and dark yellow urine. She prescribed medicine to eliminate the worm, then went on to suggest "The Way of Gurgin" to relieve her headaches.

The medicines were gathered, counseled, and assembled in the house beneath Magiryai's hammock (Fig. 7.19). A chanter named Alfaro was enlisted to sing "The Way of Gurgin." He arrived, sat on a wooden stool at the head of Magiryai's hammock, smoked a pipe, and began to place cacao seeds in the clay pot at his feet. While he was doing this he asked the women casually if the patient was a boy or a girl. Then he set his pipe aside, cleared his throat, and began to intone his chant.

"The Way of Gurgin" lasted approximately two hours. It gave a stylized account of how Magiryai's gurgin had become damaged: it was in pain, it was rising up, it was wrinkled, it was pallid, it was being attacked by "the angry ones" (*bonigana,* disease-causing spirits). He then counseled a wide array of medicines—cacao, sweet basil, a number of sweet-smelling plants, plants with spines and hooks—to set things straight, and moved into a segment called "bathing the gurgin," in which the medicines wash the patient's burba. Finally, he summoned a series of spirits to stand vigil over Magiryai's spirit, to keep dangerous spirits at bay.

The following morning, Alfaro journeyed to the forest to gather gurgin medicines, bringing them to the house around noon. He chanted the same version of "The Way of Gurgin." About half an hour after he left, an igar wisid named Rogelio appeared and sang his own version of "The Way of Gurgin."

The atmosphere in the house was bleak as Magiryai's condition worsened despite the intensified treatment involving both medicines and chants. When Rogelio finished chanting he paused briefly and then launched into "The Way of the River Agate" (Akwanusa Igar), which has the double purpose of recovering the burba and then cooling it. Shortly after he began chanting, a tub of water containing some twenty smooth river agates (*akwanusagan*) was brought forward and placed beneath Magiryai's hammock. Rogelio described the journey of the river agate shamans to the domain of the dog spirits. There, they found Magiryai's burba, calmed it down, for it had become disoriented, confused, and afraid when it had fallen from her body. With the help of a host of river plant shamans they worked to refresh the burba. This chant lasted just under two hours.

Later that evening, Magiryai's father chanted "The Way of Spanish Pepper" (Gabur Igar), the most powerful curing chant for recovering abducted burbagana. This was a sign that the illness was indeed serious. Magiryai had still not had a bowel movement; she had a deep, rasping cough.

7.20. Tomás, father of Magiryai, chanting Gabur Igar ("The Way of Spanish Pepper") at the head of her hammock. This chant is used primarily to reduce fevers.
Mac Chapin, Ustupu, 1975.

The medicines assembled beneath her hammock were the following:

- a large iron pot filled with water and sections of bamboo, pieces of cane flutes, and small tubular stems. She was bathed in the liquid to open up her anus.
- an iron pot filled with sections of roots taken from the river bank and soaking in water. She was bathed in this to cool her burba.
- a pail with twenty river agates in water, also for cooling the burba.
- a small pot with sweet-smelling plants soaking in water. The liquid was gently massaged into her scalp to refresh and repair her gurgin and eliminate the headaches.
- two small bowls with tobacco leaves soaking in water. The brown liquid was smeared on her stomach to eliminate the yellow worm.
- a small pot filled with water and broken pieces of (smoking) pipes, clay pieces with tunnels in them, and the diaphragm mechanism from the chest of a rubber doll. The liquid was poured over her throat and chest to clear her throat and lungs.
- bottled Western medicines: Pepto Bismol (for the stomach), Vick's cough syrup (for the cough), Bay Rum, and Menticol (to repair the gurgin).

At regular intervals, the women lifted Magiryai from her hammock and administered the medicines, bathing her as she sat in the large pots, rubbing her head and chest and stomach, and then drying her before returning her to her hammock. Yet she was still in the grips of illness; she was listless and her eyes were blank, empty.

The next morning, Rogelio returned and chanted "The Way of Gurgin," paused to readjust his thoughts, and began intoning "The Way of the River Agate." While he was engaged in this task, four different chanters were simultaneously performing "The Way of Cacao" in their own homes. Magiryai's father had sent each of them a packet of cacao seeds and they were chanting to the spirits of these seeds. Thus, on that afternoon, there were five curing chants being performed for her at the same time.

The nele who had made the initial diagnosis of Magiryai's illness returned to evaluate the situation. She said that the patient was now weaker than before because she had lost still another portion of her burba. She said that there was some confusion as to which bonigana had carried off the other burba; but went on to say that all they could do was continue with "The Way of Cacao," "The Way of the River Agate," and "The Way of Spanish Pepper." She also said that the gurgin was being restored to health (indeed, her headaches had abated) and the yellow worm had disappeared, but that further complications by a "frog" spirit were causing her stomach to bloat. The most immediate problem was her high fever, and her cough was as persistent as ever.

As the chanters continued virtually around the clock, the Panamanian doctor from the community clinic appeared on the scene, having heard of Magiryai's condition from a villager. He had no trouble convincing the women to take her to the clinic for a checkup. When there, he examined her and without any explanation, gave her an injection. In fact, the women were not particularly interested in his interpretation of the illness. They wrapped Magiryai up in a blanket to protect her spirit from spirits along the way and carried her home.

A chanter named Mastayans arrived in the afternoon to sing yet another version of "The Way of Spanish Pepper." His version was somewhat different from the version sung by Magiryai's father, but it covered the same general course and touched on the same elements. He was describing the shaman spirits as they entered the domain

7.21. Magiryai in medicine canoe, covered with the juice from the genipa fruit to protect her against bonigana. Wooden bowl in front has several whole fruits which are pounded into a paste for application on the skin.
Mac Chapin, Ustupu, 1975.

of the crocodile spirits in search of Magiryai's burba when the doctor strode noisily through the door, speaking in Spanish, followed by his Kuna nurse. Mastayans stopped chanting. The nurse carried a syringe her hand. The women had failed to bring Magiryai to the clinic that afternoon, the doctor said angrily; he was busy and these house calls were eating inordinately into his time. None of the women spoke; Mastayans sat silently puffing on a pipe. The nurse spoke to the women, stepped forward and injected Magiryai, who was being held by her mother, and both of them left. Mastayans waited for a few minutes and then continued his chant, describing how the shamans were exchanging their hats with the crocodile spirits.

From this point on, Magiryai's condition slowly returned to normal. The chanters continued with "The Way of Spanish Pepper," "The Way of Gurgin," and "The Way of the River Agate" over the next couple of days. As the fever diminished, her cough softened, and her bowels began to move, the chanters placed more emphasis on "standing vigil" over her burba. Fresh medicines were brought in and she was bathed with the same regularity. Now medicines to "strengthen" her niga and "firm up" and "stretch" her burba were administered. The doctor and the nurse returned and gave her another injection. The mood in the house had brightened and people were joking among themselves.

As the chanters continued, the nele returned to scan Magiryai's burba. She concluded that the shaman spirits sent into battle by the chanters had done their job well: all of the burbagana had been recovered, the "angry ones" (bonigana) had been routed, and Magiryai's niga and burba were being restored to their former strength. Her optimistic evaluation was supported by the dream of a close relative, who had seen a host of men and women wearing white hats who were standing about the house watching over Magiryai.

From this point on, things gradually returned to normal. Mastayans came for a final session of "The Way of Spanish Pepper," and Alfaro chanted "The Way of Gurgin" twice. The insular gloom in the house was replaced by neighbors who came and went on mundane errands. Some of the medicines were discontinued, while others, such as those for strengthening Magiryai's niga and burba, were replaced and continued. Injections were continued for two more days. Magiryai ate a hard-boiled egg and some crackers, and drank a can of fruit juice and some milk. She was very thin, but finally out of danger.

Kuna Picture-Writing
A Study in Iconography and Memory

Carlo Severi

Rows of small figurines, of circles, boats, flags, leaves, or flowers, accurately colored one by one, on balsawood form the oldest documents that we have; more recently they appear on ruled pages of school notebooks. Kuna healers and chiefs have produced images of this kind for at least a century (Fig. 8.2). Like other picture-writings of the American Indians, these images have been considered with some embarrassment by Western scholars. Historians of art have found them difficult to understand in purely aesthetic terms; historians of writing found them too pictorial to be sound vehicles of information.

As a result, we often find them exposed in museums hastily labeled as "drawings used as supports for memory." However, what exactly is their relation to memory? How are they actually used for memorizing? What kind of texts do they help to preserve? What indigenous notions of memory and image are involved in this technique? A drawing devoid of phonetic value is, we tend to think, a fragile, even rusty means for encoding a text. Whatever the symbolism used for transcribing words in a drawing, it will be fatally restricted to the domain of the individual. "Never mistake a drawing for a text," warned E. Gombrich rightly in his famous book on *The Sense of Order* (1979): the way to produce meaning of a design—argued the great historian of art—is totally different from that of a sign. A design should be freely appreciated aesthetically, a sign should be deciphered following implicit rules (1979, 362). As a consequence, communication through signs tends to be easy and accurate, while communication through images is difficult, always arbitrary, inevitably vague. Faced with a document that stands midway between sign and design—we will see that in a Kuna pictogram there is more than in an "arbitrary" design and less than in a "conventional" sign—we feel uneasy.

8.1. *Galu*, **spirit house mola. An illustration of spirit strongholds that are also often depicted in picture-writing. Dad Ibe, the sun, is shown in the center. 1974.** 58.5 x 73.0 cm. Private collection.

8.2 (BELOW). **Kuna picture-writing collected in 1927 by Nordenskiöld.** Nordenskiöld 1938, PLATE VII.

Yet field work shows that the Kuna still use these drawings for transcribing very long texts, and that they provide for a very effective memorization of them, even if, as Nils Holmer (1951) has demonstrated long ago, there is no representation of the sounds of the language in these pictograms. So how can Kuna drawings be almost as effective as writing, without possessing precisely the most important property of the writing systems, namely a consistent representation of the sounds of the language? How can these rather rough designs replace signs, or at least assume a similar function for the conservation of very elaborate texts? A typical reaction, still common among historians of writing, has been, as we will see, to isolate as an exception and then marginalize the Kuna tradition. In this context the effectiveness for memorization of Kuna pictograms ceases to be discussed; it is either superficially doubted, or simply denied (cf., for example, Gelb 1979, 1033–79). Kuna picture-writings, following authors like Diringer (1937), Cohen (1958), Gelb (1952), or, more recently, Defrancis (1990), is hardly worth an analysis in itself. It must be like any other American Indian pictograph: volatile, uncertain, unreliable. In this paper, I will take the opposite direction, and try to show that Kuna pictography has its own consistency, and that we find these designs difficult to understand not because they are arbitrary or confused, but because they contradict some of our most deeply rooted prejudices about "oral" traditions, writing, and the making of a social memory.[1]

When speaking of societies that we no longer wish to regard as primitive, we have got into the habit of calling them "oral" or "preliterate societies." With the exception of the early civilizations of Mexico, the American Indian societies naturally fall into this category. However, this way of defining these societies is fairly recent, and far from being obvious. The first discoverers of the New World would undoubtedly have been surprised to see them so described. For many of them, it was perfectly natural to assume that the Indians, like themselves, had always possessed a technique for preserving knowledge, legible signs, parchments, and indeed entire books (Severi 1994).

When the Spanish Jesuit Gassó—the first missionary to settle for a long duration among the Kuna in the Kuna Yala archipelago in order to undertake the difficult task of converting them to Christianity (Gassó 1910–1914)—reported the very widespread and contemporaneous practice of picture-writing, he viewed the writing of the Indians in the same perspective. In the first place, there was no doubt in his mind that it was a vestige of the past, a practice that had long since fallen into disuse: "In former times these Indians were acquainted with writing," he wrote in 1910 about a practice of which there was direct evidence before his eyes and which, it should be added, still continues today. Secondly, for him as for seventeenth-century chroniclers de Enciso (1857) or Oviedo (1851–1855), the pictograms were "hieroglyphs" altogether comparable in their function to our systems of language notation. Nevertheless, the ritual use of this picture-writing, the techniques employed, and its very appearance remained completely unknown to the missionary. Concerning the picture-writings, Gassó (1911–1914, t. 20, 253) writes:

> *Antes escribian estos indios sus escrituras de jeroglifico en unas tablillas*
> *que hacian de la madera blanda que llamamos balsa, grabando con una*
> *especie de estilete las figuritas: unas les representaban palabras o idéas,*
> *y otras, notas musicales.*

It is clear that these illusions, these mirror images between Spaniards and Indians, could persist only for lack of real documents.

The earliest real records of texts "written by American Indians"[2] were assembled in the middle of the last century, in the northeastern United States, a long way away from the Darién and its tropical forests. Among the researchers who collected this material, H.R. Schoolcraft (1851), G. Mallery (1886–1893), and W. Hoffmann (1888) were no doubt the most active. To Mallery, in particular, we are indebted for a rich corpus of Amerindian picture-writings, formed though it is of scattered examples, and almost never along with the corresponding texts. Neither Mallery nor Schoolcraft were theorists. They were men of action, one a governor of Indians and the other a colonel in the American army. They collected documents, leaving speculation to others. In the same spirit, E. Nordenskiöld, who visited the Kuna of the Darién in 1927, set about collecting the first pictographic documents of that population. He too, like Mallery and Schoolcraft, was a man of action. However, he did not confine himself, like his predecessors, to collecting pictures accompanied by vague commentaries or a few isolated words. He worked with young Indians[3] and started to collect, from the mouths of chiefs and shamans, texts (e.g., incantations, therapeutic chants, stories) believed to be transcribed by pictograms.

It was difficult work which sometimes took on a tentative character owing to Nordenskiöld's inadequate grasp of the Indian language. The first results were published in 1928 and then again ten years later, in a posthumous edition in 1938, after the work had been interrupted by Nordenskiöld's premature death. Many pictures remained without commentaries and many texts remain incomplete in the field notes that he left to the Göteborg Ethnological Museum. And yet for all that, the documents published by him are in many respects quite exceptional. For the first time, what was being offered for perusal was no longer, as in Mallery's work, rows of uncertain signs, usually very few in number, aligned on a page, followed by occasional skimpy commentaries.

The Indians that Nordenskiöld had visited painstakingly filled up pages upon pages of the small exercise books that the Swedish ethnologist had brought them. Stories relating the origin of certain mythical beings associated with the sun or moon (Nordenskiöld 1928, 30 sqq and plate VII); invocations to magic crystals to the spirits of snakes or birds; and shamanistic, funerary, and other chants linked to initiation rituals, which could require hours to recite, were recorded in long sequences of signs. Nordenskiöld also noted two important details, concerning the medium used for these writings and their internal organization: the pictograms were traditionally drawn on planks of balsawood (of which he collected a remarkable example, now in the Göteborg Ethnological Museum[4]) and always in accordance with a fixed pattern (the signs running from bottom right upwards, in boustrophedon).

The reaction of the historians of writing to this new material (which became known between 1930 and 1938) was highly circumspect. The question of writing, by which the men of the Renaissance set so little store, was crucial for these scholars who, in an evolutionist and positivist spirit, were endeavoring to establish a synoptic and chronological table of the inventions of humanity. What seemed natural to the humanists and navigators of the sixteenth- and seventeenth-centuries had become incredible. If the presence of writing was evidence of an evolution that the American Indians had never been able to achieve, how were these Kuna signs to be interpreted, where were they to be placed in the scale of the technical evolution of the human species? The question was not an easy one to resolve.[5] After being seen as the mysterious vestige of a perfect but unknowable writing (a "paleography,"[6] as Gassó still considered it), the picture-writing of the Kuna was said to derive from an imitation of the Spaniards and thus to be further evidence of the strength of one group of people and the weakness of another. The conclusion seemingly drawn by Diringer was that those who had not reached the stage of writing had no choice but to ape ours.[7] Kuna picture-writing was thus relegated to the status of an intellectual curiosity. When I. J. Gelb (1952; 1979) took a brief look at it, its place in the evolution of the techniques of humanity (which Diringer still had some trouble in establishing) had been settled. Kuna picture-writing represented a distant precursor of phonetic writing, uncertain evidence of an effort toward writing, an effort that had, of course, proved fruitless. Pictography could not be considered an effective technique by Gelb because, to his mind, no information can truly be conveyed through such a medium.[8] The metaphor that he uses to describe any pictorial images preceding phonetization is very revealing. Such images are steam. It is true that without steam no locomotive can advance, but it still remains formless, indeterminate, volatile (1979, 1045). The fact that major traditions have existed without writing (the Andean civilization and the Vedic tradition remained resolutely oral for centuries[9]) does not disturb the grammatologist. Since that time, Gelb's verdict as to the impracticable nature of picture-writing has barely been questioned. John Defrancis (1990) in his ambitious *Visible Speech*, replaced Gelb's thermodynamic metaphor with one borrowed from highway construction. In his book, pictograms are labeled once and for all "dead-end symbols" (1990, 58).

Jack Goody, for his part, in a series of studies (1977, 1987) developed an idea of orality that fully corresponds to the view of writing outlined by Gelb. The illusion entertained by the grammatologist, who wants to base his science of writing on the study of the internal properties of sign systems, almost independently of the laws of language, is matched by an idea of oral tradition that is always defined negatively[10] in relation to writing. In this approach, no visual medium or adjunct to the spoken word is taken into account. The spoken word, so Vansina writes, must be taken to comprise all that is passed down by word of mouth to the exclusion of any material object that might serve as a source for knowing the past (Vansina 1976, 61, 275). The position adopted by Goody and Watt (1968) perhaps illustrates better than any other the link between these two viewpoints: one anxious to assert the autonomy of signs in relation to forms of enunciation, the other proclaiming the autonomy of the spoken word as against material forms (objects, pictures, etc.). According to these two authors, in a work that has had considerable influence, in preliterate societies there can be no hierarchy or clear distinction where traditional knowledge is concerned. Information circulates freely in such societies, without constraints or rules, since the spoken word is by definition unstable and difficult to control. In such a situation, all knowledge directly answers the homeostatic demands of the social organism (ibid. 1–68). Consequently, no effective memory is to be found in oral traditions (Vansina 1976, 295–96). Any memory that does not directly answer the demands of social life is then excluded from traditional knowledge. It follows that, by definition, oral societies are societies virtually devoid of memory. This again, although expressed in different terms, is the same idea as Gelb's: before writing, uncertainty and disorder prevail in the realm of knowledge.

In considering the case of the Kuna, we shall be led to question this approach. However, far from putting us on the track of a vanished (or failed) writing, the Kuna picture-writings will force us rather to think again about this all too simple conception of the use of the spoken word. In order to understand the images we are examining, we need a model of tradition other than that based on the purely oral. Pictographic iconography does not have an immediate bearing on the representation of the language but rather follows the particular structure of texts fixed by tradition. We shall see that if this technique of memory is disregarded, pictographic symbolism becomes unthinkable for the Kuna, and incomprehensible for us. Among the Kuna, as in many American cultures (Zuni, Navajo, Pima[11]), any spoken word referring to traditional knowledge is ritualized. All ritual is "chant." To understand this point, it is essential to refer to the categories used by them to classify knowledge. The Kuna do not distinguish literary genres (e.g., myth, epic, legend, magical incantation), only according to their content. A crucial distinguishing criterion of knowledge concerns the type of experience of which it is the result. When it is innate, resulting from an immediate vision of the supernatural, it pertains exclusively to the *nele*, the seer who in his dreams and visions sees the future or the ultimate cause of a calamity or sickness. This knowledge can and must be ritually protected. It does not require any learning.

Learned knowledge is altogether different. While the nele's vision is unique and may apply to any circumstance, the spoken words learned from a master are specialized, specific, and local. Unable to be mastered in its totality, the knowledge to which the Kuna specialist holds the key is divided into several traditions that are learned only with difficulty, jealously protected from noninitiates, and subject to reciprocal controls on the part of specialists. The first distinction made in learned knowledge concerns those who are required to be its enunciators and guardians, and at the same time entails linguistic differentiation. Chiefs, shamans, and specialists in female initiation rituals each have their own knowledge and language. For each also, there are specific circumstances for the ritual enunciation of traditional knowledge.

The contrast between the words of the chief, those of the shaman, and those of the *gandule*—the specialist in the initiation chant reserved for the occasion of a girl's first menstruation—will suffice to give an idea of the forms taken by this ritualization of traditional words. The gandule, whose chant recalls the origins of the differentiation between the sexes, and between animals and human beings, gives public utterance to a text which is by tradition fixed and unchangeable. Joel Sherzer, with others, has produced evidence of the extraordinary precision with which these texts are preserved. It is to be noted that this is the only occasion when the actual use of pictography is included in the sequence of ritual actions to be performed in public (Sherzer 1990, 240).[12]

The shaman for his part recites his therapeutic chant (a genre of which we now know a number of examples) in a place set aside for this purpose, adopting a fixed stance, prescribed in detail by tradition (Severi 1987). Here, too, variation is in principle forbidden and pictographic notation common practice. The case of the chief is somewhat different. He is required to recite regularly (one evening in two), before the village men's assembly, the Chant of the Fathers, a cycle of chants that mixes together tales of the origins, stories of culture heroes and villages, chronicles of everyday life, moral admonishment, and political speechmaking. The chief's words are, like the others, pronounced publicly (before the men's assembly) in a language that ordinary people (and primarily women who, in this context, do not have the right to speak) cannot understand. However, the recitation of the Chant of the Fathers has two distinctive features: the chief's words are always translated and commented on by his second-in-command (the *argar*, whose role is indeed to be the chief's spokesperson). These words also, alone among traditional words, have the privilege of being more flexible, of being faithful more to the substance than to the letter of any given traditional story (Howe, Sherzer, and Chapin 1980; Howe 1986).

The use of picture-writing is keyed to these degrees of elaboration of the chief's words. Used, as will be seen, to fix cores of traditional knowledge (lists of names of places or of persons not to be forgotten), it serves no purpose in the case of a mere admonishment or a political speech that a chief chooses to formulate in words, without referring to the far stricter model of the chant.

In short, traditional texts are ritualized by the actual modes of enunciation[13] and by the use (fixed in the chanting of therapeutic, funeral, and initiation rituals, relatively fixed in the case of the cosmological and mythical tales of chiefs, and definitely improvised in the case of admonishments and chronicles) of a parallelistic style that

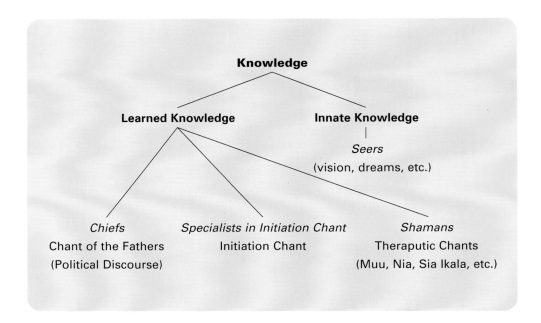

8.3. Typology of Kuna ritual words.

reduces each story to the alternation of a limited number of fixed formulas, repeated and varied in ways that we shall look at in detail later. The result of this division of languages and knowledge is a classification and a distribution of repertoires of traditional texts.[14] The division of Kuna knowledge has been sketched in this way by Howe (1974) (Fig. 8.3).

The knowledge that can be transcribed in pictograms is then intended to be enunciated, either publicly or privately, but in a strictly ritualized form. Far from being a way of dispersing knowledge in the labyrinth of any given specialist's skills, parallelistic enunciation strongly simplifies the structure of the narrative while being sufficiently flexible to adapt to any event, any story in the tradition. D. Tedlock (1983) has fully understood this phenomenon, which he has studied among the Zuni and the Maya-Quiché: "Ordinary talk not only has words in it, in the sense of strings of consonants and vowels, but it has patterns of stress, of emphasis, of pitch, of tone, of pauses or stops that can move somewhat independently of the sheer words and make the same word mean quite different things…. To fix a text without making visible marks is to bring stress and pitch and pause into a fixed relationship to the words. The Zuni call this technique 'raising it right up,' we would call it 'chant'" (1983, 234).[15]

The parallelistic structure of Kuna ritual enunciation imparts to the story its rhythm, while linking the words to a fixed threnody, which reflects a stable relationship between stress, pitch, and pause. In this sense, all traditional knowledge is transformed into *igar*, i.e. "chant" in Tedlock's sense: regulated words, which are "raised right up."

Only at that moment does the pictogram appear. Examination of the pictographic materials and corresponding texts at our disposal leads to two conclusions: 1) Whatever the degree of variation allowed by tradition, a Kuna chant is always enunciated in a parallelistic style; 2) Anything capable of being enunciated in a parallelistic style can be rendered pictographically.[16]

Some examples: images and words

Let us now take a look at some examples of this pictographic transcription of ritualized words. Among Nordenskiöld's documents (Nordenskiöld 1928, vol. II, 54), the most straightforward is a list of names of "seers" (*nelegan*), the culture heroes sent to earth by God to instruct Kuna women and men in social customs, knowledge of plants, and the proper organization of the world in which they live (Fig. 8.4).

The drawing is extremely simple, the line uncertain, the images difficult to distinguish one from the other. Although the aim is to fix the names of individuals fully identified in the cycle of the Chants of the Fathers, no story seems to be mentioned here. The memory of the person who drew the figures seems to find support in a single principle, namely alternation. The list is divided between beings said to be "above" and beings said to be "below." This rudimentary criterion of spatial organization, whose effectiveness for memorization may be doubted,[17] is developed in another picture board (Fig. 8.5), which describes the movement across the sky of the canoe that is traveled in every night by one of the central characters in Kuna mythology, Moon, who is accompanied here by a series of mythical characters, incarnations of stars, animals, and plants. Another list of names then: but how is it represented? If we follow the numbering recorded by Nordenskiöld on the board, we realize that there are two organizational principles simultaneously at work here. Parallel to the enumeration by vertical columns or by horizontal lines of the list of characters associated with Moon (the details of which are of scant importance here), we see the establishment of a spatial classification of the pictograms by territories: sea, horizon, sky. Thanks to the horizon, which divides the area represented into two distinct territories, we can on examination understand not only the succession (1, 2, 3…) of characters accompanying Moon on his voyage, but also distinguish between those who belong to the sea, the sky, and the horizon. Far from representing directly, like a drawing, the voyage of Moon's cortege across the night sky, this image provides us with a prop for memorizing a list, in which the pictograms are organized according to a classification "by succession" and "by territories" (Severi 1985).

8.4. A list of proper names of "those above" and "those below."

This superimposition of different classificatory criteria plays a fundamental role in pictography. Gelb, Goody, Defrancis, and others see recourse to memory as an irremediable defect of graphic systems. That which is of the order of memory is for them individual, arbitrary, changing, unsure, never verifiable, etc. In what sense can we speak here of mnemonics or of a relationship to memory? Do we see here a series of no doubt rather rudimentary drawings made by the shaman or the Kuna chief exclusively by the light of their talent or imagination? If this is so, does this mean that these images, rapidly sketched for their personal use, can be understood by them alone?

We have already seen that the words transcribed as pictograms are immediately organized by linguistic difference, the parallelistic structure of the text and by the ritual modes of enunciation. Howe, Sherzer, and Chapin have shown how any variation, any personal creation fits into the mold of Kuna traditional speech (1980).

8.5. Moon's canoe.

It may also be noted that a large number of the pictographic texts at our disposal, although collected at different periods and by independent researchers, reveal a surprising stylistic homogeneity. A number of rules concerning the representation of objects are always observed: the pictograms are always arranged in a particular order, and a remarkably high number of signs regularly recur. These two remarks would suffice to convince us of the extreme inadequacy of an interpretation that would claim to reduce pictographic symbolism to the realm of individual imagination alone.

8.6. Four spirits' villages from the Demon's Chant.

It should also be added that the pictograms are always used as a didactic tool. During his period of instruction (which can last for years), the pupil of a shaman, a chief,[18] or any other Kuna specialist spends long days in his master's hut, where he must show respect and obedience. Nearly every day he brings him presents and he may even work for him for many years. In return, his master, whom he invariably calls *sayla* (chief), takes the pupil into his home and passes his knowledge on to him. This teaching is based on two separate forms of learning. One, which is purely verbal, draws on the disciple's auditory memory. The master recites a passage from the igar and has the disciple recite it until he has learned it by heart. The text is treated here, in Tedlock's expression, as a relic (1983, 236), the only concern being to memorize the words, not to understand them. In accordance with custom, the pupil thus often learns words whose meaning escapes him.

The other technique used for learning is based on pictograms. Very often, a pictogram represents a proper name (designating a place or a mythical being): the master shows his disciple drawings representing particular protagonists of the *igala*: a seer whose exploits are being recounted, a particular plant spirit, the mythical villages where the gods have locked up an evil spirit, etc. These images, which he must engrave on his memory and then learn to copy, are supposed to help him to recall, with what is meant to be absolute accuracy, a text that can sometimes be of considerable length.[19] We have seen that the pupil starts by learning verses of the chant, which he must try to memorize. The master then shows the pupil series of pictograms representing variations (the lists of names of villages, spirits, etc.) contained in the verse, while teaching the pupil to decipher them. With the help of the drawings the pupil can then question the master on the content and meaning of the text. It is then that the pupil, who up to now has had to learn "without arguing," can at last embark on an exegesis of the chants and form a more detailed and more thorough idea of the shamanistic tradition.

This twofold organization of instruction matches the parallelistic structure of the Kuna igar. Let us consider some examples taken from the Demon's Chant (Severi

8.7. Picture-writing on nele-nusa.
Nordenskiöld 1938, PLATE X.

1982, Severi and Gomez 1983). Here is how the text describes the underground villages (located at the fourth chthonian level in Kuna cosmology, which has eight) which the shaman's auxiliary spirits are to visit in search of a sick man's lost soul:

> Far away, there where the sun's canoe rises, another village appeared
> The village of the monkeys appeared
> The village shows its monkeys
> Far away, there where the sun's canoe rises, further still, another village
>   appeared, the village of the threads (snakes) appeared
> The village that coils up like a thread appears
> The village that coils up like a thread reveals itself
> The village that coils up like a thread and the village of the monkeys
>   unite, like two canoes in the sea they crash into one another
> Seen from afar, from far far away, the two villages unite, they seem to
>   touch
> Far away, there where the sun's canoe rises, another village appeared
> The village of the skirt appeared
> The village shows its skirt
> Far away, there where the sun's canoe rises, further still, another village
>   appeared, the village of the creepers appeared
> The village of the creepers appeared
> The village shows its creepers

Let us compare text and picture board (Fig. 8.6). As has been noted by Kramer (1970, 115 sqq) following Nordenskiöld, Kuna pictography does not transcribe all the words that are recited. Yet, what these scholars did not notice is that the choice of the words transcribed is by no means left to chance. Following the alternation between repeated formulae and "lists of variations" which structures the parallelistic text, the pictograms refer only to certain words in the language of the chants, and indeed to those very words which, at particular moments in the course of the chant (for the master who draws and for the pupil who learns to interpret the pictograms), play the role of variants in relation to a set formula. In point of fact, the pictogram transcription translates into images only the list of variations (the names of the villages: monkeys, threads, creepers, etc.). Throughout the Demon's Chant, the verbal formula that provides the narrative structure of the text ("Far away, there where the sun's canoe rises, further still, another village appeared") is never translated into pictograms. It has to be learned exclusively by means of verbal mnemonics: the memory of sounds.

It is to be noted in Figure 8.6 that the pictorial representation, in the form of a triangle, of the spirits' village (which recurs in much of the pictographic material, even from much earlier times[20]) seems quite independent of the text, and has its own meaning. Looking at Figure 8.7, one will understand at first glance, for instance, that the text transcribed here involves, like the Demon's Chant, a series of *galugan*, of "villages inhabited by evil spirits." In this picture-writing, we recognize a series of triangles inscribed in a bigger triangle that frames them.

However, Kuna chants never describe explicitly a *galu* (village). In the passage of the Demon Chant that we are discussing here, the text provides pointers as to the spatial location of the village ("there where the sun's canoe rises" naturally signifies "eastward"); it gives the village its name, but never describes its form. The learning of a Kuna chant consequently involves three separate elements: a graphic formula and a verbal formula, both constant and independent of one another, and a variation of the text translated into pictograms.

In fact, this alternation of fixed graphic and verbal patterns with "translated variations" is the basic principle of Kuna picture-writing, and can account for a great number of documents. In the Chant of the Demon, the entire passage describing the visit of the chiefs of the auxiliary spirits of the shaman, Nele Ukuwar, to the "villages" inhabited by the evil spirits, the images (Figs. 8.8-13) consistently translate only that feature which distinguishes one village from the others (its name).

This transcription shows clearly how picture-writing reduces considerably the text, limited as it is to some names. But it shows also how the drawings can powerfully enrich it using purely pictorial means: one by one, the villages (never commented on or described here by the text) become alive before our eyes, acquiring details, colors, and forms.

This referential interdependence between word and image is the main feature of Kuna picture-writing technique: far from being completely superimposable on one another, the two graphic and oral codes along with the corresponding learning techniques each provide specific information. The formula, which completes the definition of the spirits' village each time, gives us a good example of this. Let us compare the text with the image:

> The two villages unite, like two canoes in the sea they crash with
>   one another
> Seen from afar, far away the two villages unite; seen from afar, from
>   far far away they seem to touch

It is to be noted first that in the oral text all the villages crash into one another, two by two, at that vanishing point beyond the horizon where they are placed by the gaze of the shaman's seer-spirit. This succession of villages is not immediately visible in our redaction of the therapeutic chant. Basing his chant on the material at his disposal, the shaman in fact arranged the villages in pairs (1-2, 3-4, 5-6, etc.). The oral text (along with other early pictographic documents in which the images are arranged on long strips of balsawood) tells us that this movement of union which constitutes the chain of the spirits' villages here concerns all the villages. We shall, therefore, have to read the pictographic plates in uninterrupted succession. This particular

Figures 8.8-13. Sixteen "villages" from the Chant of the Demon.

8.8.
(LOWER LEFT) **The village of the sea (1).**
(LOWER RIGHT) **The village of the sky (2).**
(UPPER LEFT) **The village beneath the ground (3).**
(UPPER RIGHT) **The village of the dead (4).**

8.9.
(TOP) **Nele Ukuwar showing the villages to the auxiliary spirits (5).**
(BOTTOM) **Nele Ukuwar and the river leading to the villages (6).**

sequential ordering of the stages of the journey (and of the variations in the oral text) reveals another, purely mnemonic aspect of the pictographic notation. As he runs through this list of villages, the shaman will in fact have to say twice the name of all the villages (except the first and the last), following the pattern 1-2, 2-3, 3-4, etc.

Furthermore, we have in the Kuna text the expression *ulu—doe—yola*, where ulu means "canoe," toe means "clash or shock," and yola is the verb "to be seen." This expression means "seem to crash like two canoes (in the sea)" and is elsewhere regularly translated into an image with divergent lines (clash, shock) which unite the two

8.10.
(LOWER LEFT) **The village of the spikes (7)**.
(LOWER RIGHT) **The curved village of the thunderbolt (8)**.
(UPPER LEFT) **The white village (9)**.
(UPPER RIGHT) **The village of the fan (10)**.

8.11.
(LOWER LEFT) **The fast village (11)**.
(LOWER RIGHT) **The village with the hair of leaves (12)**.
(UPPER LEFT) **The red village (13)**.
(UPPER RIGHT) **The low village (14)**.

villages, achieving that superimposition on the horizon, or reciprocal communication, to which the text refers. However, the "point of impact," where the two villages meet is always marked in the drawing by a circle which represents both this "union" and the sun. The sun is in fact the esoteric meaning, concealed from noninitiates, of the word *ulukwa*, which signifies "canoe."

The two notions—one manifest in the oral text and implicit in the pictographic image (canoe), the other implicit in the text and shown in the drawing (sun)—are distributed in the two graphic and oral registers with the twofold aim of preserving

8.12.
(LOWER LEFT) **The little village (15).**
(LOWER RIGHT) **The round village (16).**
(UPPER LEFT) **The rounded village (17).**
(UPPER RIGHT) **The empty village (18).**

8.13. The Village of Transformations.

them by means of a mnemonic technique based on the image and concealing their true significance from the gaze of noninitiates. Without additional knowledge, the image of a sun could not refer to the ulukwa (canoe) of the text, nor could the same word designate the sun that is seen in the pictographic image.

This interplay of reference between text and image shows that neither one code of meaning nor the other is self-sufficient. Only a parallel reading of the iconography and the text allows the entire meaning to be revealed. I will try to show that this is especially true when Kuna pictography uses a more complex symbolism than that

8.14.The Village of Transformations, (detail).

which we have just been considering. Yet this sequence of supernatural villages placed along the path of the Chant of the Demon is still a fairly straightforward case. The relationship between the image and the word can become more complex.

Let us see another example: when, later in the same chant, the shaman needs to transmit to his pupil the description of great supernatural villages, inhabited by a whole series of animal spirits whose characteristics are enumerated in the chant, he adopts another technique. Among these great villages, the most important is the one known as the Village of Transformations (Severi 1982, 49), described as the true "place of origin" of the animal spirits that bring "madness" to men. For these spirits, which result from the "transformation" of certain animals of the forest, all birth is metamorphosis. After reproducing the constant formula already known to us in order to denote the appearance of a village ("Down there, there where the sun's canoe rises…"), the text announces: "Here, in this village, the spirits are transformed, the spirits are born." Through the nominalization of the verb, common in Kuna (Holmer 1947), and the position taken by this term in the text, the verb "to be transformed" thus becomes the proper name of the village. From that point on, the chant enumerates these metamorphoses one by one. Let us look at part of it:

> Here the nias, the lords of this place, are transformed
> Here the nias are transformed into peccaries, the peccaries are there,
> with their black clothes, they cry "ya-ya-ya-ya"
> The peccaries are now changed into nias, they are transformed into
> nias, the nias are transformed
> They are transformed into lords of the animals with striped fur; above
> the trees, the nias with striped fur cry "durku-durku"
> The animals with striped fur are now changed into nias, they are
> transformed into nias, the nias are transformed
> They are transformed into *goenaga* deer, the nias are here, at the foot
> of the trees, with their black clothes, with their entangled antlers,
> they cry "me-me"
> The goenaga deer are now changed into nias, they are transformed into
> nias, the nias are transformed
> They are transformed into *wasenaga* deer, the nias are there, at the foot
> of the trees, with their black clothes, with their entangled antlers,
> with their great pointed antlers, they cry "me-me"
> The wasenaga deer are now changed into nias, they are transformed into
> nias, the nias are transformed
> Into land animals, into peccaries the nias are transformed, the nias are
> there, at the foot of the trees, with their black clothes; down there,
> at the foot of the trees, the nias cry "mos-mos"

I will soon comment on some details of this very rich text.[21] Here, let me note that the procedure followed by the pictographic representation of the text remains the same. When the object was to present the stages of the shamanistic voyage, the board translated only a list of village names. Here, where the object is to describe the nature and number of spirits dwelling in a village, the pictograms translate a list of spirits' names. From the point of view of the structure of the text, we have then here a list of "transformations" that is inserted into a list of "village names":

Following this new principle (which is, in fact, a flexible use of the same principle, parallelism) the text can eventually elaborate, in quite refined terms, the notion of the process of "transformation" itself. Let us follow here the graphic and linguistic representation of this notion, as another example of the interplay between the memorized words and the images in a Kuna chant.

Let us refer to the verbal formula, which is regularly repeated here. Its first occurrence concerns, in the first two verses of text quoted earlier, the metamorphosis of the peccaries:

> Here the nias are transformed into peccaries, the peccaries are there
>> with their black clothes, they cry "ya-ya- ya-ya"
> The peccaries are now changed into nias, they are transformed into
>> nias, the nias are transformed

Let us consider the pictographic equivalent of these verses (Fig. 8.14). We note first of all that this graphic sequence possesses the same recurrent character as its equivalent in the oral text and that all the recurrent cases are consistent with one another, as they are in relation to the verbal formula. In the graphic transposition of the verb *obinemai* (to be transformed, to become other) we see the spirit represented, in its place of origin, as an animal with a human double. Now when we recall that one of the basic meanings of the word *burba*, "the double," is "immaterial image" (as it may be represented by the image of a human face reflected in a mirror, by the shadow cast by a body, by the echo of a cry in the forest, for example), we understand that this image of a human being (after the graphic description of the animal) is in fact its essence, its hidden double. The text and the reading given of it by the shaman are very clear here: what "one sees first" is the image of an animal; the form whose existence is accessible only to the gaze of the seer spirit (the nele); its secret is the image of a human being. The spirit is not fully defined either by the presence of an animal or by that of a person or even by a juxtaposition of the two notions. The spirit can appear only when an invisible human double makes its dwelling in the body of a forest animal. The "transformation" to which the chant refers is then defined using both words and images. Text alone (which never speaks of a "human soul") or even the sole graphic representation (which obviously cannot give an idea of an invisible presence) is unable to portray it completely.

This pictographic page, which shows a more complex relationship between images and words, also develops the same principles as we saw in the previous examples. The pictograms are classified there according to the same two criteria of sequence and territory. When the Kuna scribe must, further on, distinguish between the evil incarnations of two kinds of monkeys, he does so, as in the rudimentary example shown in connection with the list of culture heroes (Fig. 8.13) by contrasting "those above" with "those below."

> The nias are transformed into *una-umaga* animals, they are down
>> there, at the foot of the trees, with their black clothes, and they
>> cry "uma-uma"

8.15. The village of dance.

The una-umaga animals are changed into nias, they are transformed
 into nias, the nias are transformed
The nias are changed into *yo-yoga* monkeys, they are up there, above
 the trees, with their black clothes, they cry like monkeys
The yo-yoga monkeys are transformed into nias, they are transformed
 into nias, the nias are transformed

Similarly, in the village which follows immediately the Village of the Transformations, where the main theme is the dance that the animal spirits perform in order to seduce the human person and make her or him crazy, the pictograms portray, one by one, the spirit-dancers (deer, birds, etc.), while the general name of the place translates the action of dancing itself (see Fig. 8.15).

Once this principle of relationship with the text through the transcription of variations (or, as we have seen, variations of variations) is established, Kuna healers and chiefs can use picture-writing in two related ways. They can draw long texts made of simple images delineated in rows, or they can combine simple pictograms in order to draw more complex images transcribing several sections of a text. In one case these sections will follow each other as in a page of a manuscript; in the other, they will be disposed in a more "figurative" way, to compose a single image. Let us look at some examples, drawn from documents collected by Nordenskiöld, by Holmer and Wassén, and by myself. The first is taken again from the Demon's Chant. It is the beginning of its first part, called "Into the House of the Shaman" (collected in Mulatupu in 1981). The second belongs to the famous Muu Igala, the chant devoted to difficult childbirth, published by Holmer and Wassén in 1953. The third is drawn from the Rock Crystal Chant collected in 1927 by Nordenskiöld, presumably in Ustupu.

In our first example, at the beginning of the Nia Igar, we find the shaman-singer seated on a "golden seat" in his house, facing the sea. A violent wind is blowing, curbing the palms of the island. The ocean is agitated, the crests of the waves are becoming white. A great tempest is coming. Here is how the chant, in its verbal and pictorial versions (Fig. 8.16), describes this situation:

1. The evil wind is blowing, the shaman is seated
   in the house, he sits on the small golden
   seat, looking around
2. The evil wind is whistling, the shaman is
   seated in the house, he sits on the small
   golden seat, looking around
3. The evil wind is whirling, the shaman is
   seated in the house, he sits on the small
   golden seat, looking around
4. The evil wind is blowing, whistling, whirling,
   the shaman is seated in the house, he sits on
   the small golden seat, looking around
5. The trunks of the palms near the ocean curb
   themselves, the shaman is seated in the
   house, he sits on the small golden seat,
   looking around
6. The palms of the ocean are curved, the
   shaman is seated in the house, he sits on the
   small golden seat, looking around
7. The leaves of the palms near the ocean are
   changing, they become yellow, they shine
   like gold, the shaman is seated in the house,
   he sits on the small golden seat, looking
   around
8. The leaves of the palms of the ocean do not
   move, the shaman is seated in the house, he
   sits on the small golden seat, looking around

8.16. The beginning of the Chant of the Demon.

9. The leaves of the palms of the ocean become blue-green, the shaman is
   seated in the house, he sits on the small golden seat, looking around
10. The leaves of the palms of the ocean make noise, the shaman is seated
    in the house, he sits on the small golden seat, looking around
11. The branches of the palms of the ocean whistle, the shaman is seated
    in the house, he sits on the small golden seat, looking around
12. The branches of the palms of the ocean become blue-green, the shaman
    is seated in the house, he sits on the small golden seat, looking around
13. The waves of the ocean raise up in the sky, the shaman is seated in the
    house, he sits on the small golden seat, looking around
14. The waves of the ocean run one after the other, the shaman is seated in
    the house, he sits on the small golden seat, looking around
15. The waves of the ocean are seizing each other
16. The waves of the ocean seized each other
17. The waves of the ocean start to speak
18. The waves of the ocean run one after the other
19. The waves of the ocean become white
20. The waves of the ocean are white
22. The waves of the ocean run one after another
23. The waves of the ocean are seizing each other, the waves of the ocean
    seized each other
24. The waves of the ocean speak
25. The waves of the ocean become white
26. The waves of the ocean look white

It is clear that in this splendid scene of tempest (where the transformation of the palm into a tree shining like gold introduces the great theme of metamorphoses which dominates the entire chant), the shaman has first translated into images only a part of the first four verses: the one describing the singer in his hut, his gaze intently fixed toward the ocean. One could say that in this case, the shaman has exceptionally depicted the constant part of the text, not the variation. However, this apparent exception is probably due to the impossibility to represent the wind itself. In fact, immediately after, pictograms and verbal formula switch roles again: this passage is never more repeated in the drawing, and it becomes the verbal formula constantly repeated in the following text. From verse 5 on, we come back to the situation we are familiar with: a verbal formula not transcribed in a graphic pattern, and the translation of a list of variations. Until now, we have seen cases where the chant was composed by a graphic formula independent from the text, a verbal formula that was never transcribed in images, and a "transcribed variation." In this case, a verbal formula introduced in the first verses is transcribed once in pictograms, and then used as a constant in the following passage. This technique of memorization is developed further in a passage taken from the Muu Igar (Holmer and Wassén 1953). Consider for instance vv. 79–91:

79. Under the hammock of the sick woman I put you *nelegan*
80. Under the hammock of the sick woman I gather you nelegan
81. Under the hammock of the sick woman I raise you up nelegan
82. They raise up along the extremity of Muu Puglip's road
83. The medicine man calls the plant chiefs, they come to call other nelegan
84. Toward the sunrise, he calls Nele Uluburwigwalele, Nele Binaisegwalele
85. They come with garments (mola) smoking like blood
86. They come with hats (*gurgin*) smoking like blood
87. They come with beads (*wini*) smoking like blood
88. Under the hammock of the sick woman I put you nelegan
89. Under the hammock of the sick woman I gather you nelegan
90. Under the hammock of the sick woman I raise you up nelegan
91. They raise up along the extremity of Muu Puglip's road[22]

8.17. A pictographic page from the Muu Igar (Chant of Muu).

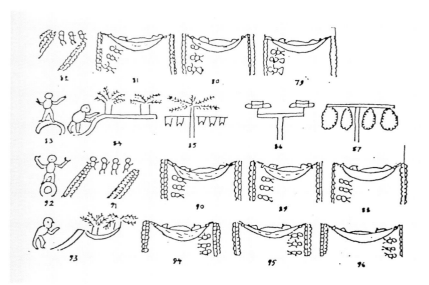

Here the text starts with a sequence of four verses (79–82), to which an identical graphic sequence always corresponds. One might notice that the variation concerns here the verbs (*urbiali*: to put; *odiali*: to gather; *odilamakali*: to raise up), and is "transcribed" for mnemonic purposes, using different colors in the same image. To this micro-variation (implicit and internal to the formula) corresponds a similar structure in the text. In this part of the chant, this formula often alternates with passages, such as vv.84–87 where the images display explicitly their usual function of translating the variations of the text—here "the garments, the molas" represented as flags, "the hats" a metaphor for "mental or spiritual power" (Severi 1996), and the beads. Finally, one notes that the expression "the medicine man calls the plant chiefs toward the sunrise" is always translated throughout this pictographic version of the chant by the same image: a standing figure raising his arms.

Among the documents published by Nordenskiöld, we find other examples of
this kind. Let us consider our third example, the Rock Crystal Chant (*Akwanele Igar*)
in Nordenskiöld (1938, 559 sqq). Rock crystals are considered to be "seers" (nelegan)
in Kuna tradition, and the shamans often include them among their auxiliary spirits.
Here, as in the Muu Igar (Holmer and Wassén 1953), the chanter alternates cosmological references concerning the place of these beings in the Kuna chthonian universe
with the offering that is made to them of the smoke from the ceremonial brazier. This
smoke from tobacco leaves, cocoa leaves, and other herbs is supposed to make them
drunk, and hence powerful.[23]

1   2   3
At the mouth of the rivers the first God set your dwelling

4   5   6
Nele-nusa-galele, Akwalele, Gunagele, I speak to you

7
(In burning) the herb innagigliba I speak to you, in burning the

8
herb innadula, I speak to you

9   10
In burning cocoa I speak to you, in burning tobacco I speak to you

11   12   13
In burning tobacco (smoking my pipe) I speak to you, Nele-nusa-galele, Akwalele,

14
Gunagele

15   16
For you the first God made shelters (*galu*)

17   18
For you the first God made fences

19   20   21
Nele-nusa-galele, Akwalele, Gunagele, I am warning you

22   23
Your fences are well established, your fences well disposed in rows

24   25
your fences are shining now, they shine like gold

26
your fences are shining now

27   28
Your fences are well established, your fences well disposed in rows

29   30
your fences are shining now, they shine like silver

31
your fences are shining now

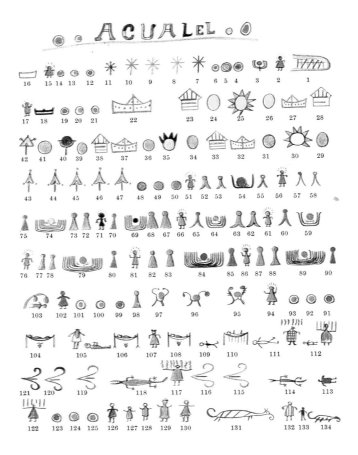

8.18. The Rock Crystal Chant.
Nordenskiöld 1938, PLATE VII.

32   33
Your fences are well established, your fences well disposed in rows

34   35   36
your fences are shining now, I am calling everything, your fences are shining now,

37   38
Your fences are well established, your fences well disposed in rows

39   40   41
your fences are shining now, like a mirror your fences are shining

If we compare once again text and image, we see that the pictographic transcription always operates in accordance with the principle of the representation of variants within verbal formulas entrusted to memory. In this last case, however, instead of there being, as in the Village of Transformations, a list (of spirits' names) which is inserted into a main list (of place names), there is an alternation of the same formulas aligned one after the other. A last feature to be noted is that the same short series of pictograms recurs, thereby constituting a visual equivalent of the parallelism of the verbal text, which makes it a valuable prop for memorizing the names. The parallelistic structure of the Crystal Chant can be notated as follows:

A B C D E F G H I L M D E F A N A O D E F...

Until now, we have seen cases where the text is memorized by the use of series of simple pictograms delineated in rows. The text can establish different relationship among these series (of inclusion or of alternation, as we have seen), but the structure of the series itself remains the same. Let us now conclude with an example of the techniques used by the Kuna specialist: the combination of several pictograms in order to construct more complex images, in what we have called a more "figurative" way. In the description of the Village of Darkness, this technique leads to a result of intense poetry, both in the image and in the text. In the case of this village, where the jaguar of the sky is seen coming down from the sky in search of its victims, we will try to read the pictographic image (Fig. 8.19), while reading and commenting on the text:

126. There where the sun's canoe lies, stops is, another Village appeared
127. The Dark Village appeared
128. The silver flower of the sun's canoe darkened, the lord of the sun's rays grew dim
129. The silver flower of the sun's canoe dims
130. The Village grows dark, the Village dazzles with light, the Village grows dim
131. Far off in the sea, in the open sea, the waves advance, the waves rise up, the waves of the sea cover the Dark Village
132. The waves of the sea go down, the waves recede, the wings of the sea waves spread like smoke, the wings of the sea waves rise up in the air
133. The wings of the sea waves interlace, they have interlaced, they are interlaced
134. The Dark Village rises in the air, the Village shakes, the Village overflows with water, out there, where the Dark Village is. The Dark Village rises up, the Village shakes, the Village overflows with water, the Village overflows, out there, where the Dark Village is.
135. The countless threads that weave the sea foam rise up in the air, the threads of the sea interlace, they have interlaced, they are interlaced
136. The Village becomes covered with clouds, the Village rises up in the air, the Village overflows with water, out there, where the Dark Village is
137. The countless threads that weave the sea foam dance in the air, they knit together, they are well knit

8.19. The Village of Darkness.

138. The Village becomes covered with clouds, the Village is invaded by mist, the Village is all full of mist, the Village overflows with water, the Village overflows, out there, where the Dark Village is

139. The countless threads that weave the sea foam fall, the threads that weave the sea foam fall from the sky like drizzle

140. The Village becomes covered with clouds, the Village is invaded by mist, the Village overflows with water, the Village overflows, the Village becomes filled with water, out there, where the Dark Village is

141. The lords of the storm hurl themselves into the sea, the lords of the storm hurl themselves into the sea

142. The Village becomes covered with clouds, the Village is invaded by mist, in the Village streams form, the Village echoes with the sound of falling rain, the Village becomes filled with puddles of water, out there, in the Dark Village

143. The jaguars of the sky move through the air, the jaguars of the sky hang in the air, they cry "swa-swa"

144. This part of the Village resounds, the Village resounds, from afar one can hear the Village

145. From the top to the bottom of the Village the Golden Dish falls; hanging from a rope-to-accompany-the-dead, the Golden Dish lets itself fall, over there, in the Dark Village

146. The teeth of the jaguar of the sky are all red, they are all *mageb* color, his nails are mageb color; hanging from a rope-to-accompany-the-dead, the Golden Dish lets itself fall in the Village

147. The teeth of the jaguar of the sky are all red, his nails are all red; hanging from a rope-to-accompany-the-dead, the Golden Dish comes down in the Village

148. The jaguar's teeth are all mageb color, all red; the Blue Golden Dish comes down over there, in the Dark Village

149. Hanging from an umbilical cord, the *ilugwa* birds calls; hanging from an umbilical cord, just like a jaguar of the sky, he is calling

150. The *balugwale* bird roars; hanging from an umbilical cord, the balugwale bird roars like the jaguar

151. Over there, at the place of the Dark Village, the Village resounds, the Village trembles, from afar one can hear it resound, over there, at the place of the Dark Village

152. The jaguars of the sky move through the air

153. The silver peccary grunts

154. The silver land peccary calls, he calls "mos-mos"

155. The land peccary who lives out there, at the foot of the trees

156. The jaguar seized him, he carried off his prey up there, in the Village

157. The Village becomes filled with blood, the Village becomes filled with the odor of blood

158. The Golden Dish carries off its prey up there, into the Village

159. The *niki-niki* jaguars come down from the sky in search of prey

160. The niki-niki jaguars of the sky are hanging up there (they move through the air) in search of prey

161. From the top to the bottom of the Village to the other the Golden Dish falls

162. From one side of the Village to the other the Golden Dish falls

163. The niki-niki jaguars of the sky are hanging up there, they are looking for

their prey, up there, at the top of the Dark Village

164. The jaguar sings like the ilugwa bird, his teeth are mageb color, his nails are mageb color; clinging to its rope-to-accompany-the-dead, the Golden Dish comes down to the Village

165. Its teeth are all red, its nails are all red; clinging to its rope-to-accompany-the-dead, the Golden Dish comes down to the Village

166. All red, the Blue Golden Dish comes down to the Village, it is clinging to its rope-to-accompany-the-dead, out there, in the Dark Village

167. The Village trembles, the Village resounds, it can be heard from afar, the Village cries "asawa-asawa"

168. At the end of the Dark Village, clinging to an umbilical cord, the palukwa bird calls, the bird rears out; clinging to an umbilical cord, the palukwa bird calls, the palukwa bird roars: clinging to an umbilical cord, the *asgogoar* bird calls, the asgogoar bird roars

169. In the distance, at the top of the Dark Village, the Village resounds, the Village trembles, the Village resounds, it can be heard from afar, out there, in the distance, at the top of the Dark Village

170. The *yo-yo* jaguars of the sky call out, the yo-yo jaguars of the sky call out

171. In the distance, at the top of the Village, the yo-yo jaguars of the sky call out, they cry "su-u-r"

172. Up there, above the trees, the jaguars of the sky seize their prey, they carry it off to the top of the Village

173. Blood flows through the Village, the Village becomes filled with the odor of blood

174. The Golden Dish caries off his prey up there

175. The jaguars of the sky move through the air, up there, at the top of the Dark Village

176. The lords of the yellow-robed flies want to go into the Village, they prowl all around the Village, they prowl all around the Village

177. Their wings can be heard, their wings buzz, the flies want to go into the Village, the flies fill the Village, the flies settle all around the Village

178. The lords of the bluish-green-robed flies want to go into the Village, they fill the Village, they prowl all around the Dark Village, they prowl all around the Dark Village

179. Their wings buzz, their wings buzz

180. The bluish-green-robed flies fill the Dark Village, they settle all around the Dark Village, up there, at the top of the Village

181. The monkeys move through the air, their prints are all over the Village, their prints are all over the Village, their prints are all over the Village

182. The Dark Village, out there, far away.

Let us see how this text is translated into a single, complex image made of pictograms. After the ritual formula signaling the appearance of the galu before the gaze of Nele Ukuwar and his army of seer spirits ("There where the sun's canoe is, another nias Village [*maigalu*] appeared"), the image at the bottom left of the pictographic plate (corresponding to vv. 128–30) translates first and foremost, as is proper, the name of the galu. The word *setokun* refers to that very moment of the darkness that immediately follows the sunset (*dad argwate*), a borderline moment situated at the threshold of the night (*nuti*). The darkening along with the slight dazzling of the eyes (*sommurgued*, "dazzling": verse 130: "The Village grows dark, the Village dazzles with light") which becomes perceptible just when the last ray of light falls combines

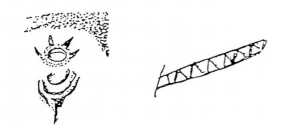

8.20. Pictograms "flower" and "canoe."

8.21. "Clouds" and "drizzle."

8.22. The lords of the storm hurl themselves into the sea.

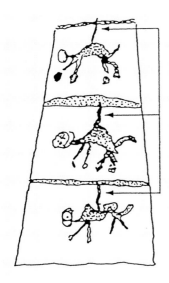

8.23. The jaguar descending from the sky.

in the definition of the Village. The image translates the esoteric formula that designates the setting sun—"The silver flower of the sun's canoe darkens"—by juxtaposing the two pictograms (flower, canoe/sun) on a surface where they are framed by the blackness of the imminent night and the dazzling glare.

Verses 131–34 describe that "stormy sea" where the sun has set. The text then describes the rhythmical movement of the waves and the transformation of the foam they produce (designated in the text as "the wing of the sea waves," v. 132) into a great mist that covers the village. The rising foam of the waves (v. 135) is formed of countless threads that interlace and tie knots in the clouds from where the drizzle comes.

The pictogram that designates the clouds here is the same as that representing the storm in verse 141.

"The lords of the storm hurl themselves into the sea." Scarcely has the village been entered (v. 143) than we see there the jaguar of the sky (*achu nipalid*) move through the air letting out his hunting cry: "swa-swa." Here (vv. 163–48), the text refers for the first time to the jaguar of the sky, in its mention of a Golden Dish (*olobate*). The shaman Enrique Gomez describes this object as a kind of skiff that transports the jaguar of the sky in its flight. But it is "also" a part of the actual body of the jaguar. In his own words, the Golden Dish is the "shoulder of the jaguar of the sky." Moreover, in speaking of the Blue Golden Dish (v. 148), the text attributes to this shamanistic skiff the color of the jaguar of the sky in the pictographic image, thus pointing to this identification of Golden Dish with jaguar which later becomes explicit (see v. 174 : "The Golden Dish carries off his prey up there"). Here the jaguar of the sky is represented in its "descent to the Village of Darkness" (Fig. 8.23).

Its nails and teeth are the color of its victim's blood and at the same time of mageb, a red-colored substance that plays a considerable role in the painting of the body (face, arms, chest) which the Kuna consider to be a powerful means of sexual seduction.

A further revealing detail is the fact that the jaguar comes down from the sky hanging from a *gwilogar*, that "rope-to-accompany-the-dead" which is always placed on the corpse of an Indian before it is buried (Severi 1982). But the jaguar of the sky is defined essentially as an animal of metamorphosis: he is at once a being of the forest (*ukusali*) and being of the sky, a bird (*uluka*). He first transforms himself into two species of bird, *ilugwa* and *ba lugwa* (vv. 149–50).

These two birds betray their predatory nature by uttering the jaguar's hunting cry ("just like a jaguar of the sky, [the bird] is calling," vv. 140, 150). Their situation in the image, which pairs them with the jaguars, translates this partial ontological coincidence of two animal species that represents here the mythical being. But the birds-with-the-jaguar's-cry do not merely attest, by combining the characteristic features of the hunting animal of the forest and those associated with the animals of the sky, to a kind of metamorphosis of one zoological species into another. By this second representation of the jaguar of the sky, they also offer a contrast with the first one in that they hang from the sky not by a rope-to-accompany-the-dead (*gwilogar*) but by a *simudub* (an umbilical cord). The fact is that the Kuna shamans can detect the presence of the jaguar of the sky both in the circumstances of an Indian's death and in certain features of his birth. The ambiguous nature of this mythical being may be revealed just as much in the unexpected death of an Indian as in certain positions assumed by the umbilical cord at the moment of birth: if the fetus emerges from the mother's womb with the umbilical cord wound all around it, say the Indians, the midwives may interpret this as a sign that the child is predestined to go mad (Prestán

1975, Severi 1996). In verses 152–58, the text completes its definition of the jaguar of the sky: pre-eminently a hunting animal, he is seen in the act of seizing his prey—the peccary—which he carries off to the top of the Village, into that black sky which conceals his presence from the sight of the Indians. The pictogram faithfully translates this "invisibility" of the jaguar's hunt by a black surface devouring his victim. But for the Indian shaman, not only can the celestial jaguar take on the visible form of a bird, but he can also speak like that bird. Thus in verses 164–67 we are told that the hunting animal "sings like the ilugwa bird."

The transformation, which until then had been in one direction only (the birds roars like a jaguar, so we were told up to now by the text), here comes full circle. The bird/jaguar relationship is made reversible, and verse 168 confirms the identical nature of the two animals by mentioning three species of bird (the third of which, *asgigiar*, is "read" here for the first time) which again utter the jaguar's hunting cry.

Other jaguars (the yo-yo jaguars) dwell in this black top of the Village that conceals them from our sight: their cry alone (suur) reveals their presence. Bluish-green-robed flies and monkeys, drawn by the stale odor of the blood of the jaguar's victims, go toward the Village and seek to enter it.

This example shows that, though certainly based on relatively simple principles of transcription and organization of the pictograms, a Kuna "pictographic text" may become fairly complex as an aesthetic image, as well as an effective support of memory (Fig. 8.18).

Iconography and memory

Let us now look again at the ways in which traditional knowledge is learned. We have seen that the pupil starts by memorizing passages. The master then shows the pupil series of pictograms representing variations (lists of names of places or characters) contained in those passages and teaches the pupil to decipher them. It is then that the relic text (Tedlock 1983) of the chant becomes an object that can be manipulated. The pupil can then question the master on the content and meaning of the text. Who was the seer who is associated with the crystal? Where are the first spirits' villages to be found? Which river is it whose mouth was the first dwelling of the messengers from the sky? Why can the jaguar of the sky sing like a bird?

It should not be forgotten that the chant is always formulated in a special language, very different from ordinary language. The learning of a chant coincides then with the learning of that variety of language. Picture-writing can be learned only in this context. This means that it can in no case transcribe words belonging to ordinary language and that, even within that language, only a relatively limited number of words are translated into images.

Pictorial symbolism then translates only a limited, specialized vocabulary. This fundamental feature would be enough in itself to show how inadequate the comparison with phonetic writing is here. All notation of language sounds must be able in principle to transcribe any word of the language by means of a limited number of signs. In the case of picture-writing, the situation is reversed: the limitation whereby the language is able to be represented in a consistent manner does not affect the number of signs used, but the number of words that can be designated by images (Severi 1985). Of course this does not mean that the vocabulary of the Kuna chants does not change in the course of time. However, changes are far from being left to individual whim. Admittedly, there may be a difference between this or that pictographic transcription of the same chant, but the difference will usually concern the style established by a master's teaching and will not be a purely individual difference. In the context of the tradition, iconography from a "shamanistic

8.24. Two birds.

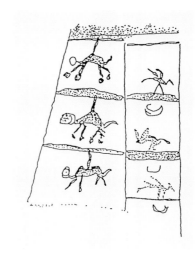

8.25. Jaguars and birds.

school," transmitted from master to pupil, reflects the slow-changing vocabulary of the chants.

Neither individual drawing nor phonetic writing, pictography has its basis in its relationship with oral instruction. For this reason, instead of it being seen as a failed or vanished form of writing, it should be regarded as an extraordinarily effective art of memory. In this context, the relationship between the pictograms and the words does not lie where the theorists of writing seek to place it (between signs and phonetic values), but rather between the order of the pictograms and the parallelistic structure of the text. Seen from this angle, the link that is established between signs and text, which Gelb (1952, 1979) and many others have described as "pictorial" and "tenuous," proves to be consistent and clearly identifiable.

Once the real effectiveness of this technique is established, it becomes possible to understand its role and its influence over the entire tradition. Each story is ritually enunciated in special language and in parallelistic style and then transcribed into pictograms. As in the examples that we have studied, it will thus receive a title, which will place it in the general catalog of stories (the great cycles of the Fathers, the Lost Souls, funeral and initiation chants, etc.). The background against which the story unfolds will then be marked by a series of lists of proper names, true points of anchorage for memory, where the mythological and cosmological knowledge of the chiefs and shamans is condensed.

Although picture-writing may be powerless to reproduce the sounds of spoken language it is capable of linking the image to the structure of a text as it is required to be enunciated by tradition. This link results from an articulation between techniques of memory (based on methods of classification), forms of ritual enunciation of traditional knowledge (parallelism), and the learning of an iconography. It results in spoken words which the Kuna describe as "strong," in the dual sense of lasting and effective.

We have seen that historians of writing and anthropologists tend to adopt two separate approaches: one anxious to assert the autonomy of signs in relation to forms of enunciation, the other proclaiming the autonomy of the spoken word as against material forms (objects, pictures, etc.). The Kuna memory-pictures, with the consistent relationship that they establish between forms of enunciation and iconography, show that a link can be established between aspects that our tradition keeps separate. It is becoming more and more clear that, in actual fact, in a number of societies where social memory is apparently based solely on the spoken word, the image has a constituent role in the process of transmission of knowledge (Severi 1994). These acts of transcription of the mythological universe of which the Kuna tradition offers us a particularly sophisticated example, far from reflecting the first faltering steps, the unsuccessful attempts, the distant precursors of the origins of writing, reveal a number of crucial features of the multiple oral and pictorial practices that constitute a so-called oral tradition. Perhaps by looking at these pictograms with a fresh eye we may begin to understand not the lost writing of the American Indians, but the force, the vitality, and the extraordinary persistence of their strong words transformed into images.

The Fiesta of San José of Narganá
Symbolic Syncretism and Persistence among the San Blas Kuna

Alexander Moore

How are we to understand a Kuna community fiesta celebrating its putative Roman Catholic patron saint, but which celebrates its adolescent girls instead? This is the fiesta of San José (St. Joseph) of Narganá, the most prominent of the three "civilized" communities. (Narganá is also known unofficially by the "more Kuna" name of Yandup.) There, the focus of the celebration has come to be not the saint or his image, but a set of unmarried adolescent women. Such women are the primary symbol of the endogamous local community in traditional Kuna culture. Yet in Narganá these young women are not celebrated in any way that overtly repeats the symbolism of traditional Kuna female life cycle rites. Nor is the fiesta Roman Catholic in a religious sense, rather, it borrows heavily from the Western Carnival. This chapter, then, investigates the hypothesis that nubile women remain a core cultural symbol to all Kuna, "civilized" or not, but that other, syncretic symbols of community identity have also taken hold. In order to conduct an analysis, however, we must first delineate the Westernized community setting for this fiesta, placing it in the context in which such extraordinarily vital syncretism could arise.

Communities among the San Blas Kuna fall within one of three blocs: the "civilized" or acculturated; the ultra-conservative; and the moderates or in-between. The communities of Narganá, Corazón de Jesús, and Río Azúcar in San Blas are the ones to call themselves *civilizados* (civilized).[1] Thus Kuna adaptation to Western civilization and modernization has not been uniform. Nonetheless the Kuna are famous among anthropologists for the relatively successful way they have retained the essentials of their own culture, while, like the Japanese of the Meiji period, taking what they want from the West, especially in terms of technology and learning (Holloman 1969).

All communities of whatever bloc have cooperated in a tribal social system which has maintained essentials of Kuna culture, while choosing "the best from the West." It is precisely because there has been a creative mix of solutions about what to choose that the San Blas Kuna as a whole have been so successful in maintaining cultural

9.1. Church mola panel. The church with elaborate towers was probably inspired by a picture in a book. 42.5 x 48.0 cm. FMCH X82.597B. Museum purchase in memory of Sidney S. Kallick.

9.2. Kuna civil servants Samuel Morris, Jr. and his wife Mina, both now retired, in a main street of Narganá. Note the modern concrete community gathering house in the right background, and the bridge to Corazón de Jesús in center background. The fiesta of 1977 took place in the former gathering house on the left.

Levon Mardikyan, 1995.

9.3. Ethnographer Alexander Moore makes a point to his Kuna friends about Narganá's most modern building, a branch of the national bank, built in the shadow of the Roman Catholic Church of San José.

Levon Mardikyan, 1995.

integrity while modernizing. Thus these three radically Westernized communities present an extreme solution, while others in the eastern part (and an enclave in the western areas as well) of the district present a nativist, traditional one. Both approaches are respected and tolerated, especially by the large number of moderate communities who explicitly seek to reconcile both approaches.

The bloc of three "civilized communities"

The "civilizing" approach among the Kuna dates from 1904 and the installation of Charles Robinson as the first chief of Narganá. He had been educated on the English-speaking Caribbean island of Providencia, and then apprenticed as a seaman. He was literate in English, and knew his Bible, but not the chants of Bab Igar, Father's Way, which traditional Kuna chiefs chant publicly on a weekly basis. Robinson launched a program of modernization by welcoming a Jesuit priest sent by the Panamanian government in 1907 to supplement his own effort to teach ABCs to community boys. In 1906 he had sent a contingent of boys to Panama City for schooling, and in 1913, after Jesuit mission funding was withdrawn by a newly anti-clerical regime in Panama in 1912, he welcomed a freelance fundamentalist Protestant missionary, Anna Coope. She in turn entered into conflict with the youth club of the returning young men educated in the capital in Roman Catholic schools. The club succeeded in getting all the public female life cycle rites, with their collective and public drunkenness, suppressed. The reformers also went after the traditional feminine dress, abolishing the mola, its associated wrap-around skirt, the gold nose ring, and short hair for the post-pubescent women. James Howe ("The Kuna and the World," in this volume) asserts that this policy was actively abetted by the Panamanian colonial administration of the district at the time. To this day, then, the three communities most notably differ from the others in their lack of these key symbols of Kuna identity: molas, gold nose rings, short hair. Their women wear Western dress and do not undergo any of the collective life cycle rites. Some however, do sew molas for sale. In addition the chiefs of the three communities do not chant Bab Igar, the traditional body of mythology. Not having to come from a select few with special knowledge, chiefs instead are elected at large from the local citizenry.

In 1925 members of the youth club, having supplanted Robinson in power with government backing, were targets of the organized tribal revolt of that year, and would have lost their lives had they not fled to the government post at El Porvenir. However, in typical Kuna fashion, once the relations of the Kuna to the Panamanian government had fundamentally shifted, the modernizers were tolerated, and even welcomed in the counsels of tribal government, especially as local leader Estanislao López became a power broker with the national government.

Because of their head start with literacy, families from these communities were the first to supply schoolteachers to the wider district, and are currently disproportionately represented in the emerging Kuna social class of educated government officials and urban professionals.

For example, the household which hosted me, that of the widely respected elder Samuel Morris, contained three such professionals in the late 1970s: Samuel Morris, Jr., then head of educational sports for the San Blas schools; his wife; who was the health care aid at the maternity clinic (Fig. 9.2), and Samuel himself, retired from school teaching. Samuel Sr.'s then long deceased first wife had been the sister of native Baptist missionary Alcibiades Iglesias and herself was among the first schoolteachers. Next door to us, her niece, an Iglesias, was also a school-teacher. Like her aunt, and Samuel Morris himself, she had started her teaching career in another community. A full census of the descendants of Claudio and Alcibiades Iglesias and their siblings would find numerous profes-sionals, many of them living in urban Panama and even in the United States. In the future, educated families from the moderate bloc may overtake the Narganenses, who nonetheless have a considerable head start by one or two generations.

9.4. Four girls in Narganá, wearing Western dress rather than the traditional molas, enjoy one of the town's wide streets, next to a quite traditional home whose owners are renewing the thatched roof. Note the spacious plaza in front of the Roman Catholic church.
Levon Mardikyan, 1995.

As the home base of Estanislao López (Fig. 9.7), the modernizing cacique favored by the Panamanian government through a number of regimes (see Howe, in this volume), the bloc acquired a reputation for political influence in Panama far out of proportion to its size and population. The regime of General Omar Torrijos carved San Blas up into three *corregimientos* or legislative assembly districts. It is probable that the government always confused Estanislao López's field of influence with that particular administrative unit, that is, all the communities of western San Blas, rather than only three of them. Indeed, to the contrary, one enclave of communities in the western area, the Carti group, was traditionalist.

However, Narganá has become the unofficial capital of San Blas because it is the seat of a number of government agencies' local headquarters. These include not only the first and for a long time only junior high school in the district, but Cedulación (the electoral registry), Digedecom (a community development agency), the judge for the entire district, as well as the commanding National Guard post for all San Blas. In the past decade Narganá has become the seat of the district jail, which houses some sixty inmates as of my count in 1995. The community also now has a branch of the Banco Nacional de Panamá (Fig. 9.3).

9.5. These adult married women of Narganá are contributing one day's work to a communal labor party helping to extend the town's airstrip at the northwest end of the island. The group's secretary notes the names of participants. (The local gathering or congress levies fines on no-shows.) Eventually the town leaders expect to fill in the sea out to the line indicated by stakes.
Levon Mardikyan, 1995.

Geographically the three communities are located perhaps one fourth of the way southeast on the San Blas Coast line past the start of the district at Porvenir, and well past the small gulf of Mandinga and the Carti communities. Their waters, well protected by numerous coral islets further out to sea, have been rich in fish, and the islets are all planted in coconut palms, providing relative abundance to the three and their neighbors. Of these the traditionalist communities of Tigre and Tikantikí are composed of dissidents who fled the others early in the century, and who consequently maintain kin and some property ties with their modernist relatives.

The twin communities Narganá and Corazón de Jesús are better known than the smaller and more isolated community of Río Azúcar, situated at some distance near its own river and fresh water. Corazón de Jesús is smaller both in area and population than Narganá, with whom it is connected by a graceful arched bridge over the channel separating the two islands. Both communities have prominent Roman Catholic churches, and both have Mediterranean style plazas. Narganá's plaza boasts a round central kiosk housing a community store. This plaza sports benches made of concrete and painted with slogans celebrating the Día de la Civilización. It also has raised flower beds.

Corazón is relatively more crowded than Narganá, and has more houses of reinforced concrete or of wood frame, often two stories. Narganá has its share of such dwellings too, but the great majority of its buildings are spacious thatched houses in traditional style (Fig. 9.4). Both communities are laid out in a grid plan, a consciously "civilized" trait, but Narganá, having more land, has wide and spacious streets. Because of emigration to the cities for schooling and work, Narganá's population has remained relatively constant at fourteen hundred persons over the last two decades.

Although adjacent and tied by multiple kin relations, the two communities are militantly separate in all things civic, maintaining separate airstrips, for example, Corazón's on a nearby island, Narganá's on a point on its own island, which for over twenty years the citizens have been busily extending through communal labor parties (Fig. 9.5).

In spite of the grid plan, the spacious streets, the many "modern" buildings, and government installations, and in spite of the lack of molas except those worn by numerous visiting women, Narganá is nonetheless Kuna, as evidenced by the housing of the great majority of its inhabitants, those who do not have professional jobs, and who have not made a "fortune" in such jobs or in trade in the city. Most live under traditional thatched roofs, and all speak Kuna. Animated conversations in that language abound on either side as the visitor, often beset upon by welcoming small children, walks through the spacious and scrupulously clean streets.

The ostensibly Roman Catholic Feast of San José de Narganá

In Narganá a curious pageant has emerged in the feast of San José, the official, spiritual patron of the community.[2] This feast is not the occasion to celebrate the statue or icon of San José as I had anticipated (unwittingly forming expectations based on previous fieldwork in a highland Maya community). Rather the festival focuses upon and celebrates a company of teenaged girls. They form a court of a queen and her attendant princesses, and appear in different costumes on successive nights. In addition, each evening a ballroom dance is held after the ceremonial entry and installation of the young women upon a raised tableaux. The mothers of the girls feast the community with funds they raise themselves. In addition the entire community is also feasted by a communal cash levy imposed by the village chiefs through their commission on festivities (Spanish: *festejos*).[3] Pubescent girls, then, have emerged in this modern community as the paramount symbol of community life, although the content of the actual celebration is very different from the traditional female puberty rites which, perhaps, serve the same function.

More specifically, preparations for the fiesta are started months in advance when the families of adolescent girls decide to launch their candidacy for the fiesta court. They canvas friends and relatives, soliciting cash contributions for tickets. Their activity is coordinated with the town's

9.6. The Queen of the Fiesta de San José de Narganá enthroned upon the dais that dominates the interior space of the town hall. The painted backdrop combines elements from the Panamanian national flag with portraits of Narganá's legendary tribal forbears. Note the two adolescent male escorts and the three little girl attendants. This experience prepares them to become queens and princesses themselves as adolescents. Alexander Moore, 20 March 1977.

9.7. The banner embellishes the home of Su Majestad (Her Majesty) Teresita I, who stands in front of it flanked by her maternal grandmother and grandfather (the patriarch of her matrilocal household). To their right is Narganá's own tribal high chief, the late Estanislao López.
Alexander Moore, 21 March 1977.

festivities commission, headed by one of the second ranking hierarchy of officials: "interpreters" (Spanish: *voceros*; Kuna: *argar*, pl. *argargana*). At some point the vote is officially tallied, and the girl with the greatest cash contribution and hence the most numerous votes, wins. She is the fiesta queen. A ranked cohort of princesses is selected by the same principle, the more numerous the votes and hence the greater the cash, the higher the rank of the princess. I do not know if the number of princesses is limited to four, or whether all candidates achieve some place in the ranking and hence a place on the fiesta court.

Competition is most keenly felt for the first place, that of queen. Girls win not only by their beauty and popularity, but far more by the extent of their kinship connections and by the wealth of their natal household. Indeed, in 1995, I am told, the winning candidate was the daughter of a townsperson who lives in Cativá, a Kuna settlement in the outskirts of Colon, Panama's second city, on the Atlantic side of the Canal. That settlement is, in effect, a colony of Narganá. The fiesta provided the means for a second generation daughter of the community to return to her parents' hometown in triumph. Detractors claimed the victory was bought. Indeed it did provide the girl's parents the opportunity to attempt to turn urban cash into rural prestige.

The fiesta itself falls on 19 March, a date set by the Roman Catholic almanac, and not—as in the traditional rites to be discussed below—by the exigencies of tropical forest horticulture and the best time for harvesting sugarcane (January and February). The fiesta is not a movable feast. However, the date is a convenient one for the families involved because the Panamanian school calendar provides for a break in classes from mid-January to the last week in March. If their daughters are in school, participating in the fiesta is not a problem.

Clearly, weeks of effort and planning go into the celebration. An essential element is the cooking of great quantities of food, going on both at the home of the mother of the queen and at the town's community center. The latter was, in 1977, a European-type building housing a schoolroom on one end and a "basilica" style gathering chamber on the other. A partition between the chambers had been removed and a dais with a throne and canvas backdrop had been set up to dominate the hall (Fig. 9.6). At the home of the queen, another dais, complete with throne, and streamers and balloons instead of a backdrop had also been set up (Fig. 9.7).[4]

9.8. Flanked by her two young escorts, the fiesta queen has left her traditional thatched home (marked by a line of streamers in the background) to march in a ceremonial procession to the town hall to be invested in her office.
Alexander Moore, 19 March 1977.

9.9. On the first evening of the fiesta the queen enters her ballroom wearing a change of gown from the afternoon investiture.
Alexander Moore, 19 March 1977.

At some point the girls and their mothers had also decided on costumes for each event. On the afternoon of Saturday, 19 March, the Day of San José itself, (and the first event I myself observed), the girls were attired in formal ballroom gowns, the queen wearing a tightly fitting white one. Thus attired, the group made a formal procession from the queen's home to the town hall for her investiture in office (Fig. 9.8). At night that same day, the "Court" wore another version of formal ballroom dress (Fig. 9.9). On Sunday night they wore the *pollera*, the traditional Panamanian peasant costume highly identified as a nationalist symbol (Fig. 9.10). On the final night they were back to ballroom gowns.

Each night after the girls had made their formal progress from the queen's house to the community center and installed themselves on the dais, two male youth dance clubs (Spanish: *comparsas*), named Santana and Los Campesinos, entered one after the other to stage a dance. Each comparsa has its own young musicians playing drums, maracas, and guitars (Fig. 9.11). The male comparsa members recruit young children and adolescent females to dance with them. Some official group of adults (most likely the festivities commission) serves as a dance jury and awards a prize each year to the better club. After the comparsas perform, there is a general ballroom dance open to the entire public but, as can be imagined, frequented more by unmarried youths and young married couples than anyone else. Elder kinspersons of the queen and princesses attend to watch.

Each day food is distributed to married women who go to the community center or to the home of the queen as the case may be with a bowl to collect what is offered: a dish of rice and either beef or pork, purchased in the city.

Finally, smaller children had their hand in events the year I observed them as they constructed a stuffed Judas figure and hung it up for display (Fig. 9.12), quite a common custom around Panama during Lent and Holy Week. This dummy was burned on Sunday afternoon in front of a procession of the queen and her princesses and members of one of the comparsas disguised as devils, whom other members drove off, amid general merriment among small children.

9.10. A fiesta princess, next to her mother, happily displays her pollera, Panama's national folklore dress. Such a costume costs a great deal and most likely is seldom worn.
Alexander Moore, 20 March 1977.

9.11. Their backs to the photographer, comparsa musicians play while the queen and her escort dance.
Alexander Moore, 20 March 1977.

9.13. Two adolescent male "devils" menace a mother and child on Narganá's plaza. The bench on the right is commemorating "Civilization Day."
Alexander Moore, 20 March 1977.

9.12. Small boys mug for the camera while tormenting the effigy of Judas on display by the Narganá Roman Catholic church.
Alexander Moore, 19 March 1977.

9.14. Judas in flames. These youths have made their own devil masks, rather less expensive for them than the formal dresses were for the young women of the fiesta. Alexander Moore, 20 March 1977.

The day after the fiesta, the community center was left open to the small children for them to play among the stage settings and props.

The traditional complex of female life cycle rites

Kuna communities in the traditional and moderate blocs all practice a series of female life cycle rites very different from the one described above. In common with the other indigenous peoples of the tropical forest culture area, the Kuna observe female puberty by a set of isolating and purifying rituals, the most common element of which is the separation and isolation of the newly menstruating pubescent female, and, perhaps, some body paint and hair cutting as well. Groups differ in the attention they pay to the ritual; but generally they are individual and family rather than collective affairs, and are limited to the immediate period of the first menstruation.[5] The Kuna have, however, elaborated female rites of passage from birth to marriage into a series of very public rituals culminating in the—usually post-pubescent—collective hair-cutting-and-naming coming of age ceremonies.[6] While some girls came of age, several "graduates" of the rite might also be married in weddings staged toward the end of four days of intense community ritual and associated feasting.

Kuna symbolic recognition of the importance of women starts with the newborn female's nose and ear-piercing rite, accompanied by ceremonial distribution and consumption of *chicha* (Kuna: *inna*), a fermented mead made of sugarcane juice and maize, flavored with cacao. This feast is not generally for the entire community, but for the infant girl relatives and the community elders. The rite is followed next in the life cycle by a ritual at first menstruation. This is a family and household event, but a few months later it is followed by a collective drinking bout sponsored by the girl's family in common with those of the other newly menstruating females. In this feast several young women are isolated together in a *surba*, a rectangular enclosure, where they are painted black with the dye of the genipa fruit.

The culmination of all these rites is reached in a three-day hair-cutting ceremony with two days of an almost nonstop drinking bout, as well as communal food feasts each day. It is not strictly necessary that the young female initiate in this rite have undergone the first menses and subsequent rite. That is, prepubescent girls may be inducted with other young women into the hair-cutting. In the past this ritual, however, was considered a prerequisite for marriage.

Weddings were traditionally staged at the close of the hair-cutting ceremony, although the bride was a woman initiated in previous years, not a new initiate. Weddings were arranged by the parents of the young couple, who well might not be informed ahead of time. A commission of young men appointed by the chiefs would fall upon the unsuspecting bridegroom, carry him forcibly to the house of his equally unsuspecting bride, and thrust him into her hammock. They would then thrust the young woman into the hammock on top of him, holding the prospective pair there an instant while one of the commission would place a burning brand under the hammock. When the captors released the couple, the man and woman would jump up and flee the scene. This event would be repeated for three nights. On the last night, if the couple agreed to the match, they would remain together all night. At dawn the bride-groom would go with his new father-in-law to gather firewood, two stout logs which his bride might then place in a cross, and create a hearth at their center. Once she had done that, the marriage was sealed. For our purposes it is important to note that the young woman was forcibly claimed by the community for one of its young men.

Discussion of the series of traditional rites

In common with other tropical forest peoples, the Kuna have elaborated a ritual life that reflects the ecological conditions of their existence, as well as the rhythms of the human life cycle. Their sacred, mind-altering elements include chicha, made from the products of their gardens, and tobacco, another such product. Genipap fruits and annatto leaves for dyes are gathered from the rain forest and basil leaves are collected for sweet, purifying scented water for bathing female initiates. The flesh of game animals and fish are obligatory foods to be mixed with horticultural products in their feasts. They Kuna must go to their gardens, the forest, and the rivers and sea in order to effect these rites.

Likewise the isolation and purification of the young newly menstruating woman makes use of forest products, water, and natural dyes. She is at once purified and darkened to identify her with the new moon, who hides its face.

Animistic belief informs these practices. Food offerings are made to the spirit dogs of the chicha; the spirit shaman and its dogs within the genipap tree must be awakened. Expert cantors chant to the spirits of the needle (in the infant piercing rite), of the chicha, and of the sacred flutes (in the hair-cutting, coming-of-age rite). According to Sherzer (1983), each such chant is very detailed description of the event itself. In other words the *gandule*, who addresses the spirit of the flute (*gammu*), and the *inna sobet*, who addresses the spirit of the inna or chicha, are telling them exactly what is happening, or has happened, almost like a camera's eye chant. This text is, according to Sherzer, the *most* invariable of all Kuna texts, every morpheme must be exact from one rendition to another (ibid. 139–52).

What is unusual in all of this is the elaboration of a complex of rites to include, not merely puberty alone, but birth, and two other elaborate rites with feasts, one clearly post-puberty, the other pre-marital. That last one is associated with hair-cutting, a very common trait of first menses purification among many groups (and also a very common trait in the purification rites for warriors who have killed their first victim).[7] This is also the rite in which ritual flutes—initially as reeds forbidden to view— accompany chanting and dancing. Sacred flutes are a common part of the ritual repertory of tropical forest peoples, as symbols of masculinity.

In these successive elaborations of what is usually one single, simple and private rite, sponsoring family members must contract specialists to perform specific stereotyped activities in each rite. These specialists may be otherwise quite everyday sorts of people, it was just their "path" (Kuna: *igar*) to learn and perform a particular specialty. The Kuna believe that every individual is born with certain talents and callings, mythologically explained by the lullabies of the spirit grandmother, Muu, who keeps spirits of unborn fetuses in her dwelling in the bottom layer of the underworld. The content of her songs determines the path or igar an individual ought to take in life. In this complex of rites, the two most prestigious specialists are the gandule, who may gain great renown by being the titular chief of the inna suid or climactic rite, and his female partner, the haircutter or *ied*.

Old and new female coming of age rites among the Kuna

While in the field in Narganá, I would sometimes remark that the Fiesta de San José appeared to be the functional equivalent of the *inna suid*, the long chicha or hair-cutting rite. My remark was met with immediate dismissal, sometimes offhand, sometimes indignant: "Oh no, it's nothing like that!" Of course, the Narganenses were right, the fiesta is nothing like that. The content, the symbols, many of the activities, are totally different. The fact remains, however, that these Kuna have transformed the celebration of a Roman Catholic saint's day into the celebration of adolescent girls. The saint's day is now a female coming-of-age rite.

First, some salient differences. In spite of its Roman Catholic context, the fiesta de San José is totally secular. The supernatural is simply not addressed, as the spirits are so movingly and beautifully addressed in such chants as *gammu igar*, the chant to the flute spirit, in the hair-cutting rite.

Moreover, the entire interdependence upon the tropical forest horticultural cycles is gone. The two natural forest dyes, annatto or achiote and genipap, are not made from scratch from ritually gathered materials, nor are they applied to the initiates. The flesh of game animals is no longer mandatory; meats grown beyond San Blas for sale will do. The locally fermented mead is not prepared at all, and the necessary collective planting and harvesting is foregone. The mothers of the girls do serve unfermented meads, especially from chocolate, but they are inclined to use purchased chocolate more than homegrown cacao. Similarly each youth of the comparsas contributes two bunches of plantains to the queen's mother, to be distributed out again, cooked, but the bulk of the starchy food distributed is not plantains, but rice, again purchased on the market.

It is not only fermented chicha, the sacred inna, that is missing; alcohol is simply not served at all. There simply is no collective, community drinking bout with all its revelry. The comparsas and the ballroom dancing is relatively restrained revelry when compared to the traditional rites. The fiesta is the occasion for community fun, not for collective catharsis.[8]

Indeed, although it seems that every household in town is feasted, not all attend. The festivities are mainly for children, adolescents, and some adults, those more closely related to the young women.

Out of the *surba*, onto the throne

Moreover, the treatment of the adolescent women is quite different in the western fete. Traditionally the young women were hidden, isolated in a seclusion hut (*surba*). Indeed in the climactic rite, she is half-buried there. Their appearance was changed, so that when they emerged, either with threads through their pierced apertures as babies, or painted black as young women, and finally with their hair cut as marriageable women, their changed status was visible to all. In the new fiesta the young women may be singled out but they are not hidden and buried. Quite to the contrary, they are elevated as objects of veneration on a throne itself placed upon a dais in a typical basilica form of architecture.

The overall form of the fete in Narganá is quite clearly borrowed from the Western Carnival, in its Panamanian form. Panama City has a very strong public tradition of celebrating Carnival on the weekend before and up to and including Ash Wednesday. Dance clubs (comparsas) dance in the streets, and the high point of the parade is always the float bearing the Carnival queen! Narganá is on dangerous ground here in terms of ethnic nationalism. One particularly strong grievance giving rise to the organized revolt of the Kuna in 1925 against Panama was the forced dancing of Kuna girls at Saturday night dances (sarabandas), held by the local National guardsmen in Kuna communities. It was precisely during Carnival night that the uprising struck.

Nowadays traditional communities stage pageants commemorating that history. In Tigre, an island of traditionalists founded by families fleeing modernizing Narganá early in this century, an elaborate pageant each year presents a pantomimed re-enactment of the events of the revolt of 1925 in the community. The narrative is first declaimed by a chief, and then enacted without speech. The revolt, as reenacted today, had Kuna conspirators fall upon drunken Panamanian guardsmen in 1925. The Kuna portraying the guardsman are shown forcibly dancing with young woman wearing paper Carnival crowns. The conspirators slay them, liberate the young women, and cooperate with North Americans in an effort to confine the Panamanians to their proper place, that is outside the boundaries of the district.

As I maintain elsewhere (1983), the revolt itself mirrored the spiritual strategy of Kuna exorcists in their rite of exorcism, in which by means of chants, magical spirit helpers get evil spirits drunk (evil spirits who have come too close and are causing sickness or some misfortune), and then fall upon them and transport them back to their home on the bottom level of the underworld.

Carnival, then, is replete with ambivalent symbolism about Kuna identity. Narganá was not a party to the revolt; and was itself enthusiastically celebrating Carnival when the revolt struck. To revive the symbols of Carnival would seem to courting harsh criticism from other communities. In fact, however, this has not been the case.

There are no doubt a number of reasons why other Kuna do not find the Narganá fiesta offensive. First of all, Carnival remains an attractive event, especially to youth. Indeed the community of Playón Chico has it both ways. It incorporates a re-enactment of the 1925 Carnival in its four-day, twenty-four-hours re-enactment of the revolt of 1925. The town is delivered over to a youth group, the "Policía Colonial," who with entirely too much gusto re-enact all the abuses of the pre-1925 Panamanian colonial administration. They draft young women as Carnival queen and princesses, and stage a baile obligatorio on Carnival night, during which in the wee hours of the morning they are fallen upon by another, red-shirted youth group of revolutionaries and symbolically slain. Young people who have participated tell me that the forced dance is "fun" (divertido). The community symbolically rejects the event but insists on practicing it, with modern gusto and glee.

Moreover in Narganá, young women are clearly being claimed by and for the community, not for outsider guardsmen. Their most prominent courtiers are two male youth groups. Carnival dancing has been incorporated into the age and sex classes of the community. The same youths who are doing the dancing are likely to marry the girls at a later date. Indeed their organization is reminiscent of the commission of young men who must, traditionally, carry both groom and bride to their wedding by force.

Third, Narganá has for some decades been the site of a junior high school and the schoolteachers, mostly Kuna themselves, have encouraged the kind of pageants that the festival enacts. Kuna schoolteachers use pageants for the ritual cycle of schooling: beginning and ending the year, inaugurations of new buildings, fetes welcoming new boarding students to the junior high school, Schoolteacher Day, and retirement ceremonies for outgoing teachers. Teachers join with pupils in acts which emphasize individual artistic achievements. They sing songs, play musical instruments, declaim poetry, put on skits, and make speeches. At the junior high school they make elaborate use of pubescent girls as a dominant symbol: a plethora of queens, princesses, and godmothers (*madrinas*) are installed and exalted in ceremonial costume and language.

Thus, it is the schoolteachers who have strongly encouraged the kind of fantastic drawing upon the world's cultural traditions that the fete displays. The girls have learned their lessons well, and now undertake them on their own. They portray themselves as participants in other traditions (i.e., European royalty, Panamanian peasants in traditional dress). In one junior high school fete, girls even don the unfamiliar but culturally correct mola as well. The schoolteachers have shown them that modernity is a stance that embraces many traditions. They are merely repeating the lesson here.

Last, there is the theme of exorcism. Judas is the evil spirit to be purged by fire, but youths impersonate devils that other youths may drive out.

A traditional coming-of-age rite in disguise?

The western fiesta we have examined is in some degree the functional secular equivalent of the inna suid, the hair-cutting ceremony. The entire community is feasted, and most if not all households have contributed economically to the feast, this time by the modern device of paying cash for subscription votes. A party is held, but the emphasis has shifted from the entire community to its younger segments. The Kuna emphasis on specialists, persons who learn a particular task, often highly stereotyped and ritualized, and repeat it constantly throughout adulthood, has shifted. Now it is youth itself, male and female, who learn to impersonate themes from world culture, to tap into the broad ecumenical heritage which is now available to them. Now it is not adult men who play ritually fabricated flutes and sing traditionally fixed chants about and to the spirits. Rather it is young men who demonstrate recent mastery over a larger array of musical instruments. Young women gain honor and prestige from the young men's music and dance. A good time is had by all.

What we have in the Narganá feast is a secularized ritual, one in which the Roman Catholic sacred meanings and associations have been largely lost, or transformed into a carnival. The traditional ceremony is a ritual of catharsis, especially for adults; this festival is largely for youth. The performance aspects have shifted away from chanting altogether toward performance. The mythology invoked is that of the Western fantasies that Carnival enacts. It is a productive mythology, a secular one, which also opens up a world of yearning, of wish-fulfillment for the youth involved. For those who are, in fact, boys and girls headed for more education, the future is indeed open and many such fantasies may be fulfilled as more and more Kuna enter the educated professional and bureaucratic groups in Panama and abroad.

Our central hypothesis, that young unmarried women remain a core symbol of Kuna culture, seems to be validated. We see that the modernizing Kuna of Narganá have found one way to reaffirm the central symbolic importance of young women, the key symbol of each endogamous community. They enthrone her rather than enclose her, but they surround her by troops of young males, her implicit guards . She belongs to the community. Her celebration may not be as cathartic, the sacrament

9.15. Welcome to Yandup! This poster painted on the wharf side of the Narganá (Yandup) town hall presents a young man alone on his sailing canoe with a young woman in a fantasy garb of a bathing beauty. The endogamous community continues to claim exclusive rights to its young women for local young men. Levon Mardikyan, 1995.

may be less extensive and less deep, but nonetheless the key symbol of the community has been affirmed and exalted. Every community needs its own celebration, secular or religious, to affirm its identity. When the citizens of Narganá found their former collective rite, all celebrating local females, abolished, they made use of another occasion and brought back their nubile females to claim and celebrate, but they did so in a creatively syncretic manner.

Acknowledgments

The initial field work upon which this paper is based was supported by a National Science Grant No. BNS76-11900, "Consensus as a Mechanism of Self-Government." The expedition to videotape an inna suid rite in Playón Chico in March 1996 was supported by a University of Southern California grant-in-aid to the Center for Visual Anthropology at USC. I thank James Howe and Gillian Goslinga for comments on an earlier draft. I thank Gillian, too, and Levon Mardikyan for accompanying me to videotape the rite at Playón Chico.

Puberty Ceremonies

James Howe

Kuna boys have traditionally entered puberty without ceremony or outward sign except putting on their first pair of long pants. Kuna girls, on the other hand, as they reach physical maturity, undergo three separate series of rituals. The first begins on the morning after a girl has her first period. The men of her village assemble to build a ritual enclosure in her house, where she spends the following week. During this week, she is bathed repeatedly in seawater, her hair is cut off, her body dyed black with juice from the genipa plant, and at the end of the week a feast is served to the village.

Months later, villagers are repaid for their support with a one-day communal celebration, in which they enthusiastically consume an alcoholic drink brewed from sugar cane juice called *inna* (*chicha* in Spanish). The girl, once again painted black, spends hours serving the inna drink through a slit in a sail. Finally, if her father can afford it, he sponsors a celebration lasting three or four days, in which ritualists called *gandule* (flute persons) perform a long cycle of chants, and the whole village, along with visitors from neighboring islands, drinks inna and rum.

The preparations for the extended celebration, called the long chicha or *inna suit*, commence months or years ahead of time, as a young girl's father begins saving money, planting extra bananas, and arranging to have forest animals from several different species shot for feasting and ritual payments. Two weeks before the chosen date, villagers cut sugarcane and squeeze its juice, which is cooked in great cauldrons and set to mature in huge clay pots (Figs. A, B). Thereafter, the inna is periodically tasted by the master brewer and his assistants to judge its readiness.

As the day approaches, each household in the village contributes bananas, corn, and smoked fish, and when the brew reaches maturity, preliminary rituals begin. Specialists weave the ropes and strings for the hammocks in which the gandule will

A

B

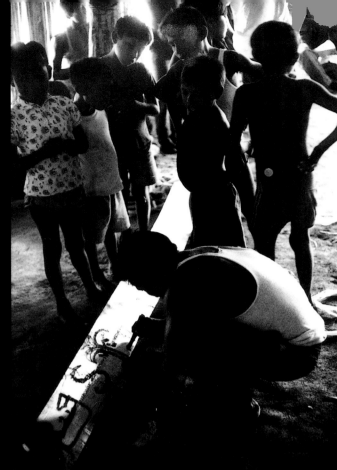

C Q D

soon chant, construct the flutes and rattles with which
they will accompany their chant (Fig. C), and paint
ong boards with symbolic designs (Fig. D). Each step
s carried out with formal ceremony, and each has its
esoteric symbolism concerning the pubescent
girl's maturation and her future marriage,
sexual life, and childbearing—none of which
should be overtly mentioned.

Once the ritual preparations are completed
and the first of several feasts consumed, the
assembled villagers begin the ceremonial
drinking, men at one end of the great inna
house, women at the other. Servers bring
large calabashes of the brew, now dark and
potent, to waiting men and women, who salute
their friends before draining the calabashes
(Fig. E). At each round of drinks, ritualists
wearing clattering necklaces of pelican bones
dance and blow smoke from long cigars in
the drinkers' faces, while other specialists tend
braziers in which cacao beans burn: the smoke
from the cacao and tobacco turns into food

and drink for spirit masters who are watching over the ceremony, some of them in the form of invisible jaguars perched on the house beams, who if not appeased would harm the human drinkers.

After the end of the ceremonial phase of drinking, the gandules begin the long cycle of chants, which describe the ceremony in exhaustive detail and elaborate its sexual and reproductive symbolism. The chanters eventually move to the hammock prepared for them, and at several points in the following days, when it is said that a great spirit wind is blowing, the hammock is swung violently back and forth while they continue chanting (Fig. H).

Since the gandules chant to spirit beings in a language unintelligible to ordinary

H

humans, other participants pay them little attention, devoting themselves instead to drinking and socializing (Figs. F, G). Women dance and sing to each other, first of their happiness at being with kin and friends and later of their sadness at losing others who are dead or far away. Some men play panpipes; others show off their knowledge of foreign languages; others sing songs for amusement or display or perform passages from curing chants; and everyone talks and observes their neighbors' behavior. The revelry, sometimes boisterous or emotional, seldom turns violent.

The young girl herself spends these days isolated in a small enclosure outside the inna house. At one point, her parents and a gandule choose a long traditional name for her, and at another, a female ritualist cuts off all her hair a second time (Fig. I). Otherwise, however, she plays little part in the celebrations given in her honor.

I

Twice during the festivities, other activities stop, and people turn to dancing. Lines of men and women, some of them wearing the feather headdresses of the gandules, whirl and stomp through the inna house, forming tight circles and then wheeling off again in long lines (Figs. J, K, L). Young men, who take the lead in dancing, imitate animals and perform bravura displays of manhood in which they dance with lengths of a thorny, poisonous vine, grinding it between them (Fig. M).

Eventually the gandules finish their chant cycle, the young girl is ready for marriage and adult life, and everyone else goes home to rest.

M

Photographs by James Howe, Niatupu and Tigre, 1970 and 1971.

ASOCIACIÓN DECENTRO DE
NOKAKOPENASIS.
KUNA YALA
SIANAL
GOGUE
SUPE
METE

The Musical Arts of the Kuna

Sandra Smith

Introduction

Music is found in association with every aspect of Kuna life. There are chants to assist in childbirth, puberty, and death, songs that teach children about their family responsibilities, dances to celebrate puberty rites, and inter-island dance festivals. Although the Kuna perform much of their music publicly, they are notably guarded about communicating the specialized knowledge of the musical arts to foreigners and also to each other.

The Kuna have an unusual array of musical instruments. These are flutes, panpipes, and rattles. There are no drums and no stringed instruments even though neighboring cultures use those instruments. Even more unusual, though, is that no unifying musical system or repertory is common to all of the Kuna instruments. Each of their instruments is associated with a unique repertory based on unique compositional rules.

Kuna musical compositions unfold according to principals that involve assumptions different from our own about music as a human endeavor and means of cultural expression. I will describe some of the unique characteristics of the musical arts in relation to the verbal, visual, and performance arts.

The relationship between Kuna musical arts and the verbal, visual, and performance arts

Kuna musical arts are intimately tied to the verbal, visual, and performance arts. Friendship songs, lullabies, laments, and gathering chants employ the art of verbal improvisation. The highly stylized chants associated with curing and ceremonial practices require years of study and memorization of archaic forms of language and special delivery styles. The study of these chants also involves the visual arts. Chanters learn to interpret and produce a traditional form of chant notation consisting of colorful pictographs. Each pictograph, measuring one to two centimeters square, corresponds to an event, an episode, a character, or an entity that is portrayed in a

10.1. Noga Kope center mola panel. This panel depicts and names some of the musical instruments used by the Noga Kope dance groups in Kuna Yala.
29.5 x 37.5 cm. Private collection.

10.2. The Noga Kope Dance Group from the island of Tigre performs with the large six-part *guli* "panpipe" that is distributed among six men. Each musician has one flute, a bamboo tube cut to produce a different pitch. To create sound, the tube is held with the first and second fingers placed front to back across the opening of the tube to create a mouthpiece. This particular dance depicts the courtship display of the golden collared manakin bird.
James Howe, 1997.

chant. A long tabulation of pictographs, running in boustrophedon, visually represents the path or way of a chant, depicting spirits and spirit-helpers on their travels to spiritual abodes. Masters of medicinal and exorcistic chants also learn to carve wooden representations of their spirit helpers to whom they address their chants.

Other uses of the visual arts in musical expression include the construction and decoration of musical instruments and the fabrication of dance costumes. Dancers sew special clothing so that the members of a group will match in color and also in the thematic representations depicted in their molas. They also paint designs on their rattles that are coordinated with their molas.

Although Kuna musical arts closely involve the verbal and visual arts, they are, above all, performance arts—they direct cultural expressions toward specific audiences: the family, the village, the spirit world, and foreigners. The musical arts are believed by the Kuna to be essential to certain areas of cultural knowledge. This will be my starting point for a discussion of Kuna beliefs about their musical traditions. Following this, I will briefly describe the different types of songs and chants and look at the unique features of Kuna musical composition by comparing the compositional schemes used with two different panpipes. Next there will be a description of the performance settings in which a wide array of music is found: the puberty celebrations and inter-island dance festivals. To close, I will discuss the aesthetic evaluation of musical performance by Kuna musical specialists.

Kuna beliefs about music

Kuna beliefs about their musical traditions offer several clues about how they conceive of and use music. To understand what Kuna music is, how it works, and how it functions, we must first locate Kuna musical arts properly in the domain of specialized cultural knowledge. Cultural knowledge is broadly classified as nonspecialized and specialized in Kuna society. Nonspecialized knowledge, such as cooking, child rearing, clothes making, basketry, farming, fishing, hunting, and house building, is held commonly, although some individuals might be recognized as more accomplished than others.

Specialized knowledge, by contrast, requires specific talents or abilities and long periods of training. The Kuna classify specialized cultural knowledge as historical and political knowledge; knowledge for conducting puberty celebrations; medicinal knowledge, curing, and magical knowledge including exorcism and funeral rites; knowledge of all the different kinds of flutes and panpipes and their associated dances; knowledge of the *gammu burwi* panpipe music and dance repertory; and the interpretive knowledge mastered by seers. Except for the last mentioned area which is used for prophecy and prognosis, each of the disciplines of specialized cultural knowledge is practiced in the form of musical performance. Music is the necessary medium for the transmission of these important areas of cultural knowledge.

The origin and function of music

The Kuna explanation for the origin and function of music rests on two fundamental concepts concerning creativity and performance. The first derives from the Kuna belief that cultural ways, including musical traditions, were introduced to the Kuna people by the gods Great Mother and Great Father, and that the forms or expressions of these cultural traditions exist in a realm of their own. In the Kuna view of things, people have a cultural responsibility for learning how to express the traditions in their proper ways and for transmitting their knowledge about them to others, but they are not responsible for creating the traditions as such. The second is based on the idea that musical activities are essential to the well-being of the Kuna people and that musical performances are used to demonstrate the strength and vitality of Kuna culture to the Kuna themselves as well as to foreigners.

The Kuna presume that there have been and will continue to be periods of cultural advancement, decline, and revival. They believe that cultural continuity is maintained even though traditions may be modified during times of cultural revival in response to changing situations. At the heart of this Kuna perspective on continuity and change in cultural traditions lies the legendary example of the great cultural leader, Ibeorgun, who helped reintroduce traditional ways to the Kuna people in mythical times.

A summary of the chanted history of the origin and function of music was related to me by a cultural leader from Nalunega (Smith 1984, 194–96). This man is a specialist

10.3A, B. Panpipes and rattles mola. Figure 10.3A shows a Kuna woman shaking a rattle with two pairs of *gammu burwi* panpipes in the background. Figure 10.3B shows the woman playing the panpipe with decorated rattles in the background. Note that she is depicted in traditional dress with large gold earrings, beaded arm bands, a gold nose ring, and a mola blouse.
A. 33 x 41 cm. FMCH X97.3.11A.
B. 33 x 40 cm. FMCH X97.3.11B.

in medicine and history. Originally from Usdup, he settled in Nalunega after he was a practicing specialist.

There was a time when the beings on the Earth were uncivilized and animal-like. At this time the gods enjoyed all aspects of culture including knowledge of the important skills and ceremonies needed to live in a civilized manner. To help the Earthly beings, the gods sent them teachers equipped with examples of cultural knowledge. Ibeorgun was one of these cultural teachers for the Kuna.

One time, Ibeorgun brought many different kinds of flutes to the Kuna people. In the realm of the gods, the flutes were animate beings; they spoke by singing and they walked by dancing. Each type of flute had its unique music and dance and was accompanied in this by its spouse or by one or more companions.

To reach the Earth, the flutes had to pass through a perilous whirlpool full of harmful spirits. To protect themselves, they traveled together and sounded their different musical styles all at once, producing a cacophony to frighten the spirits. In the confusion of the whirlpool, some of the flutes lost their spouses and others grouped together in new ways.

Ibeorgun presented the somewhat modified flutes and their musical traditions along with other cultural traditions, to the Kuna people. The Kuna became partially civilized, but reverted back to a state of corruption. There have been subsequent periods of cultural advancement and decline. Each time, Kuna cultural leaders reconstruct their traditional ways by listening to the voices of the ancestors.

Ibeorgun's example demonstrates that specialized cultural knowledge is managed by cultural leaders. We will look at who these leaders are today, how they learn and teach the musical arts, and what role they play in aesthetic evaluation. We will also look at the unusual characteristics attributed to the flute traditions—that they employ several different musical "languages," and that many of the instruments are constructed and used in pairs or groups that parallel social groupings in Kuna society.

Lullabies, friendship songs, and death laments

In Kuna society, lullabies, friendship songs, and death laments are the purview of women. Women sing lullabies daily to their children. Periodically, during puberty celebrations, they sing friendship songs to each other in their section of the festival hall. At the side of a dying relative, they sing laments.

In each of these genres, singing is improvised around common themes in ordinary language. Musically, the songs follow certain melodic and rhythmic conventions, but there is individual freedom of expression.

Lullaby singing occurs every day and throughout the day to calm and quiet young children (see McCosker 1974; 1976, 29–66). Lullabies are performed within the privacy of the matrilocal household by female relatives of the child: an older sister, cousin, aunt, mother, or grandmother. They are improvised around several common themes, but they always address the particular circumstances of the child at hand. Musical phrases are short and rhythmically regular. Their melodic shapes are oscillating, each ending on a low tone. The last phrase ends with

10.4. Children are quieted by their mother or an older sister who sings to them while swinging in a hammock. The lullabies, which are improvised, describe the day-to-day tasks and duties that children are expected to perform for their families.
Mari Lyn Salvador, Ubigandup, 1997.

a long tone. The singer sits in a hammock with a child and shakes a
rattle at a fast and steady pace close to the child's head (Fig. 10.4). This
sound, combined with the rapid swinging of the hammock, quickly
puts the child to sleep.

Friendship songs are performed when a village's adult women
gather together in the festival hall during the first few days of a puberty
celebration. They gather in a small area and are served fermented
drink by younger girls. Sitting as close to each other as possible in two
facing rows with shoulders, hips, and knees touching each other, they
sing to each other for several hours. They sing one-at-a-time about their
mutual friendships. The musical style is like lullaby singing but without
rhythmic accompaniment.

Laments are sung at the side of a dying relative. Sometimes several
individuals will sing simultaneously although each is singing about her
own feelings and memories. There is no rhythmic accompaniment to
this kind of singing, and the singing is not rhythmically regular. The
singing continues after the relative dies and is taken to the burial site,
and it continues there for a short while after the burial.

10.5. Women from the island of Tigre
enjoying a *chicha* celebration.
Mari Lyn Salvador, 1997.

The chanting traditions

The chanting traditions are performed primarily by men who are
specialists. Masters of the chanting traditions are given official titles which identify
them as cultural leaders. These different types of cultural leaders preside over their
communities in turns whenever the circumstances call for their particular areas of
expertise. For example, when a village suffers an epidemic caused by a multitude
of harmful spirits, an exorcism chanter, of which there are very few, is called in to
preside over the community during the curing period. He isolates the villagers from
other villagers and specifies what they should and should not do during a month-long
period. For eight successive nights, he performs a repertory of lengthy chants in the
presence of all the members of the village (see Howe 1976, 67–76).

Puberty celebrations also involve the community as a whole and usually require
a specialist from outside the community who brings several assistant chanters with
him. He presides over twenty to thirty members of the community who have been
appointed to carry out all of the preparations, and he directs all of the ceremonial
activities during the several days of the event.

This chanting tradition is performed in duet by two men. Each one uses a flute
and a rattle. The flutes are made as a male-female pair. The male flute is longer than
the female flute. Together they produce four tones. The bamboo flutes are constructed,
washed, and decorated by two villagers who have been appointed and trained for
this purpose.

The two chanters perform in a standing, sitting, or reclining position. When
standing side by side, they slowly rotate their bodies as a pair while stepping in place.
They shake their rattles in a continuous, steady rhythm. Each man holds his flute
loosely in his mouth, to one side, while chanting to voice the chant through the flute.
Sherzer describes the linguistic features of this form of chanting (1974, 276). At times,
the flutes are played in succession to introduce a chanted line. When they are played
in this way, the male flute is sounded first. Its tone is held so that the sound of the
female flute overlaps it.

Each village has at least two history-political chanters and several specialists who
know some of the curing chants. History-political chanters convene the villagers in
nightly or weekly gatherings. Howe has made a complete study of the different kinds

Instrumental musical genres

Instruments used for improvised music during puberty celebrations and dance festivals

Dolo. Single, end blown, external duct bamboo flute; performed by specialists.

Goenono and achunono. Deer and jaguar skull voice amplifiers; performed in pantomime by nonspecialists.

Instrumental traditions performed by specialists during puberty celebrations

Gammu suid. Paired, end blown bamboo flutes and calabash rattles used by chanters.

Galabigbili. Single, horizontal bone or wood flute.

Dede. Single, end-blown armadillo skull flute used to purify performance spaces.

Gorgigala, sulupgala, uasgala, and mulagala. Sets of end-blown, internal duct, wing bone flutes that are also strung onto necklaces and used percussively by male dancers.

Suara. Paired, end-blown, notched bamboo flutes played by men who are sometimes accompanied by women dancers.

Supe. Paired, end blown, external duct bamboo flutes played by men who are sometimes accompanied by women dancers.

Instrumental traditions performed by nonspecialists but organized by specialists. Men play these instruments and are sometimes accompanied by women dancers who use rattles.

Guli dodoged. Unbound six-part bamboo panpipe.

Goke dodoged. Bound three-part bamboo panpipe.

Gammu burwi dodoged. Bound two-part bamboo panpipe.

of gatherings (1986). Their chants describe mythical and historic events. They are not as long as the exorcism or puberty rite chants, but the repertory is very large.

Curing chanters specialize in certain treatments and work with a wide variety of chants associated with particular conditions. One may specialize in headaches, insanity, special mental talents, and learning abilities, while another may specialize in broken bones, fever, or choking. Each one masters a large part of the total chant repertory, but no two specialists have exactly the same training or professional skills (see Sherzer 1986, 169–212).

Musically, the performance of all of the following types of chants, except for the puberty rite chants, share stylistic features. These have been analyzed by Sherzer and Wicks (1982). They are performed without musical instruments; their statements consist of short parallel phrases which begin on a high pitch and end on a low pitch while diminishing in volume and tempo; the final phrase of each statement ends with a long-held tone. The overall melodic shape of the phrases suit each chant, but all of them contain strings of syllables on a single pitch: some descend in a steady pattern; others seesaw up and down; others cluster in sets of repeating patterns corresponding to repeated linguistic phrases. As the chanter proceeds, the overall range of the chanting ascends and increases in volume, strength, and tempo.

Puberty rite chants have a different musical style. The statements are chanted in short note values with a change of pitch on nearly every syllable. Flutes and rattles are also used with this form of chanting.

Instrumental music

Kuna musical instruments consist only of wind instruments (aerophones) and rattles, even though neighboring cultural groups use a variety of drums and stringed instruments. Kuna instruments include gourd rattles, shell trumpets, voice amplifiers made of animal skulls

10.6. The audience responds to a hilarious moment during a drinking vessel dance, which imitates the antics of men and women during the puberty festivals.
Mari Lyn Salvador, Tigre, 1997.

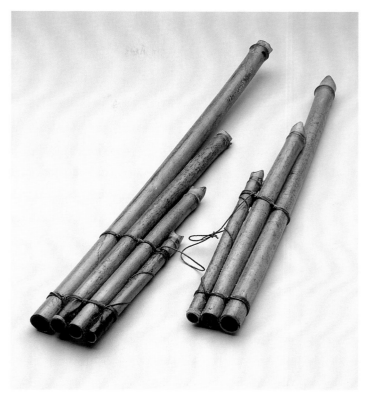

and bamboo, as well as several different types of flutes and panpipes made of wood, bone, and bamboo. Knowledge of instrument construction and musical composition associated with the different types of aerophones is restricted to the few men who are musical specialists. Not every village has a musical specialist even though it may have a dance society that is organized and directed by a nearby musical specialist. The dance societies are a relatively new phenomenon, having been first formed in 1947 in the village of Tigre. They are used to promote the participation in the traditional forms of music and dance associated with each type of flute and panpipe. The *gamma burwi* panpipe in particular has been the most popular because it has the largest repertory and its dance tradition involves the greatest number of dancers.

The Kuna do not construct their flutes and panpipes according to a single scale at a standardized pitch. Each type of instrument is made to produce a particular array of tones, but its size and range can vary. When matching sets of instruments are used, as when a dance society needs three sets of the paired gammu burwi panpipe, then the sets are constructed exactly alike. Different types of instruments are not played together in concert except to produce a cacophony which is used to drive away harmful spirits.

Most of the instruments are designed to be played in sets of two, three, or six component parts divided among two or more players. It is interesting to note how the Kuna describe these sets. Some of the paired instruments are said to consist of a complementary male-female couple, while others are said to consist of a primary and secondary speaker. A three-part panpipe contains members that are arranged in a sequential hierarchy, with the members providing different numbers of pitches. A six-part panpipe contains members that are similar, each one producing a different, single pitch.

Other forms of Kuna artistic expression also depict the roles and relationships characteristic of Kuna social groupings. In the art of house construction, for example, the naming of the beams and structural components parallel the names for different kinds of cultural leaders and villagers and the names for the different members of a

10.7. *Dede*, **armadillo skull flute used to purify performance spaces. Armadillo skull, incised bird bone, natural resin, beetle shell with white beads.**

Armadillo skull, pelican bone, beads, cotton string. 34.0 cm. Private collection.

10.8. One set of the paired gammu burwi panpipes. The thin, straight-walled bamboo used to construct this instrument can only be found sin the highlands.

Bamboo, string. 45.0 cm. FMCH X97.5.28.

10.9. Cluster rattle. Museum collections contain Kuna rattles made from seed pods, such as this one, or other materials such as crab claws, coconut shells, wood, and gourds.

Wood, seed pods, seeds, plant fiber. 27.5 cm. Private collection.

10.10. *Nasis*, gourd rattle. Women use this type of wooden-handled rattle when singing lullabies and also when dancing. A similar rattle made with a deer bone handle is used by the puberty chanters.

Gourd, cotton string, wood, pigment. 10.5 cm. FMCH X83.506. Gift of Dorothy M. Cordry in memory of Donald B. Cordry.

matrilocal family unit. Without reducing all Kuna artistic expression to this principal, it is worth noting that the art of musical composition in particular explores the patterns of interaction among two or more members who stand in certain relationships to each other.

A comparison of the music associated with two types of panpipes illustrates how the art of musical composition is based on specific patterns of interaction between the players. One type is the paired gammu burwi panpipe; the other is the three-part *goke* panpipe.

The paired gammu burwi panpipe

The paired panpipe is made up of fourteen different lengths of bamboo tubes in total, giving fourteen consecutive pitches of an equal seven-step scale. The fourteen tubes are distributed alternately between a male and female set that are played in duet. The seven tubes of each set are again distributed alternately between two bound rafts. Each player holds a three-tube raft and a four-tube raft side-by-side with the shortest tubes in the center. By this distribution scheme, the tubes of the two sets are arranged identically, but each tube of the male set is one step longer and lower in pitch than the corresponding tube of the female set. Melodic statements are produced in an alternating and interlocking pattern between the two players. In dance performances, three matching sets are used so that six panpipe players, all men, dance with six women who each have a rattle.

The musical relationship between the two players is explained by Kuna musicians as leader-follower or husband-wife. The relationship corresponds to the male-female labeling of the sets. When playing, the two men alternate back and forth with notes to make up the melodic lines. The alternation is nearly one-to-one, but the leader's part is rhythmically regular and musically predictable, while the follower's part is not, making it the more difficult part to learn and to play. The leader-follower relationship of this music is not easily understood by Western musicologists because standard musical notation and analysis make it seem that the indicated leader part is following, while the follower part is leading.

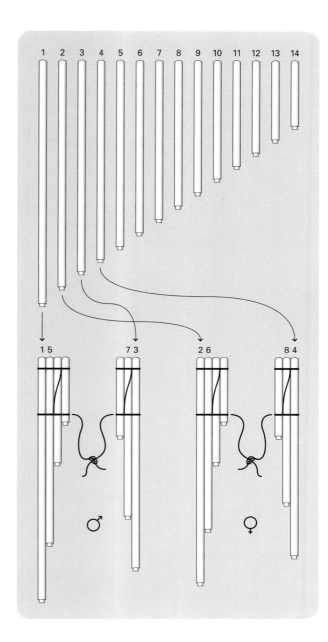

10.11. Construction of the gammu burwi panpipe. Fourteen lengths of bamboo are distributed alternately between a set of male and female panpipes that are played in duet.

10.12. The paired gammu burwi panpipe is played by two men in an alternating and interlocking manner. This type of panpipe is used by the dance societies in their inter-island festivals.
Sandra Smith, Nalunega, 1979.

10.13. The Noga Kope dance groups usually perform with six men using three matching pairs of panpipes and six women each using a rattle. The dance step is a step plus hop-in-place which becomes a skip when traveling.
James Howe, Niatupu, 1975.

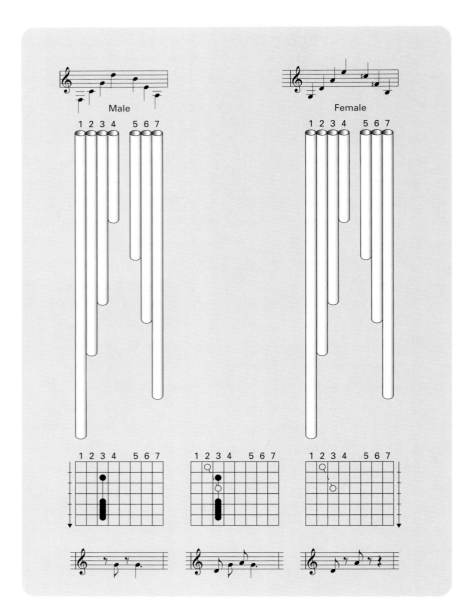

10.14. Graphic transcriptions of panpipe music.

The musical pitches of the male and female panpipes are shown at the top of the figure. The tubes are numbered from left to right to correspond to numbered columns on the grid. Horizontal lines mark equal units of time. A musical piece proceeds down a graph from top to bottom.

Transcription by Sandra Smith.

associated with the different types of aerophones is restricted to the few men who are musical specialists. Not every village has a musical specialist even though it may have a dance society that is organized and directed by a nearby musical specialist. The dance societies are a relatively new phenomenon, having been first formed in 1947 in the village of Tigre. They are used to promote the participation in the traditional forms of music and dance associated with each type of flute and panpipe. The *gamma burwi* panpipe in particular has been the most popular because it has the largest repertory and its dance tradition involves the greatest number of dancers.

The Kuna do not construct their flutes and panpipes according to a single scale at a standardized pitch. Each type of instrument is made to produce a particular array of tones, but its size and range can vary. When matching sets of instruments are used, as when a dance society needs three sets of the paired gammu burwi panpipe, then the sets are constructed exactly alike. Different types of instruments are not played together in concert except to produce a cacophony which is used to drive away harmful spirits.

Most of the instruments are designed to be played in sets of two, three, or six component parts divided among two or more players. It is interesting to note how the Kuna describe these sets. Some of the paired instruments are said to consist of a complementary male-female couple, while others are said to consist of a primary

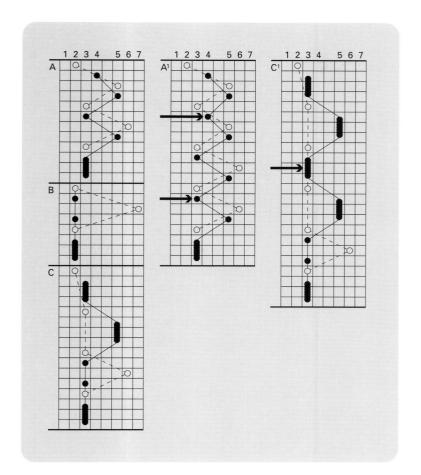

the tubes are identical in the two sets, because of the distribution scheme of the tubes overall, and since the two players rarely play at the same time, I have superimposed the transcriptions of the two sets onto a single grid in order to more easily see the interaction between the two musical parts.

The female player's part is notated with white circles connected by dashed lines; the male player's part is shown with black circles connected by solid lines. Musical statements are created by the two players as they alternately blow down certain tubes. Their playing is rhythmically even and regular for the most part, each one blowing down a tube while the other one takes a short breath. The musical statements are notated beginning at the top row and proceeding row by row with each pulse of sound. When a player blows down a tube for two or three consecutive pulses, the sound is represented in the transcription as a vertical bar of connected circles. A piece consists of one or several themes, notated as A, B, C. Expanded versions of themes are notated as A', B', C'. The following piece is an example of how the leader-follower relationship works in a musical composition.

The leader-follower relationship in musical composition

The piece "Achu Make Dule" (The Jaguar Hunter) is represented by my own notation (Fig. 10.15), as well as by conventional musical notation (Fig. 10.16). The female part initiates each of the three themes A, B, and C. The male part terminates each one with a long-held tone. The male part moves back and forth across the panpipe in more balanced movements than the female part. The movement of the male part is most often between tubes three and five, as shown in themes A and C. The movement of the female part is more erratic, and it moves across a greater number of tubes—between tubes two and five, six, or seven. The male part uses

10.15 (ABOVE LEFT). **Graphic transcription of "Achu Make Dule."**

The seven numbered columns represent the panpipe tubes which are arranged with the four-tube raft held to the left of the three-tube raft. White circles indicate the female panpipe part; black circles indicate the male part. Both parts are superimposed onto a single grid. Vertical rows represent equal units of time. Arrows mark the male part's choices of tones in themes A' and C' that signal the female part to repeat a section before continuing the themes. Transcription by Sandra Smith.

10.16 (ABOVE RIGHT). **Western notation of "Achu Make Dule."**

Each theme is notated in succession with the overall compositional structure indicated below. The notes with stems drawn upward are played by the female (follower) panpipe; those with downward stems are played by the male (leader) panpipe. Transcription by Sandra Smith.

pitch than the corresponding tube of the female set. Melodic statements are produced in an alternating and interlocking pattern between the two players. In dance performances, three matching sets are used so that six panpipe players, all men, dance with six women who each have a rattle.

The musical relationship between the two players is explained by Kuna musicians as leader-follower or husband-wife. The relationship corresponds to the male-female labeling of the sets. When playing, the two men alternate back and forth with notes to make up the melodic lines. The alternation is nearly one-to-one, but the leader's part is rhythmically regular and musically predictable, while the follower's part is not, making it the more difficult part to learn and to play. The leader-follower relationship of this music is not easily understood by Western musicologists because standard musical notation and analysis make it seem that the indicated leader part is following, while the follower part is leading.

The analogy used by Kuna musicians to explain the musical relationship of the duo is a husband and wife journeying by canoe: The man enters first, sitting mid-canoe, and the woman follows, sitting in the stern. The man uses his strength to paddle a few strokes on one side and then a few on the other, back and forth in an even rhythm, propelling the canoe to its destination. The woman only paddles now and then, and she mostly uses her paddle as a rudder to keep the canoe on course. The husband's role is to indicate the direction of course and provide strength and regularity. The wife's role is to follow her husband's directions, to initiate movement by pushing off, and to guide the canoe to its destination.

I have devised a form of musical notation which graphically represents the interaction of the two musical parts to display the leader-follower relationship. Columns represent the tubes of the panpipes; rows represent equal units of time, much like metronome pulses, moving from top to bottom, down the page. Melodic statements are recorded by marking the sequence of tubes blown by each player.

For consistency in the transcriptions, the seven tubes of each player's set are numbered and arranged alike with the four-tube raft to the left of the three-tube raft. I have placed an empty column between the rafts so that the back-and-forth movement between the rafts is more noticeable. Since the relationships of the intervals between the tubes are identical in the two sets, because of the distribution scheme of the tubes overall, and since the two players rarely play at the same time, I have superimposed the transcriptions of the two sets onto a single grid in order to more easily see the interaction between the two musical parts.

The female player's part is notated with white circles connected by dashed lines; the male player's part is shown with black circles connected by solid lines. Musical statements are created by the two players as they alternately blow down certain tubes. Their playing is rhythmically even and regular for the most part, each one blowing down a tube while the other one takes a short breath. The musical statements are notated beginning at the top row and proceeding row by row with each pulse of sound. When a player blows down a tube for two or three consecutive pulses, the sound is represented in the transcription as a vertical bar of connected circles. A piece consists of one or several themes, notated as A, B, C. Expanded versions of themes are notated as A', B', C'. The following piece is an example of how the leader-follower relationship works in a musical composition.

The leader-follower relationship in musical composition

The piece "Achu Make Dule" (The Jaguar Hunter) is represented by my own notation (Fig. 10.15), as well as by conventional musical notation (Fig. 10.16). The female part initiates each of the three themes A, B, and C. The male part terminates each one with a long-held tone. The male part moves back and forth across the panpipe in more balanced movements than the female part. The movement of the male part is most often between tubes three and five, as shown in themes A and C. The movement of the female part is more erratic, and it moves across a greater number of tubes—between tubes two and five, six, or seven. The male part uses heavier, long-held tones, especially in theme C. The female part does not use any long-held tones.

If we compare the expanded themes A' and C' to their original short forms, A and C, we can see that the male part introduces a different note, by playing on a different tube, as in theme A' at the point marked by the first arrow in the transcription, or the part plays a short tone instead of a long-held tone, as in the second arrow in A', or a long-held tone instead of a short tone, as in theme C' at the arrow. These changes are signals to the female part that the theme is going to be expanded by the internal repetition of melodic material at this point. The female part then proceeds with the change by repeating the last two sounds it made before continuing on with the remaining notes of the theme. In this way, the male (leader) part, with each expansion, signals to the female (follower) part a repetition of internal segments of the themes. The female part then carries this directive out by playing the next appropriate note which actually defines the section which is to be repeated.

The expansion and contraction of musical themes

The performance of a single piece can continue for half an hour, with themes expanding little by little, and entire sections being repeated in a slowly unfolding process. After a gradual expansion of the themes, the players quickly shrink them back to their original short forms to end the performance. Another piece "Burwigwad Dummad" (The Little Ones, The Big Ones) provides a good example of the expansion and contraction process. The compositional structure consists of themes A and B which are expanded to create the modified, longer themes A' and B'. Sections are defined by the manner in which the themes are repeated. An outline of the compositional structure is as follows:

Section 1: AABB (4 times)
Section 2: A'A'B'B' (4 times)
Section 3: AABB, A'A'B'B' (1 time)
Section 4: AAB'B' (1 time)

In Section 1, the short forms of the themes are played and repeated. In Section 2, the long forms are played and repeated. In Section 3, the entire piece to this point is contracted into a single statement of Sections 1 and 2. Finally, in Section 4, Section 3 is further contracted.

Successful performances are those in which the players are able to increase their speed and intensity of playing while following a gradual course of thematic expansion and then returning the themes to their original short forms at the end of the piece.

10.17. In preparation for the annual dance festival, members of the Tigre dance society paint the dance rattles with designs that will match the designs in the molas that they will wear.
Sandra Smith, Tigre, 1979.

The three-part goke panpipe

The music played on another type of panpipe, the three-part goke, follows a different compositional process. This bamboo panpipe is constructed in three sets: one consists of a raft of three bound tubes; another has two bound tubes; the third is a

10.18. The dance society from the village of Usdup has earned a reputation for innovative choreographies. In this performance in 1979, the dancers used a new cross step, and the women each used two rattles instead of one. The composition and choreography were newly composed to commemorate their cultural leader Sayla Nele Kantule.
Sandra Smith, Usdup, 1979.

10.19. The jaguar skull voice amplifier (*achunono*) is cleaned and reassembled in preparation for a dance festival. It is used with a deer skull voice amplifier (*goenono*) in a pantomime of a hunt.
Sandra Smith, Tigre, 1979.

dance groups which are all organized within one society directed by two brothers. In the larger village of Usdup, there are several different dance societies. Each one is given equal weight in village decisions and equal time in village performances. Their directors secretly develop innovative performance arrangements to unveil during these joint performances. For example, one society has the women dancers use two rattles instead of the customary one (Fig. 10.18). The innovation characteristic of Usdup dancers is unusual in light of the overall conformity of the repertory as performed by all dance societies throughout Kuna territory.

Annual inter-island dance festivals provide a good setting for observing this conformity. In the festival hosted by Tigre, for example, dance societies from as far away as Galet, located at the far southeastern tip of the archipelago, come to perform. Their arrangements of pieces in the repertory are very close to those performed by the dancers of Gwebdi to the west of Tigre.

The dance societies differ mainly in the extent of their repertory. The society of Tigre is one of the most diversified. Its directors learned to construct and play a variety of musical instruments from their father, who was a musical specialist, and they have continued their training with other musical specialists. They, in turn, have taught some of their own members how to perform the music and dance repertories of many different types of flutes.

There are several inter-island festivals held in different locations, each drawing together groups from a few villages. There is no tribalwide festival, and many dance groups never have the opportunity to encounter each other. The primary force that keeps each repertory of music and dance intact and homogeneous, even though they are sporadically performed, is the manner in which aesthetic evaluation is exercised by musical specialists.

Aesthetic evaluation

In dance society practice sessions, learning is mostly accomplished by imitation. The gammu burwi players and dancers follow a lead pair through the choreographic formations as well as the musical compositions. When mistakes disrupt a piece, the dance society director will usually stop the piece and start it again without much explanation. The dancers repeat pieces over and over again until they are perfected. They practice to develop the intensity and vigor of their dancing and playing, working to keep their formations tight while they increase the speed of the music.

Members of a dance group rarely discuss or evaluate their performances or those by other groups. Most performances, however, take place under the watchful eyes of musical specialists and other cultural leaders. These men usually sit together in a prominent "front row" spot, and they observe the performers very seriously.

Musical specialists, like the other cultural leaders, at times travel from their villages to visit other specialists in distant villages. While on their travels, they will attend political gatherings, puberty celebrations, and other public performances including dance society performances. For this reason, the chanters of history and puberty chants as well as the dance groups expect that there might be cultural leaders from other villages present whenever they perform.

The aesthetic evaluation of musical performances by cultural leaders takes into consideration their conformity to the tradition as well as the special attributes of the performer or group. Musical specialists judge the tightness and complexity of inter-locking musical and choreographic parts, the control of increasing and decreasing the intensity of delivery or speed of performance, the control of gradually expanding thematic material and quickly contracting it to its original state, and the vigor and clarity of the expression.

Many of these same qualities are also found in the verbal and visual arts. For example, skillful gammu burwi players and dancers can interlock their musical parts with precision while playing rapidly and vigorously. Their circular dance formations and the expansion and contraction of musical themes as they play bring to mind the concentric outlining of images in mola design. The vigor of their performance is like the clarity of the expression achieved in mola making by the use of contrasting colors in the layers of fabric. Mola images interlock in complex ways not only as seen on the top layer, but also in relation to the parts of the design that are expressed in the different layers of cloth. Skillful sewers can heighten this complexity by incorporating many layers of cloth and by creating many concentric outlines which are narrowly and evenly spaced. Controlling the narrow and even spaces, seen as contrasting colors of outlining, is very difficult to do, especially when the images are curved. Molas that contain two, three, four, or more colors each require different structural schemes for working out the layered relationship of the images.

When gammu burwi dancers increase the tempo of the music, they travel greater and greater distances through the air with each dance step without changing their step or their body position. They pass each other more closely twirling at that moment. This dynamic way of dancing is greeted with enthusiastic audience approval. In some curing chants, the chanter himself is depicted as moving very slowly, as if viewed from another dimension in which time moves more rapidly. The pictographs show him being called to the patient's house.

10.20. Young girls learning a dance.
Mari Lyn Salvador, Ailigandi, 1974.

10.21 (ABOVE LEFT). **Noga Kope dancers are trained to comport themselves seriously even as the dancing increases in speed and intensity.**
Mari Lyn Salvador, Tigre, 1997.

10.22 (ABOVE RIGHT). **The dancer in front is wearing a necklace made of pelican wing-bone flutes. The bones rattle percussively as he dances.**
Mari Lyn Salvador, Tigre, 1997.

He moves as if in very slow motion—picking up his foot, moving his foot forward, placing his foot down—step-by-step to the house.

The depiction of different dimensions of time or movement in chants and gammu burwi dances brings to mind the final line dance performed by villagers at the close of a puberty celebration. Men and women entwine their arms at the shoulders and form lines that race around the two chanters at a running pace. The lines gradually connect to each other to form one single, long line of dancers, comprising all of the villagers. They spiral around and around the two chanters who are slowing rotating in place as a duo. The spirals of dancers closest to the chanters travel around more slowly than those whipped about the outer perimeter. If one could view the scene from above, one would see the entire village tightly rotating around the central two chanters.

Perhaps this dance is a choreographic analogy of the whirlpool that the flutes had to pass through to reach the Earth. The idea of swirling down through the spiritual dimensions to reach the earth where things move more slowly might also have some relationship to the layering of images by reverse appliqué in mola design. The central focus of the images is created in the bottom layer of fabric. Successive upper layers create outward outlining of the images until, on the top layer, the outermost outlining tends to merge the images with smaller surrounding images that look like they are circling around the central images. In some types of molas, the outward outlining

10.23. The Noga Kope dance group is performing with a single *suara* **flute. This type of notched bamboo flute is similar to the** *quena* **flute that is found throughout the Andes. The specific types of flutes and panpipes used by the Kuna are unusual for the Central American lowlands, and they are not shared by neighboring groups in Panama. Kuna musical instruments and the music and dance traditions suggest a cultural affinity with groups from the South American highlands.**
Mari Lyn Salvador, Tigre, 1997.

blurs the central images seen in the bottom layer, incorporating parts of their shapes into each other in an interlocking manner.

Together, the verbal, visual, and musical arts depict the complexity of life with a clarity of expression, strength of delivery and display, and control of movement or time—often with a good amount of humor mixed in. This is the essence of being Kuna.

Kuna Migration into Urban Areas

Marta Lucía de Gerdes

"There is very little information available about Kuna who have left San Blas permanently or about Kuna enclaves" (Swain 1978, 238). These words written almost twenty years ago by Mary Swain, a student of Kuna culture, describe today's situation accurately. With few exceptions, little data exists on Kuna migration into Panama, particularly on the formation of Kuna communities in the cities of Panama and Colon.

In the past twenty-five years, Kuna migration into these areas has increasingly changed from seasonal to permanent, and its main characteristics can be described rather well in spite of the lack of records. Above all, it can be said that the resettling of Kuna people in the cities of Panama and Colon has not been random. Instead, it has developed as rather systematic, coordinated, and goal oriented, particularly if compared with the flow of other groups from rural Panama. Kuna migration certainly shows a less organized facet ridden with contradictions, internal power struggles, and the surfacing of old rivalries. There have also been many complications derived from gender and economic inequalities in the migration process.

The reasons behind Kuna migration (out of the Comarca or Kuna Yala) into the cities of Panama and Colon, and to a lesser extent into other areas of Panama, are varied and have changed through time. Although up to now the desire to acquire a formal education and to engage in wage work have been predominant, deteriorating socio-economic conditions in the islands have become in themselves another significant factor. The high density of population in most communities makes great demands over the carrying capacity of the territory, and pollution looms already as a serious problem in the Comarca. The availability of land has decreased in proportion to the population growth; there are frequent confrontations with *colonos* (illegal settlers in the Kuna territory) and with clandestine gold diggers. The coconut trade has turned into a losing enterprise because of the price drop, decreased involvement of youth, and the recent impact of a tropical disease that affects palm trees. In addition, there is a marked increase in criminality and drug trafficking. All of these factors, and others—disagreement with the traditional

11.1. Stadium mola panel. Flags shown on top of a stadium. Inspired by an exposition poster.
50.5 x 63.5 cm. FMCH X82.597A. Museum purchase in memory of Sidney S. Kallick.

order, for example—have driven many Kuna out of their islands.

Today there are more than eleven thousand Kuna in the Province of Panama according to the 1990–1991 national population census (DNEC 1990), and approximately nine thousand of them live in Panama City (CEASPA 1992). These figures are significant in proportion—roughly one fourth of all Kuna are in Panama City. But in spite of the numbers, the average Panamanian is rather indifferent to the growing presence of Kuna in their surroundings. This attitude of denial has sometimes been reinforced by the nation-state discourse which turns Kuna people simply into objects of folklore. Such distorted perception of the Kuna, referred to as "invisibility" by Raúl Leis (1991) in his novel about Kuna in the city, is not without its potential for strategic use by the Kuna themselves.

Although motives such as education, wage work, and economic hardship seem clear-cut and self-explanatory, they overlap each other and become complicated by the intrigues of local, national, and international politics. The history of Kuna migration shows the strategic thinking of a small and brave community of Amerindian people, while it also reveals the schemes of global ideological and economic interests.

Tracing educational migration

Shortly after its independence, Panama's ruling government gave priority to the "civilization" and integration of the Kuna to mainstream society, and held education to be a fundamental component of this endeavor. The task,

11.2. A woman sews a mola in Kuna Nega.
Marta Lucía de Gerdes, 1993.

however, was delegated to the Catholic Church. In 1907 a missionary was sent to the island of Narganá, whose well-traveled chief was known to admire Western education. Shortly after the arrival of the Spanish priest a Protestant missionary, a British woman, established herself in the smaller and more conservative island of Mono. In spite of their convictions and persistence, both missionaries met with little immediate success. Nonetheless, they started a flow of Kuna children into Panama and the United States for the purposes of schooling, and each party achieved this in a different style. The children sponsored by the Catholic mission, then and in the following years, were often sent to *acudientes*. These were hosts, generally Catholic families, for whom the children were required to do housework in exchange for an education in a public or Catholic school. (It should be remarked here that word "acudiente" is not restricted only to this meaning in Kuna culture.)

The mission led by the British crusader, in contrast, first arranged for Kuna children to be sent to Bible boarding schools in the United States; later, with the arrival of other Christian denominations financed by communities in the United States, Kuna children were also lodged in boarding houses or orphanages in Panama City. They were to attend schools affiliated to Protestant churches where the English language was emphasized.

In general, educational migration into Panama City grew rapidly. In 1924 there were already sixty Kuna students in Panama City schools, most of them from Narganá

(Stout 1947, 89). Already in 1928 there was an umbrella organization in Panama City for young Kuna who attended school there. Only during the years that followed the 1925 Kuna revolution was there an obvious decline in educational migration.

In the 1930s Panama's government began to take over the role it had delegated to the Catholic Church. It offered scholarships to Kuna youth who would be active in spreading the political goals of national government in the islands and who would actually engage in political party campaigns.

Educational migration continued a growing trend up until the 1950s when a number of elementary and secondary schools were established in the Comarca. Then, in the 1960s, a new cycle of educational migration began with a small but steady flow of Kuna university students. Those coming from the island of Ailigandi, in particular, were sponsored by the Baptist Mission which encouraged them to pursue careers in the health field, after the opening of a hospital on the island (Vandervelde and Iglesias 1982, 152). This group of Ailigandi students contrasted with those from other islands who soon became organized and politically active. But this aspect of Kuna student life was only a reflection of what occurred at other levels. On the one hand, Kuna were offered education and political training in countries of the then Socialist block (see, for example, Holloman 1969, 370), while the U.S.-based Christian denominations continued to send other students to Bible colleges in the United States and Latin American countries.

11.3, 11.4. The community of Abya Yala.
David Mayo, 1997.

This stage of educational migration crystallized a new leadership that had been emerging since the 1950s. Younger men with different levels of education marked themselves as powerful individuals in their respective communities in the Comarca, since they could effect immediate change through their contact with outside authorities. The core of the conflict between this leadership and the traditional authorities has been, beyond the question of their lack of traditional knowledge, the challenge they present to class-age authority, one of the pillars of Kuna social structure.

Wage work migration

In 1930 the Kuna Chief Nele Kantule signed a historic treaty with the United States Army which marked the beginning of an organized wage-work migration into the cities of Panama and Colon. While the treaty strengthened the autonomous nature of the Kuna region, the contracts were not fair to Kuna workers; they reserved only low-wage menial jobs for them, and stipulated a thirty-nine-hour work week which circumvented their rights to benefits.

Parallel to this labor migration another smaller but equally significant migration took place. The Canal Zone Kuna workers began to make arrangements on an individual basis to find positions for younger Kuna, mostly for boys, as house-help in well to do residences in Panama, Colon, and the Canal Zone. For each of the cases, the authorities

of the respective villages had to give approval, issuing written permits when possible. But as it can be anticipated, these mediated arrangements for very young people meant below minimum wages most of the times, no benefits, and unlike the *acudiente* arrangement, responsibility for the formal education of the child was not always guaranteed.

During World War II the demand for Kuna labor grew in the U.S. Army bases and in the Panamanian service sector that catered to the American military. By the mid-1940s there were more than four thousand Kuna men in the cities of Panama and Colon; most were seasonal workers who returned to the islands for at least several months each year (Stout 1947, 57).

Living arrangements of these immigrants varied, but one characteristic was aggregation. Immigrants stayed in groups as it was desirable to maintain social control and traditional culture, and to minimize spending. The pattern of aggregation generally followed native village membership, which most of the times overlapped kinship ties. Men who worked within the Canal Zone system, namely those who had contracts with the U.S. Armed Forces, paid for space in the barracks provided for single male workers in the military bases. The conditions there were better and relatively less expensive than the rooms that other men shared in dilapidated apartments in the downtown area or low-income neighborhoods in Panama City.

With the end of World War II the need for Kuna labor in the Canal decreased, while Panama entered an economic crisis and a decade of grave sociopolitical instability. This situation coincided with a new era in the relations between the Kuna and the Panamanian nation-state. In 1945 the Panamanian government passed a law which institutionalized a ranked system of chiefs for the Kuna Reservation (Herlihy 1989, 18). The Comarca was divided into three political sectors, each with a high chief. Two of these sectors could be traced at least to nineteenth-century affiliations. The creation of the third sector was rather a strategy from the national government, alleging that there was a group of islands so much more "modern" and acculturated that did not fit any of the other two sectors. The chief of the island of Narganá was appointed as the highest local authority for this new third sector (see Howe 1986, 20). The national government attempted there first its strategies for integration and nationalization, but in the long run the new sector was more the target of politicking than actual modernization. However, the public school system did spread rapidly. This permitted Kuna from other islands to receive an education without leaving the territory. This situation favored the chiefs of the most conservative regions who, aware of the crisis Panama experienced after World War II, made an effort to curb migration. They tried to keep a steady labor pool in the islands while reinforcing social control in the Kuna territory.

In 1953 Panama committed itself to recognize the autonomy of the entire territory of San Blas through a new law. It not only conferred special territorial status to the Kuna land, but it also served to confirm a new labor treaty between Kuna authorities and a transnational company. In 1952 the United Fruit Company (UFC) had signed a treaty with a Kuna chief, mediated and facilitated by the U.S. government. The UFC, owner of vast banana plantations in the westernmost provinces of Bocas del Toro and Chiriquí, obtained temporary cheap labor from the Kuna this way.

The UFC, like the Canal authorities, did not provide any benefits to Kuna employees (cf. Bourgois 1989, 163) and banned unionization. The majority of Kuna hired by the UFC came from poorer islands where there were no alternative sources of income and coconut farms were scarcer. This profile contrasted with the Canal Zone Kuna labor where most workers came from acculturated Narganá, or the more conservative, more pro-U.S. Ailigandi. Nonetheless, because of the particular mechanics of each arrangement, plantation workers could contribute more money to their very needy communities.

While the UFC Kuna workers were not permitted to organize, in another region of the country the opposite happened. Workers from less wealthy islands had also come to work in the docks in the Province of Colon. They worked in deplorable conditions, earning an average of fifteen dollars per month (Moncada Vargas 1990). The Marine Workers Union of the Province of Colon approached the Kuna who were already organized in regional groups to join them in their general struggle for workers' rights. In 1957, the Kuna, as part of the Marine Workers Union, joined the Federation of Workers of Colon (Moncada Vargas 1990).

In the 1960s the traditional chief in charge of the discipline of UFC migrant laborers lost much of his authority over the growing number of Kuna, who in contrast to previous years, migrated with family and children to the United Fruit enclaves in the Province of Bocas del Toro. In his study of Kuna life in the banana plantations, Bourgeois (1989, 171) recorded these words from an elder Kuna who remembers that period: "It got so bad that we lived all dispersed, one separate from the other, like Hispanics!" During this period some of these workers decided not to return to San Blas after finishing their contract in the plantations. Instead, they moved or reunited with their families in the cities of Colon or Panama.

Reinforcing the links between the city and the Comarca

In the 1970s there was a reaffirmation of the authority of the chiefs over Kuna living outside the Comarca. The system of *capítulos* became an important, although rather symbolic mechanism in this process. The word capítulo, borrowed from Spanish, basically refers to regional branch offices that represent the authorities of each of the major Comarca villages in Panama City, and sometimes also in the City of Colon. The first capítulos appear to have emerged in the mid-1940s (Lasso 1962), but other regional associations, as indicated above, preceded their formation.

Each capítulo operates much like an embassy or a consulate. It keeps track of island residents by recording the destination or the permanent residence of village members and their families in the city. Travel permits into the Comarca are only extended to Kuna who have paid the required monthly fees or "tax contribution" to the local government of the parent island through the corresponding capítulo.

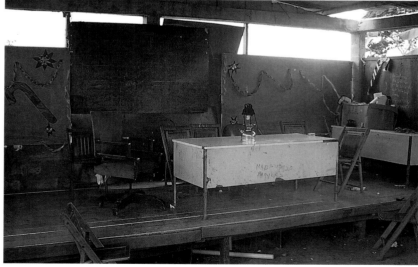

The practice of issuing travel permits among the Kuna actually dates back to the 1915 restrictions placed by the Panamanian government on their mobility, which catalyzed the 1925 Kuna Revolution. According to R. Holloman, the permit system was implemented in the capítulos as a control mechanism and as a symbol of the authority of the chiefs of all islands. In theory, no island will let into its territory a delinquent member of another community (Holloman 1969, 251). In this way, at least symbolically, all Kuna who leave the Comarca continue to be answerable to their native villages.

11.5. A meeting space in Abya Yala.
David Mayo, 1997.

All capítulos are structured similarly; they are led by a board of directors elected by direct vote from the members. In years past Kuna have indicated that the criteria for electing the president of a capítulo are "his knowledge of the tradition, his behavior, his education, his age [usually men over fifty years old], his level of energy, and his verbal skills,… in addition to being a role model for young people" (Rodríguez 1961, 58). All adult members are required to attend weekly meetings, and excessive absences result in an interest fee which tends to accumulate rapidly.

One of the most important aspects of the capítulo life is their role as a community facility. Among other purposes, they serve as post offices, fund-raising headquarters, and cafeterias where traditional Kuna meals are prepared and sold every weekend. And although capítulos tend to be located in small apartments they also function as hostels or shelters for newcomers and authorized visitors.

The capítulos also play a role in the coordination of Kuna cultural performances in the cities. Committees within each capítulo, or sometimes from different ones, coordinate and develop artistic projects such as dance and theater groups. The themes of these performances range from local political issues to traditional culture. But in the city, even the latter have an urban outlook.

The larger capítulos have been increasingly dedicated to the periodic organization of cultural programs in tribute to important chiefs, especially in memory of Cimral Colman and Nele Kantule both protagonists of the Kuna Revolution. These tributes feature poetry, songs, dances, short theatrical pieces, and carefully selected narrators or masters of ceremony. The general structure of the events seems to be patterned after the cultural programs that are a trademark of the Panamanian school

11.6. A woman speaks at an interregional meeting.
Marta Lucía de Gerdes, Cartí Suitupu, 1993.

system, with a heavy emphasis on oratory and poetry. Among Kuna communities in the city, the tribute programs tend to reinforce intracommunal identity, and furthermore, they remind the participants of larger regional affiliations that can be traced back at least to the late nineteenth century.

Beyond cultural performances, the sports events are another very important aspect of the capítulos, especially for young people. One of the most vivid ways of displaying island affiliation, of socializing, and experiencing the body as part of Kuna identity is found in Kuna sports leagues. Young Kuna participate passionately in these activities and speak of feeling honored when they are chosen to be a part of the team that represents the capítulo of an island.

It is true also that not all capítulos invest equally in sports. However, other differences are more significant in marking the "character" of a capítulo. Among these are the kind, amount, and number of fees and taxes that must be paid by each member, the importance given to religious interests and party politics, and the level of the organization itself.

One concrete expression of these differences is the degree to which capítulos have come to be urban schools of the Kuna oral tradition. Sherzer (1994, 904) has indicated that chiefs "visit from time to time and formally counsel the assembled members of the chapter," but one chief informed him that he does not perform traditional chants for fear that people would make fun of him.

At least two capítulos have well organized groups of young men, high school or university students, dedicated to learning traditional knowledge directly from the chiefs. As one member indicated, the group meets once a week "to discuss the philosophy of the elders, and to write and interpret myths." The capítulo actually makes "contracts" with a given chief from the parent island, and less often with respected chiefs from other islands, to lecture to these groups of young men.

The visiting chiefs meet with their students in a room of a capítulo reserved for this purpose. A chief will address the young men in a style that differs significantly from the narrative or the distinctive chief chanting that characterizes the island nightly gatherings, but which is a very formalized style, nonetheless. The chief's role becomes more that of a "guest lecturer" who attempts not only to teach a body of texts but to interpret their symbolism and philosophy in Western style, interacting freely with the students who take notes or record the talks.

Besides the issues addressed above, there is also the fact that some islands are too small in size and population to have a capítulo of their own. These communities can resort to less structured "associations," such as voluntary societies (cf. Costello 1986, 96–97), but they also find indirect representation in the larger capítulos. As of 1994 there were sixteen capítulos that coordinated their activities through an umbrella organization called the Unión de Capítulos. The Union was established in 1990, and serves to link the capítulos to the General Congress, the highest authority of the Comarca.

Capítulos present good evidence of the importance of intracommunity affiliation among the Kuna, which Mary Swain called "community centrism" in her 1978 ethnographic study. By reproducing the small-island bound structure in the city, the capítulo system ensures a sameness at a microlevel that, like most Kuna traditional discourse, reproduces not a boring homogeneity but a defined space for embellishment and creativity.

11.7. Sporting activites in Kuna Nega.
Marta Lucía de Gerdes, 1993.

Although there seems to be no antagonism between the operation of the capítulos and other long-standing organizations such as the Cooperative of the Panama Canal Kuna Employees, other emerging allegiances have affected capítulo activism. A survey carried out by this author in a community where only Kuna live, revealed that approximately eighty percent of the households did not participate in the weekly or monthly meetings of the capítulos. Availability and the cost of public transportation were intervening factors. In addition to this, the administrative meetings of the community coincided with those of the capítulo.

Some people also objected to the financial demands made by the capítulos, and criticized in particular the management of funds. However, all survey participants knew the location of the larger capítulos, and many indicated that they did visit them to pick up correspondence or to take socializing breaks when running errands in the downtown area.

To keep its central position in Kuna urban life, the capítulo system will have to deal effectively with the situation of the many Kuna children who are now born and raised in Panama City; their affiliation to a capítulo is certain to develop in entirely different terms than that of the preceding generations.

Becoming visible in the city

The fact that Kuna males who migrate as wage workers tend to secure an employment prior to the arrival of the nuclear family to the city, and that, at least in theory, they count on reliable regional and kin support networks, can obscure some of the

11.8. A "seer" visits a Kuna community in the city. Women concerned about the health of their children and grandchildren consult her for advice.
Marta Lucia de Gerdes, Kuna Nega, 1993.

serious problems that Kuna families encounter in the migration process. One of those often overlooked situations is the fact that the men may be away from their homes in the urban areas even for weeks at a time because of the nature or location of their jobs (from military sites in the Canal area to banana plantations close to the Costa Rican border). Economic stability is not always assured for the family during these periods, and Kuna women face many pressures during these absences.

Kuna women are indeed affected by all the other situations experienced by women from other migrant communities around the world: health issues, lack of safety, and other situations poverty brings about; conflicting ideas of morality with the dominant society, discrimination, language barriers, and lack of access to natural resources. Then, there are also the more personal concerns—there have been cases where Kuna men have repudiated their wives and moved in with other women during their prolonged absences. This has occurred in spite of surveillance and pressure from the chiefs, who themselves are not immune to such situations. For example, it is said, that the today legendary Chief Nele Kantule not only left his original island when he reestablished himself in Ailigandi; he also left a first wife behind.

Not least is the fact that in traditional Kuna culture the domain of women is highly marked as the household, and that it is there, as much as in the so-called "public" cultural events, where Kuna culture is reconstructed. By keeping these facts in mind, it is not surprising then to realize that Kuna women took the initiative in finding alternatives for better and more permanent housing.

The turning point was the beginning of the 1980s when a group of women organized themselves, their kin, and acquaintances to find legal land for Kuna people in the city. With the support of local grassroots organizations and international funding agencies they secured fully legal access to land that was to be reverted by the Panama Canal Treaties. The neighborhood which resulted from these efforts, still developing today, was named Kuna Nega. N*ega*, a term with a broad semantic field and which is often glossed as "house," is very symbolic in this case. Nega can also mean "land," "country," or "territory." Holmer's 1952 dictionary of Kuna already featured Kuna Nega at the same conceptual level of Merki Nega, which can be glossed as "the land of the Americans, the U.S." Kuna Nega, as all other Kuna neighborhoods, is much more than a plot of land; nega means also "space"—a space where the Kuna world can be recreated. And the Kuna world is as definite as it is diverse and dynamic; it is as open as the nature of "air," "time," or "world," all of which can also be translated as *nega*.

The success of the Kuna and their supporters in obtaining governmental approval for the Kuna Nega project was based on an in-depth knowledge of Panamanian politics, in particular of local bureaucracy. But it also demanded patience, solidarity, and good strategies from the Kuna involved.

To this day, the rich lands of the areas reverted by the Canal treaties are coveted by many powerful groups. The Kuna, thus, achieved something that the most influential groups in Panamanian society were not able to do. This resulted in a series of veiled reactions against the Kuna, such as the decision to place the Municipal Landfill approximately one kilometer away from the land assigned to the Kuna neighborhood. The landfill, which receives more than 1,450 tons of waste per day, started to operate officially in 1985 (Susman 1984, 18).

Most sources agree that the pioneer of the neighborhood initiative was a woman named Andrea Mendoza, supported by six other Kuna women. Mendoza, who is still active in the administrative structure of the community, remembers well the beginning of what is now her neighborhood. She and the other founding members used to take a bus ride at 4 a.m., and then a twenty-minute walk to the densely forested area that was the construction site. Families camped out on weekends, sharing at first the tasks of clearing the tropical bush and building temporary latrines, among others. The work presented several health hazards because the area was infested with mosquitoes and snakes, and families had sometimes to work and sleep out in the rain. This stage of the formation of the neighborhood is remembered as one of much value. The founders proudly talk about how the group of people that worked there persevered, how they managed to accomplish defined goals, and more importantly, how they worked together by themselves, independently. The founding members in particular overtly acknowledge this time of hardship as an experience that now binds them together.

Although people that did not take part in this initial stage have moved now into the neighborhood, and have even taken up positions within the administrative structure, the newcomers themselves praise the "pioneers" and their hard work and make the disclaimer that they moved in to Kuna Nega more recently and did not share the experience of the founders.

Parallel to the Kuna Nega initiative, other all-Kuna neighborhoods started to take clear shape in the outskirts of Panama City, always directly linked to the dynamics of urban life. There are at least three other well known Kuna neighborhoods, each of them reproducing to some degree part of the traditional social structure of the Comarca villages. Their population ranges from five hundred to fifteen hundred, but it is always in flow as many visitors come and go with regularity. However, up to the present only Kuna Nega has been granted full legal status from the concerned national authorities.

Even if each one of the all-Kuna neighborhoods is located in the outskirts of the city where the living conditions are still urban-rural (*urbano-barrial*), the lives

MARTA LUCÍA DE GERDES

11.9. One of the occasions in which experts in traditional house architecture came from the community of Bayano to help the community of Kuna Nega build its gathering house. Unfortunately, each of the houses they have built has burned down, and the community is taking its time before investing in a new one.
Marta Lucía de Gerdes, 1994.

11.10. Community work for the construction of a pedestrian bridge across the Mocambo. The women hand picked stones from the river and transported buckets of sand to the site where the men built the bridge.
Marta Lucía de Gerdes, Kuna Nega, 1993.

of the residents are so tightly linked to the city sphere that for all practical purposes they are not related to rural affairs. The lack of utility installations in these communities is not so much related to their location, but rather to the low-income bracket of the residents. It is a common feature of many Third World cities that adjacent communities of sharp economic contrasts differ in the type of modern facilities available to them.

The Kuna-only neighborhoods lie next to other communities of clear socioeconomic and sometimes well defined ethnic membership. In spite of the fact that there is sometimes tension, there have been no proved incidents of aggression or animosity between the Kuna and their neighbors.

The desire to live in a Kuna neighborhood is affected by regional and kin ties—which may expedite approval of membership into the community—availability of land, and certainly, socio-economic status. For example, Kuna Nega the only neighborhood where regional affiliation was overtly downplayed, required the deposit of an initial membership fee, as well as the verification that the new member would be able to afford the monthly payments of the future home to the rotating fund. While such economic expectations disqualified some people who were interested in the project, others who had achieved higher social status within the national society would have not joined the enterprise just in order to live with other Kuna. The purpose of the initiative at any rate was not to recall those Kuna who had accommodated themselves to other spaces in Panamanian society, but rather to provide an alternative to those with limited economic resources, and who wanted a lifestyle more in accordance with traditional Kuna values.

This need of Kuna people for a space to grow, adapt, and change in the cities can easily be misread as a segregationist strand by the dominant society, and can unleash fears and distrust. This is a situation that many immigrant communities around the world confront each day; and by some twisted turn of history, Amerindian communities have become immigrants in their own land.

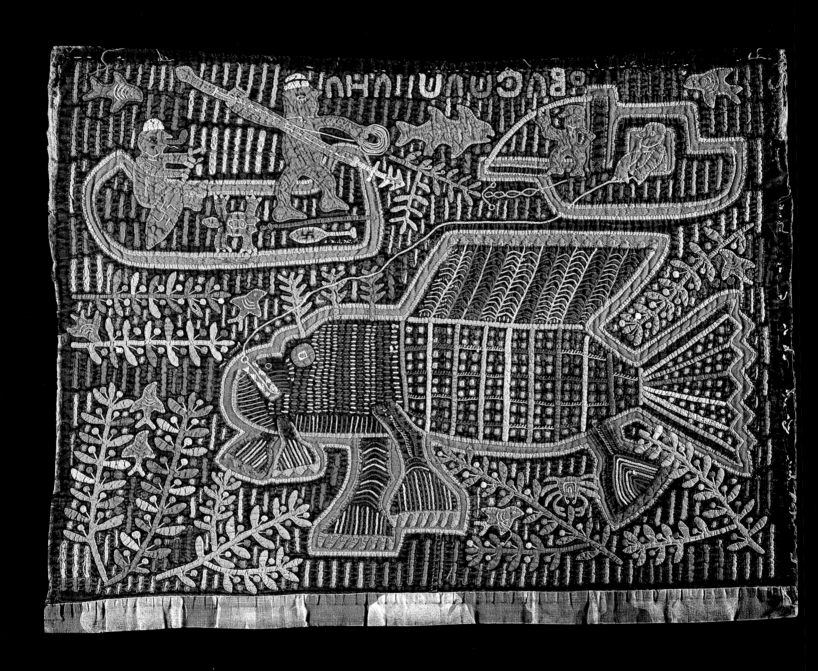

Catalog

Kuna objects from the Field Museum

The Field Museum in Chicago has some of the earliest Kuna material anywhere. The Museum owns at least three significant collections. The earliest is a small group of materials dating from the 1893 World's Columbian Exposition in Chicago. It includes a bow, several arrows, panpipes, flutes, and at least one headdress. This collection was followed by ninety works, including twenty molas, assembled in Panama before 1918 by Mr. G. L. Fitz-William, a chemical and mining engineer from Hammond, Indiana. The exact dates of his collecting efforts are not known but he offered the collection to the Museum in a letter dated 8 April 1918. Besides the molas there are a number of *nuchus*, staffs, baskets, necklaces, paddles, and musical instruments. Many of these pieces have island names associated with them; and a seven-page document, "Notes on the San Blas Indians" by Fitz-William, is on file at the museum. The third collection is a fascinating group of 148 mola blouses and panels dating from between 1954 and 1965 possibly assembled by a woman named Diana Chiari Gruber, based on a reference in the 21 May 1965 issue of *Panama American* found with the material. The whole collection was bought sight unseen at a Railway Express auction and subsequently given to the museum in 1966. Selections from all three collections are presented on pages 322–333.

Cat. 1 (OPPOSITE). **Fishing mola. The man in the boat on the right catches a huge fish with a hook and line. In the boat the man at the back paddles as the man in the front spears a fish.** 55.0 x 42.5 cm. The Field Museum, Chicago. Cat. #190453; Neg. #A113284c.

Cat. 2. Bird mola blouse. The bird seems to be on top of a beetlelike figure; the serrated outline is called *dientes*. 64.0 x 78.0 cm. The Field Museum, Chicago. Cat. #5825; Neg. #A113288c.

Cat. 3. Figures mola blouse. Line of figures in three vertical bands. 73.0 x 85.0 cm. The Field Museum, Chicago. Cat. #5818; Neg. #A113291c.

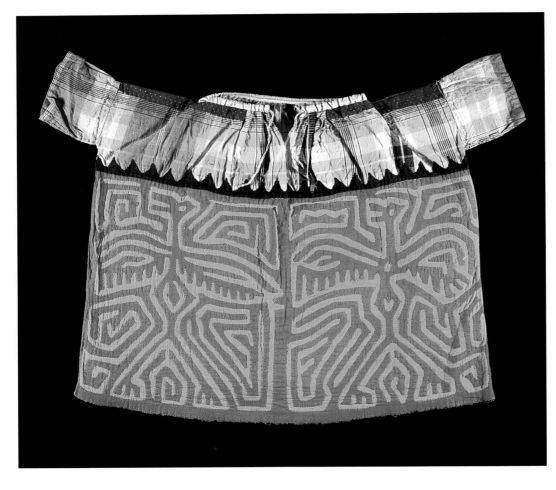

Cat. 4A,B (TWO VIEWS). Double birds mola blouse. This type of mola is called *mor gwinagwad,* one color. The front and back are the same type and have similar designs. Plaid fabric was particularly popular in the early 1900s.
48.0 x 69.0 cm. The Field Museum, Chicago. Cat. #5813; Neg. #A113285c, A113286c

Cat. 5A,B (TWO VIEWS). **Early geometric mola blouse. The side shown on the bottom has four figures depicted on their sides.**

64.0 x 80.0 cm. The Field Museum, Chicago. Cat. #5820; Neg. #A113297c, A113298c.

**Cat. 6. Geometric mola blouse.
This type of mola has several
overall layers.**
62.0 x 87.0 cm. The Field Museum, Chicago.
Cat. #5815; Neg. #A113289c.

Cat. 7. *Ulu* **(canoe) mola blouse.
Here, the canoe design is depicted
in a vertical format. It is the same
design shown in Figs. 6.12 and 6.79.**
62.0 x 78.0 cm. The Field Museum, Chicago.
Cat. #5816; Neg. #A113293c.

**Cat. 8. Ovaltine mola blouse.
Multicolored mola showing a
cheerful, dancing Ovaltine jar.**

57.0 x 70.0 cm. The Field Museum, Chicago.
Cat. #190347; Neg. #A113295c.

**Cat. 9. *Gammu burwi* (panpipes).
One of a pair of panpipes.**

Bamboo, string. 54.0 cm. The Field Museum,
Chicago. Cat. #5886.1-2, Neg. #A113314c.

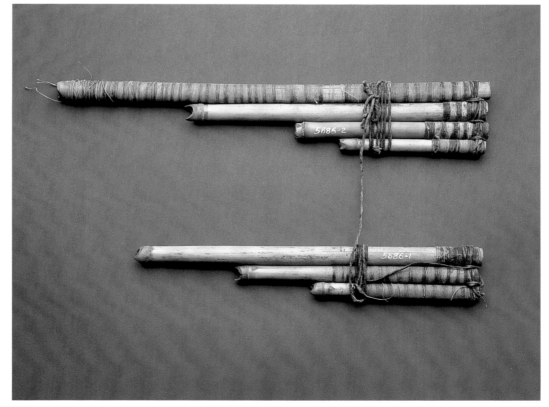

Cat. 10. *Gandule gurgin* (ritual specialist's headdress). Mr. G. L. Fitz-William, the collector, describes the headdress as having white hawk feathers with bunches of heron aigrettes in bamboo tubes and the tail feathers of a red macaw.

Feathers, bamboo, plant fiber. 78.0 cm. The Field Museum, Chicago. Cat. #5835; Neg. #A113312c.

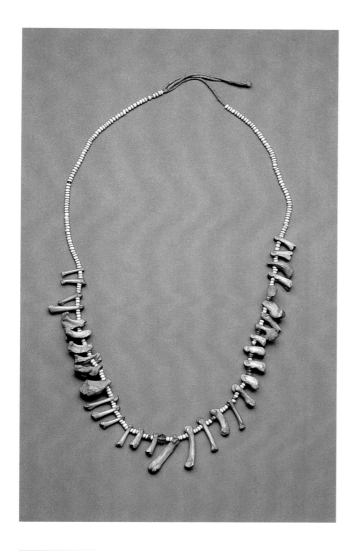

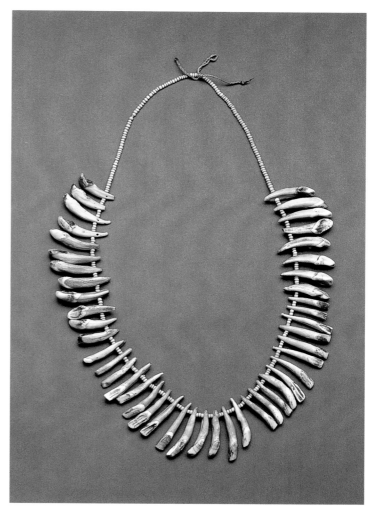

Cat. 11 (ABOVE LEFT). **Necklace. Young boys wear this type of necklace made from animal teeth and beads.**
Animal teeth, beads, string. 7.0 cm. The Field Museum, Chicago. Cat. #5881; Neg. #A113306c.

Cat. 12 (ABOVE RIGHT). **Necklace. Necklaces like these are also sold by the hundreds to tourists.**
Animal teeth, beads, string. 18.0 cm. The Field Museum, Chicago. Cat. #5878; Neg. #A113310c.

Cat. 13. Necklace.
Animal teeth, beads, string. 27.0 cm. The Field Museum, Chicago. Cat. #5882; Neg. #A113311c.

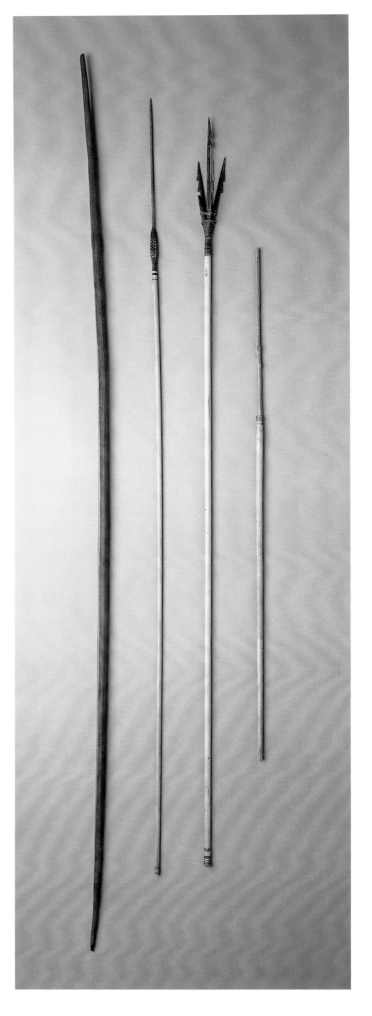

Fishing spears and hunting implements. The arrows are made from the flowering stems of white cane, the tips from black palm.

AT RIGHT, LEFT TO RIGHT:

Cat. 14.
188.0 cm. The Field Museum, Chicago. Cat. #6470; Neg. #A113304c.

Cat. 15 (DETAIL ABOVE).
161.0 cm. The Field Museum, Chicago. Cat. #5860; Neg. #A113304c, A113305c (detail).

Cat. 16 (DETAIL ABOVE).
153.0 cm. The Field Museum, Chicago. Cat. #5858; Neg. #A113304c, A113305c (detail).

Cat. 17.
104.0 cm. The Field Museum, Chicago. Cat. #6466; Neg. #A113304c.

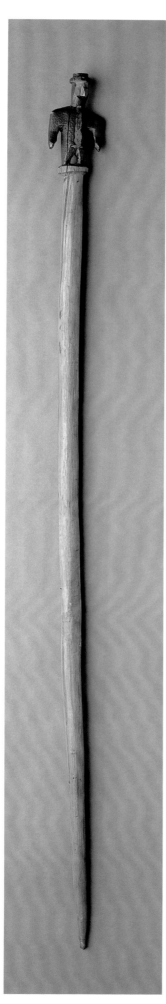

Authority staffs. Wooden staffs with designs carved on the top are carried by policemen and curers.

Cat. 18 (FAR LEFT).
95.0 cm. The Field Museum, Chicago. Cat. #5895; Neg. #A113299c.

Cat. 19 (LEFT, DETAIL ABOVE).
109.0 cm. The Field Museum, Chicago.Cat. #191582; Neg. #A113300c, A113301c (detail).

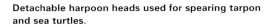

Cat. 20. *Dede,* flute made from an armadillo skull and bird bone. The pieces are held together with a natural resin.
15.5 cm. The Field Museum, Chicago.
Cat. #6476; Neg. #A113309c.

Detachable harpoon heads used for spearing tarpon and sea turtles.

Cat. 21 (ABOVE).
Iron, plant fiber. 22.0 cm. The Field Museum, Chicago.
Cat. #5876; Neg. #A113308c.

Cat. 22 (ABOVE RIGHT).
Iron, plant fiber. 32.0 cm. The Field Museum, Chicago.
Cat. #5875; Neg. #A113307c.

Cat. 23 (FAR LEFT). *Nuchu,* **carved wooden figure used for curing.**
35.0 cm. The Field Museum, Chicago. Cat. #5840; Neg. #A113303c.

Cat. 24 (LEFT). *Nuchu.*
19.5 cm. The Field Museum, Chicago. Cat. #5848; Neg. #A113302c.

Cat. 25. Basket with lid. This type of basket is generally used to store clothes.
Plant fiber. 28.0 cm. The Field Museum, Chicago. Cat. #5866A-B; Neg. #A113313c.

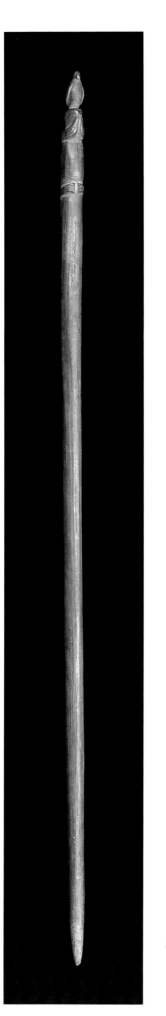

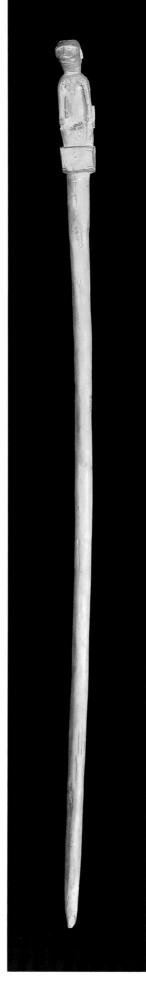

Cat. 26 (ABOVE AND RIGHT).
Authority staff.
Wood. 92.5 cm. NMAI 25/2259. From the
Museum Gift Shop.

Cat. 27 (LEFT AND ABOVE).
Authority staff.
Wood, pigment. 100.0 cm. NMAI 12/9112.
Collected by A. Hyatt Verrill.

Cat. 28. Plate mola blouse.
Opposite side of Fig. N, p. 77.
72.0 x 85.0 cm. NMAI 22/4836. Presented by
Elena Eritta.

Cat. 29. Basketball mola blouse.
Opposite side of Fig. 1.30, p. 41.
61.0 x 68.0 cm. NMAI 24/7986. Presented by
Elena Eritta.

Cat. 30. Ali Baba mola. Based on the story of Ali Baba and the Forty Thieves, this panel depicts Morgiana pouring hot oil into the jars in which robbers were hidden.

32.0 x 42.5 cm. Private collection.

Cat. 31. *Chicha* mola. This design illustrates a dance performed as part of girls' puberty ceremonies. The two figures with the hats in the center represent the ritual specialist and his assistant, each playing a flute and shaking a rattle.

38.0 x 46.0 cm. Private collection.

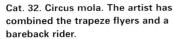

Cat. 32. Circus mola. The artist has combined the trapeze flyers and a bareback rider.

40.5 x 50.0 cm. Private collection.

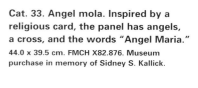

Cat. 33. Angel mola. Inspired by a religious card, the panel has angels, a cross, and the words "Angel Maria."
44.0 x 39.5 cm. FMCH X82.876. Museum purchase in memory of Sidney S. Kallick.

Cat. 34. Crèche mola. Angels hover above the Holy Family. This design could have been inspired by a Christmas card or the small Nativity scenes sold in Panama during the holidays.
49.0 x 39.0 cm. FMCH X82.877. Museum purchase in memory of Sidney S. Kallick.

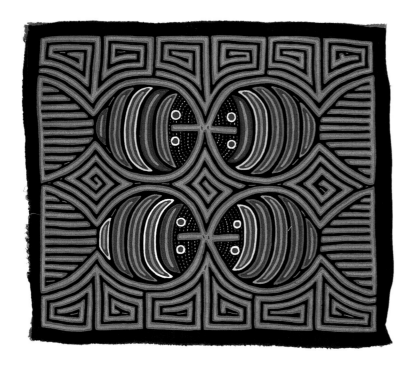

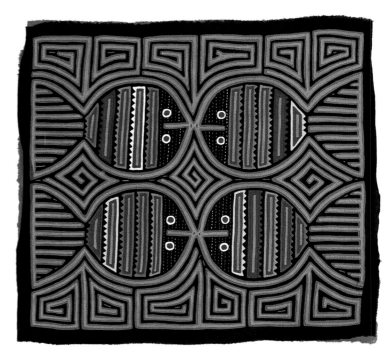

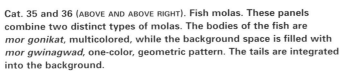

Cat. 35 and 36 (ABOVE AND ABOVE RIGHT). Fish molas. These panels combine two distinct types of molas. The bodies of the fish are *mor gonikat*, multicolored, while the background space is filled with *mor gwinagwad*, one-color, geometric pattern. The tails are integrated into the background.
Both, 42.5 x 38.5 cm. FMCH X96.25.2A,B.

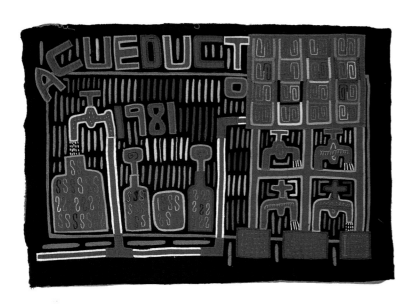

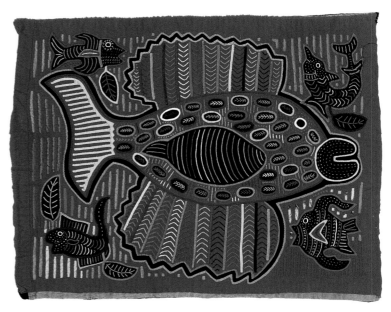

Cat. 37. Aqueduct mola. Some islands have fresh water piped from the mainland. Here, faucets are shown with water flowing into the bottles.
31.0 x 43.0 cm. FMCH X91.1648.

Cat. 38. Fish mola. Underwater scene depicts fish and shells. This color combination is unusual in molas the women make for their own blouses.
31.0 x 39.0 cm. FMCH X97.3.13.

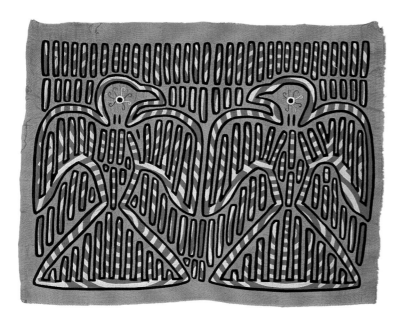

Cat. 39 and 40 (ABOVE AND ABOVE RIGHT). Birds molas. Made in 1996, these panels represent a renewed interest in a type of mola popular in the 1920s. A geometric design is first cut and sewn onto a base layer. Then another layer of fabric is put on top and a different design is cut out and sewn to expose the pattern below.
Both, 42.0 x 51.0 cm. FMCH X96.25.1A,B.

Cat. 41. "Puss in Boots" mola. Depicting a children's story, the artist shows the whiskers on the cats and detail on the boots.
49.5 x 41.0 cm. FMCH X82.874A. Museum purchase in memory of Sidney S. Kallick.

Cat. 42. Dogs in baskets mola. Reverse side of Cat. 41. It may have been inspired by a greeting card.
48.0 x 41.5 cm. FMCH X82.874B. Museum purchase in memory of Sidney S. Kallick.

Cat. 43. Comic mola. An elephant steps gingerly onto a scale as a bird and a rabbit look on. The design may be from a comic book or a children's story.
46.0 x 49.0 cm. FMCH X96.25.8.

Cat. 44. Santa Claus mola, showing Saint Nick in his sleigh, with a stocking and a candle in the background.
38.0 x 40.5 cm. FMCH X96.25.6.

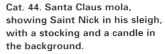

Cat. 45. "Jesus Murio" mola. Christ is depicted in the tomb with flowers and a candle.
35.5 x 44.0 cm. FMCH X96.25.7.

Cat. 46. Drummer mola. A man in fancy boots is shown playing the drums. "Hombre Anta" is sewn at the top.
35.0 x 42.0 cm. FMCH X88.597. Gift of the United Nations Association, World Center.

Cat. 47. Geometric mola. Designs like this one may have been inspired by the print fabric Kuna women used to make their skirts.
44.0 x 50.0 cm. FMCH X82.883. Museum purchase in memory of Sidney S. Kallick.

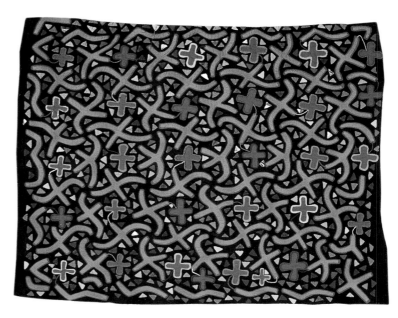

Cat. 48. Floral pattern mola. This design, called *flores* (flowers), has been popular for decades.
50.0 x 43.0 cm. FMCH X82.879. Museum purchase in memory of Sidney S. Kallick.

Cat. 49. Circles mola. The mola design is created over the top of print fabric and utilizes the printed pattern in some areas rather than cutting each section. Some women expressed concern about this way of creating a mola.
34.5 x 42.0 cm. FMCH X96.25.10.

Cat. 50. "S" mola. An old fashioned design.
38.0 x 45.5 cm. FMCH X84.667. Gift of Dorothy M. Cordry in memory of Donald B. Cordry.

Cat. 51. Two figures mola. This early design showing a small figure on top of or inside of another larger figure raises questions regarding interpretation.

39.0 x 48.5 cm. FMCH X82.881. Museum purchase in memory of Sidney S. Kallick.

Cat. 52. *Gole igar*, path of the hermit crab, also shown in Figures 6.5 and 6.6.

49.5 x 41.0 cm. FMCH X84.657. Museum purchase in memory of Sidney S. Kallick.

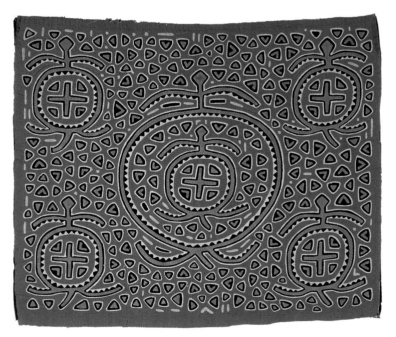

Cat. 53. Anchor mola design. Intricate design that may be based on an anchor motif taken from a trademark or package.

38.0 x 51.0 cm. FMCH X83.436. Gift of Dorothy M. Cordry in memory of Donald B. Cordry.

Cat. 54. Turtle mola design. A central turtle with smaller turtles in the corners, this early design is being made again today.

43.0 x 51.0 cm. FMCH X82.614. Museum purchase in memory of Sidney S. Kallick.

Cat. 55. TV logo mola. Television stations in Panama use logos based on motifs found on ceramics from archaeological sites.

44.5 x 49.5 cm. FMCH X82.607. Museum purchase in memory of Sidney S. Kallick.

Cat. 56. Political party mola. The National Liberation Movement mola, similar to the one shown in Figure 3.9, shows the flag of the CPN, Patriotic Coalition Movement.

41.0 x 49.0 cm. FMCH X82.602. Museum purchase in memory of Sidney S. Kallick.

Cat. 57. Sea Slugs mola. The design depicts two wood-boring sea slugs.

33.5 x 40.0 cm. FMCH X88.1366.

Cat. 58. Succarath mola. The embroidered lettering identifies this as Succarath, a beast who lived in South America.

50.5 x 48.0 cm. FMCH X82.880. Museum purchase in memory of Sidney S. Kallick.

Cat. 59. Toy airplane. Airplanes come daily to Kuna Yala, and children enjoy playing with toy planes.
Wood, cloth. 64.5 cm. FMCH X97.5.15.

Notes

1. Artful Lives *Mari Lyn Salvador and James Howe*

1. This passage is from a ritual greeting between chiefs on July 5, 1970. The chanter was Chief Mandiweginya of Muladupu and the responder was a visiting chief from Niadupu. Personal communication, Joel Sherzer.
2. Oral history 1985 from Jimmy Solis. Recorded by Jesus Alemancia, transcribed by Reinaldo Sody and translated by James Howe and Reinaldo Sody.
3. For other references regarding Kuna structuralism: see Hirschfield 1976, 1977a, 1997b; Kramer 1970; Howe, Sherzer, and Chapin 1980; Reverte 1968; Salvador 1978.
4. I3eorgun is one of the great culture heroes, responsible for founding most of the institutions of Kuna life.

3. The Kuna and the World *James Howe*

1. For this article, documentation has been kept to a minimum. Fuller documentation can be found in Howe (forthcoming, Spring 1998).

4. Kuna Language and Literature *Joel Sherzer*

1. For further information about Kuna language and literature, see Chapin (1970), Howe (1986), Howe, Sherzer and Chapin (1980), McCosker (1974), and Sherzer (1983, 1990).

6. Contemporary Kuna Women's Arts *Mari Lyn Salvador*

1. Print fabric was popular in the early 1900s and is still widely used by mola makers today.
2. Thanks to Lynn Felsher for drawing my attention to the possibility of patterns from trade fabrics being used as motifs for molas.
3. For a discussion of Kuna economics, see Holloman 1969 and Tice 1995.
4. For a discussion of ethnic tourism, gender, and economics see Swain 1977 and 1978.
5. See Hatley 1967 for a discussion of the early history of the Mola Co-op.
6. See Hartmann 1980, Parker and Neal 1977, and Puls 1988 for a general discussion of molas and Hirschfeld 1977 for a quantitative analysis of molas.

8. Kuna Picture-Writing *Carlo Severi*

1. I have been working on this text during my 1994–1995 stay as a Getty Scholar at the Getty Center for the History of Art and the Humanities, Santa Monica, California. I have greatly benefited from the Scholar's Seminar organized there on the theme of "Image and Memory." I wish to thank all the participants and, in particular, Salvatore Settis, Carlo Ginzburg, Randolph Starn, Michel Baxandall, Mary Carruthers, Christian Jacob, Ian Assmann, Ann and Patrick Poirier, and Michael Roth for their comments and friendly help.
2. I shall not be talking here about the discovery of Maya or Nahua picture-writing, which would take us too far away from our subject.
3. Among these young Kuna workers, mention should be made of the indefatigable Ruben Perez, who truly deserves to be called the first Kuna ethnologist, soon followed by Guillermo Hayans.
4. See the painted balsa planks in the Göteborg Museum (N.27271431) reproduced in E. Nordenskiöld (1928, plates V, VI, VII).
5. In fact, the whole issue was clouded by a particular type of Western rhetoric. To the mind of David Diringer, for instance, who published a hefty tome on these matters in the Fascist Italy of the 1930s, the development of writing, or rather "the way of the alphabet," coincided with the civilizing mission of Rome and the Christian religion (1937). In his *The alphabet in the history of civilization*, while recognizing their astonishing similarity to the Ojibwa pictograms, he considered the material published by Nordenskiöld to be the result of a recent invention (1937, 605). A true armchair anthropologist, he took the view that it had sprung belatedly from a modernization of the Kuna culture which he assumed had already ended (and which, in 1937, when he published his book, had barely begun).
6. In Miguel Triana's term, with reference to the Chibcha (1921).
7. Some twenty years later, M. Cohen, another eminent historian of writing, took a less categorical, more flexible attitude. After initially going along with Diringer, he revised his views (Cohen 1958, t. 1, p. 30, and t. 2, pp. 45 sqq). Keeping more closely to Nordenskiöld's text in his account of the situation of the Kuna, and more attentive also than many of his colleagues to the social uses of the writings, Cohen points out that the Kuna pictograms are used in many circumstances, and that this presupposes a less rudimentary developed technique and less improvisation than might have been thought. He concluded that the use made of these signs should be looked at in greater detail, adding that there was a far greater likelihood than Diringer thought that this picture-writing was of Amerindian origin. However, the research that Cohen wished to see undertaken was not carried out for a long time. Nordenskiöld's pupils concerned themselves with publishing major shamanistic texts, sometimes accompanied by their pictographic transcription (Holmer and Wassén 1958), but without the pictography itself being studied as such. The realization by N. Holmer (1951) that there was no phonetization was apparently the signal for the matter to be brought to a close.
8. For Gelb, whose perusal of this material is rather summary (and who, while quoting Nordenskiöld, does not devote a single line to the use made of Kuna pictograms), this is demonstrated by the formal characteristics of the signs. These, in a nutshell, are three. The first two, the "tenuous relationship" between signs, writing, and language (1979, 1035) and the lack of order between the signs, inevitably result in the main

characteristic of such systems, which is sterility. For Gelb (ibid. 1036), all logography is sterile: how could such techniques, still too akin to "artistic pictures," transcribe the "thousands and thousands" of words in a language? In short, such systems always come to nothing because they cannot evolve. And they cannot evolve because they cannot spread. If there seem to be some situations that give evidence of a more widespread, less episodic use of logography, as in the case of the writing of Easter Island, Gelb immediately condemns it as a "pictorial concoction for magical purposes." In other words, something basically alien to the field of writing. The distinction that he proposes between descriptive signs and mnemonic signs is directed to the same end, since in both cases what he is seeking to show is the fragility of the graphic image: any dependence on memory is for Gelb a fatal flaw in a system of signs.

9. These facts are recalled for instance by M. Detienne (1988, 10 sqq). Gelb's position must be clearly understood because there is an extreme side to it which distinguishes it from that taken by other historians of writing. It is one thing to seek to ascertain in what way the practice of writing is instrumental in producing a particular type of knowledge, which develops as a written tradition. It is quite another thing to exclude what is not written not only from the field of any knowledge worthy of the name ("a pictorial concoction for magical purposes") but also from that of communication. There is in this judgment, which confuses radically different sociolinguistic contexts, not only, as will be seen, an ethnocentric attitude, but also an anachronistic one.
10. In this connection, see Severi (1993a; 1994).
11. For the Zuni, see in particular D. Tedlock (1983). For the Pima, R. Bahr (1974). More generally, see D. Hymes (1981).
12. "In the performance of magical chants for curing and disease protection," writes Sherzer, "slight variations of an essentially nonreferential nature occur […] The magical chants performed for Kuna girls' puberty rites by contrast are completely fixed. Not the slightest variation is tolerated. The degree to which they are fixed in form is reflected in a personal experience. In 1970 I made a tape recording of a puberty rites specialist teaching a chant to several students. Between 1970 and 1978 I never discussed this chant with him. In March 1979, nine years after the recording, I brought him a transcription in order to translate it in ordinary Kuna, from which it differs considerably. Since he does not read or write, he asked me to read him the text. I did so […] Typically I barely began a line and he finished it, never missing a morpheme or even a phoneme from my transcription." (Sherzer 1990, 240). Sherzer also adds, like Tedlock and practically all the anthropologists who have concerned themselves with Amerindian literature, that "the Kuna [like many Amerindian cultures] provide still another counter-example to the view that there is no pure, verbatim memorization of fixed text in nonliterate, oral societies." In this connection, see above the discussion of J. Goody's arguments. Concerning the use of picture-writing on such occasions, see A. Prestán (1975).
13. The modes of enunciation are often verbalized in the chant itself. In this connection, see Severi 1990.
14. This typology, strict in its general categories, becomes more lax only within the repertoire of any given specialist. Attention should be drawn once again to the special position of the chief. Whereas the words of the shamans and ritual chanters are in principle unchangeable, the chief can choose to speak (*sunmake*) or to chant (*namake*). When he chooses to chant the linguistic variety, the parallelistic style and the absence of any reference to personal experience necessarily follow. Accordingly, it is explicitly forbidden for chiefs to relate their dreams on these occasions (which seers, on the other hand, are required to do).
15. Interesting examples of this regularity are given by Sherzer ("Kuna Language and Literature," in this volume).
16. The great majority of the texts that I am studying here (often of cosmological inspiration) form part of the universe of shamanistic tradition, which is perhaps at the present time the most favored, though not the exclusive, field for the pictographic tradition. F. Kramer (1970, 150–51), in his catalog of the Kuna texts held in Göteborg, mentions an "exceptionally high" number of *sayla igalas* in pictographic form. The texts in question relate the origins of animals, medicinal plants, etc.
17. In this case Nordenskiöld himself expresses reservations regarding the pictographic style of his informant.
18. Concerning the Zuni, see Tedlock (1983, 235). The sayla's apprenticeship is altogether similar to the shaman's (Howe 1986, 83 sqq).
19. Concerning the memorization of the therapeutic chants, my experience confirms that of Sherzer point by point (cf. note 12). At an interval of several years, the text of the Nia Igala which I collected in the field was chanted in exactly the same way.
20. Concerning the oldest representations of these spirits' villages, cf. note 4.
21. For an analysis of the village of transformations, see Severi (1982, 50–59).
22. I have referred here to the Kuna version of the Mu Igar, and slightly corrected the Holmer and Wassén translation.
23. While correcting some of Nordenskiöld's translations, I reproduce his numbering of the pictograms.

9. The Fiesta of San José of Narganá *Alexander Moore*

1. *Civilización, civilizado* are the terms members of the three communities use to describe themselves. While they extol civilización, they also extol traditional Kuna culture, and feel no contradiction between the dual poles of their cultural participation.

2. Not all Narganenses are Roman Catholics. There is a sizable Baptist congregation. In recent years a Mormon mission has established a toehold, not to say beachhead, on the island. I suspect that the majority, or near majority, are unchurched and would describe their beliefs as "traditional Kuna." I do not have a census on religious affiliation or belief, however.

3. My field notes assert that one of the several free meals that my host household received during the fiesta was from public funds, but I did not verify that by any cross-checking inquiries. The fiesta occurred scarcely one month after I took up residence in the field to study political events, especially the local and tribal gatherings. I took notes on what was happening as a matter of course; I also photographed events. But I did not subject the event to active follow-up research. Indeed, one attempt, weeks after the fiesta, to interview its queen and her mother, first showing them slides of the fiesta, was not successful. They watched the slides with some interest, but the mother had a full slate of women's commission meetings that evening and in the foreseeable future. She was not in my universe of informants with whom I had achieved smooth rapport. Since I was focusing on other problems and other persons, she never became a key informant. However, the fiesta continues to flourish in Narganá, or so my friends there have assured me in recent years.

4. See my discussion of the competition in Narganá between the basilica style of public building and the traditional gathering house supported by three or more central king posts (1981).

5. Napoleon Chagnon (1992, 127) describes the Yanomamö variation on the first menses rite. The young girl is isolated and hidden. She must not touch her body or her food with her hands, rather she scratches herself with sticks and eats with sticks also.

6. Although Nordenskiöld (1938, 56–78) collected some material on the menstruation rite and the "puberty feast" and "second puberty feasts," the most thorough and detailed description is contained in Prestán (1972). I was able to observe an inna suid in Playón Chico from 16–26 March 1996.

7. See my discussion of this for the Tupinambá warrior (1992, 252–56). Chagnon (1992, 200) asserts quite convincingly that the Yanomamö warrior who had killed a man must undergo a purification ritual which exactly resembles the first menstruation rite, without haircutting however.

8. In traditional Kuna societies these drinking bouts in the female life cycle rites were the only occasions to imbibe alcohol. Collective, complete inebriation for a few days, a few times a year at most, was the society's way of enjoying and handling strong drink. Nowadays beer is imported and available at small stores. Schoolteachers and other government employees in particular, enjoy socializing over a beer or two every afternoon after work. This is an entirely new approach to alcohol and one that is on a daily, not seasonal schedule.

Photography and Illustration Credits

Cover (background): Don Cole.
Pages viii-ix, x-xi (background), xxvi: Don Cole.
Pages xxvi-xxvii: Map by Jim Drobka.

1. Artful Lives *Mari Lyn Salvador and James Howe*
1.1, 1.45: Don Cole.
1.10, 1.30, 1.41A, 1.41B, 1.44A, 1.44B: Courtesy of the National Museum of the American Indian, Smithsonian Institution. Photograph by Gina Fuentes.
1.38: Mari Lyn Salvador.

2. Baba's Creation *Jorge Ventocilla*
2.1, 2.14-2.18B, 2.26: Don Cole.
2.7. Drawings by Ologuagdi, reprinted from *Plants and Animals in the life of the Kuna* by Jorge Ventocilla, Heraclio Herrera, and Valerio Núñez, Copyright ©1995, by permission of the University of Texas Press.
2.22, 2.25A, 2.25B: Courtesy of the National Museum of the American Indian, Smithsonian Institution. Photograph by Gina Fuentes.

The Artfulness of Everyday Life *Mari Lyn Salvador*
G, H, O, P, Q, R, S, U, W, Y, Z, AA, BB, CC: Don Cole.
B, N, DD, EE: Courtesy of the National Museum of the American Indian, Smithsonian Institution. Photograph by Gina Fuentes.
C: Mari Lyn Salvador.

3. The Kuna and the World *James Howe*
3.1: Mari Lyn Salvador.
3.8, 3.9: Don Cole.

4. Kuna Language and Literature *Joel Sherzer*
4.1, 4.2, : Don Cole.
4.10: Mari Lyn Salvador.

5. The Gathering House *James Howe*
5.1, 5.5, 5.11A, 5.11B: Don Cole.

6. Looking Back *Mari Lyn Salvador*
6.1, 6.6-6.10, 6.24, 6.25, 6.27-6.33, 6.42, 6.43, 6.47, 6.48, 6.56, 6.57, 6.60, 6.61-6.63, 6.69, 6.70, 6.72, 6.73-6.79, 6.86, 6.92, 6.94, 6.96, 6.98, 6.100, 6.103, 6.104, 6.106-6.112, 6.14-6.136, 6.140-6.142, 6.147, 6.148, 6.152-6.153B: Don Cole.
6.5, 6.37, 6.39, 6.46, 6.71, 6.82, 6.101: Mari Lyn Salvador.
6.36, 6.41, 6.44, 6.45, 6.84, 6.85, 6.87, 6.89-6.91, 6.93, 6.95, 6.97, 6.99, 6.102: Courtesy of the National Museum of the American Indian, Smithsonian Institution. Photograph by Gina Fuentes.
6.113: Courtesy of Ann Parker and Avon Neal.

The Spirit of the Flute *Mari Lyn Salvador*
A, C, D, E, F, H, I, K: Don Cole.
G, P: Courtesy of the National Museum of the American Indian, Smithsonian Institution. Photograph by Gina Fuentes.

7. The World of Spirit, Disease, and Curing *Mac Chapin*
7.1, 7.5, 7.7, 7.9: Don Cole.
7.12: Mac Chapin.
7.15, 7.16: Courtesy of the National Museum of the American Indian, Smithsonian Institution. Photograph by Gina Fuentes.

8. Kuna Picture-Writing *Carlo Severi*
8.1: Don Cole.
8.4-8.25: Carlo Severi.

9. The Fiesta of San José of Narganá *Alexander Moore*
9.1: Don Cole.

10. The Musical Arts of the Kuna *Sandra Smith*
10.1, 10.3A, 10.3B, 10.7-10.10: Don Cole.
10.11, 10.14-10.16: Illustration by Anthony A.G. Kluck.

11. Kuna Migration into Urban Areas *Marta Lucía de Gerdes*
11.1: Don Cole.

Catalog
CAT. 1-25: ©1997 The Field Museum, Chicago. Photograph by John Weinstein.
CAT. 26-29: Courtesy of the National Museum of the American Indian, Smithsonian Institution. Photograph by Gina Fuentes.
CAT. 30-59: Don Cole.

References Cited

Andagoya, Pascual de

1865   *Narrative of the Proceedings of Pedrarias Davila.* Clements Markham, ed. and transl. London: Publications of the Hakluyt Society 34.

Bahr, R.

1974   *Pima Shamanism.* Tucson: University of Arizona Press.

Bell, Eleanor Yorke

1910   "Republic of Panama and Its People." *Smithsonian Institution Annual Report for 1909*, pp. 607–37. Washington D.C.: Smithsonian Institution.

Bourgeois, Philippe

1989   *Ethnicity at Work. Divided Labor on a Central American Banana Plantation.* Baltimore: Johns Hopkins University.

Brown, Lady Richmond

1925   *Unknown Tribes, Uncharted Seas.* New York: D. Appleton.

Castillero Calvo, Alfredo

1995   *Conquista, Evangelización, y Resistencia: ¿Triunfo o Fracaso de la Política Indigenista?* Panama: Instituto Nacional de la Cultura.

CEASPA (Centro de Estudios Y Accion Social Panameno)

1992   "Compilación de Datos Sobre la Población Kuna en la Ciudad de Panamá, Proporcionados por Secretaría Indígena." Manuscript. Panama: Centro de Estudios y Acción Social de Panamá.

Chagnon, Napoleon

1992   *Yanomamö*, 4th rev. ed. (earlier eds., 1966, 1978: *Yanomamö—The Fierce People*). New York: Holt, Rinehart, & Winston.

Chapin, Mac

1970   *Pap Igala: Historias de la Tradición Kuna.* Panama City: Universidad de Panamá.

Chapin, Norman Macpherson (see Chapin, Mac)

1983   "Curing Among the San Blas Kuna of Panama." Ph.D. diss. Ann Arbor: University Microfilms International.

Cohen, M.

1958   *La Grande Invention de l'Écriture.* Paris: CNRS Editions.

Conniff, Michael

1992   *Panama and the United States: The Forced Alliance.* Athens: University of Georgia Press.

Coope, Anna

1917   *Anna Coope: Sky Pilot of the San Blas Indians.* New York: American Tract Society.

Core, Sue Pearl

1925   *Trail of Progress of The Story of Panama and Its Canal.* New York: The Knickerbocker Press.

Costello, Richard

1986   "Política de Congreso en un Medio Urbano: Un Estudio del Proceso Político Cuna." P. Vanela, transl. Thesis, Universidad de Panamá. ([1983] "Congreso politics in an urban setting: a study of Cuna political process." *Panama in Transition: Local Reaction to Development Policies.* Monographs in Anthropology 6. J.R. Bort and M.W. Helms, eds. Columbia: The University of Missouri.)

de Enciso, M. Fernando

1857   *Descripción de las Islas Occidentales* (first edition 1519), Santiago de Chili.

Defrancis, John

1990   *Visible Speech: The Diverse Oneness of Writing.* Honolulu: Hawaii University Press.

Detienne, M.

1988   "L'Écriture et ses Nouveaux Objets Intellectuels en Grèce." In *Les Savoirs de l'Écriture en Grèce Ancienne*, M. Detienne, ed. Lille, France: Presses Universitaires de Lille.

De Puydt, Lucién

1868   *Account of Scientific Explorations in the Isthmus of Darién in the Years 1861 and 1865*, vol. 38. London: Journal of the Royal Geographical Society.

Diringer, David

1937   *L'Alfabeto nella Storia della Civiltà* (The Alphabet in the History of Civilization). Florence: La Barbera.

DNEC (Dirección Nacional de Estadistica Y Censo)

1990   "Población Indígena por Grupos de Edad, Según Sexo y Grupo Indígena a que Pertenece." *Censo de Población de 1990, Cuadro 19.* Panama: Dirección Nacional de Estadística y Censo.

Dunham, Captain Jacob

1850   *Journal of Voyages.* New York.

Gassó, Leonardo

1911–1914   "La Misión de San José de Narganá entre los Karibes (República de Panamá)." In *Las Misiones Católicas* 18-22, Barcelona.

Gause, Frank A., and Charles Carl Carr

1917   *The Story of Panama: The New Route to India.* Boston: Silver, Burdett, and Company.

Gelb, I.J.

1952   *A Study of Writing.* Chicago: University of Chicago Press.

1979   "Writing." In *Encyclopaedia Britannica*, pp.1033–45.

Gombrich, E.

1979   *The Sense of Order: A Study in the Psychology of Decorative Art.* London: Phaidon Press.

Goody, J.

1977   "Mémoire et Apprentissage dans les Sociétés avec et sans Écriture: La Transmission du Bagré." *L'Homme* 17(1): 29–52.

1987   *The Interface between the Oral and the Written.* Cambridge: Cambridge University Press.

Goody, J., and J. Watt

1968   *Literacy in Traditional Societies.* Cambridge: Cambridge University Press.

Hartmann, Gunther

1980   *Molakana: Volkskunst der Cuna, Panama.* Berlin: Museum für Volkerkunde.

Hatley, Nancy Brennan

1976   "Cooperativism and Enculturation Among the Cuna Indians of San Blas." In *Enculturation in Latin America*, pp. 76–94. Johannes Wilbert, ed. Los Angeles: Latin American Center Publications, University of California at Los Angeles.

Helms, Mary

1979   *Ancient Panama: Chiefs in Search of Power.* Austin: University of Texas Press.

1981   "Cuna Molas and Cocle Art Forms: Reflections on Panamanian Design Styles and Symbols." *Working Papers in Traditional Arts* 7. Philadelphia: Institute for the Study of Human Issues.

Herlihy, Peter

1989   "Panama's Quiet Revolution. Comarca Homelands and Indian Rights." *Cultural Survival Quarterly* 13(3):15–24.

Hirschfield, Lawrence

1976   "A Structural Analysis of the Cuna Arts." In *Ritual and Symbol in Native Central America*. Philip Young and James Howe, eds. Eugene: University of Oregon Anthropological Papers 9, pp. 43–56.

1977A   "Art in Cuna Ideology and Cultural Adaptation" *Man* n.s.(12): 104–23.

1977B   "Cuna Aesthetics: A Quantitative Analysis." *Ethnology* 16: 147–66.

Hoffmann, W. James

1888   "Pictography and Shamanistic Rites of the Ojibwa." *American Anthropologist* 1: 209–29.

Holloman, Regina

1969   "Developmental Change in San Blas." Ph.D. diss., Northwestern University. Ann Arbor: University Microfilms.

Holmer, Nils

1947   *A Critical and Comparative Grammar of the Cuna Language*. Göteborg, Sweden: Göteborgs Etnografiska Museum.

1951   *Cuna Crestomathy*. Göteborg, Sweden: Göteborgs Etnografiska Museum.

1952   *Ethno-linguistic Cuna Dictionary*. Etnologiska Studier 19. Göteborg, Sweden: Göteborgs Etnografiska Museum.

Holmer, Nils, and H. Wassén

1953   *The Complete Mu-Ikala in Picture Writing*. Etnologiska Studier, No. 21. Göteborgs Etnografiska Museum. Göteborg, Sweden: Elanders Boktryckeri Aktiebolag.

1958   *Nia Ikala, Canto Magico para Curar la Locura*. Göteborg, Sweden: Göteborgs Etnografiska Museum.

Howe, James

1974   "Village Political Organization Among the San Blas Kuna." Ph.D. diss., University of Pennsylvania.

1976   "Smoking Out the Spirits." In *Ritual and Symbol in Native Central America*, Anthropological Papers 9. Philip Young and James Howe, eds. Eugene, Oregon: University of Oregon.

1978   "Algunos Problemas no Resueltos del Este de Panamá." *Revista Panameña de Antropología* 2:30–47.

1986   *The Kuna Gathering: Contemporary Village Politics in Panama*. Austin: University of Texas Press.

1990   "Mission Rivalry and Conflict in San Blas, Panama." In *Class, Politics, and Popular Religion in Mexico and Central America*, pp. 143–66. Society for Latin American Anthropology Publication Series 10. Lynn Stephen and James Dow, eds.

1991   "An Ideological Triangle: The Struggle over San Blas Kuna Culture, 1915–1925." In *Nation-States and Indians in Latin America*, pp. 9–52. Greg Urban and Joel Sherzer, eds. Austin: University of Texas Press.

1992   "Protestant, Catholics, and 'Gentiles': The Articulation of Missionary and Indigenous Culture on the San Blas Coast of Panama." *Journal of the Anthropological Society of Oxford* 23:139–55.

In press   *A People Who Would Not Kneel: Panama, the United States, and the San Blas Kuna*. Washington: Smithsonian Institution Press. (Spring 1998)

Howe, James, Joel Sherzer, and Mac Chapin

1980   *Cantos y Oraciones del Congreso Cuna*. Panama City: Editorial Universitaria.

Hymes, D.

1981   *In Vain I Have Tried to Tell You. Essays in American Indian Ethnopoetics*. Philadelphia: University of Pennsylvania Press.

Kramer, F.

1970   *Literature among the Cuna Indians*. Göteborg, Sweden: Göteborgs Etnografiska Museum.

Lasso, Aminta

1962   "Los Fenómenos de Aculturación de los Indios Cunas Residentes en Panamá." Thesis, Universidad de Panamá.

Leis, Raúl

1991   *Machí: Un Kuna en la ciudad*. Panama: CEASPA.

Luengo Muñoz, Manuel

1959   "El Darién en la Política Internacional del Siglo XVIII." *Estudios Americanos* 18:96–97, 139–56.

1961   "Génesis de las Expediciones Militares al Darién en 1785–6." *Anuario de Estudios Americanos* 18:335–416.

Major, John

1993   *Prize Possession: The United States and the Panama Canal, 1903–1979*. Cambridge: Cambridge University Press.

Mallery, G.

1886–1893   *Picture Writing of the American Indians*, 2 vols. Washington: Bureau of American Ethnologists.

Marsh, Richard

1934   *White Indians of Darien*. New York: Putnam.

McCosker, Sandra Smith (see Smith, Sandra)

1974   *The Lullabies of the San Blas Cuna Indians of Panama*. Etnologiska Studier, No. 33. Göteborgs Etnografiska Museum. Göteborg: Elanders Boktryckeri Aktiebolag.

1976   "San Blas Cuna Indian Lullabies: A Means of Informal Learning." In *Enculturation in Latin America, An Anthology*. UCLA Latin American Studies, vol. 37. Johannes Wilbert, ed. Los Angeles: UCLA Latin American Center Publications.

McCullough, David

1977   *The Path Between the Seas: The Creation of the Panama Canal, 1870–1914*. New York: Simon & Shuster.

Moncado Vargas, Marta

1990   "National Identity in Panama between 1948 and 1958." Thesis, University of Texas at Austin.

Monod, A., and J. Galarza

1977   *Doctrina Christiana*. Paris: Société d'ethnographie, Nanterre.

Moore, Alexander

1981   "Basilicas and King Posts: A Proxemic and Symbolic Event Analysis of Competing Architecture Among the San Blas Cuna." *American Ethnologist* 8(2):259–77.

1983   "Lore and Life: Cuna Indian Pageants, Exorcism and Diplomacy in the 20th Century." *Ethnohistory* 30(2):93–106.

1992   *Cultural Anthropology: The Field Study of Human Beings*. San Diego, California: Collegiate Press.

Nordenskiöld, Erland

1928   "Picture-Writings and Other Documents." *Comparative Ethnographical Studies* 7.

1938   "An Historical and Ethnological Survey of the Cuna Indians." *Comparative Ethnographical Studies* 10.

Oliver, Frederick

1916   "The San Blas Indians of Darien." Manuscript, National Archives of Anthropology. Washington, D.C: Smithsonian Institution.

Otis, Fessenden Nott

1867   *Isthmus of Panama: History of the Panama Railroad; and of the Pacific Mail Steamship Company*. New York: Harper & Brothers.

Oviedo y Valdes, G. Fernandez

1851–1855   *Historia General y Natural de las Indias*, t. 4. Madrid.

Parker, Ann, and Avon Neal

1977   *Molas: Folk Art of the Cuna Indians*. New York: Barre Publishing.

Pittier, Henry

1912   "Little Known Parts of Panama." *National Geographic* 23 (July):627–62.

Prebble, John

1968   *The Darien Disaster*. London: Secker & Warburg.

Prestán, Arnulfo

1975   *El Uso de la Chicha en la Sociedad Kuna*, Ediciones Especiales 72. Mexico City: Instituto Indigenista Interamericano.

1991   "Organizacion Social y Politica de Kuna Yala." *Hombre y Cultura* 2:107–59.

Puls, Herta

1988   *Textiles of the Kuna Indians of Panama*. Princes Risborough, U.K.: Shire Publications Ltd.

Reclus, Armando

1958   *Exploraciones a los Istmos de Panama y Darien en 1876, 1877 and 1878*. Panama: Publicaciones de la Revista Loteria. (Reprinted from 1881 edition.)

Reverte, José Manuel

1968   *Literatura Oral de los Indios Cunas*. Ensayo Literario Sobre una Cultura Aborigen Panameña. Panama: Ministerio de Educación.

Roberts, Orlando

1827   *Narrative of Voyages and Excursion on the East Coast and in the Interior of Central America*. Edinburgh: Constable and Co.

Rodríguez, Cristina

1961   "Fenómenos de Aculturación de Indios Cunas en la Ciudad de Colón." Thesis, Universidad de Panamá.

Rojas y Arrieta, Guillermo

1929   *History of the Bishops of Panama*. T.J. McDonald, transl. Panama: Imprenta de la Academia.

Romoli, Kathleen

1987   *Los de la Lengua Cueva: Los Grupos Indígenas del Istmo Oriental en la Época de la Conquista Española*. Bogota: Instituto Colombiano de Antropología.

Salcedo, Gonzalo

1979   "Una Consejo Matrimonial." In *Cantos y Oraciones del Congreso Cuna*, pp. 64–72. James Howe, Joel Sherzer, and Mac Chapin, eds. Panama: Editorial Universitaria.

Salvador, Mari Lyn

1978   *Yer Dailege! Kuna Women's Art*. Albuquerque: University of New Mexico Press.

Sauer, Carl O.

1966   *The Early Spanish Main*. Berkeley: University of California Press.

Schoolcraft, H.R.

1851   *Historical and Statistical Information Respecting the History, Condition and Prospects of the Indian Tribes of the United States,* (6 vols.), Part 1. Philadelphia: Lippincott.

Selfridge, Thomas Oliver

1874   "Reports of Explorations and Surveys to Ascertain the Practicability of a Ship-Canal between the Atlantic and Pacific Oceans by the Way of the Isthmus of Darien." Washington, D.C.: Government Printing Office.

Severi, Carlo

1982   "Le Chemin des Métamorphoses: Un Modèle de Connaissance de la Folie dans un Chant Chamanique Cuna." *Res—Anthropology and Aesthetics* 3:32–67.

1985   "Penser par Séquences, Penser par Territoires: Cosmologie et Art de la Mémoire dans la Pictographie des Indiens Cuna." *Communications* 41:169–90.

1987   "The Invisible Path: On the Ritual Representation of Suffering in Cuna Shamanistic Tradition." *Res—Anthropology and Aesthetics* 14:66–85.

1990   "Cristallizzazione e Dispersione del Sapere nella Tradizione Cuna." In *La Trasmissione del Sapere*. G. Cardona, ed. Rome.

1993A   "Talking about Souls—The Pragmatic Construction of Meaning in the Cuna Shamanistic Chants." In *Cognitive Aspects of Religious Symbolism*, pp.165–81. P. Boyer, ed. Cambridge: Cambridge University Press.

1993B   "La Mémoire Rituelle—Experience, Tradition, Historicité." In *Mémoires de la Tradition*, pp. 347–64. A. Monod and A. Molinié, eds. Paris: Société d'ethnologie, Nanterre.

1994   "Protée ou la Propagation d'une Forme—Art Primitif et Mémoire." In *Actes du Colloque International d'Histoire de l'Art*, pp.121–38. T.W. Gahetegens, ed. Berlin: Akademie Verlag.

1996   *La Memoria Ritual. Locura e Imagen del Blanco en una Tradicion Chamanica Amerindia*, pp. 1–306. R. Pochtar, trans. Quito: Ediciones Abya Yala.

Severi, Carlo, and E. Gomez

1983   "Nia Ikala, Los Pueblos del Camino de la Locura. Texto Cuna y Traducción Española." *Amerindia: Revue d'Ethnolinguistique Amérindienne* 8:129–79.

Severino de Santa Teresa, Padre

1956   *Historia Documentada de la Iglesia en Urabá y el Darién, IV, Segunda Parte, América Española, 1550–1810*. Bogota: Editorial Kelly.

Sherzer, Joel

1974   "Namakke, Sunmakke, Kormakke: Three Types of Cuna Speech Event." In *Explorations in the Ethnography of Speaking*. Richard Bauman and Joel Sherzer, eds. Cambridge: Cambridge University Press.

1983   *Kuna Ways of Speaking: An Ethnographic Perspective*. Austin: University of Texas Press.

1986   "The Report of a Kuna Curing Specialist: The Poetics and Rhetoric of an Oral Performance." In *Native South American Discourse*, Joel Sherzer and Greg Urban, eds. New York: Walter de Gruyter & Co.

1990   *Verbal Art in San Blas: Kuna Culture Through its Discourse*. Cambridge: University of Cambridge Press.

1994   "The Kuna and Columbus: Encounters and Confrontations of Discourse." *American Anthropologist* 96(4):902–24.

Sherzer, Dina, and Joel Sherzer

1976   "Mormaknamaloe: The Cuna Mola." In *Ritual and Symbol in Native Central America*. University of Oregon Anthropological Papers, no. 9. Philip Young and James Howe, eds.

Sherzer, Joel, and Sammie Ann Wicks

1982   "The Intersection of Music and Language in Kuna Discourse." *Latin American Music Review* 3:147–64.

Smith, Sandra (see McCosker, Sandra Smith)

1984   *Panpipes for Power, Panpipes for Play: The Social Management of Cultural Expression in Kuna Society*. Ann Arbor: University Microfilms International.

In press "Music of the Kuna of Panama." In *Music of Latin America and the Caribbean*. Dale Olsen and Daniel Sheehy, eds. of Vol. 9 of *Garland Encyclopedia of World Music*. T. Rice and J. Porter, eds., New York: Garland Publications.

Stout, David B.

947   *San Blas Cuna Acculturation: an Introduction*. New York: Viking Fund Publications in Anthropology 9.

Susman, Daniel

1984   "La Basura en Panamá." *Revista Diálogo Social*. 172:18.

Swain, Margaret

1977   "Cuna Women and Ethnic Tourism: A Way to Persist and an Avenue to Change." In *Hosts and Guests: The Anthropology of Tourism*, pp. 71–81.

1978   "Ailigandi Women: Continuity and Change in Cuna Female Identity." Ph.D. diss., University of Washington. Ann Arbor microfilms.

Tedlock, D.

1983   *The Spoken Word and the Work of Interpretation.* Philadelphia: University of
       Pennsylvania Press.

Tice, Karen E.

1995   *Kuna Crafts, Gender, and the Global Economy.* Austin: University of Texas Press.

Triana, Miguel

1921   *La Civilisación Chibcha.* Bogota: Biblioteca Banco Popular.

Vandervelde, Marjorie, and Marvel Iglesias

1982   *Born Primitive.* Emmetsburg, Iowa: Velde Press.

Vansina, J.

1976   *La Tradition Orale.* (Italian edition). Rome: Officina Edizioni.

Ventocilla, Jorge, Heraclio Herrera, and Valerio Nuñez, eds.

1995   *Plants and Animals in the Life of the Kuna.* Elizabeth King, transl. Austin:
       University of Texas Press.

Verrill, A. Hyatt

1918   *Indian Tribes of Panama.* Manuscript, National Museum of the American Indian,
       Smithsonian Institution Archives.

Wafer, Lionel

1970 [1699]   *A New Voyage and Description of the Isthmus of America.* George Parker
             Winship, ed. New York: Burt Franklin.

Ward, Christopher

1993   *Imperial Panama: Commerce and Conflict in Isthmian America, 1550–1800.*
       Albuquerque: University of New Mexico Press.

Contributors

Mac Chapin is an anthropologist who conducted initial field work among the Kuna and has worked with indigenous peoples of Central America for thirty years. He is currently the director of the Center for the Support of Native Lands, a nongovernmental organization that works with Central American Indians to defend their lands and natural resources.

Dr. Marta Lucía de Gerdes is a Panamanian journalist and anthropologist whose work with the Kuna people focused on discourse and migration, with a gender perspective. She currently works in Zurich, Switzerland, on issues of migration and integration.

James Howe, professor and head of the Anthropology Program at Massachusetts Institute of Technology, has carried out ethnographic and ethnohistoric research in Panama since 1970. He is author of *The Kuna Gathering* (1986) and of the forthcoming *A People Who Would Not Kneel: Panama, The United States, and the San Blas Kuna* (1998).

Alexander Moore is a professor and chair of the anthropology department at the University of Southern California. He did field work among the Kuna for eighteen months (1977–1978), and has visited the area periodically since then. His most recent book is *Cultural Anthropology: the Field Study of Human Beings* (San Diego: Collegiate Press, 1992).

Mari Lyn Salvador is the chief curator of the Maxwell Museum of Anthropology and an associate professor of anthropology at the University of New Mexico. She began field work with the Kuna in 1966 and continues to study Kuna women's arts from an ethnoaesthetic perspective. She also studies the aesthetics of ritual performance in the Azores, Portugal, and in the Portuguese American community in California. Recently, she began a collaborative project with Hispanic artists in Northern New Mexico. Her publications include *Cuando Hablan los Santos*

(1995); *Festas Açoreanas: Portuguese Religious Celebrations in the Azores and California* (1981); and *Yer Dailege: Kuna Women's Art* (1978).

Carlo Severi obtained his Doctorat d'Ethnologie from the École des Hautes Études en Sciences Sociales in Paris, and is now a Chargé de Recherche at the Centre National de la Recherche Scientifique. He has published two books, one on the Kuna shamanistic tradition and the other on ritual transvestism among the Iatmul (Sepik, Papua New Guinea).

Joel Sherzer is a professor of anthropology and linguistics at the University of Texas at Austin. He has carried out anthropological and linguistic research among the Kuna since 1969. He is the author of *Kuna Ways of Speaking* (1983) and *Verbal Art in San Blas* (1990).

Sandra Smith conducted her field work with the Kuna in San Blas, Panama in 1970–1971, briefly in 1976, and again in 1979–1980. Her recent publications include *Panpipes for Power, Panpipes for Play: The Social Management of Cultural Expression in Kuna Society* (1984) and "Music of the Kuna in Panama" in the *Garland Encyclopedia of World Music* (1997). She is a research associate of the California Academy of Sciences and an independent scholar.

Jorge Luis Ventocilla Cuadros is a biologist (zoologist) who has worked since 1980 at the Smithsonian Tropical Research Institute in Panama as an environmental specialist in the Office of Education and Conservation. He has participated in several conservation projects in Panama and elsewhere, and maintains strong personal and professional relationships with the Kuna people. He has traveled throughout the Kuna territory; in the community of Cangandi he studied the practices of subsistence hunting. He has published books and articles about environmental education and on the relationship of communities with the wildlife.

UCLA Fowler Museum of Cultural History

Doran H. Ross *Director*
Clarissa M. Coyoca *Assistant Director for Administration and Finance*

Accounting
Dina M. Ogle *Accountant*
Michael Bermudez *Accounting Assistant*

Administration
Betsy R. Escandor *Administrative Specialist*
Lori A. LaVelle *Administrative Assistant*

Center for the Study of Regional Dress
Patricia Anawalt *Director*
Barbara Sloan *Assistant Director*

Collections
Fran Krystock *Collections Manager*
Dwight Gorden *Assistant Collections Manager*
Aileen Dugan *Collections Assistant*

Conservation
Jo A. Hill *Conservator*

Curatorial
Patricia B. Altman *Curator Emeritus*
Roy W. Hamilton *Curator of Southeast Asian and Oceanic Collections*
Doran H. Ross *Curator of African Collections*
Glenn S. Russell *Curator of Archaeology*
Anne Summerfield *Visiting Curator*
John Summerfield *Visiting Curator*

Development
Kyrin Ealy Hobson *Director of Development*
Lynne K. Brodhead *Assistant Director of Development*

Education
Betsy D. Quick *Director of Education*
Stacey J. Hong *Assistant Director of Education*
Kristen Quine *Education Assistant*

Exhibitions
David A. Mayo *Exhibition Designer*
Victor Lozano, Jr. *Exhibition Production*
Ann McNamara *Graphic Technician*
Don Simmons *Exhibition Production*
Karyn Zarubica *Traveling Exhibitions Coordinator*

Information Systems
Ray Huang *Director of Information Systems*
Donald H. McClelland *Imaging Consultant*
Eric Anderson *Imaging Technician*
Ledda J. Macera *Imaging Technician*
Branislav Unkovic *Imaging Technician*

Membership
Kathlene Kolian *Director of Membership*
Vickie Reese *Membership Assistant*

Museum Store
Polly Svenson *Museum Store Manager*
Sue Kallick *Assistant Store Manager*
Marilyn Liebman *Special Events Coordinator*

Photography
Donald Cole *Senior Photographer*
Jonathan Molvik *Photography Assistant*

Public Relations
Christine Sellin *Director of Public Relations*
Lisa Rosen *Public Relations Assistant*

Publications
Daniel R. Brauer *Director of Publications*
Anthony A.G. Kluck *Assistant Director of Publications*
David Svenson *Publications Processor*

Registration
Sarah Jane Kennington *Registrar*
Farida Sunada *Assistant Registrar*

Security
Francisco J. Muñoz *Director of Security*
Jose A. Garcia *Assistant Director of Security*
Emry Thomas *Facilities Supervisor*

Security Guards
Joseph Eubank *Security Supervisor*
Roger Palmer *Console Supervisor*
Fernando Martin *Console Relief*
Steven Faison *Console Relief*
Michelle Oskoui *Cashier*
Pejman Akhlaghi
German Bracamonte
Domingo Caldona
Nuvia Flores
Pablo Orduño
Francheska Peters
Gina Denora Ruiz
Marika Sotin
Fabian Torres
Lisa Wong

Interns
Karen Abend
James J. Clark
Aphrodite Dielubanza
Priscilla Herbilla
Alicia Katano
Taaji Rauf-Madyun
Luciana Scrutchen
Danielle Smith

Support Staff
Cathy Barrow
Angel Haro
Kathy Marquez
Paula Padilla

Volunteers
Ruth Parsell *Volunteer Coordinator*
Margaret Abraham
Lyn Avins
Jane Bardwell
Virginia Beckwith
Simone Civet
Linda Clougherty
Josey Dodd
Monica Eiserling
Doris Finck
Elaine Fleischman
Helen Goebel
Moonlight Gurfield
Kimberly Herzog
Marillyn H. Holmes
Betsy Keliher
Rose Korsak
Deborah R. Last
Mary Jane Leland
Roz Lipkis
Mickey Loy
Jovita Luglug
Frances Martin
Robert McClelland
Nancy McCreery
Rosemary Murray
Nancy Porter
Caroline Sakaguchi
Batyah Schtrum
Stuart Shaffer
Jill Stein
Ellen Vener
Andrea Williams

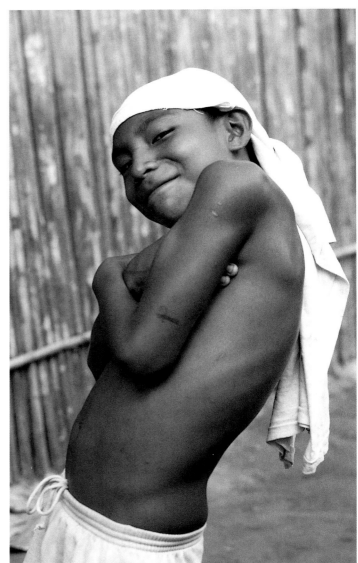